REGULATION AND CRIMINAL JUSTICE

While regulatory institutions and strategies have been the subject of increasing academic attention, there has been limited application of regulatory theories to criminal justice scholarship. This collection of essays from a range of outstanding international scholars adopts a critical, interdisciplinary approach, providing an innovative application of regulatory theory to the practice of criminal justice and offering suggestions for further research. Part I explores the aims and values of criminal justice and other regulatory networks and the synergies and tensions between these fields; Part II examines criminal justice as a regulatory force to control 'deviant' and antisocial behaviour; and Part III examines the regulation and oversight of criminal justice through the operation of prison inspectorates, and explores notions of responsive justice.

HANNAH QUIRK is a lecturer in criminal law and justice at the University of Manchester, where her research interests include the right of silence and wrongful convictions.

TOBY SEDDON is a reader in regulation at the School of Law, University of Manchester, and Director of the Regulation, Security and Justice Research Centre.

GRAHAM SMITH is a senior lecturer in regulation at the School of Law, University of Manchester, and Deputy Director of the Regulation, Security and Justice Research Centre.

REGULATION AND CRIMINAL JUSTICE

Innovations in Policy and Research

Edited by

HANNAH QUIRK

TOBY SEDDON

and

GRAHAM SMITH

CAMBRIDGE
UNIVERSITY PRESS

CAMBRIDGE UNIVERSITY PRESS
Cambridge, New York, Melbourne, Madrid, Cape Town, Singapore,
São Paulo, Delhi, Dubai, Tokyo, Mexico City

Cambridge University Press
The Edinburgh Building, Cambridge CB2 8RU, UK

Published in the United States of America by Cambridge University Press, New York

www.cambridge.org
Information on this title: www.cambridge.org/9780521190701

First published 2010

Printed in the United Kingdom at the University Press, Cambridge

A catalogue record for this publication is available from the British Library

Library of Congress Cataloguing in Publication data
Regulation and Criminal Justice : Innovations in Policy and
Research / [edited by] Hannah Quirk, Toby Seddon, Graham Smith.
p. cm
Includes bibliographical references and index.
ISBN 978-0-521-19070-1 (hardback)
1. Criminal justice, Administration of. 2. Punishment. 3. Sanctions,
Administrative. 4. Administrative procedure. 5. Law enforcement.
I. Quirk, Hannah, 1973– II. Seddon, Toby, 1970– III. Smith, Graham, 1957–
K5001.R44 2010
364–dc22
2010045704

ISBN 978-0-521-19070-1 Hardback

CONTENTS

FIGURES AND TABLES

Figures

Tables

NOTES ON CONTRIBUTORS

John Flint is Professor of Housing and Urban Governance in the Centre for Regional Economic and Social Research at Sheffield Hallam University. He has conducted studies of the governance and regulation of antisocial behaviour for the Home Office, DWP, Department for Children, Schools and Families and the Scottish government. He has written a series of reports and articles about his research and he is the editor of *Housing, Urban Governance and Anti-social Behaviour* (2006).

Jan Froestad is Associate Professor in the Department of Administration and Organization Theory at the University of Bergen. He wrote his dissertation on the education of deaf people and the care of disabled people in Norway, Denmark and Sweden in the nineteenth century. He has published several articles on Norwegian school policy and, together with M. Söder and P. Solvang, edited a book on disability, politics and society. His ongoing project deals with conditions for mobilizing local knowledge and self-directed capacity in poor communities in South Africa.

Peter Grabosky is a professor in the Regulatory Institutions Network, in the College of Asia and the Pacific at the Australian National University. A Fellow of the Academy of the Social Sciences in Australia, he holds a Ph.D. in political science from Northwestern University, and has written extensively on criminal justice and public policy. His general interests are in harnessing resources outside the public sector in furtherance of public administration, and in the use of incentives and inducements as regulatory instruments. Among other appointments, he has been a Russell Sage Fellow in Law and Social Science at Yale Law School, and a Visiting Professor at Chuo University (Japan) and the Chinese People's Public Security University. He is past president of the Australian and New Zealand Society of Criminology and is currently Vice President of the Asian Criminological Society.

Barbara Hudson is Professor (Emeritus), Lancashire Law School, University of Central Lancashire. Her publications include *Justice in the Risk Society* (2003), and many articles and book chapters on criminal justice. Her research interests include justice and gender, race/ethnicity, poverty and restorative justice. She is currently working on aspects of cosmopolitan justice, including work on migration (2007), cosmopolitanism and divided societies (2008), justice and the war on terror (2009). Professor Hudson is a collaborator with a research project on justice and security at the University of Oslo; she is an adviser on the Master's programme on justice and security at Erasmus University, Rotterdam. Since 2003 she has spent part of each year working in Brazil, where she is a Visiting Professor on the LLM in Law and Inequality at the State University of Paraná (Jacarezinho) and also lectures on the LLM in Human Rights at UniBrasil (Curitiba). She is conducting research on the Ministério Público in Paraná.

Caroline Hunter is Professor of Law at the York Law School, University of York. She has written extensively on the regulation of antisocial behaviour, particularly by housing organizations. She has been involved in a number of empirical research projects which have examined the use of legal remedies and alternatives to legal remedies to deal with antisocial behaviour including: Hunter *et al.*, *Neighbour Nuisance, Social Landlords and the Law* (2000); J. Nixon *et al.*, *ASB Intensive Family Support Projects: An Evaluation of Six Pioneering Projects* (2006).

Palash Kamruzzaman is a teaching fellow in sociology at the University of Leicester. He has degrees in sociology, social policy and anthropology. His Ph.D. research has examined poverty reduction strategies in Bangladesh, and whether civil society participation was really used to enhance the Poverty Reduction Strategy Paper in that country. He has been an overseas research student and Wingate scholar, and his main current teaching and research interests are in international development, participation, civil society, poverty and community cohesion.

Gary Lynch-Wood is a lecturer in law and regulation and the Director of the Sustainability, Policy and Regulation Research Centre at the School of Law at the University of Manchester. He lectures on a range of undergraduate and postgraduate courses in areas of environmental law, regulation and corporate social responsibility. He is also the Course Director for Legal Methods and Systems. His research interests are the impact of regulation on organizations and the role of regulation in promoting corporate social responsibility and sustainable development.

Gabriel Mythen is Senior Lecturer in Sociology at the University of Liverpool. His present research investigates the ways in which risks are politically managed by the state and the modes of risk regulation deployed by government and criminal justice agencies seeking to secure order and social control. He is author of *Ulrich Beck: A Critical Introduction to the Risk Society* (2004) and, with S. Walklate, co-editor of *Beyond the Risk Society: Critical Reflections on Risk and Human Security* (2006). He is presently writing a book entitled *Understanding the Risk Society: Crime, Security and Justice.*

Anthony Ogus is Emeritus Professor at the School of Law of the University of Manchester (where he was Dean 1990–2); he is also part-time Erasmus Professor of the Fundamentals of Private Law at the University of Rotterdam. He has held visiting positions at the Universities of Antwerp, California (Berkeley), Maastricht, Paris II and Toronto, and the Bucerius Law School at Hamburg He has written books and articles on the law of damages, social security law, law and economics and regulation. He was joint founding editor of the *International Review for Law and Economics.* In 2002 he received a CBE for services to the Social Security Advisory Committee. He is a Fellow of the British Academy.

Anne Owers was General Secretary of the Joint Council for the Welfare of Immigrants (1985–90). She was Director of JUSTICE, working on human rights, asylum and the provision of legal services (1992–01). She was a member of the government task force on the implementation of the Human Rights Act 1998. In 2001 she was appointed HM Chief Inspector of Prisons, and made a Dame Commander of the Order of the British Empire (2009). She has contributed chapters and articles to a number of publications on aspects of prisons, inspection and immigration, and provided evidence at the hearings of the Vera Institute's Commission into Abuse in America's Prisons.

Hannah Quirk is a lecturer in criminal law and justice at the University of Manchester. She worked previously for the Legal Services Commission and the Criminal Cases Review Commission. Her current research interests include the right of silence and wrongful convictions.

Andrew Sanders has held academic posts at several universities, including most recently the Universities of Oxford, Bristol and Manchester. He took up his present post as Professor of Criminal Law and Criminology at the University of Birmingham in 2010. His teaching and research interests are in the areas of criminal law, criminal justice, and socio-legal studies. He is author of *The Case for the Prosecution* (with M. McConville and R. Leng, 1991) and of *Criminal Justice* (with R. Young and M. Burton, 4th edn, 2010). In recent years his research has been particularly concerned with the role of victims in criminal justice, and has been published in journals such as the *Criminal Law Review* and *British Journal of Criminology*. He is also a Parole Commissioner for Northern Ireland.

Toby Seddon is a reader in regulation at the School of Law at the University of Manchester and Director of the Regulation, Security and Justice Research Centre. He is author of *Punishment and Madness* (2007) and *A History of Drugs* (2010).

Clifford Shearing is Professor in the Department of Public Law, Faculty of Law, University of Cape Town. His work has focused on the development of theoretical understandings that can be used to enhance the quality of security and justice governance. A particular focus of his work has been contributing to the development of institutions and processes that enhance the ability of poor collectivities to both direct and add value to their security and justice. He is currently engaged in research and writing on environmental security. He holds the National Research Foundation Chair on African Security and Justice, and the Chair of Criminology and is Director of the Centre of Criminology at the University of Cape Town.

Graham Smith is a senior lecturer in regulation at the School of Law, University of Manchester and is Deputy Director of the Regulation, Security and Justice Research Centre. He has written extensively on remedies to police misconduct and is the police complaints Consultant to the Council of Europe Commissioner for Human Rights.

David Whyte is a reader in sociology at the School of Sociology and Social Policy, University of Liverpool. His research interests include corporate crime, state crime and the social impacts of counter-terrorism. He has recently completed studies on the social construction and criminalization of deaths and injuries at work, and on the role of corporations in the occupation and reconstruction of Iraq. Recent publications include *Crimes of the Powerful: A Reader* (2009) and *Safety Crimes* (2007, with S. Tombs).

David Williamson is a senior research fellow in Regulation and a Director of the Sustainability, Policy and Regulation Research Centre at the School of Law at the University of Manchester. David has a longstanding interest in how regulation affects small firms and has carried out research for a number of agencies in this area. In recent times this has been extended to include a consideration of how receptive differences to regulation shape regulatory success. This includes areas as diverse as ecological modernization and legal transplants, and more generally, why civil regulation may be a necessary form of regulation in modern pluralistic societies.

FOREWORD

John Braithwaite

Whatever the upshot of enquiries into the legality of the invasion of Iraq in 2003, we can feel confident that criminal justice journals will not be full of articles that argue 'if it was right to convict Prime Minister Tojo and his cabinet for crimes of aggression, should not western cabinet ministers hear the clang of the jailhouse door over Iraq?' We might excuse US journals for not being engaged with such a debate because the US does not acknowledge the jurisdiction of international criminal law over its leaders. We know this will not happen anywhere for Iraq because journals concerned with crime have never engaged in any major way with such debates when past leaders were Anglo-Saxon, or friends of the dominant western powers. We can have a debate over whether President Saddam Hussein should hang for crimes against the Kurds once he is a pariah in the west, but it is not a question worth discussing among criminologists when he is an ally during the period when he actually commits the crimes. Criminology can have a debate over whether Pol Pot and his communist Cambodian leadership should have been convicted, but not over whether President Suharto should have been convicted for the slaughter of half a million Indonesian communists, or for the invasion of West Papua or the invasion of East Timor. Suharto was also arguably the most successful white-collar criminal of the twentieth century, in terms of the scale of his crimes. Even though many western criminologists were victims of Suharto family embezzlement from joint ventures between his Indonesian government and western firms in which we have pension funds invested, this is unlikely to cross the minds of criminologists as a central question for discussion in our journals.

The sheer duplicity and arbitrariness that some criminologists, inspired by Edwin Sutherland (1949/1983), saw in the way that the crimes of the powerful are exempted from criminological scrutiny is the beginning of the journey that leads to a book as interesting as *Regulation and Criminal Justice*. Those of us who made crimes of the powerful our intellectual passion took different courses, however. Some like Frank Pearce and Steve Tombs (1990) pushed for balancing the books by locking up powerful criminals wherever possible. Others like myself looked at a big case like the crimes of Suharto in killing over 100,000 Timorese and saw the important thing when Suharto was deposed and replaced by his Vice President as persuading the new cabinet to repair the harm and to surround itself with new checks and balances that would make the crimes of the past more difficult in the future. Repairing the harm in East Timor meant doing exactly what the post-Suharto cabinet did – giving the people of East Timor a referendum in which they could vote to separate from Indonesia. Rightly or wrongly, scholars of this persuasion gave priority to regulatory and restorative means that might prevent ongoing suffering. They give this priority over punitive equality in the criminal law. It would have been desirable to have prosecuted some members of the post-Suharto cabinets as well as Suharto himself, and in some cases it is still not too late to do so, but it was more important to secure peace and democracy in East Timor.

Yet because equality was a value that led so many scholars of white-collar crime to be troubled over impunity for crimes of the *powerful* in the first place, we also became interested in regulatory and restorative solutions to preventing future harm from crimes of the *powerless*. It follows that scholars of this persuasion think what the University of Manchester has attempted in the workshops that led to this book is an endeavour of great merit. I will not delve into the definition of regulation in this Foreword, as the editors have provided an excellent discussion of that matter in their introductory essay.

The criminal law was a modern invention of European legal systems. All the rule breaking it came to regulate – murder, assault, theft, usury, arson, sexual misconduct, tax evasion, kidnap – was regulated by other means for millennia before the invention of the criminal law. The European state system and its state legal systems almost completely globalized in the nineteenth and twentieth centuries, exceptions being fewer than ten states that clung to Islamic or Hindu–Buddhist national legal systems. At the same time, administrative systems of western criminal law – paramilitary police specializing in crime, prisons, western training in the discipline of law – also globalized. But nowhere, for no form of crime, did the criminal law completely take over from other forms of regulation. Even for the most quintessentially criminalized form of rule breaking, homicide, when it is homicide by chief executives of corporations against their workers or by prime ministers against the people of nations they invade illegally, the criminal law applies in theory but not in practice. For other very common forms of serious crime, such as assaults of children on one of their parents, tax cheating that most Australians indulge in most years of their working life, regulation remains almost totally in the care of instruments other than the criminal law. The form of tax cheating that involves the largest frauds – profit shifting (e.g. into tax havens) by multinational corporations – in Australia, as in most nations, is never criminally prosecuted. Ironically, as this book documents, non-criminal forms of inspection and improvement orders, rather than the criminal law itself, remain the tools of choice for regulating the institutions of the criminal law itself when prisoners are treated unconscionably. When judges abuse the human rights of those who appear in their courts, their abuse is often regulated by reversing their decisions on appeal, by counselling from peers or other forms of legal professional self-regulation, not by imprisonment. Imprisonment is often inflicted on defendants or witnesses who rudely abuse a judge, never when it is the judge who inappropriately abuses them.

For the rural majority of the bulk of the world's population who live in developing countries, offences that are criminal according to their nation's law are rarely reported to the police. Rather, these are resolved by customary law normally led by legally untrained elders. For still a surprisingly large though uncertain proportion of the world's population, this continues to be true even for murder.

This reality makes it a difficult project for the criminal law paradigm to become even more imperially ambitious by aspiring to proportionate application to all the human rights abuses of greatest culpability. One problem is that costs of criminal enforcement are particularly high where the stakes are high. We see this with even middling war crimes trials. We also see it with the huge costs borne by the only national tax authority I know that regularly runs criminal prosecutions against fraudulent profit shifting into lower tax jurisdictions by large multinational corporations, the US Internal Revenue Service. And we see the opportunity cost when we consider the evidence of how effective non-criminal responsive regulatory enforcement innovations have been in Australia – returning more than a billion dollars to the taxpayer for every million spent on the responsive regulation programme (Braithwaite 2005: 89–97).

That said, the criminal law is a great European invention that, used prudently, can enhance the effectiveness of other forms of regulation. Some of this power comes from the intensity of the productive normative debates modern societies experience over what should be and should not be a crime. An upshot is that once a form of misconduct is accepted in the society as criminal conduct, it becomes much more possible to educate and persuade the community to the shamefulness of the conduct. Australian society has seen in my lifetime the criminal law constitute the shamefulness of drink driving and domestic violence that they did not have when I was young. The deepening of the normative furrows of the criminal law in my society has saved lives as a result. With domestic violence, my hypothesis is that the criminal law does less of its good work directly through deterrence, more of it indirectly through deepening the legitimacy of the change feminism as a social movement has wrought in thinking across the society. With drink driving, there is some Australian evidence to suggest that criminal enforcement has contributed less to saving lives via deterrence–rehabilitation–incapacitation, more by signalling a cultural change in drinking behaviour, strengthening the hand of friends who insist, 'You should not drive, I will get you home' (Homel 1988). The criminal law is a great institution because it has productive synergies with other forms of regulation more powerful than itself. That is not to deny that deterrence, rehabilitation and incapacitation can also do much more good than harm when deployed with wisdom.

The second important historical accomplishment of the globalization of the criminal law tradition is the way it imposed limits on the circumstances where the most onerous sanctions – deprivation of liberty through imprisonment, capital punishment, corporal punishment and torture could be used. The criminal law does the profound service to human rights of defining upper limits on the severity of such impositions even in circumstances where the nature of the wrongdoing permits their use. It also is a tradition that protects against excess by blocking any access to it unless a 'beyond reasonable doubt standard' and other evidentiary tests are passed (that need not be passed for non-criminal sanctions). The war on terror, as this book shows, has set back this momentum of the criminal law as a regulator of state violence. While the exposure of Abu Ghraib halted some of the worst torture, the debate that ensued has in some ways strengthened the impregnability to criminal law procedural regulation of practices like sleep deprivation during interrogation.

Notwithstanding the virtues of the criminal law paradigm discussed in this book and in my previous paragraph, one of its vices is that criminal law professionalism promotes a myopic tendency to see a right outcome to criminal wrongdoing as proportionate criminal punishment. This renders the criminal law vulnerable to capture by retributivist excess and by law and order auctions in politics. There is a case for depoliticization of criminal law to guard against such capture (Lacey 2008). But because punitive myopias internal to criminal law professionalism are also a danger, and because law and order politics will never go away, there is also a need for countervailing social movement politics against the excesses of criminal law globalization. The social movement for rehabilitation and reintegration of criminals, the human rights movement (particularly its prisoners' rights and its children's rights arms that in India has completely prohibited the criminalization of children) and the social movement for criminal law professionalism were in a sense each productively checking the excesses of the other for more than a century of declining punitiveness in most western societies until the late 1970s. Then the movement for rehabilitation of criminals was discredited, partly by an unfair reading of the state of the evidence on the effectiveness of rehabilitation. Movements for indigenous justice and legal pluralism have similarly suffered setbacks at the hands of criminal law fundamentalisms in western societies with large ethnic minorities since the 1970s. The social movement for restorative justice has sought in a new way to regulate the excesses of criminal law myopia. But it has little hope of substantially reducing that excess unless the movements for rehabilitation, customary law and prisoners' rights are also rejuvenated and become respectable again.

Regulatory studies also has an important intellectual contribution to make in tempering tendencies to simplify thinking about wrongdoing into crime and non-crime. This is not to say that a regulatory lens implies any kind of unified value position or unified epistemology. Indeed diversity is on display in the consistently fine essays in this collection. Whether regulatory approaches crush freedom more or less than criminal law approaches depends on the methods and values that frame each of them (Sanders 2010). Which approach is more effective in solving the problem is also contingent. This is a volume full of insights into how research might specify the contingencies where regulatory approaches might be more effective and decent than standard criminal justice responses to crime, and vice versa. It gives us by far the most fertile assembly of fine thinkers in the literature on the virtues and vices of looking at crime through a regulatory lens. My congratulations to Hannah Quirk, Toby Seddon and Graham Smith, and to all their authors, for their vision and for the quality of the research it has spawned.

References

Braithwaite, J. (2005) *Markets in Vice, Markets in Virtue*. New York, NY: Oxford University Press.

Homel, R. (1988) *Policing and Punishing the Drinking Driver: A Study of General and Specific Deterrence*. New York, NY: Springer-Verlag.

Lacey, N. (2008) *The Prisoners' Dilemma: Political Economy and Punishment in Contemporary Democracies*. Cambridge University Press.

Pearce, F. and Tombs, S. (1990) 'Ideology, Hegemony and Empiricism: Compliance Theories of Regulation', *British Journal of Criminology*, **30**(4), 423–43.

Sanders, A. (2010) 'Reconciling the Apparently Different Goals of Criminal Justice and Regulation: The "Freedom" Perspective' (this book, Chapter 3).

Sutherland, E. (1949/1983) *White-Collar Crime: The Uncut Version*. New Haven, CT: Yale University Press.

ACKNOWLEDGEMENTS

This book is based on a selection of papers presented to an Economic and Social Research Council-funded international seminar series entitled 'Regulation and Criminal Justice: Developing a New Framework for Research and Policy Development' (ESRC reference no. RES-451–26–0342). The series was organized by the Regulation, Security and Justice Research Centre based at the School of Law, University of Manchester. Four seminars were held at the University in November 2007, April and September 2008 and February 2009. The editors wish to express their gratitude to all of the participants who made the project so enjoyable and worthwhile. They are: Carolyn Abbot, Daniele Alge, Kevin Brown, Elizabeth Burney, Alex Carlile, Adam Crawford, Phil Edwards, John Flint, Richard Garside, Tom Gibbons, Joanna Gilmore, Peter Grabosky, Danielle Griffiths, Kate Hammond, Paddy Hillyard, Barbara Hudson, Caroline Hunter, Imogen Jones, Tammy Krause, Charles Loft, Gary Lynch-Wood, Nigel Meadows, Gabe Mythen, Anthony Ogus, Anne Owers, Andrew Sanders, Clifford Shearing, Frank Stephen, Lindsay Stirton, Clive Walker, Dave Whyte, Dave Williamson and Sarah Wilson.

1

Regulation and criminal justice: exploring the connections and disconnections

GRAHAM SMITH, TOBY SEDDON AND HANNAH QUIRK

This book explores the relationship between regulation and criminal justice. It comprises a selection of papers presented to an international seminar series hosted by the School of Law, University of Manchester, UK, between November 2007 and February 2009.[1] The majority of seminar participants were criminologists and interdisciplinary scholars involved in research across a range of criminal justice fields, invited to engage in a 'long conversation' with several regulation scholars and practitioners. One of the strengths of interdisciplinary discourse is the cross-fertilization of ideas between specialisms that facilitates comparative study and knowledge transfer. Socio-legal research and analysis, in explanatory and normative forms, has played a crucial part in the recent development of regulation (Morgan and Yeung 2007) and criminal justice (Sanders *et al.* 2010) as distinct areas of scholarship. But, as we will see, the two areas do share some common heritage, and so it is not surprising that connections have been established – most persuasively in the fields of policing (Ayling *et al.* 2009; Johnston and Shearing 2003) and restorative justice as an alternative to penal orthodoxy (Braithwaite 2002).

Grabosky (see Chapter 4, this book) describes regulation as a 'mansion with many rooms', an image that captures its scope, multifaceted character and conceptual diversity. Contemporary regulation discourse is rooted in public sector innovation dating back some three decades, which led to the transformation of governance in, and between, democratic polities regionally and globally (Levi-Faur 2005; Majone 1996). Keeping abreast

[1] Entitled 'Regulation and Criminal Justice: Developing a New Framework for Research and Policy Development', the Economic and Social Research Council-funded series was organized by the three co-editors, Kevin Brown and Andrew Sanders, to whom, with Phil Edwards (2008), we are grateful for their contributions to this chapter. In addition to the chapters in this collection, seminar papers have been published in regulation and criminology journals (Crawford 2009; Smith 2009; Tombs and Whyte 2009).

of the rapidly developing policy terrain scholars have theorized on the opening up of regulatory spaces (Hancher and Moran 1989; Scott 2001), (new) regulatory and post-regulatory states (Moran 2002; Parker and Braithwaite 2003; Scott 2004; Sunstein 1993) and regulatory capitalism (Braithwaite 2008; Levi-Faur 2005). Research has sought to understand and inform practice in analyses of governing from a distance (Osborne and Gaebler 1992), responsive regulation (Ayres and Braithwaite 1992), risk regulation regimes (Hood *et al.* 2001), decentred or polycentric regulation (Black 2002), problem-solving (Sparrow 2002) and regulation of regulation, or meta-regulation (Grabosky 1995).

Among this wealth of scholarly enterprise many definitions have been crafted. For Braithwaite, 'steering the flow of events' (2008: 1) suffices in an endeavour to portray regulation's vast reach and the growth of 'regulatory capitalism'. Moran adopts a similarly straightforward approach, 'to govern in the sense of balancing a system' (2002: 5) like the regulator in a steam engine. Developing a law-and-economics approach, Ogus (see Chapter 2, this book), limits its meaning to public governance, which is characterized by state intervention in markets to override individual preferences and private governance in order to address what are perceived to be undesirable outcomes. Black also adopts a purposive approach but, in contrast to Ogus, she conceives regulation to be decentred and not restricted to state activity. Thus, 'regulation is the sustained and focused attempt to alter the behaviour of others according to defined standards or purposes with the intention of producing a broadly defined outcome or outcomes' (Black 2002: 26; see also Shearing and Froestad's treatment of polycentric governance, Chapter 5, this book). In her examination of techniques available to regulators to secure compliance with Australian competition law, Yeung draws on Ogus and Black to conceptualize regulation as 'the sustained and focussed attempt by the state to alter behaviour thought to be of value to the community' (2004: 5). Clarifying her standpoint Yeung accepts the important part that non-state actors play in regulation, but declares there is no space for them in her definition because she is investigating the role of public regulators. Her reason for restricting the type of behaviour that is subject to regulation, as that which is thought to be of value to the community, is because if it were not, it would be subject to punishment and censure by criminal sanction.

Criminal justice research is also a relative newcomer to the academy.[2] Devoted to study of the criminal process it does not boast the same

[2] Until recently it was customary to refer separately to the administration of justice, criminal law or criminal procedure, as typified by the title of Sir Leon Radzinowicz's five-volume

intersectoral credentials as regulation, which partly explains the poverty of criminal justice theory.[3] In their attempts to contextualize criminal law and explain innovation in the criminal justice system scholars have tended to rely on normative models (Ashworth and Redmayne 2005; Packer 1968; Sanders, Chapter 3, this book). There are signs that the reluctance to define criminal justice is changing, arguably as a result of the emergence of regulation as an alternative control system which challenges conventional criminal justice practice and ideas. The development of regulation as a governing force is sharpening its relief with substantive and procedural criminal law and focusing the minds of criminal justice scholars to think more about what criminal justice is (Zedner 2004), what it is not, and how it is different to regulation. Thus, in their examination of recent criminal justice reform in England and Wales, Ashworth and Zedner present a liberal conception of criminal justice 'that emphasises both the purpose of the criminal law in providing for censure and punishment and the need to respect the autonomy and dignity of individuals in the criminal process' (2008: 22). Analysing the UK government's reliance on regulatory tools in its antisocial behaviour agenda, Crawford (2009)[4] stops short of offering a definition of criminal justice. In arguing that regulation language has intruded upon criminal justice practice, however, he outlines core elements of criminal justice. These include 'command-and-control-style rule', '[u]niform standards and universal principles' and 're-ordering and accounting for past conduct' (Crawford 2009: 813–14). Sanders (Chapter 3, this book, and see more below) goes one step further and, although qualifying his definition by restricting its reach to the purpose at hand, broadly conceives of criminal justice as 'legal state coercion that is determinable in the criminal courts'.

The aim of the Manchester seminars was to examine the nexus between regulation and criminal justice with a view to developing a new framework for research and policy development. We wanted, above all, to explore how regulatory scholarship from other fields might inform our understanding of contemporary criminal justice developments. There appeared to us to be some new policy directions in the field for which

History of English Criminal Law and Its Administration (1948–86). Sanders and Young wrote the first textbook on criminal justice in England and Wales, in 1994, now in its fourth edition.

3 The exception here is the end point of the criminal justice process, punishment, which has been the subject of extensive theorising, both normative and explanatory, for a very long time. See Garland (1990) and Duff and Garland (1994).

4 A participant in the Manchester seminar series, Adam Crawford presented an earlier draft of this chapter to the first seminar.

the application of more conventional criminal justice approaches was of only limited usefulness. We were interested in exploring the extent to which cross-cutting perspectives may help to advance knowledge and thinking about policy. It is apparent that the connections between these two social control systems extend beyond policing and restorative justice. For example, the criminal sanction is one of several regulatory interventions intended to modify behaviour; criminal justice operates as a regulatory regime that may influence behaviour whether or not a sanction is issued; and the organizations that make up the criminal justice system are subject to regulation. Moreover, the introduction in England and Wales of hybrid interventions, which combine civil orders and criminal penalties, most particularly the Anti-Social Behaviour Order (ASBO) and the Control Order for the purpose of regulating antisocial behaviour and terrorist risk, respectively, point to overlapping regulatory and criminal justice practices. On closer inspection, however, it is also evident that there is much in principle and practice to distinguish regulation and criminal justice, and disconnections were repeatedly articulated in seminar discussions. Connections or disconnections are made depending on how regulation and criminal justice are conceptualized, the nature of the issue problematized and whether analysis is explanatory or normative. In consequence, the relationship between regulation and criminal justice is characterized by blurred and uncertain boundaries. The distinction, for example, between conduct that is controlled by regulatory measures and that which is subject to the criminal law, often appears unclear or even arbitrary. Yet it is a distinction which is frequently accepted as the basis for much scholarship and policy-making.

In the first of the four seminars, we focused on the idea of criminal justice, attempting to specify its parameters and boundaries, as a prelude to looking at its relationship with regulation. In fact, discussions about concepts and definitions continued throughout the series and the chapters in Part I of this book, by Ogus (Chapter 2), Sanders (Chapter 3) and Grabosky (Chapter 4) are products of this debate.

Several important perspectives in regulatory, socio-legal and criminological scholarship can be understood as extended efforts to transcend the divide between regulation and criminal justice. Founded on the seminal contributions of Richard Posner, Gary Becker and others, the law-and-economics movement that emerged in the USA in the late 1950s is a major regulation perspective. Influential on both sides of the Atlantic and elsewhere it seeks to provide a framework which can be applied in diverse fields that sweep across the boundaries of regulation and criminal justice. The founding principle of law and economics is the Benthamite notion that 'people are rational maximizers of their satisfactions' (Posner 1983: 1) who weigh up costs and benefits before taking decisions about how to act. The central insight of the approach is that this is true not only when people engage in markets but more broadly in other areas and activities of life. As Becker puts it:

> I have come to the position that the economic approach is a comprehensive one that is applicable to all human behavior, be it behavior involving money prices or imputed shadow prices, repeated or infrequent decisions, large or minor decisions, emotional or mechanical ends.
>
> (1976: 8)

A key moment in this literature is Becker's famous paper published in 1968, in which he applies an economic approach to the problem of crime and criminal justice. He defines 'crime' very broadly in this paper, including 'not just felonies – like murder, robbery, and assault [...] but also tax evasion, the so-called white-collar crimes, and traffic and other violations' (1968: 170). Becker's economic model sets out the impact of enforcement actions and punishment on motivations to offend:

> There is a function relating the number of offenses by any person to his probability of conviction, to his punishment if convicted, and to other variables, such as the income available to him in legal and other illegal activities, the frequency of nuisance arrests, and his willingness to commit an illegal act.
>
> (1968: 177)

This model provides a generic method for determining the most efficient and effective strategy for securing compliance with rules and standards concerning human behaviour – a model, in other words, for optimizing enforcement. Expressed in this way, it is an analytical perspective which can potentially cut across the boundaries of regulation and criminal justice.

Law-and-economics proponent Anthony Ogus examines the relationship between regulation and criminal justice, Chapter 2 of this book. Cost–benefit analysis rests at the heart of what he describes as a continuum between 'mainstream criminal law offences' and 'regulatory offences' and in the proposition that mainstream criminal offences – against the person, property, public order – are more appropriately regulated by criminal justice; and regulatory offences by compliance strategies and administrative or civil interventions. Excepting, of course, where the seriousness of the offence committed requires criminal sanction. In accordance with the economic theory of deterrence, as the object of enforcement is to modify behaviour, it follows that it should be practised optimally in a way that involves minimum cost and produces maximum benefit. Based on the assumption that regulatory offences are committed in furtherance of activity which is of value to the community, high administrative and error costs and welfare losses (reduced activity as a precaution against the risk of prosecution) associated with criminal proceedings, renders criminal justice deterrence ineffective relative to less costly regulatory enforcement. Standard criminal behaviour does not generate significant social value and, without the need to offset administrative and error costs against welfare losses, the same calculus does not apply when controlled by criminal justice.

Thus, for Ogus, a standard formula that calculates the utility of different methods of enforcement for different types of offence connects regulation and criminal justice. However, in making the connection, law-and-economics deterrence principles simultaneously disconnect regulation and criminal justice in the separating out of regulatory from criminal offences to justify the imposition of different enforcement interventions. For some, including Sanders and Whyte in their contributions to this book (Chapters 3 and 7, respectively) a consequence of this disconnection may be inequitable distribution of sanctions commensurate with the power, wealth and status of the offender.

Socio-legal criminal justice scholar, Andrew Sanders, offers an expansive definition of criminal justice, Chapter 3 of this book, which encompasses criminal and regulatory offences and enforcement techniques under the rubric of criminal justice, consistent with a toolkit approach. His objective is to develop a normative argument in support of the 'freedom model' he has collaboratively developed (Sanders and Young 2000; Sanders *et al.* 2010). For Sanders, regulation and criminal justice are connected by innovation in both fields and he sets out to establish some ground rules for how their respective goals and principles, some of which conflict, should be prioritized. Adopting a polemical style, he is critical of the failure of human rights, currently considered the dominant normative approach to criminal justice, to balance competing human rights adequately and maintains that their goal-setting capacity is limited. After Gearty (2006), his concern is that human rights cannot usurp democratic politics and serve as the basis for positive law. Addressing the apparent conflict between compliance and punishment approaches, cornerstones of regulation and criminal justice, respectively, he reminds us they are not goals, and concludes in favour of an integrated strategy to offending per se. Although he rejects Ogus's analysis restricting regulatory interventions to regulatory offences, Sanders accepts his argument on the cost-effectiveness of compliance, and extends it in his freedom perspective beyond the realms of regulation and criminal justice. With the assertion that 'criminal justice is a matter of social justice' he points out that effective resource allocation in criminal justice has positive consequences for other public services. Thus, state intervention, whether in regulation or criminal justice form, should only be exercised if the net effect is to enhance freedom. This may mean doing nothing if the activity contemplated, stop and search for example, is ineffective in the prevention or detection of crime and interferes with individuals' human rights; the resources required could be reallocated for more effective use elsewhere.

Sanders attaches major importance to regulation theory in his chapter, the ideas of eminent criminologist turned regulation scholar John Braithwaite in particular. To Braithwaite and colleagues in the Regulatory Institutions Network (RegNet) at the Australian National University the study of regulation has emerged at the cutting edge of paradigmatic change in the social sciences (Braithwaite 2000). For Braithwaite the organization of disciplines around categorical referents like 'crime' or 'markets' no longer makes sense. Instead, work organized around theoretical themes like regulation has much greater scope for delivering advances in knowledge, advances which may cut across categories (Braithwaite 2005). In broadly defining regulation as all attempts to steer the flow of events, crime becomes simply another regulatory problem and the apparent divide between regulation and criminal justice largely disappears. One of the 'big ideas' of the RegNet School – responsive regulation and the regulatory pyramid (Ayres and Braithwaite 1992; Braithwaite 2002; Grabosky, Chapter 4, this book) – illustrates this nicely. Developed and refined over the course of more than twenty-five years, it has been the focus of empirical research in diverse fields, from corporate crime to coal mine safety, tax evasion to youth offending. Empirical work in one field has shed light on research in others. It has been a site for genuine cross-boundary and cross-disciplinary conversations, facilitated through the deployment of the cross-cutting theme of regulation. And it is conversations of this kind which have proved more fruitful in terms of advancing knowledge and developing practice, rather than work located more conventionally within single disciplines.

In Chapter 4 Peter Grabosky, RegNet scholar in regulation and criminal justice, examines criminal justice as an instrument of regulation. His main point, in keeping with regulation orthodoxy, is that in comparison to the more informal tools preferred by regulators the *criminal process* is slow, costly, unpredictable, ineffective and only used as a last resort.

Grabosky's principal contribution to research and policy is to locate and expand on the role of third parties in regulation and criminal justice. Dissatisfied with the capacity of Braithwaite's pyramidal heuristic to capture the complexity of multi-agency arrangements, he illustrates[5] the value of a three-dimensional Regulatory Tetrahedron; of which, more in a moment. Turning his attention to regulation as an instrument of criminal justice, Grabosky relies on a broader conceptualization of criminal justice. He conceives it more as *crime control*, which facilitates inclusion of crime prevention strategies designed to inhibit crime and forestall the need to engage the criminal process. Again, major importance is attached to third parties and Grabosky focuses his attention on their role in an examination of the application of regulatory principles to the crime control process. These include, *inter alia*, conscripting third parties to assist with law enforcement or regulation, a duty to maintain and disclose records (facilitating self-regulation), the availability of incentives to encourage compliance and contracting out of functions. Like Sanders, Grabosky is mindful of the importance of cross-sectoral resource management and organically connects regulation and criminal justice. Conscious of several normative problems, damage to transparency and accountability in particular, he stresses the greater potential of regulation for effective and efficient control in contrast to Sanders's emphasis on the expansion of criminal justice.

Sanders also refers to a new cross-cutting approach connecting regulation and criminal justice developed from within criminology: the 'social harm' or zemiology perspective (Hillyard *et al.* 2005).[6] This starts from the view that not only is the category of 'crime' a social construction with no ontological reality, it is also a term that encompasses an extremely wide range of behaviours and acts. Consequently, it is unlikely that a single type of intervention in the form of criminal justice will be appropriate or effective. Zemiologists argue further that many serious harms either lie outside the ambit of the criminal law or else tend to be

[5] Literally. In the first Manchester seminar he wowed participants with an impressive Powerpoint presentation which included moving three-dimensional images of the Regulatory Tetrahedron!

[6] Paddy Hillyard responded to Sanders's paper in the first Manchester seminar. Charles Loft, Local Authorities Co-ordinator of Regulatory Services Policy Officer, triggered a fascinating discussion by outlining a practitioner's concerns with cost–benefit analysis; namely, problems quantifying incommensurable variables and the probability of erratic or misleading outcomes. Discussion quickly moved onto the advantages of principles-based approaches and the relative merits of 'freedom' and 'harm' as alternative – positive and negative – indices of social control.

handled outside of it. Examples include workplace injuries, corporate crime and police violence. In this view, the conventional criminal justice or crime control approach is a failure which allows many serious dangers and harms to continue relatively unchecked while focusing unduly on relatively minor or petty acts simply because they are defined by the crime label. To address this, they propose abandoning the concept of crime and replacing it with the idea of social harm – and in the process abandoning criminology for the new discipline of zemiology. 'Social harm' is defined broadly to cover a range of potential harms to individuals: physical; financial/economic; emotional/psychological; sexual; cultural. They argue that this perspective would open up the possibilities for much wider investigations of responsibility for producing harms and for much broader and more ambitious social policy solutions. There is an obvious affinity worth noting here between zemiology and law and economics: the term 'harm' shares many characteristics with the economic notion of 'cost'. Indeed, Becker's (1968: 198) seminal article even raises the speculative idea that the criminal law might become a branch of the law of torts with the public collectively suing for 'public harms'. There is also a connection with the regulation perspective. The zemiologists seek to build a new theoretical approach around the concept of social harm which can cut across existing boundaries, in much the same way as Braithwaite attempts in using the concept of regulation. Like regulation scholars, the zemiologists are not confined by conventional views on the limits of criminal justice or regulation. Indeed, they explicitly aim to break down barriers between them.

Returning to the definitions presented at the beginning of this introductory chapter, they help differentiate the three comparative approaches developed by Ogus, Sanders and Grabosky. Ogus adheres to a type of criminal justice definition similar to that of Ashworth and Zedner (2008), alongside his public governance conception of regulation. Sanders's criminal justice as state-coercion approach is consistent with Yeung's definition of regulation. Grabosky's conceptualization of regulation compares to Black's and he relies on a narrow definition of criminal justice in keeping with Ashworth and Zedner when considering it as an instrument of regulation, broadening this out to crime control when examining regulation as an instrument of criminal justice.

Different metaphors also feature in the comparative approaches presented here. Ogus and Sanders rely on a one-dimensional spectrum to illustrate the relationship between regulation and criminal justice. Grabosky presents a version of Braithwaite's two-dimensional pyramid and develops his own three-dimensional tetrahedron.[7] Each metaphor facilitates analysis, explanatory and normative, of the appropriate regulatory or criminal justice intervention used or required to achieve a desired outcome or censure and punish wrongdoing. Interventions are located dimensionally or spatially in each metaphor, and normative assumptions may also be represented by movement along, up and down, or inside each heuristic. Ogus uses type of offence and intervention, whether regulatory or criminal justice, to distinguish between regulation and criminal justice. Location on the spectrum is by cost–benefit analysis, using social welfare as a key determinant, and movement in either direction is resource driven. Sanders uses the notion of freedom and whether it is enhanced or eroded by interventions that pre-empt or remedy wrongdoing of any description; the desired goal is the pursuit of freedom which is located at one end of the spectrum. In Braithwaite's regulatory pyramid, degree of compliance combined with severity of intervention determines vertical location and frequency of application is represented horizontally. Responsiveness is portrayed by movement up and down, which is achievable by the escalation and de-escalation of interventions. Grabosky's tetrahedron, which fully incorporates Braithwaite's pyramid on one face, additionally portrays the relationship between regulatee and regulator. One face represents the regulatee individually and collectively, in the form of professional body or association for example, and depicts self-regulation; state regulation is represented on the second face (Braithwaite's pyramid); and the contribution of third parties on the third. The contribution of different parties, compliance and severity pinpoints interventions inside the tetrahedron, which provides the heuristic with the capacity to measure collaborativeness in addition to responsiveness.

In light of this brief discussion of definitions and metaphors, what account do these scholars offer for the condition of the criminal justice estate? This is not of significance for Ogus, as he does not trespass on criminal justice territory.[8] Neither does it particularly exercise Braithwaite – as already mentioned his regulation landscape includes criminal justice

[7] Sanders also finds the toolkit image helpful. An advantage of this metaphor is its flexibility and the degree of discretion it affords the decision-maker; it suggests addressing a problem by choosing a remedy from an unordered range of interventions. The problem remains, however (as Sanders points out), how does the decision-maker prioritize conflicting goals and principles and choose the right tool for the job?

[8] In challenging the appropriateness of regulation and criminal justice referents and championing social harm as an alternative, zemiologists also maintain a critical distance from this question.

research and policy fields. For Ashworth and Zedner (2008) regulatory innovation and its incursion into criminal law and procedure represent a retreat from principle and the contraction of criminal justice in recognition of the diminishing importance of the criminal trial. Although concerned that his observations on regulation challenge criminal justice principles, Crawford (2009) does not venture into normative analysis and he is agnostic on this point. Sanders and Grabosky, in contrast, hold that criminal justice is expanding, and incorporates regulatory innovations, and neither is unduly troubled in principle by the general trend, although they each raise particular problems.

Grabosky borrows from another metaphor developed in regulation discourse, 'regulatory space' (this book: p. 90), and makes a passing reference to 'crime space' in the context of pluralistic crime control and associated resource management pressures. Whereas Grabosky speaks of separate regulatory and crime spaces, reading Sanders's contribution to this book a distinctive 'criminal justice space' is discernible, which includes the use of regulatory interventions but, unlike Grabosky, not crime prevention. Applied crime prevention is a cross-cutting crime control approach that draws on economic analysis, rational choice theory and routine action theory (Felson and Clark 1998). Crime prevention is evidently in 'crime space', 'crime control space' and 'regulatory space'; but not 'criminal justice space' if any one of the definitions outlined above by Ashworth and Zedner, Crawford or Sanders is accepted. Thus, it is possible to identify a range of approaches, on a continuum once again, to the relationship between regulation and criminal justice developed by Braithwaite, Sanders and Grabosky. Braithwaite understands criminal justice as a part of regulation, or in regulatory space, at one end; Sanders understands regulation in criminal justice space, towards the other; and, somewhere between the two, Grabosky understands regulation and criminal justice as overlapping spaces.

There is, of course, some irony in the defence of criminal justice principles that Ashworth and Zedner (2008) and others put forward, given that the criminal process has failed, and continues to fail, so many, including victims, offenders and innocent suspects subjected to miscarriages of justice. This is what makes the search for alternative means of maintaining good social relations so crucial. The introduction of innovative regulatory interventions designed for the purpose of protecting the public, on one hand, and preventing entry into the criminal justice system, on the other, is commendable in principle. Pragmatic attempts to achieve these conflicting goals do, however, give rise to problems of principle, which, in turn, have repercussions for the effectiveness of regulatory and criminal justice interventions. In the remaining three Manchester seminars we embarked on a number of case studies which focused on two key dimensions of the nexus between regulation and criminal justice: criminal justice as a means of behavioural regulation; and the regulation of criminal justice itself. Conceptual and theoretical discussions concerning the relationship between regulation and criminal justice continued to play a central part in our discussions.

Criminal justice as regulation

One criminal justice field where regulation discourse has proved highly influential is policing, and deep connections have been established between police practice and regulation (Gill 2002). Since Bayley and Shearing (1996) famously presented their thesis on the transformation of policing there has been a shift in the locus of police scholarship. Discourse on the governance of plural policing, securitization and democratization of policing in transitional states has flourished (Bayley 2006; Johnston and Shearing 2003; Loader 2000; Zedner 2009). Debate has blossomed between 'nodal governance' scholars, on the one hand, who argue that the rise of plural policing is reorganizing the landscape to make the public police one of many providers of security services (Shearing and Wood 2006). Their adversaries, on the other hand, claim that there is much life, and good, left in the public police that its status as the principal protector of community safety is assured (Crawford 2006; Loader and Walker 2007).

This reawakening of interest in regulation has also prompted several historical reappraisals of the practice of policing (O'Malley and Hutchinson 2007; Zedner 2006). In *The Culture of Control*, Garland observes that:

> The early modern idea of 'police' referred not to the specialist agency that emerged in the nineteenth century but to a much more general programme of detailed regulation, pursued by urban authorities in their efforts to create an orderly environment for trade and commerce. The aim of this kind of 'police' regulation was to promote public tranquillity and security, to ensure efficient trade and communications in the city, and to enhance the wealth, health, and prosperity of the population. To this end, city authorities promulgated detailed by-laws calling for the inspection of weights and measures, censuses of the population, programmes of street lighting, the regulation of roads and buildings, trade and foodstuffs. (Garland 2001: 31)

The establishment by Peel of the Metropolitan Police in 1829 thus marked a significant fork in the road, as 'police' took on its modern meaning of a uniformed civil agency with a paramilitary structure dedicated to regulating matters of crime and disorder. In a European context, Pasquino (1991: 109) traces this development back a little further but suggests that this new meaning can be found no earlier than the 1770s. In an important review essay on Garland's book, Braithwaite (2003) criticizes him for mentioning this fork but then proceeding largely to ignore it in his subsequent analysis. He argues that this unduly restricts his analytical vision, as it erases the 'pre-history' of police and obscures its common roots with forms of business regulation in the pre-industrial police economy.

Contemporary securitization literature draws on insights provided by regulation scholarship into public sector reform, the interconnectedness of institutions that span the public–private divide and informal regulatory mechanisms. Clifford Shearing's ideas are prominent in this discourse, and in this book, Chapter 5 he and Jan Froestad trace the development of the 'nodal governance' perspective culminating in the development of the Zwelethemba Model. Shearing's contribution to policy development is impressive. He was a member of the Independent Commission on Policing in Northern Ireland (1999, Patten Commission) that has influenced police reform far beyond the borders of contested UK territory in Ireland (Bayley 2008). Scepticism of command and control regulation is at the core of Shearing and Froestad's nodal governance narrative. In opposition to top-down ordering that stifles innovation, growth, effectiveness and efficiency, they prefer bottom-up mobilization of local capacity and resources engaged in 'democratic experimentalism' and the design of new security arrangements. In their view, pluralization of policing creates openings for marginalized populations to gather together and establish their own node of security governance. This is demonstrated in Shearing's personal journey from provision of safer housing in Toronto, to peaceful marches leading up to South Africa's first free election, to dispute resolution in Zwelethemba.

In Chapter 6 environment regulation researchers Gary Lynch-Wood and Dave Williamson probe responsive regulation premises based on comparative study of compliance by large and small and medium enterprises (SMEs) and in Chapter 7 criminologist Dave Whyte responds to effective failure to sanction corporate crime. The popularity of responsive regulation has meant it has been subject to critical scrutiny, and it has not survived unscathed (Abbot 2009). For example, serious consequences of non-compliance may render non-coercive intervention inappropriate and require immediate resort to criminal sanction;[9] it may not be practicable to escalate or de-escalate interventions; differential intervention is inconsistent with the principle of equality before the law (Ashworth 2000); and under or over-enforcement may contravene principles of proportionality and consistency (Yeung 2004).

In their chapter, Lynch-Wood and Williamson are interested in the receptive capacity of regulatees to comply with interventions. Rather than approach the question of responsiveness from the standpoint of the regulator, and the need for understanding of the regulatee's circumstances (Baldwin and Black 2008), they analyse the attitudes of regulatees. Their argument, in a nutshell, is that size matters. Compliance with environmental regulation is better in large organizations than SMEs and there is more non-compliance among smaller than larger organizations. In their resource-based model, Lynch-Wood and Williamson identify a range of regulatee responses based on organizational capability and compliance orientation.[10] Their evidence suggests that current regulatory strategies, targeted as they are at compliant large firms, are of limited effectiveness and they conclude in support of the reallocation of regulatory resources targeted at SMEs for whom the risk of non-compliance is greatest. For these two environmental scholars, there is a clear disconnection between regulation and criminal justice along the same lines as suggested by Ogus, evidenced by rare mention of criminal sanctions. Rather than assume that a more coercive intervention is required to respond to non-compliance, they suggest insufficient attention has been paid to the reasons why SMEs do not comply. In Chapter 7 of this book Whyte does not pull his punches in dismissing this alternative approach to existing risk-based regulation strategies and vigorously attempting to reconnect regulation and criminal justice. In zemiological language and Marxist dialect he condemns neo-liberal and pluralistic apologists for corporate offending. Citing the Environment Agency's record of declining inspections and enforcement interventions and increasing audits in the last decade or so, Whyte argues that a new politics of regulatory consensus has emerged, of which prosecutions of corporate crime are a casualty. Rather than size, the asymmetries, including resource distribution, between regulatory and criminal justice agencies matter more.

[9] For example, prosecution of the Office of the Commissioner of the Police for the Metropolis under the Health and Safety at Work Act 1974 following the shooting of Jean Charles de Menezes by police officers in London (Independent Police Complaints Commission 2007).

[10] Not to be outshone by Peter Grabosky, their graphics are also impressive.

Discussion of preventive and risk-based strategies designed to pre-empt crime featured prominently in the seminar series, reflecting the wider 'rise of risk' across the social sciences (Garland 2003). As well as a paper on recent risk-oriented innovations in drug policy (Seddon *et al.* 2008), three papers were presented on the UK's antisocial behaviour programme, by Adam Crawford (2009), Elizabeth Burney (2008) and John Flint and Caroline Hunter (Chapter 8, this book), and three on counter-terrorism policy, by Alex Carlile, the UK's Independent Reviewer of Terrorism Legislation (2008), Paddy Hillyard (2009) and Gabe Mythen (Chapter 9, this book). Innovations in the latter two fields, involving the regulation of behaviour that may not involve criminal conduct, have had a major impact on criminal justice.

The Anti-Social Behaviour Order introduced under the Crime and Disorder Act 1998 is not a criminal sanction. It is a hybrid intervention that involves a *civil* order, issued by a magistrate on application by police and local authority, or landlord, but where failure to comply may result in *criminal* sanction. It embodies, in this sense, the responsive regulation principle of the escalation of sanctions where there is non-compliance, albeit in a crude two-step form (Simester and von Hirsch 2006). The ASBO is a pluralistically managed intervention that requires an individual to act, or not, in a prescribed way for preventive purposes. The statutory intention is to prevent behaviour that causes, or is likely to cause, harassment, alarm or distress to other persons and protect them from further suffering. Further intentions are to curtail the subject of the order from developing a criminal career and prevent entry into the criminal justice system. John Flint and Caroline Hunter, geographer and lawyer, respectively, consider some recent developments in the government's Respect antisocial behaviour programme in Chapter 8, this book. They explore hybrid interventions, related to the ASBO, that target the family as a cause of problem behaviour and widen multi-agency involvement in an ever-expanding regulatory regime. The Respect Task Force's twin-track approach – *supporting* individuals who wish to fulfil their parental responsibilities and *making* those who will not – is scrutinized in their examination of four interventions. In addition to the familiarly pessimistic conclusion that hybrid interventions are exclusionary, disciplinary and punitive, they also cautiously welcome their capacity to be inclusionary, supportive and transformative.

The first Manchester seminar took place shortly after reorganization of the machinery of government in the UK, which involved the creation of a new Ministry of Justice (Smith 2007). Lead responsibility for counter-terrorism was given to the Home Office with the aim of producing 'a step change in our [the government's] approach to managing the terrorist threat to the UK and winning the battle for hearts and minds' (Cabinet Office 2007: 2) In furtherance of this goal a new Ministerial Committee and Office for Security and Counter-Terrorism were established to take responsibility for the Contest strategy (HM Government 2009). Another aim of the reorganization was to bring together management of the criminal justice system in the Ministry of Justice, 'meaning that once a suspect has been charged, their journey through the courts, and if necessary prison and probation, can be managed seamlessly' (Cabinet Office 2007: 3). This distinction, drawn in regulatory terms, between counter-terrorism and criminal justice has become all too familiar around the globe since the fateful events in the USA on 11 September 2001. Examples include increasing reliance on executive power, detention without trial, judicial deference, military trial and non-disclosure of intelligence (Parry 2006; Walker 2009). In light of these developments much has been written about the normalization of exceptional powers introduced to combat terrorism and, then, being applied to criminal justice (Flyghed 2002; McCulloch and Pickering 2009; Wolfendale 2007). Another concern is what sociologists term 'othering' (Bauman 1989; Jamieson and McEvoy 2005), referring to the process by which the state and sections of majority populations manage to ostracize minorities perceived to be a threat to dominant interests. This provides some context for Gabe Mythen and Palash Kamruzzaman's fascinating ethnographic study, this book, Chapter 9, in which they recount young British Muslims' experiences of anti-terrorism legislation. In their opening commentary on 'new' terrorism and the UK's pre-emptive counter-terrorism strategy they pose some awkward questions. Most significantly, they ask whether the threat to a nation not unused to withstanding terrorist violence has 'changed so dramatically' or whether the UK is drifting towards a 'risk averse and punitive political climate' (p. 222). Mythen and Kamruzzaman describe as 'disconcerting and sobering' (p. 227) their respondents' experiences of surveillance, stop and search and suspicion and the commonly held view that they are targeted not as a consequence of their behaviour, but because of their race.

Designed for the purpose of controlling and subverting sub-criminal behaviours and radicalizing ideas that may lead to the commission of criminal acts, antisocial behaviour and counter-terrorism strategies, like crime prevention, are developing regulation regimes that are connected to, yet separate from, criminal justice. Description of the ASBO as 'quasi-criminal',[11] for example, reflects its hybridity and capacity to control a broader range of behaviours than conventional criminal justice. Much counter-terrorism policy is similarly devoted to pursuing aims alien to traditional criminal justice goals and principles, the disruption of suspected future acts without resort to the courts for example. Rather than define and pigeon-hole these innovations, a more valuable exercise, given current levels of knowledge and understanding, is arguably to contextualize them in regulatory and criminal justice spaces along similar lines to Braithwaite, Sanders or Grabosky.

Regulation of criminal justice

The police are primary state actors in crime prevention, criminal justice, antisocial behaviour and counter-terrorism policy. Among their many responsibilities they protect communities against crime, serve as gatekeepers to the criminal justice system, make ASBO applications and operate on the frontline combating terrorism. A wide range of discretionary coercive powers are available to the police to enable them to perform these functions. Like other criminal justice agencies, they are subject to regulatory and accountability arrangements for the purpose of ensuring effective, efficient and human rights-compliant performance. Self-regulation is predominant, consistent with the principle of independent and impartial law enforcement and the command and control character of criminal justice. For this reason, among others, New Public Management innovations that transformed other public services in the 1980s reached criminal justice late (McLaughlin *et al.* 2001). Surging reform since the turn of the millennium, however, is now ushering in a complex and intricate governance network.

Take, for example, two 'exceptional' counter-terrorism interventions which operate beyond traditional criminal justice principles: the police power to stop and search without reasonable grounds for suspicion under the Terrorism Act 2000, and the issuing to a terrorist suspect of a Control Order under the Prevention of Terrorism Act 2005, a hybrid intervention similar to the ASBO (Walker 2009). The overarching purpose of these interventions is to protect against terrorism, and in pursuance of this objective they are subject to a range of standards which are not entirely complementary. Effectiveness and efficiency are maintained by performance standards and, because these interventions interfere with the right

[11] *R (on the application of McCann)* v. *Manchester Crown Court* [2003] 1 AC 787.

to liberty, respect for privacy, freedom of expression and association, they are subject to standards laid down in the European Convention on Human Rights (ECHR). Thus, their use is regulated legally and administratively in several ways, including by time and geographical restrictions, requirements of prior political or judicial authority, Code of Practice guidance, regular independent operational review, judicial review and application to the European Court of Human Rights (ECtHR). The regulation regime involves self-regulating police services, the Inspectorate of Constabulary, Home Office, Parliamentary Joint Committee on Human Rights, courts including the Special Immigration Appeals Court, Council of Europe Committee for the Prevention of Torture, Degrading and Inhuman Treatment, non-governmental organizations (NGOs) such as Liberty, along with many other state and non-state organizations. Mythen and Kamruzzaman devote space to the controversies associated with stop and search and Control Orders in their chapter, and it is worthy of note that the ECtHR is proving to be an effective meta-regulatory institution, although its influence is delayed. In *Gillan and Quinton* v. *UK*[12] the ECtHR ruled that stop and search under the 2000 Terrorism Act constituted a violation of the right to respect for privacy; this was nearly four years after the House of Lords ruled it was a proportionate intervention in consideration of the terrorism risk.[13] Following the ECtHR's lead, the House of Lords reconsidered the lawfulness of Control Orders and remitted several for a judge to consider what is essential to the fairness of the trial.[14] In light of these judgments the Home Secretary subsequently requested a review of the viability of the Control Order regime (*Guardian*, 19 September 2009).

Several seminar sessions were devoted to the regulation of criminal justice, including examination of the criminal courts (Quirk 2008), the Independent Police Complaints Commission (Smith 2009) and the Independent Reviewer of Terrorism Legislation (Carlile 2008). Five separate inspectorates – of Constabulary, Crown Prosecution Service, Courts Administration, Prison and Probation – are key to the criminal justice regulation regime. In Chapter 10 the former Chief Inspector of Prisons, Anne Owers, offers a wide-ranging treatment of the regulation of criminal justice in England and Wales and developments in prison inspection, including in France and the USA. Reading Owers's inside account it is apparent that inspection of the separate criminal justice agencies has

[12] Application no. 4158/05: Judgment 12 January 2010.

[13] *R (on the application of Gillan (FC) and another (FC))* v. *Commissioner of Police for the Metropolis and others* [2006] UKHL 12.

[14] *Secretary of State for the Home Department* v. *AF and another* [2009] UKHL 28.

developed ad hoc. Bereft of clear principles, regulation has been imposed on existing structures in pragmatic response to dysfunctional regulation. The impression of inconsistent and incoherent regulation of criminal justice was reinforced as recently as 2006 when the government withdrew its plans for creating a unified criminal justice inspectorate. Since then, there has been increased cooperation between inspectorates and some reorientation. The Inspectorate of Constabulary, for example, has become more public-facing and human rights aware. For Owers, cooperation between independent inspectorates is crucial, and regulatory effectiveness would benefit if they were to report to a joint committee of Parliament (which would weaken ties with government departments and enhance independent oversight). In response to Owers, criminologist Toby Seddon accentuates the commonalities between prison inspection and other regulation regimes in Chapter 11. Taking his lead from Braithwaite's responsive regulation research, especially on nursing homes, he suggests prison inspection would benefit from a less ritualistic and more informal approach. This would help focus on continuous improvement rather than just on ensuring minimum standards are met. For Seddon, the unavailability of enforcement powers to the Chief Inspector of Prisons is particularly problematic as responsive regulation requires the availability of coercive interventions at the peak of the pyramid as a last resort if persuasion fails.

The limits imposed on the prison inspection regime reflect the state's reluctance to relinquish command and control of criminal justice in the same way it has for other public services. Despite the inexorable rise of regulation in the recent past, criminal justice agencies survive as independent, powerful and primarily self-regulating state institutions. This situation is slowly changing, however, as new ideas about partnership and interdependence challenge traditional, and much criticized, accountability arrangements based on the separation of responsibilities between independent agencies. In the final chapter of this book (Chapter 12), Barbara Hudson distances herself from more recognized socio-legal approaches and explores the potential of cosmopolitanism to enhance regulation research and practice. In her examination of the responsibilities and achievements of the office of the Ministério Público in Brazil she considers how democracy may be regulated in transitional states. Hudson presents an optimistic account of the protection of the 1988 Constitution and the powerless, demonstrated in the readiness to prosecute the powerful. With regard to criminal justice, however, much remains to be done if democratic professionalism is to succeed where political allegiance once protected corrupt officials from prosecution.

Regulation, security and justice

Criminal justice is founded on principles of independence and impartiality and regulation promotes pluralistic and flexible pragmatism. Considered this way, they appear as conceptually incongruous control systems suggesting there is little scope for synthesis or fusion. Comparative analysis is likely to reveal as many disconnections as connections, something we discovered at the very outset of the Manchester seminar series. Where we presumed connections, in hybrid interventions such as the ASBO and Control Order for example, on closer inspection we found a greater divergence between regulation and criminal justice than we imagined.

There was much agreement among seminar participants in two areas: that people are subject to greater state intervention, either directly or by proxy; and that criminal justice, including constituent agencies, is in a period of transformation. There were significant differences about whether to conceptualize interventions as regulatory or criminal justice, which is the fairer, more effective and efficient, and how innovation is reorganizing the relationship between regulation and criminal justice.

The seminar series was a major success. The long conversation between scholars with diverse research interests and speaking different technical languages was exceptionally productive. The participants, from the internationally renowned professor to the doctoral student, declared that they enjoyed the experience of engaging with foreign yet strangely familiar ideas. Midway through the series Peter Grabosky, Anne Owers, Clifford Shearing, Andrew Sanders and Toby Seddon joined regional senior criminal justice practitioners in a round-table discussion to launch the Regulation, Security and Justice Research Centre in the University of Manchester School of Law. As the name of the Centre indicates, we are of the view that criminal justice does not stand alone as a discrete area of research and policy and needs to be studied in the context of regulation.

References

Abbot, C. (2009) *Enforcing Pollution Control Regulation*. Oxford: Hart.

Ashworth, A. (2000) 'Is the Criminal Law a Lost Cause?', *Law Quarterly Review*, **116**, 225–56.

Ashworth, A. and Redmayne, M. (2005) *The Criminal Process*, 3rd edn. Oxford University Press.

Ashworth, A. and Zedner, L. (2008) 'Defending the Criminal Law: Reflections on the Changing Character of Crime, Procedure, and Sanctions', *Criminal Law and Philosophy*, **2**, 21–51.

Ayling, J., Grabosky, P. and Shearing, C. (2009) *Lengthening the Arm of the Law: Enhancing Police Powers in the Twenty-First Century*. Cambridge University Press.

Ayres, I. and Braithwaite, J. (1992) *Responsive Regulation: Transcending the Deregulation Debate*. Oxford University Press.

Baldwin, R. and Black, J. (2008) 'Really Responsive Regulation', *Modern Law Review*, **71**(1), 59–94.

Bauman, Z. (1989) *Modernity and the Holocaust*. Cambridge: Polity.

Bayley, D. (2006) *Changing the Guard: Developing Democratic Police Abroad*. New York, NY: Oxford University Press.

(2008) 'Post-Conflict Police Reform: Is Northern Ireland a Model?', *Policing*, **2**(2), 233–40.

Bayley, D. and Shearing, C. (1996) 'The Future of Policing', *Law and Society Review*, **30**(3), 585–606.

Becker, G. (1968) 'Crime and Punishment: An Economic Approach', *Journal of Political Economy*, **76**, 169–87.

(1976) *The Economic Approach to Human Behaviour*. University of Chicago Press.

Black, J. (2002) 'Critical Reflections on Regulation', *Australian Journal of Legal Philosophy*, **27**, 1–35.

Braithwaite, J. (2000) 'The New Regulatory State and the Transformation of Criminology', in D. Garland and R. Sparks (eds.), *Criminology and Social Theory*. Oxford University Press, pp. 47–69.

(2002) *Restorative Justice and Responsive Regulation*. Oxford University Press.

(2003) 'What's Wrong with the Sociology of Punishment?', *Theoretical Criminology*, **7**(1), 5–28.

(2005) 'For public social science', *British Journal of Sociology*, **56**(3), 345–53.

(2008) *Regulatory Capitalism: How It Works, Ideas for Making It Work Better*. Cheltenham: Edward Elgar.

Burney, E. (2008) 'Regulating behaviour', paper (unpublished) presented at the ESRC Regulation and Criminal Justice Seminar, University of Manchester, 9 September.

Cabinet Office (2007) *Machinery of Government: Security and Counter-Terrorism, and the Criminal Justice System*. Available at: www.cabinetoffice.gov.uk/media/cabinetoffice/corp/assets/publications/reports/government_changes/pdf/machinery_govt.pdf. Accessed 27 January 2010.

Carlile, A. (2008) 'Terrorism and the legislative process', paper (unpublished) presented at the ESRC Regulation and Criminal Justice Seminar, University of Manchester, 9 April.

Crawford, A. (2006) 'Networked Governance and the Post-Regulatory State? Steering, Rowing and Anchoring the Provision of Policing and Security', *Theoretical Criminology*, **10**(4), 449–79.

(2009) 'Governing through Anti-Social Behaviour: Regulatory Challenges to Criminal Justice', *British Journal of Criminology*, **49**(6), 810–31.

Duff, A. and Garland, D. (eds.) (1994) *A Reader on Punishment*. Oxford University Press.

Felson, M. and Clark, R. V. (1998) *Opportunity Makes the Thief: Practical Theory for Crime Prevention*. London: Home Office Police Research Series Paper 98.

Flyghed, J. (2002) 'Normalizing the Exceptional: The Case of Political Violence', *Policing and Society*, **13**(1), 23–41.

Garland, D. (1990) *Punishment and Modern Society: A Study in Social Theory*. Oxford: Clarendon Press.

(2001) *The Culture of Control*. Oxford University Press.

(2003) 'The Rise of Risk', in R. Ericson and A. Doyle (eds.), *Risk and Morality*. University of Toronto Press, 44–86.

Gearty, C. (2006) *Can Human Rights Survive?* Cambridge University Press.

Gill, P. (2002) 'Policing and Regulation: What is the Difference?' *Social and Legal Studies*, **11**(4), 523–46.

Grabosky, P. (1995) 'Using Non-Governmental Resources to Foster Regulatory Compliance', *Governance: An International Journal of Policy and Administration*, **8**(4), 527–50.

Hancher, L. and Moran, M. (1989) 'Organizing Regulatory Space', in L. Hancher and M. Moran (eds.), *Capitalism, Culture and Economic Regulation*. Oxford University Press.

Hillyard, P. (2009) 'Regulating state political violence: some reflections on Northern Ireland', paper (unpublished) presented at the ESRC Regulation and Criminal Justice Seminar, University of Manchester, 10 February.

Hillyard, P., Pantazis, C., Tombs, S., Gordon, D. and Dorling, D. (eds.) (2005) *Criminal Obsessions: Why Harm Matters More Than Crime*. London: Crime and Society Foundation.

HM Government (2009) *Pursue Prevent Protect Prepare*. London: Stationery Office.

Hood, C., Rothstein, H. and Baldwin, R. (2001) *The Government of Risk: Understanding Risk Regulation Regimes*. Oxford University Press.

Independent Commission on Policing in Northern Ireland (1999) *A New Beginning: Report of the Independent Commission on Policing in Northern Ireland*. Available at: www.nio.gov.uk/index/nio-publication.htm. Accessed 27 January 2010.

Independent Police Complaints Commission (2007) *Stockwell One: Investigation into the Shooting of Jean Charles de Menezes at Stockwell Underground Station on 22 July 2005*. London: Independent Police Complaints Commission.

Jamieson, R. and McEvoy, K. (2005) 'State Crime by Proxy and Juridical Othering', *British Journal of Criminology*, **45**(4), 504–27.

Johnston, L. and Shearing, C. (2003) *Governing Security: Explorations in Policing and Justice*. London: Routledge.

Levi-Faur, D. (2005) 'The Global Diffusion of Regulatory Capitalism', *Annals of the American Academy of Political and Social Science*, **598**, 12–32.

Loader, I. (2000) 'Plural Policing and Democratic Governance', *Social and Legal Studies*, **9**(3), 323–45.

Loader, I. and Walker, N. (2007) *Civilizing Security*. Cambridge University Press.

McCulloch, J. and Pickering, S. (2009) 'Pre-Crime and Counter-Terrorism: Imagining Future Crime in the "War on Terror"', *British Journal of Criminology*, **49**(5), 628–45.

McLaughlin, E., Murji, K. and Hughes, G. (2001) 'The Permanent Revolution: New Labour, New Public Management and the Modernization of Criminal Justice', *Criminology and Criminal Justice*, **1**(3), 301–18.

Majone, G. (1996) *Regulating Europe*. London: Routledge.

Moran, M. (2002) *The British Regulatory State: High Modernism and Hyper-Innovation*. Oxford University Press.

Morgan, B. and Yeung, K. (2007) *An Introduction to Law and Regulation: Text and Materials*. Cambridge University Press.

O'Malley, P. and Hutchinson, S. (2007) 'Reinventing Prevention: Why Did "Crime Prevention" Develop so Late?', *British Journal of Criminology*, **47**(3), 373–89.

Osborne, D. and Gaebler, T. (1992) *Reinventing Government: How the Entrepreneurial Spirit Is Transforming the Public Sector*. Reading, MA: Addison-Wesley.

Packer, H. (1968) *The Limits of the Criminal Sanction*. Stanford University Press.

Parry, J. T. (2006) 'Terrorism and the New Criminal Process', *William and Mary Bill of Rights Journal* **15**, 765–835.

Pasquino, P. (1991) 'Theatricum Politicum: The Genealogy of Capital – Police and the State of Prosperity', in G. Burchell, C. Gordon and P. Miller (eds.), *The Foucault Effect: Studies in Governmentality*. University of Chicago Press, pp. 105–18.

Posner, R. (1983) *The Economics of Justice*. Cambridge, MA: Harvard University Press.

Quirk, H. (2008) 'Self-regulation by the criminal courts – the regulatory black hole at the heart of the system', paper (unpublished) presented at the ESRC Regulation and Criminal Justice Seminar, University of Manchester, 9 February.

Radzinowicz, L. (1948–86) *History of English Criminal Law and Its Administration*, 5 vols. (vol. 5 with R. Hood). London: Stevens & Son.

Sanders, A. and Young, R. (1994) *Criminal Justice*, 1st edn. London: Butterworths.
(2000) *Criminal Justice*, 2nd edn. London: Butterworths.

Sanders, A., Young, R. and Burton, M. (2010) *Criminal Justice*, 4th edn. Oxford University Press.

Scott, C. (2001) 'Analysing Regulatory Space: Fragmented Resources and Institutional Design', *Public Law*, 329–53.

(2004) 'Regulation in the Age of Governance: The Rise of the Post-Regulatory State', in J. Jordana and D. Levi-Faur (eds.), *The Politics of Regulation*. Cheltenham, Glos.: Edward Elgar, pp. 145–74.

Seddon, T., Ralphs, R. and Williams, L. (2008) 'Criminal justice as risk-based regulation: the case of recent British drugs-crime policy', paper (unpublished) presented at the ESRC Regulation and Criminal Justice Seminar, University of Manchester, 9 September.

Shearing, C. and Wood, J. (2006) *Imagining Security*. Cullompton, Devon: Willan.

Simester, A. and von Hirsch, A. (2006) 'Regulating Offensive Conduct through Two-Step Prohibitions', in A. von Hirsch and A. Simester (eds.), *Incivilities: Regulating Offensive Behaviour*. Oxford: Hart.

Smith, G. (2007) 'The parameters of criminal justice', paper (unpublished) presented at the ESRC Regulation and Criminal Justice Seminar, University of Manchester, 7 November.

(2009) 'Citizen Oversight of Independent Police Services: Bifurcated Accountability, Regulation Creep and Lesson Learning', *Regulation and Governance*, **3**(4), 421–41.

Sparrow, M. (2002) *The Regulatory Craft*. Washington, DC: Brookings Institution Press.

Sunstein, C. (1993) *After the Rights Revolution: Reconceiving the Regulatory State*. Cambridge, MA: Harvard University Press.

Tombs, S. and Whyte, D. (2009) 'A Deadly Consensus: Worker Safety and Regulatory Degradation under New Labour', *British Journal of Criminology* **50**(1), 46–65.

Walker, C. (2009) *Blackstone's Guide to the Anti-Terrorism Legislation*. Oxford University Press.

Wolfendale, J. (2007) 'Terrorism, Security, and the Threat of Counter-Terrorism', *Studies in Conflict and Terrorism*, **30**, 75–92.

Yeung, K. (2004) *Securing Compliance: A Principled Approach*. Oxford: Hart Publishing.

Zedner, L. (2004) *Criminal Justice*. Oxford University Press.

(2006) 'Policing Before and After the Police: The Historical Antecedents of Contemporary Crime Control', *British Journal of Criminology*, **46**(1), 78–96.

(2009) *Security*. Abingdon: Routledge.

PART I

Regulation and criminal justice: framing the debate

2

Regulation and its relationship with the criminal justice process

ANTHONY OGUS

The purpose of this chapter is to provide an overview of the nature of regulation and its relationship with the criminal justice process.[1] I begin with a short exploration of the meaning of 'regulation' and its (generally agreed) characteristics. I then proceed to show how the enforcement of regulation, so understood, potentially involves both administrative and criminal justice processes. The main part of the chapter will be a comparison of those processes as regards principles of liability, sanctions, institutions and procedures. In addressing the normative question of when use of the criminal justice process may be justified in relation to regulatory contraventions, I adopt a predominantly economic perspective. The use of economics to analyse law and legal institutions has generated major insights for legal scholarship (Ogus 2006) but is, perhaps, still insufficiently familiar to those working in the field of criminal justice.

The nature of regulation

'Regulation is a phenomenon that is notoriously difficult to define with clarity and precision, as its meaning and the scope of its inquiry are unsettled and contested' (Morgan and Yeung 2007: 3. For an elaborate discussion, see Mitnick 1980: ch. 1). I define regulation by reference to its politico-economic significance, its essential characteristic being that of public governance. The state intervenes in the market to override individual preferences and private governance, arising from property and market transactions (Ogus 2004b: 1–4 and 2006: 83–6). As this statement implies, the intervention is considered to be justified because the unregulated market

[1] This chapter draws on a chapter 'Criminal Law and Regulation', in N. Garoupa (ed.), *Criminal Law and Economics* (Cheltenham, Glos: Edward Elgar, 2009).

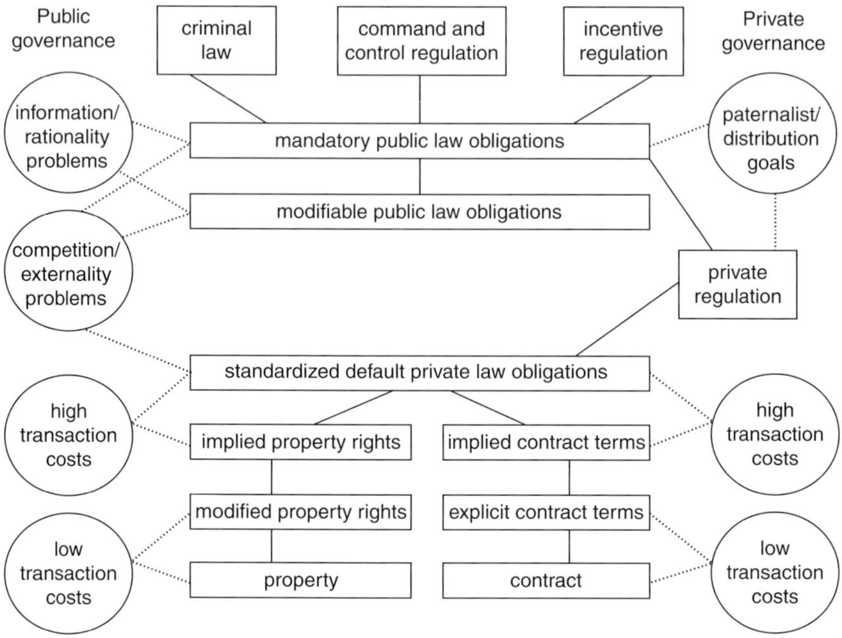

Figure 2.1 Private and public governance (Ogus 2006: 78)

generates outcomes which are perceived to be undesirable. The 'market failure' may (in economic terms) result from inadequate competition, externalities, inadequate information; or rather, from a non-economic perspective, reflecting for example paternalist or redistributional goals.

State interventions can take place within private law by imposing mandatory obligations which can only be enforced by the party in whose favour they are created, for example a consumer who is given the power to resile from a contract if the information supplied is inadequate. As indicated in Figure 2.1 above, this phenomenon may be referred to as 'private regulation'. However the concept of 'regulation' is invariably used by lawyers to refer to public law interventions and thus is represented in Figure 2.1 as 'public law obligations'. Normally these obligations cannot be varied by private agreement but reflect the fact that there may be some degree of delegation from public institutions to private institutions under a system of 'co-regulation'. I include in the concept both modifiable and mandatory public law obligations.

As Figure 2.1 indicates, there are three main categories of mandatory public law obligations. 'Command and control' may be considered the archetypal form of regulation: legislation prescribes, or authorizes the prescription of, the obligation and renders those failing to comply subject to a sanction or sanctions. As will be seen, those sanctions may be administrative, civil (i.e. imposed by proceedings in civil courts) or criminal (as a consequence of a criminal justice conviction).

Incentive regulation covers those regulatory instruments which are used to secure behavioural change not through the threat of a sanction but by creating financial or other incentives, such as taxing the existence or amount of an undesired activity or subsidizing a desired activity. It is not always easy to distinguish in practice between regulatory taxes or charges and administrative financial penalties, but the theoretical difference is that the latter is imposed for an *illegal* act or omission, whereas the activities subject to taxes or charges are, in a formal sense, *legal*.

In Figure 2.1, I distinguish between 'command and control regulation' and 'criminal law'. This is imprecise, but important. I assume that there is a significant difference between mainstream criminal law (predominantly offences against the person, property and public order), sometimes referred to as *mala in se*, and regulatory offences which are formally part of the criminal law but which are not mainstream crime – *mala prohibita* (Wells 1993: 7–8). Since the distinction is not always easy to apply, it is best to treat the matter as on a spectrum between the two concepts (Sutherland 1945).

A key to the distinction lies in an observation by Selznick that the central meaning of regulation involves control 'over activities that are valued by the community' (1985: 363). Expressing this in other language, while mainstream crime may generate utility gains (for example, financial profits made from a theft or satisfaction derived from an assault) for the offender and perhaps for some associates or family, it is assumed to possess no social utility. In deciding what is the optimal level of law enforcement in relation to such crimes (Stigler 1970), the point where the costs of law enforcement approximate to its benefits, the reduction in the social harm caused by crime, it is appropriate to disregard the utility of mainstream crime to offenders and others. Therefore there will be no social benefits to offset against the social harm. In contrast most regulatory contraventions arise out of activities, for example industrial productive activity, which are socially beneficial. In consequence, in determining the optimal level of enforcement it is appropriate to take into account the gains to the offender.

It is convenient here to refer to another difference between mainstream crime and *some* regulatory instruments. Criminal liability usually arises only *ex post* the engagement in the undesired, generally harm-creating, activity and a principal function of the law is deterrence, in that the threat of the penal sanction is intended to induce compliance with the law. The same applies to most regulatory instruments which apply *ex post* sanctions to those who fail to comply, but some instruments operate *ex ante* to prevent the illegal activity. The classic example is where an individual or firm must, prior to supplying a service or product, obtain formal approval from some public agency, and to secure the approval the applicant must show that the product or service satisfies certain standards (Ogus 2004b: ch. 10).

Role of criminal justice in the regulatory enforcement process

My next task is to identify the role played by the criminal justice system in the regulatory enforcement process. Across different jurisdictions and even within jurisdictions, there is a huge variety in the methods and practices of enforcing regulation. Nevertheless there is a general pattern, made familiar in the celebrated 'enforcement pyramid' of Ayres and Braithwaite (1992: 35), that agencies typically respond to non-compliant behaviour by applying to offenders pressure and sanctions of increasing severity until compliance is secured. At the bottom of the pyramid are various informal methods of persuasion undertaken by enforcement agencies. Then there is usually some formal administrative measure such as a warning, a 'cease and desist order' or a notice of intention to prosecute. For some contraventions and in some, but not all, jurisdictions, the enforcement agency may have power itself to impose a financial penalty. Otherwise, or in addition, the agency may take proceedings in a civil court for a financial penalty, a compensation order or an injunction (or equivalent formal order), breach of which will give rise to proceedings for contempt. At the apex of the pyramid is normally a criminal penalty[2] secured as a result of prosecution in the criminal justice system.

In some jurisdictions, criminal prosecutions are reserved for flagrant or very serious breaches while in others, for example, the United Kingdom, in theory at least they constitute the principal sanction for most regulatory contraventions; and indeed, there is evidence that enforcement agencies are increasingly relying on them (Baldwin 2004). This approach has been

[2] For regulatory measures involving a licence (see Ogus 2004a and text above), suspension or revocation of a licence will in practice be a more serious sanction than most criminal penalties, especially fines.

criticized on the ground that it is unduly heavy-handed and unnecessarily expensive (Macrory and Woods 2003; Ogus 2004a). Following a review of the question undertaken under the aegis of the Better Regulation Initiative by Professor Richard Macrory (2006) the government in 2008 introduced the Regulatory Enforcement and Sanctions Act. If and when fully implemented, this should lead to a radical shift in many areas of regulation away from reliance on the criminal justice system, since it will enable regulatory agencies to impose administrative financial penalties.[3]

In what follows, I shall compare the systems of regulatory enforcement with and without recourse to the criminal justice system, in an effort to identify in what situations and under what conditions use of that system might be regarded as justifiable. To address this normative issue, I am solely concerned with the deterrence function of the law and I next provide an introduction to the economic theory of deterrence which will form the basis of my analytical approach.

Introduction to the economic theory of deterrence

The economic theory of deterrence is premised on the assumption that those making decisions on whether or not to commit a crime, explicitly or implicitly, weigh up the costs and benefits of doing so. It predicts that the costs ($\boldsymbol{D}$) incurred by offenders as a result of the liability, when discounted by the probability of being caught ($\boldsymbol{p}$), will be sufficient to deter them from engaging in the undesired activity, because $\boldsymbol{pD}$ exceeds the benefit ($\boldsymbol{U}$) to the offender of the offence (Becker 1968). In most cases, the costs arising from detected offences are significantly broader than the penalties imposed by the law since they include also the 'hassle' and personal inconvenience arising from encounters with enforcement officials, legal and other defence expenditures, as well as any loss of market reputation resulting from the detection. It follows that some of the costs to the offender will be incurred even if there is no formal condemnation by a tribunal or other authorized institution. Because not all cases reach the ultimate stage of a court condemnation, involving the imposition of the formal sanction, we can rewrite the *ex ante* additional cost arising from the contravention as $\boldsymbol{qE + pD}$ where $\boldsymbol{qE}$ represents the probability and the associated costs of the relevant act being detected, and $\boldsymbol{pD}$ the probability of a formal condemnation and its associated costs, including notably

[3] At the time of writing this, the relevant provisions of Part 3 have not been brought into effect in relation to any regulatory sector.

the prescribed sanction (Ogus 2006: 102–5). The condition of compliance thus becomes $\boldsymbol{U} < \boldsymbol{qE} + \boldsymbol{pD}$.

An inquiry as to optimal enforcement policy, whether of mainstream crime or of regulation, involves selecting appropriate values for particular regimes and for different types of offender: for $\boldsymbol{q}$ and $\boldsymbol{p}$, in the light particularly of monitoring costs and the costs of determining liability; and for $\boldsymbol{E}$ and $\boldsymbol{D}$ having regard, in particular, to the costs of imposing sanctions and other informal costs, notably hassle. There is, of course, a considerable literature on these questions (for overviews, see: Eide 2000; Polinsky and Shavell 2000a).

Sanctions

A criminal justice system can impose sanctions, for example very large fines and imprisonment, which are otherwise not available for the enforcement of regulation. From a deterrence perspective, we need to hypothesize on the circumstances in which use of the criminal justice sanctions might be optimal. We note first that the cost to the offender following conviction in the criminal process will generally be significantly higher than that which follows non-criminal procedures. This is not only because the formal sanctions available in the criminal process are generally more severe; it is also because stigma attaches to a criminal conviction much more than to other forms of condemnation (Funk 2004). Indeed, there is empirical evidence that loss of market reputation following criminal proceedings may be of greater consequence to some regulatory offenders than the penalty imposed (Baldwin 2004: 361–4; Karpoff *et al.* 2005).

Now if the criminal process can be used to ensure that the offender, on conviction, will face costs ($\boldsymbol{pD} + \boldsymbol{qE}$) sufficiently high to exceed the utility ($\boldsymbol{U}$) to be derived from the contravention, why should it not be invoked in all cases? There are four important answers to that question and it is a consideration of these which should lead us to the means of identifying when criminal sanctions might be optimal for regulatory contraventions.

Two arguments relate to the lowering of costs which are generated by the imposition of criminal penalties. The first has regard to the costs incurred by the offender. Although it is of the very essence of a deterrence system that individuals and firms should incur costs if they offend, social welfare is increased if the same level of deterrence can be achieved when those costs are smaller, rather than larger. Second, account has to be taken of administrative costs. Of course, some criminal penalties, notably imprisonment, are much more expensive to apply than administrative or civil penalties; but more significant is the comparison of process costs, since (as we shall see) the procedural requirements of criminal liability are much more exacting than their administrative and civil equivalents.

The third consideration is that of marginal deterrence: other things being equal, the severity of penalties should increase proportionately with the severity of the harm caused by illegal activities (Friedman and Sjostrom 1993; Mookherjee and Png 1994). This is because offenders contemplating committing a less serious offence should not be motivated, perversely, to commit a more serious offence for the same penalty.

Fourth, excessively severe penalties can lead to over-deterrence (Bierschbach and Stein 2005). If, as argued above, the activity giving rise to the regulatory contravention enhances social welfare, the prospect of a severe penalty may induce the actor either to reduce the amount of the activity or to invest in an excessive level of care, or both, and social welfare losses are incurred.

If the discussion above indicates why criminal penalties should not be used for all regulatory contraventions, there are other powerful arguments suggesting that administrative sanctions are preferable for most such contraventions. Take, first, the question of the offender's knowledge and information concerning legal obligations (Craswell and Calfee 1985). This is generally not a problem in relation to mainstream crime because it can be assumed that everyone with mental capacity knows of the wrongful character of what we have already referred to as *mala in se*. In contrast, many regulatory contraventions arise from conduct which is not obviously wrongful and many regulatees may have only a sketchy knowledge of what is required. A regulatory contravention may thus occur through an inadequate understanding of the law, as well as through simple inadvertence. In such circumstances, it is inefficient to secure future compliance by the costly imposition of a criminal penalty if the communication of appropriate information by the regulatory agency will be equally effective in securing this outcome (May and Wood 2003). If this is right, it is not likely that imposing a penalty on first offenders will ensure future compliance better than dismissing the case with advice and/or an informal warning (Scholz and Gray 1997; Nyborg and Telle 2004). The argument does not apply where a regulatory contravention gives rise to large losses, either to the immediate victims or to society more generally: here even a first offence should be deterred. Subject to that important caveat, the reasoning leads to the conclusion that generally, in a regulatory context, substantial, particularly criminal, penalties should not be imposed for a first offence. In theory, of course, ignorance of the law is not a defence to criminal liability, but it is a matter which can be properly taken into account in the exercise of the discretion whether or not to prosecute.

Take next the Ayres and Braithwaite pyramid. This, as indicated above, shows how an enforcement agency should compare the marginal benefits of proceeding up the pyramid (increased prospect of compliance) with the marginal (particularly administrative) costs of applying an increasingly severe sanction. It also reveals the problem of excessive reliance on criminal sanctions in deterring regulatory contraventions (Macrory and Woods 2003; Ogus 2004a). Although the costs ($\boldsymbol{D}$ and $\boldsymbol{E}$) to offenders increase with each higher stage, so also will there be a significant reduction in the *ex ante* probabilities, $\boldsymbol{p}$ and $\boldsymbol{q}$, that the relevant next stage will be reached. In relation to the criminal sanction at the apex of the pyramid, $\boldsymbol{p}$ is likely to be small particularly because of the disproportionately high cost to the agency of procuring evidence sufficient to satisfy the procedural standards of liability in the criminal courts (see further on this below). If criminal liability constitutes the only significant penalty, then, for deterrence purposes, this must be sufficiently large when discounted by $\boldsymbol{p}$ to exceed the profit to the offender from the contravention. Since courts are typically reluctant to impose large penalties for most regulatory contraventions such a system is likely to suffer from under-deterrence. Clearly this problem should not arise if the agency is able to impose an administrative financial penalty at an intermediate point in the pyramid, where $\boldsymbol{p}$ will have a relatively high value.

None of this is to deny the importance of criminal liability as a residual deterrent for certain categories of regulatory offences and regulatory offenders, notably where a single contravention gives rise to a significantly large amount of harm and, for repeated contraventions, when other sanctions provide inadequate deterrence. Criminal prosecution may also be important where the enforcement by an administrative agency proves to be inadequate (Garoupa and Gomez-Pomar 2003). For example, the imposition of an administrative sanction may be hindered by political influence or a conflict of interests between members of the agency and the regulated industry; so also where, for one reason or another, there is likely to be collusion between the agency and offenders, because of 'capture' by the latter.

Procedural arrangements

A criminal penalty can be imposed only by a court – this is a requirement of human rights law (Guinchard 2004) – and only following completion of prescribed procedures. These vary between jurisdictions and particularly across legal cultures, but the procedures generally include: (for more serious offences) trial by jury; a burden of proof on the prosecution to a standard higher than that used in non-criminal cases; a condition of mental responsibility (*mens rea*); and rules of evidence protecting the defendant. In contrast, some administrative sanctions, for example small fines and financial charges, can be imposed without an oral hearing or other formality, to a lower standard of proof and on the basis of strict liability. In England and Wales there has been increasing use by the police of conditional cautions (Blakeborough and Pierpoint 2007), an approach which, in many respects, is similar.

The principal purpose of the criminal procedural requirements is to reduce the number of errors that can result from the adjudication process, including notably the wrongful imposition of a penalty on those who are innocent, and the costs that arise from such errors. But since the procedures designed to reduce errors are themselves costly, there is in principle an optimal level of error reduction where the benefits of such reduction approximate to their costs (Posner 1973; Lando 2000). For the differences between criminal and administrative procedures to be economically justified we therefore need to identify the relevant variables and variations in the values to be attributed to them.

Take, first, the benefits to be derived from reducing inappropriate penalty impositions, sometimes referred to as Type I errors. Most obviously, the innocent parties themselves benefit from the procedural arrangements since the penalties and other losses associated with them are avoided and it seems appropriate to add to these a set of less concrete benefits, in that society gains from increased confidence in the quality of justice generated by its institutional processes (Polinsky and Shavell 2000b).

To be set against these benefits are the costs. These may include any increase in administrative resources which have to be spent on the adjudicative process. Further costs arise from the impairment of the deterrence function of the law, resulting from the fact that some guilty defendants will avoid the penalty (Type II errors). It is important to appreciate that the reduced deterrence resulting in such cases occurs for two related but independent reasons. Some of the 'guilty' cases processed will not satisfy the higher procedural standards and will fail for that reason. Others will not be prosecuted because, with limited resources, the enforcement agency will concentrate those resources on clear-cut cases requiring less preparation (Polinsky and Shavell 1989; Miceli 1991. For empirical evidence, see Ogus *et al.* 2006).

To compare the incidence of these benefits and costs in relation to criminal and administrative procedures, take, first, by way of example, the question of burden of proof which in criminal law is on the prosecution but which in many administrative systems is, in practice at least, on the suspected offender. A simple guideline here is to place the burden on the party who can supply the information at lower cost, and it may be that, in this respect, the regulatee–regulator relationship has different characteristics from the criminal defendant–prosecutor relationship (Lewis and Poitevin 1997). Regulatees are normally firms with access to, and an ability to supply, detailed relevant information for the purposes of an administrative determination, at least as cheaply as regulators. Greater weight attaches to evidence produced for criminal trials and imposing the burden of proof on defendants, particularly individuals, is likely to increase, rather than reduce, the costs of adjudication.

But there are also other, more important, variables involved, notably the phenomenon of error costs. Placing the burden of proof on prosecutors reduces Type I error costs at the expense of Type II error costs (Lee 1997).

In the context of the criminal justice system, the burden of proof rule is economically appropriate because adjudication and post-adjudication administrative costs are particularly heavy, and because, given the stigma attaching to criminal law convictions, Type I error costs are assumed to be significantly higher than Type II error costs: it is 'better that ten guilty persons escape, than one innocent suffer' (Blackstone 1836: 358). Adjudication and post-adjudication administrative costs are generally lower in a regulatory non-criminal context, but the principal economic justification for the alternative burden of proof rule must be that, given typically relatively modest penalties and, perhaps even more importantly, an absence of stigma, Type I error costs are not so significant and, indeed, may be outweighed by Type II error costs.

The analysis has similar implications for other protections conferred on criminal defendants. The *mens rea* requirement, for example, in its concern to establish mental responsibility for the offence, must, in contrast to strict liability, significantly reduce Type I errors. This is also a justification for the rules restricting the evidence on which the prosecution can rely (Schrag and Scotchmer 1994), as well as the principles governing the standard of proof, there being a striking contrast between the criminal rule ('beyond reasonable doubt') implying a level of accuracy above 0.95 and the equivalent administrative standard which is just above 0.5 (Kokott 1998: 134. See also Hylton and Khanna 2006).

Institutional considerations

There are many institutional differences between regulatory processes and criminal justice processes, but we need only highlight those which are the most significant for the purposes of this chapter. Undoubtedly the major such difference relates to the separation of powers. Compliance with the criminal law is principally monitored by the police. They may undertake prosecutions but in many jurisdictions this is the responsibility of an independent authority; liability is determined by a court (often by a jury) and the appropriate penalty is selected by the judiciary. In contrast, in relation to regulatory controls, the regulatory agency is normally responsible for monitoring behaviour and initiating administrative enforcement proceedings. In some jurisdictions liability for, and selection of, the administrative sanction is the responsibility of an independent authority or tribunal, but in others they are undertaken by the regulatory agency, with the offender having access to an independent authority only by way of appeal.

Generalizing on these arrangements, it may be said that regulatory institutions and functions (monitoring, enforcement and adjudication) are, to a large degree, vertically integrated, whereas in the criminal sphere they are separated. The integration generates considerable savings in the coordination and information costs of regulatory processes, but of course it also has adverse consequences. An independent assessment of the application of the rules can reduce intertemporal inconsistency and hence error costs (Stephenson 2006). Further, some form of competition of, or overlapping between, decision-makers can inhibit collusive behaviour between prosecutors and offenders, including corrupt transactions (Rose-Ackerman 1978).

Delegation to the regulatory agency for fleshing out the skeletal legislative principles is common and can be justified in terms of economizing both on information costs and on the costs of rule promulgation, given the likelihood of frequent amendment. Indeed, the borderline between rule-making and enforcement is not always easy to define because the more general the regulatory requirement, the greater the agency's discretion and the more important interpretation becomes in the enforcement process.

Explicit, or more usually implicit, bargaining between regulator and regulatee can help to generate a wide range of efficient outcomes (Yeung 2004). In analogy to plea-bargaining, agencies may agree to informal standards, lower than those required by the law, in return for a commitment to compliance (Kambhu 1989; see also Johnston 2001). The agency may have technical expertise not available to small firm regulatees and can assist the latter by supplying information as to low-cost methods of meeting regulatory requirements. Of course, the phenomenon of arm's-length bargaining between offender and enforcement agency raises the possibility of private agreement which serves to benefit both parties, but not the public interest. In the absence of adequate controls involving transparency and accountability, this can lead to corrupt transactions with major negative consequences (Polinsky and Shavell 2001; Garoupa and Klerman 2004).

A final issue concerns the role of enforcement agencies in formally determining that a regulatory contravention has occurred and selecting and imposing the administrative sanction. Some penalties, for example 'on the spot' fines, can hardly be administered otherwise than by the agency responsible for detecting the contravention. In other respects, the issue turns on the familiar trade-off between error costs and administrative costs. There are, of course, large savings of the latter if the same institution is responsible for different stages in the enforcement process. But such arrangements can also generate large error costs, and decision-makers can be prone to commit such errors if the agency itself benefits from the volume of formal condemnations recorded for contraventions (Posner 1973: 416–17). Such benefits may arise in two forms: an enhancement of the public reputation of the agency for effective performance of its enforcement responsibilities; and additions to the agency's income if financial payments accrue directly to it. The normative implications are clear: although there is little that can be done to moderate the first benefit, the second should not be permitted; and, in any event, the offender must be able to initiate some form of appeal against, or review of, the decision. The optimal trade-off between administrative and error costs is dependent on several important variables. These include notably the probability of error which itself is a function of the procedural arrangements, in particular the facilities for appeals, and the size of the penalties imposed.

Conclusions

In this chapter I have sought to demonstrate the importance of distinguishing between regulatory contraventions and mainstream crime. For the purposes of determining the level of resources to be allocated to law enforcement, the gains arising from crime should not be taken into account, whereas the gains from regulatory contraventions are relevant.

In comparing regulatory enforcement with and without resort to the criminal justice process, I have highlighted differences regarding sanctions, procedural arrangements and institutional considerations. In the light of these, I conclude that although the criminal justice system may play an important residual role in dealing particularly with repeat offenders and those causing large amounts of social harm, deterrence of regulatory contraventions can adequately be secured by non-criminal processes, provided that financial penalties are available in that context.

In economic terms, I have explored the differences in terms of their cost implications. Reliance on the criminal justice systems generates increased administrative costs and (for most regulatory contraventions) greater welfare losses from reduced deterrence, but avoids the high error costs arising from the wrongful impositions of sanctions.

References

Ayres I. and Braithwaite, J. (1992) *Responsive Regulation: Transcending the Deregulation Debate*. Oxford University Press.

Baldwin, R. (2004) 'The New Punitive Regulation', *Modern Law Review*, **67**, 351.

Becker, G. S. (1968) 'Crime and Punishment: An Economic Approach', *Journal of Political Economy*, **7**, 169.

Bierschbach, R. A. and Stein, A. (2005) 'Overenforcement', *Georgetown Law Journal*, **93**, 1743.

Blackstone, W. (1836) *Commentaries on the Laws of England, vol. IV*, 19th edn. London: Sweet & Maxwell.

Blakeborough, L. and Pierpoint, H. (2007), *Conditional Cautions: An Examination of the Early Implementation of the Scheme*. London: Ministry of Justice.

Craswell, R. and Calfee, J. E. (1985) 'Deterrence and Uncertain Legal Standards', *Journal of Law, Economics and Organization*, **2**, 279.

Eide, E. (2000) 'Economics of Criminal Behavior', in G. De Geest and B. Bouckaert (eds.), *Encyclopedia of Law and Economics*. Cheltenham, Glos.: Edward Elgar.

Friedman D. and Sjostrom, W. (1993) 'Hanged for a Sheep: The Economics of Marginal Deterrence', *Journal of Legal Studies*, **22**, 345.

Funk, P. (2004) 'On the Effective Use of Stigma as a Crime-Deterrent', *European Economic Review*, **48**, 715.

Garoupa, N. and Gomez-Pomar, F. (2003) 'Punish Once or Punish Twice: A Theory of the Use of Criminal Sanctions in Addition to Regulatory Penalties', *American Law and Economics Review*, **6**, 410.

Garoupa, N. and Klerman, D. (2004) 'Corruption and the Optimal Use of Nonmonetary Sanctions', *International Review of Law and Economics*, **24**, 21.

Guinchard, A. (2004) 'Fixing the Boundaries of the Concept of Crime: The Challenge for Human Rights', *International and Comparative Law Quarterly*, **54**, 719.

Hylton, K. H. and Khanna, V. S. (2006) 'A Public Choice Theory of Criminal Procedure', *Supreme Court Economic Review*, **15**, 61.

Johnston, J. S. (2001) 'The Law and Economics of Environmental Contracts', in E. W. Orts and K. Deketelaere (eds.), *Environmental Contracts: Comparative Approaches to Regulatory Innovation in the United States and Europe*. The Hague: Kluwer, ch. 12.

Kambhu, J. (1989) 'Regulatory Standards, Noncompliance and Enforcement', *Journal of Regulatory Economics*, **1**, 103.

Karpoff, J., Lott J. R. and Wehrly, E. W. (2005) 'The Reputational Penalties for Environmental Violations: Empirical Evidence', *Journal of Law and Economics*, **48**, 653.

Kokott, J. (1998) *The Burden of Proof in Comparative and International Human Rights Law*. The Hague: Kluwer.

Lando, H. (2000) *The Optimal Standard of Proof in Criminal Law When Both Fairness and Deterrence Matter*. Copenhagen Business School.

Lee, T. R. (1997) 'Pleading and Proof: The Economics of Legal Burdens', *Brigham Young University Law Review*, 1.

Lewis, T. and Poitevin, M. (1997) 'Disclosure of Information in Regulatory Proceedings', *Journal of Law, Economics, and Organization*, **13**, 50.

Macrory, R. and Woods, M. (2003) *Environmental Civil Penalties: A More Proportionate Response to Regulatory Breach*. Centre for Law and the Environment, University College London.

May, P. and Wood, R. (2003) 'At the Regulatory Front Lines: Inspectors' Enforcement Styles and Regulatory Compliance', *Journal of Public Administration Research and Theory*, **13**, 117.

Miceli, T. J. (1991) 'Optimal Criminal Procedure: Fairness and Deterrence', *International Review of Law and Economics*, **11**, 3.

Mitnick, B. M. (1980) *The Political Economy of Regulation*. New York, NY: Columbia University Press.

Mookherjee, D. and Png, I. P. L. (1994) 'Marginal Deterrence in Enforcement of Law', *Journal of Political Economy*, **102**, 1039.

Morgan, B. and Yeung, K. (2007) *An Introduction to Law and Regulation*. Cambridge University Press.

Nyborg, K. and Telle, K. (2004) 'The Role of Warnings in Regulation: Keeping Control with Less Punishment', *Journal of Public Economics*, **88**, 2801.

Ogus, A. (2004a) 'Enforcing Regulation: Do We Need the Criminal Law?', in H. Sjögren and G. Skögh (eds.), *New Perspectives on Economic Crime*. Cheltenham: Edward Elgar, 42–56.

(2004b) Regulation: Legal Form and Economic Theory. Oxford: Hart Publishing.

(2006) *Costs and Cautionary Tales: Economic Insights for the Law*. Oxford: Hart Publishing.

Ogus, A., Faure, M. and Philipsen, N. (2006) *Best Practices for Consumer Policy: Report on the Effectiveness of Enforcement Regimes*. Paris: OECD.

Polinsky, A. M. and Shavell, S. (1989) 'Legal Error, Litigation, and the Incentive to Obey the Law', *Journal of Law, Economics, and Organization*, **5**, 99.

(2000a) 'The Economic Theory of Public Enforcement of Law', *Journal of Economic Literature*, **38**, 45.

(2000b) 'The Fairness of Sanctions: Some Implications for Optimal Enforcement Policy', *American Law and Economics Review*, **2**, 223.

(2001) 'Corruption and Optimal Law Enforcement', *Journal of Public Economics* **81**, 1.

Posner, R. A. (1973) 'An Economic Approach to Legal Procedure and Judicial Administration', *Journal of Legal Studies*, **2**, 399.

Rose-Ackerman, S. (1978) *Corruption: A Study in Political Economy*. New York, NY: Academic Press.

Scholz, J. T. and Gray, W. B. (1997) 'Can Government Facilitate Cooperation? An Informational Model of OSHA Enforcement', *American Journal of Political Science*, **41**, 693.

Schrag, J. and Scotchmer, S. (1994) 'Crime and Prejudice: The Use of Character Evidence in Criminal Trials', *Journal of Law, Economics, and Organization*, **10**, 319.

Selznick, P. (1985) 'Focusing Organizational Research on Regulation', in R. Noll (ed.), *Regulatory Policy and the Social Sciences*. Berkeley, CA: University of California Press.

Stephenson, M. C. (2006) 'Legislative Allocation of Delegated Power: Uncertainty, Risk, and the Choice Between Agencies and Courts', *Harvard Law Review*, **119**, 1036.

Stigler, G. (1970) 'The Optimal Enforcement of Laws', *Journal of Political Economy*, **78**, 526.

Sutherland E. (1945) 'Is "White Collar Crime" Crime?', *American Sociological Review*, **10**, 132.

Wells, C. (1993) *Corporations and Criminal Responsibility*. Oxford University Press.

Yeung, K. *Securing Compliance: A Principled Approach*. Oxford: Hart Publishing.

3

Reconciling the apparently different goals of criminal justice and regulation: the 'freedom' perspective*

ANDREW SANDERS

Criminal justice and regulation: what do we mean by 'criminal justice'?

Before looking at the goals of the criminal justice system, I first ask what is meant by 'criminal justice'. In other words, what are the structures and processes with which this chapter will deal? The purpose of a definition is not to identify an absolute truth, but to further an objective. My objective is to show the value of looking at criminal justice and regulation together, both intellectually and in terms of policy development: to show, in part, how what we conventionally think of as 'criminal justice' can learn from 'regulation' and vice versa. Thus, I choose to define 'criminal justice' in an expansive way: to include many areas that are often thought of as 'regulatory', as will become apparent.

Phil Edwards raises the interesting question: is criminal justice a form of regulation, or is regulation a form of criminal justice?[1] The answer, in abstract, is both. At one level, criminal justice is just one way of attempting to regulate our behaviour. The 'Zwelethemba Model' discussed by Shearing and Froestad (Chapter 5, this book) is a good example, showing how regulatory systems can, and often do, incorporate criminal justice as just one (not necessarily dominating) element. From this point of view 'regulation' should not be seen as part of criminal justice.

* This chapter draws heavily on my book, *Criminal Justice*, ch. 1, co-written with Richard Young and Mandy Burton (4th edn, 2010), in which we set out the 'freedom approach' advocated here. Without Richard this chapter (on which he gave me valuable comments), indeed much of my work, would not have been possible. I also thank Kevin Brown, Phil Edwards, Imogen Jones, Richard Garside, Toby Seddon and Graham Smith for their comments on drafts of this chapter, all of which have led to improvements over the original.

[1] Unpublished comment on a selection of the seminar papers.

At another level, we can distinguish between regulation that aims at, or could lead to, an official criminal sanction (List A below); and regulation that cannot (List B below):

> **List A:** This includes regulation carried out by agencies such as the Health and Safety Executive (HSE), Environment Agency (EA) and Financial Services Authority (FSA) in relation to health and safety, pollution and financial matters; 'civil-penal' orders (most notoriously the ASBO) and counter-terrorism legislation. For example, the Health and Safety at Work Act 1974, which created the HSE, also creates a series of obligations for employers. These, broadly, give employers and managers the duty to ensure, as far as is reasonably practical, that working conditions are safe. This applies to people working and members of the public entering the area or premises concerned. Breach of the duty is generally a civil and criminal matter. Like all criminal offences, it is up to the enforcement body to decide whether to prosecute for an alleged breach, and up to the injured party, if there is one, to decide whether to sue in the civil courts. Thus nothing, in principle, distinguishes these 'regulatory' crimes from crimes enforced by the police (Sanders *et al.* 2010: ch. 7).
>
> **List B:** This includes the civil legal system through the law of tort, inspections (of, for example, schools and hospitals) and professional self-regulation (if we are, for example, doctors, lawyers, accountants, financial advisers).

The forms of regulation comprising List A should therefore logically be considered to be part of criminal justice. It might be argued that this is a formalistic distinction. Ogus, for example, argues (Chapter 2, this book) that 'regulatory crime' (the category created to cover List A-type offences) is socially valued activity that has gone wrong in some way, while 'normal' crime is not. But there are too many exceptions to this for it to be a valid generalization. Demonstrations, for example, are – in political rhetoric at least – socially valued, but demonstrators are increasingly treated by police as 'real' criminals. Is obtaining money or services by deception intrinsically bad behaviour or socially valued behaviour 'gone wrong'? How about 'date rape', speeding, public drunkenness? And are the pharmacists who misuse their market position by selling drugs most similar to businesses that misuse their market position by price-fixing, or 'real' criminals who sell drugs on the street? It also might be thought that regulatory crime rarely leads to formal criminal sanctions. But this is true of many 'normal' crimes too. Thus crimes involving cannabis and prostitution, for example, rarely end up in the criminal courts either. And the majority of child offenders are warned, not prosecuted.

Thus, as argued by an increasing number of scholars from a variety of theoretical perspectives (e.g. Yeung 2004; Tombs and Whyte 2007; Abbot 2009), the old distinction between 'real' (i.e. 'normal') and 'regulatory' crime that Ogus tries to perpetuate simply does not hold up. For the purposes of this paper I therefore define 'criminal justice' as legal state coercion that is determinable in the criminal courts. This includes List A-type forms of regulation. As we shall see not only is there more convergence between police and regulatory agencies that deal with List A-type activity than is generally thought (in principle, though not in scale) with regard to dispositions, but both types of agency also constantly weigh up how to utilize scarce resources. A different objection to my approach might come from the authors of *Beyond Criminology* (Hillyard *et al.* 2004). For them, confining discussion of 'regulatory crime' and agencies such as the HSE within criminology and 'criminal justice' distorts and minimizes the nature of that activity. I hope that by the end of this chapter it will be apparent that this need not necessarily be so.

Subject to the kinds of exceptions referred to above, 'criminal justice' includes the following institutions and processes:

1 police and other enforcement agencies (e.g. HSE, HM Revenue & Customs);
2 non-prosecution dispositions (e.g. cautions, enforcement notices, financial penalties);
3 pre-trial and trial agencies and processes;
4 review of conviction: appeals and CCRC;
5 complaints investigation; and
6 sentencing and punishment.

The arguments in this chapter could be applied to all of these. In practice, discussion will be confined to 1, 2 and 3.[2]

This expansive view of criminal justice is consistent with a 'toolkit' approach. We can conceptualize the criminal justice system as a set of 'tools' including surveillance and covert action, stop–search, civil-penal orders, compliance mechanisms, controls/detention (such as 'kettling', a public order policing tactic to contain protestors in a confined area), arrest, sanctions (including prosecution), enforced compensation, etc. These can be chosen, almost at will by enforcement agencies to deal with a range of

[2] Note that my definition excludes private policing, except where private agencies are given specific powers; policing functions that do not involve the (potential) exercise of powers (e.g. much crime prevention work); illegal state activity (e.g. torture and 'extraordinary rendition' of terrorist suspects).

issues including 'normal' crimes, 'regulatory' crimes, antisocial behaviour, suspected terrorist activities, illegal immigration, disorder, oppositional activity, etc.[3] Seeing criminal justice in this way does not identify any one type of process or activity as more 'core' than any other. Instead, one can see the 'tools' being chosen at will as being in the service of the broader aims of the criminal justice system, however one might conceive of them.[4]

Criminal justice goals

At one level, discussion of criminal justice goals is inevitably trite, but at another it is impossibly complex. It is trite because who could disagree with a list of normative goals such as this?

- prevention of crime;
- reduction of reoffending;
- bringing offenders to justice (whether through prosecution or other methods);
- respecting victims and witnesses, and not creating secondary victimization;
- protecting the innocent;
- invading the rights and liberties of suspects and offenders (whether guilty or not) proportionately rather than disproportionately;
- adversely affecting only people directly involved;
- using scarce resources that could be put to better use proportionately, not disproportionately; and
- securing appropriate public respect for, and trust in, the criminal justice system (including public involvement in criminal justice).

It is true that radical critics – including Richard Young and me, to some extent – argue that repression of one kind or another (see fn. 4) is the central goal of criminal justice in the UK, and that many of the above goals are grossly subordinated to the reduction and prevention of 'normal' crime. But my focus in this chapter is primarily normative, not analytical.

[3] Crawford (2009) refers to a version of this approach propounded by government as value neutral. A differently nuanced version emerged through discussion at the 4th (and final) seminar). I am particularly grateful to everyone who participated in that seminar, though this should not be taken to imply that anyone except myself necessarily subscribes to this approach.

[4] In *Criminal Justice*, Mandy Burton, Richard Young and I (2010) see this broad aim in practice as 'crime control' (broadly conceived in the sense Packer (1968) conceived it). Others – e.g. Zedner (2007) – might see the overarching aim as different, but the toolkit would be equally applicable to both.

The discussion is complex because these goals often conflict with each other, at least some of the time. For example, if resources were limitless, more offenders could be apprehended while using repressive measures less; but scarce resources lead the police to cut corners by often restricting suspects' rights and using stop–search, arrest and interrogation powers in either discriminatory or indiscriminate ways (Sanders *et al.* 2010: chs. 1–5). To take another example, the commendable objective of preventing secondary victimization led to the restriction of the use of sexual history evidence in rape trials, but in some cases this prevents defendants securing a fair trial (McEwan 2005). These conflicting goals therefore have to be prioritized, but on what basis? This will be the central question tackled in this chapter.

A secondary issue is that many of the above goals are not really goals. The best way of protecting innocent people, for example, is to simply not use coercive powers against anyone who might be innocent and to not prosecute except where guilt is certain. But this would be intolerable, as criminal justice powers would then rarely be invoked. Thus this 'goal' (like the final four goals in the list) is really a *constraining principle* to limit the actions of criminal justice agencies in pursuit of the first four.

This chapter will discuss the main attempts to reconcile these competing goals and principles. All the traditional models are flawed. I therefore go on to outline the 'freedom' approach. This seeks to achieve that elusive reconciliation, and to do so by seeing criminal justice and regulation as part of a continuous spectrum, rather than as separate spheres of conceptual and practical activity. Drawing on both traditions, four core values, or building blocks, are identified as being at the heart of the freedom approach: equality of esteem, legality (i.e. 'justice'), democracy and effective use of resources

Models of criminal justice and their implicit goals

There are several models of the criminal justice system. Models have two main purposes. The first is analytical: i.e. in an attempt to help understand the criminal justice system. The second is normative: i.e. an argument for a particular type of criminal justice system, or one that prioritizes particular goals or values. In practice most models combine the two: they analyse what currently exists and offer an evaluation by reference to an implicit or explicit normative model. I will not attempt to analyse the system in detail in this chapter, but will highlight some key features in order to show why the freedom model is preferable to those currently most favoured.

Due process and crime control

These concepts were most famously coined by Packer (1968) some forty years ago. Briefly, in a 'due process'-based criminal justice system the principle of 'innocent till proven guilty' would drive laws, policies and practices governing all parts of the criminal justice system. Thus suspects and defendants would have extensive rights, and the police and other criminal justice agencies would have to respect these rights. The innocent would be protected at the expense of convictions of people strongly suspected to be, but not proven to be, guilty. By contrast, in a 'crime control'-based system, conviction of the probably guilty would take priority at the expense of some probably, innocent people. To varying extents (variance being both between jurisdictions and over time) European criminal justice systems proclaim themselves to be largely 'due process'-based, but in reality are largely 'crime control'-based (McBarnet 1981; Sanders and Young 2010: ch. 1). Packer argued that no system actually does, or could, correspond entirely with due process or crime control; criminal justice in western-style liberal democracies were, he postulated, generally on a spectrum, with due process and crime control at each end. Packer tried to be as analytical as possible, but his distaste for the erosion of due process rules and policies is clear in his analysis of the disjuncture between criminal justice practice and the rule of law.

Some writers (e.g. Ashworth and Redmayne 2005; Smith 1997) are misled by the terminology of due process and crime control into thinking that the former model has no law enforcement goal, and that the latter incorporates no constraints on the power of criminal justice agencies. This was not Packer's argument. Indeed, 'due process' as a concept cannot be a criminal justice goal; it is, instead, a set of procedural standards. As such it is a set of standards to be applied to a process that must have an identifiable goal. Ashworth and Redmayne, and Smith, both suggest 'reformulations', whereby crime control is seen as the aim of the process, constrained by due process principles. This is actually what Packer himself argued: that both models have crime control goals (construed in a broad sense), constrained by due process procedures, and that the difference between the two models is a matter of balance between the two ends of the spectrum.

The need to employ the metaphor of 'balance' when using Packer's models is one of Ashworth and Redmayne's main sources of dissatisfaction with these models. The problem with the idea of 'balance' is that, in itself, there is no basis for judging whether a particular 'balance' is struck well or not, for without outside reference points, we cannot know what we mean by 'well struck'. Part of the problem, that I shall return to later, is that the balance is between apples and pears, rather than between different kinds of apples.

The usual way of characterizing the 'balance' problem is to ask how to balance an increased probability of conviction against reduced civil liberties (and vice-versa). In an era when the 'culture of control' (Garland 2001a) continues to tighten its grip, the 'balance' can shift ever further towards the crime control end of the spectrum. We shall see that Ashworth and Redmayne tackle this by resorting to a human rights-based approach to criminal justice.

Another way of characterizing the 'balance' problem is by widening our view of 'criminal justice' beyond that used by most writers to the set of institutions highlighted above (p. 43). In the world of tax evasion, health and safety, pollution, etc. the issue of civil liberties rarely arises: few non-police inspectorates have coercive powers such as stop–search and arrest, so in most situations their powers to detain and question are minimal. Depending on the context, they can however, prevent processes or businesses running. They therefore have potentially powerful financial tools with financial and economic consequences that go far beyond the bottom line of a particular business (closing down major businesses or creating an environment that leads them to relocate has major effects on employment, for example). On the other hand, these enforcement bodies have limited resources, so investigation and the invocation of these powers at any one time has to be considered against what else could be done with the resources those actions would consume (see e.g. Hawkins 2003; Abbot 2009). As the Chair of HMRC said, 'We cannot prosecute everybody', and this is why thirty-six barristers repaid £605,000 to HMRC in 2008 instead of being prosecuted (*Guardian*, 9 December 2008).

Balances are therefore constantly being struck by enforcement agencies: between the cost of enforcement action in a particular instance (cost to the agency, to the 'offending' individual, firm or organization, and to employees and consumers connected to the 'offenders') and the likely harm done by the 'offence(s)' in question. This is endorsed in a Code introduced in 2007 for agencies such as the HSE. The Regulators' Compliance Code states that: 'Regulators should recognise that a key element of their activity will be to allow, or even encourage, economic progress and only to intervene when there is a clear case for protection.'[5] The 'benefits' must

[5] BIS 2007 (Statutory Code of Practice for Regulators). Para 3. See Whyte (2007/8) for a critique.

justify the 'costs'. Prosecutions are not mentioned once. But these are not the balances discussed by Packer, Ashworth and Redmayne or most other criminal justice writers, and the Packer model does not seem able to incorporate this issue. A key feature of the freedom model that will be outlined later is that, unlike other models, it takes scarcity of resources into account.

Another problem with Packer's models is that they allow for no coherent consideration of the role and rights of victims of crime. Again, I return to this issue later when we will see why victims cannot be located on the crime control–due process spectrum.

Clearly Packer's models do not provide us with an adequate basis for formulating criminal justice goals. To establish 'crime control' as the primary goal means that concern for both the accused and the victim will always be secondary. The pursuit of crime control can be qualified by respect for due process and for victims, but no one has provided a coherent basis for calibrating 'how much' due process (or the rights of victims) should intrude. And the cost, both in financial and human terms, of both enforcement and non-enforcement is a largely neglected issue.[6] It is 'largely' but not completely neglected. For while in a world of scarce resources there will always be a tendency for agencies to attempt to become more efficient. While 'crime control' is a dominant goal this efficiency drive generally includes clearing away due process obstacles (such as comprehensive access to free high-quality legal advice for suspects; rights to jury trial; full disclosure to the defence of evidence collected by the police). We shall see that the freedom model seeks efficiencies in other ways, as for many practitioners and commentators erosions of due process are also erosions of freedom.

Human rights

Ashworth and Redmayne (2005) argue that their vision of the ideal criminal process differs fundamentally from the type of process implied by Packer's models. In their vision, the goal of bringing cases to effective trial would be authoritatively constrained by human rights principles instead of merely compromised to a varying extent by conflicting due process principles. These principles would be drawn from the European

[6] Though it is pleasing to see that, after Richard Young and I made this issue central to the 'freedom model' in the 2nd edn, in 2000, of our *Criminal Justice* text, Ashworth and Redmayne picked the issue up in their 3rd edn (2005: 39).

Convention on Human Rights (ECHR). The groundwork for this has already been done, as the ECHR has, in effect, been incorporated into UK law by the Human Rights Act 1998. Since the human rights approach is now the dominant normative approach to criminal justice (e.g. Hudson 2007; Padfield 2008: 10–11; Doak 2008), we need to assess how persuasive this ideal is.

Ashworth and Redmayne suggest that we resolve conflicts between different rights (e.g. of the accused and of victims) and between the protection of rights and the goal of bringing cases to effective trial as follows. The problem may be solved by the absolute status of one of the rights in conflict, as is the case with the prohibition by Art. 3 of the ECHR of the use of torture or inhuman treatment. These methods of controlling crime are absolutely forbidden, regardless of what overall social benefits they might bring in a particular case or context.

Most of the relevant principles and rights (e.g. to a fair trial under Art. 6), however, are 'strong' rather than 'absolute' and breaches are not allowed in some circumstances. Ashworth and Redmayne (2005) support this partly on resource grounds and partly because statements of rights cannot be allowed to stand in isolation from their overall justification for having a criminal process – i.e. to bring cases to effective trial. As Ashworth (1998: 52) acknowledges:

> It would be foolish to deny that conflicts will arise here, and equally foolish to deny that ultimately such conflicts will need to be resolved by means of some compromise or balancing. What is distinctive about the approach advocated here is that the process of resolving the conflicts should be securely based on facts established by research, and firmly grounded in a proper appreciation of the rights and interests of all relevant parties.

There are a number of problems here. First, Ashworth's proposition is insufficiently concrete to resist the encroachment of crime control concerns on due process protections. For one person's 'proper appreciation' of someone's rights will not accord with that of someone with a radically different standpoint. Second, for human rights to underpin all the important elements of the criminal justice system the network of human rights would have to go far beyond the ECHR. Though Ashworth accepts this, he does not discuss who would be responsible for formulating new, and equally powerful, human rights for, for example, vulnerable suspects or the majority of people wishing to make complaints against the police (neither of which are currently catered for in the ECHR or the case law based on it). Third, most ECHR rights, apart from the few absolute rights, are subject to many broadly drawn exceptions, many of which reduce their status from 'strong' to 'qualified'. For example the right to privacy under Art. 8 may be breached when it is:

> necessary in a democratic society in the interests of national security, public safety or the economic well-being of the country, for the prevention of disorder or crime, for the protection of health or morals, or for the protection of the rights and freedoms of others.

The tension between due process and crime control values is as much in evidence in the structure of the Convention and in the jurisprudence of the European Court of Human Rights (ECtHR) as it is within English law. Thus the ECtHR (and English courts) often allows considerable room for manoeuvre to states through the 'margin of appreciation' doctrine. Under this doctrine a state's assessment of the need to invade rights is subjected to a relatively undemanding standard of judicial review. As Ormerod observes (2003: 65):

> On one level, it is impossible to regard Strasbourg rulings otherwise than as pronouncements of the very minimum protection to be afforded... The margin of appreciation afforded to all States in all aspects of the Convention is well established.[7]

This illustrates a further problem – the vagueness of many 'rights' especially when the courts fill the gaps left by the ECHR itself. This can be seen in relation to the 'human rights' of victims in particular (see below, pp. 58–60).

Finally, the human rights approach has little to say about the balancing of resource costs of law enforcement against the costs of crime identified earlier (economic, emotional, etc.). It is true that a 'proportionality' principle is sometimes applicable, but it has very limited effect. The criminal justice system cannot operate without making decisions on priorities, for – as with the National Health Service, for example – the demands on law enforcement agencies far exceed the supply of their time and resources, and will always do so. An adequate model of the criminal justice system has to incorporate this consideration. We saw earlier that this is a particular problem in the 'regulation' arena, but it applies equally to areas of 'normal' crime such as public order, offences relating to prostitution, drug abuse, antisocial behaviour, etc. There have even been court cases brought by victims who are aggrieved that prioritization did not

[7] Little has changed in the last few years: see, e.g. Ewing and Tham (2008: 682).

work in their favour. These decisions have always been decided in favour of the police, the courts recognizing that law enforcement agencies have to decide how best to expend resources themselves (subject to general guidelines set through established mechanisms of accountability).[8] This does not mean that the police and other agencies necessarily *do* prioritize intelligently. To take a few examples, powers of arrest have been increased in recent years, allowing the police to pick off 'low hanging fruit', instead of tackling more serious crime, in order to improve their 'figures'. And in a dubious use of anti-terrorist powers, much police time is spent harassing photographers taking pictures of public buildings (*Guardian*, 11 December 2009). If there was a meaningful proportionality principle it would surely bite on these activities.

Many of these points are illustrated by the 'speed camera' cases of *O'Halloran and Francis* v. *UK*, decided by the ECtHR.[9] They concerned two offences created by road traffic legislation: speeding and failing to give the name and address of the driver of a car found by a speed camera to have been speeding. In one of the cases the defendant admitted he was the driver but pleaded not guilty to speeding. He argued that his confession should be excluded from trial because his privilege against self-incrimination – protected by ECHR Art. 6[10] – had been violated by the compulsion created by the second of these two offences. In the other case the defendant simply refused to provide the required information on the same grounds.

On any normal interpretation of 'right to silence' these defendants would have to be vindicated. Take the erosion of the right of silence in the Criminal Justice and Public Order Act 1994. This provides that 'adverse inferences' can, in some circumstances, be drawn from silence – i.e. silence can be used as evidence against a defendant. But in a case concerned with the Northern Ireland forerunner of these laws the courts made clear that convictions must not be based 'solely or mainly' on silence,[11] and in *Saunders* v. *UK* it was held that Art. 6 would be violated if coercion was used to procure self-incriminating statements.[12] So on the face of it, our two defendants should have won their cases – especially as *Saunders* concerned legislation that made silence, in the context of that case, criminal. But not surprisingly, the ECtHR was no more willing than the domestic

[8] See e.g. *Chief Constable of Sussex ex p. ITF* [1999] 1 All ER 129 (a police case); *IRC ex p. Mead* [1993] 1 All ER 772 (a tax case). See discussion by Sanders *et al.* (2010: ch. 7.2).

[9] (2008) 46 EHRR 21.

[10] *Condron* v. *UK* (2001) 31 EHRR 1.

[11] *Murray* v. *UK* (1996) 22 EHRR 29.

[12] (1997) 23 EHRR 313.

criminal courts had been to reach this logical conclusion, for to do so would completely undermine this way of regulating road safety.

The ECtHR could take one of two routes to deciding against the defendants. One would have been to say that making silence a crime in this context is not a denial of the right of silence. The other would have been to admit that it obviously does undermine the right of silence but to say that that right had to be balanced against other considerations. Both routes are problematic, as the first is logically fatuous, and the second undermines the idea that 'human rights' are somehow special. Bizarrely, the ECtHR combined the two, saying that Art. 6 had not been violated because the compulsion had to be balanced against the fairness of a regulatory scheme that imposes limited obligations (i.e. to provide the name and address of the guilty driver).

As Ashworth in his commentary on the cases observes,[13] this judgment does not merely see the Art. 6 right as not 'absolute'; it is also incompatible with *Saunders*, in which the courts rejected the idea that 'public interest' or relative triviality of offence was relevant. He notes that in reality the ECtHR took the former route (the fatuous 'no violation' route) when, he argues, it should have taken the latter on the grounds that road safety justifies a limited exception to the Art. 6 right. The point about all this is that even the arch-defender of the human rights approach is obliged to accept the case for undermining it in some circumstances.

To those who might say 'no harm was done, so why make all the fuss?' one could point to *A (FC)* v. *Home Secretary*.[14] In this case the House of Lords decided that the Anti-terrorism, Crime and Security Act 2001 breached the Human Rights Act 1998 because it was discriminatory, allowing non-nationals to be detained under certain circumstances if suspected of terrorism. The government response was the Prevention of Terrorism Act 2005 (as amended and extended by the Counter-Terrorism Act 2008) which established a new 'control order' regime for nationals and non-nationals alike. Respect for the rights of one group could, it seems, be established by denial of the rights of everyone (Campbell 2009). There must surely be a better way.

A rather different, and more fundamental, critique of the Ashworth–Redmayne approach – but which is completely consistent with the points made in this section – comes implicitly from within the human rights movement itself. Gearty (2006) defends the idea that human rights should

[13] [2007] Crim LR 898. Also see Birdling (2008).

[14] [2004] UKHL 56.

underlie law and legal processes, and indeed, that respect for human rights should be an integral part of political and social discourse. But in asking what we mean by 'human rights' he acknowledges that the term can have no fixed concrete meaning – that human rights have no autonomous existence outside democratic politics.

It follows from the lack of fixed meaning of human rights that positive laws cannot be 'read off' from them as if they were Dworkinian principles. Gearty takes as an example the famous American case of *Roe* v. *Wade*.[15] This declared the right to abortion to be a constitutional right of all pregnant women. Gearty argues that however much we might approve of this and similar decisions – and most human rights advocates would be of a liberal mind that would tend to approve of it – 'rights' decisions like this are actually a threat to the idea of human or constitutional rights. For Gearty argues that whether women have, or should have, the 'right to choose' is essentially a political matter. This should be argued out in public, in the media and in legislatures. The argument should be informed by human rights principles, which should not, however, predetermine the answer. For he argues that there is no right or wrong answer to the question whether women have the 'right to choose'. It seems to me that the same argument applies to criminal justice matters such as the right of silence, the right to representation and most other controversial matters based on Art. 6 of the ECHR.

But why not take the opportunity to enshrine progressive policies into entrenched law (as is the case with most concrete 'human rights')? First, there is what Gearty (and I) regard as the intellectual dishonesty of a claim that simply does not bear scrutiny. Second there is the tendency to argue that anything that is compatible with such entrenched laws is fine – rather than to argue over the merits of laws on the grounds, *inter alia*, that one particular legal solution would be more in keeping with human rights principles than another. Third, there is the danger that political decisions masquerading as human rights decisions simply devalue human rights principles. Finally, and related to this point, political manoeuvring in judicial appointments becomes more prominent as governments of different hues seek to appoint to the highest benches in their own images in order to reverse rulings of these types (the US Supreme Court being an obvious example). In short, the short-term gains for progressives achieved through the legalization of human rights is likely to be outweighed by long-term losses. Thus Gearty (2006: ch. 3) actually sees developments

[15] 410 US 113 (1973).

like *Roe* v. *Wade* – and, implicitly, the characterization of new fair trial rights for victims of crime, for example, as 'human rights'[16] – as *threats to the survival of human rights*: the 'crisis of legalism'.

It follows that in seeking concrete goals for criminal justice we need to look beyond human rights. However, it will be shown below (pp. 60–2) that human rights form an essential part of the foundation of a progressive set of criminal justice goals. The human rights approach also establishes certain points – with greater or lesser degrees of precision – beyond which the balance between due process and crime control cannot slip. For the UK this has been (so far) of largely theoretical interest as the 'culture of control' has not yet given way to outright authoritarianism. But it may become important in practical terms in the future, and it is certainly important in many other jurisdictions that are even more authoritarian than the UK and USA.

Compliance approaches

The earlier discussion of crime control and due process did not specify the sense in which the former approach attempts to control crime. It is usually assumed that the focus is on 'bringing offenders to justice' by prosecution and punitive sentencing. While this may aim, among other things, to prevent crime and reduce reoffending (through deterrence, rehabilitation and incapacitation), it appears at first glance that government policy over the last two decades has regarded ever-tougher law enforcement as a goal in its own right. Some writers identify a 'new punitiveness' both in Britain (Downes and Morgan 2007) and in many other industrialized countries (Pratt *et al.* 2005).

This is an overly simplistic view. First, there is a differentiated approach to low and high-level offending. While serious crime is indeed dealt with ever more punitively, alternatives to prison, and indeed to prosecution, are still advocated for relatively minor crime committed by non-prolific offenders; arguably, there is little 'new' about this twin-track approach (Matthews 2005). Significantly, when government talks about 'bringing offenders to justice' it includes non-prosecution dispositions such as warnings and fixed penalties, the use of which has increased hugely in recent years (Young 2008). Second, the punitiveness that we associate with 'crime control' is aimed particularly at the most marginalized

[16] e.g. *Doorson* v. *Netherlands* (1996) 22 EHRR 330. For a powerful argument in favour of human rights for victims, see Doak (2008).

sections of society (Garland 2001b). Third, it is relevant primarily to the police and police-enforced crime, including youth crime.

These three points all go together, and 'regulatory' offences are generally perceived as low-level crimes committed by the least marginalized sections of society. Indeed, as Whyte shows (this book, Chapter 7; see also Abbot 2009: 115 and 150), most of the (few) prosecutions carried out against polluters are against individuals or very small firms burning tyres and the like – not the big producers who cause most pollution. With most 'regulatory' crime and the agencies concerned with such crimes – health and safety, tax authorities, pollution control bodies, etc. – there is, for most offenders, no punitive policy and there probably never has been.[17] But that does not mean that these agencies are unconcerned about crime control in the broader sense of preventing crime and reducing reoffending. Far from it. This is precisely what the 'compliance approach' – which characterizes regulatory theory – is supposed to be about, as is evident from Ogus (this book, Chapter 2).

Moreover, the manner of this approach is not so different from the non-prosecution strategies referred to above that the police increasingly adopt for minor crime. According to the Environment Agency, for example:

> The Agency regards prevention as better than cure. It offers information and advice to those it regulates and seeks to secure co-operation avoiding bureaucracy or excessive cost… The purpose of enforcement is to ensure that preventative or remedial action is taken to protect the environment or to secure compliance with a regulatory system… the institution of a prosecution is a serious matter that should only be taken after full consideration of the implications and consequences. (Environment Agency 1998: paras. 4, 6, 20)

As the North-West Region of the Agency puts it, 'We are a firm but fair regulator using prosecution as a last resort. We try to seek voluntary co-operation to resolve issues but sometimes this isn't enough and we need to use prosecution to prevent recurrence and to act as a deterrant to others. We take environmental crime [but not spelling] seriously' (Environment Agency 2006).

It follows that, at an analytical level, the separation of 'compliance' approaches for 'regulatory crime' and punitive approaches for 'normal' crime is irrational and artificial (Hillyard *et al.* 2004). But we should not

[17] Social security fraud is a major exception. Significantly, and like the tyre burners, the criminals in question are, as with police-enforced crime, largely poor and marginalized. Fraud is a more complicated issue. See generally, Cook (2006); Sanders *et al.* (2010: ch. 7).

be misled into ignoring the important differences between the approaches of police and non-police agencies. Regulatory crime is very rarely prosecuted, while the police and Crown Prosecution Service (CPS) adopt compliance approaches for a minority of 'normal' crimes. The Regulatory Code requires regulators to justify any strong enforcement action, while the Code for Crown Prosecutors requires police and CPS to justify not prosecuting. The suffering of victims of 'normal' crime is invoked to justify punitiveness for 'normal' criminals, while the victims of 'regulatory' offences are largely ignored (Whyte 2007). And there is little evidence that the desire to control 'normal' crime is matched by a similar zeal in relation to 'regulatory' crime (Whyte, this book, Chapter 7; Donaghy 2009) – largely because of the different cost balances highlighted earlier in relation to these two types of crime.

At a normative level, as Braithwaite (2002) argues, we should integrate compliance and punitive approaches in respect of all types of crime, both in our theoretical thinking and in policy-making. Neither compliance nor punishment should, in themselves, be seen as goals of criminal justice; rather, they should both be seen as means of achieving broader crime control goals. Further, this thinking should be applied to all crimes, without an artificial separation of 'normal' from 'regulatory' crime.

While this may not seem even worth mentioning, in fact the point is ignored by all policy-makers and most academics. Among the latter, two exceptions should be mentioned. First, the new zemiologists (Hillyard *et al.* 2004) have been important in highlighting the harm caused by 'regulatory' crime. They argue that we should transcend the artificial political construct of 'crime' and replace it with the concept of 'social harm'. But beyond arguing that social and legal responses should be graded according to the degree of harm involved, the policy prescription is unclear.

Second, Abbot (2009) has recently argued that a 'deterrence' strategy, drawing on the law-and-economics approach of Becker (1968), should be explicitly adopted for regulatory crime (and, by implication, for 'normal' crime). Abbot's insight is to see that there is no contradiction between a compliance approach that seeks genuine compliance and the use of deterrent sanctions, for the threat of the latter is often necessary in order to secure the former. Nor need deterrent approaches necessarily rely solely on criminal sanctions, as administrative sanctions can be equally effective. But the question is one of effectiveness – not just in securing quanta of compliance, but in securing compliance regarding the crimes with most impact and in the most cost-effective way.

Victim-centred approaches

I identified 'respecting victims and witnesses, and not creating secondary victimization' as one of several criminal justice goals about which there is little controversy (above, p. 45). We have also seen that inability to take this into account is one of the failings of the crime control–due process approach. Although the human rights approach advocated by Ashworth–Redmayne puts that omission right, simply throwing 'victims' into an ever-growing pot of goals exacerbates the problem of prioritization. Moreover, the more that rights of victims are characterized as 'human rights', the greater the 'crisis of legalism'; and the fewer that are so characterized, the less likely our victim goal is to be achieved.

The answer, in the view of some, is to create a victim-centred criminal justice system in which all the other goals would be subordinated. Government rhetoric claims to be doing just this (minus acknowledgement of clash of goals with crime control aims) (see e.g. Home Office 2002; and, more recently, *Guardian*, 27 October 2008). Let us leave aside the analytical implausibility of this claim, both in intention and result (Jackson 2003) and concentrate on its normative desirability.

A pure victim-rights approach would allow victims to determine all decisions. This would be a long way away from not only all current Western criminal justice systems, but from any historical system of which I am aware. In the so-called 'golden age' of the victim in eighteenth-century England and Wales, for example, the actions of the victim were a necessary but not sufficient precondition for arrest and prosecution. Arrest warrants had to be sought from, and decisions whether to prosecute were made by, judges and magistrates. Thus although victims had an important role, due process protections for suspects and defendants were in place.

A pure victim-rights approach would have no due process or human rights protections for the accused. Vengeful (and falsely accusing) victims would be able to insist on arrest and prosecution when there was no evidence, and on wildly disproportionate sentences. This could not be countenanced. A human rights backstop would be required if only to comply with our international obligations, but a backstop would, by definition, provide only minimal protection. Disparity – and consequent discrimination and unfairness – would be rife. Further, as Cavadino and Dignan (1996) point out, not only would the personal interests of victims subsume the interests of the accused, the interests of the community in reducing reoffending would also be sidelined. Thus if, for example, a police officer happens upon a violent attack by one person against another, if the victim does not seek official action the assailant would be released. Even leaving aside paternalistic arguments about whether the victim in this example is able to safeguard his/her own interests, the interests of other members of the public at risk from the assailant are clear. It is difficult to dispute Cavadino and Dignan's view that it would be unacceptable to sideline the interests of the community like this – and, in any number of different types of example, to sideline the interests of the accused. Consequently, when victim-rights approaches are advocated, they are generally combined with other approaches.

Beloof, for example, seeks to systematize what he sees as implicit in the language of many modern US statutes and state constitutions – and, we might add, in many European laws and policies including those of the UK. This language includes three important concepts: fairness to the victim, respect for the victim and dignity of the victim. His object is a system designed 'to ensure that the interest of the individual victim in the case is promoted' (1999: 291). But, as he also acknowledges, 'A core interest of the victim is that the truth be revealed and an appropriate disposition reached' (1999: 291). He recognizes that the interests or desires of victims, if acted upon, can undermine due process values of truth and fairness, crime control values of efficiency, and the state's interest in many cases of prosecuting (or not prosecuting) regardless of the victim's wish. Thus he advocates a 'three model' approach to understanding criminal justice. This combines Packer's two models with one that promotes the interests of victims. Unlike a pure victim-rights advocate, Beloof recognizes that the accused and the community have rights and concerns that are as important as those of the victim.

Just as Packer's approach presents irreconcilable conflicts between crime control norms that favour conviction at the expense of the rights of suspects and defendants and due process norms that favour the rights of suspects and defendants at the expense of convictions, so does Beloof's. But Beloof's approach presents, in addition, conflicts between the rights of victims and those of suspects and defendants on the one hand, and between victims and crime control on the other. What Beloof gives us is, essentially, a list of features of the criminal justice system similar to those outlined above (p. 43). When some of those features conflict with others he gives us no basis on which to understand how some are prioritized over others, nor how prioritization should take place. Beloof takes an analytical model that sets out to illuminate irreconcilable conflicts of values and adds to it a further set of irreconcilable elements.

Cavadino and Dignan (1997) advocate a victim-rights approach only within the context of a (yet-to-be-created) restorative justice-based system. Even then, they advocate giving the state the right of veto over prosecution decisions and the right to set desert-based maxima and minima for punishment. They do not discuss what rights victims should have in the non-restorative justice system that currently predominates in England and Wales and is likely to continue to do so for the foreseeable future. They clearly lack confidence in a system where victims would have a profound influence. In similar vein, Roach (1999) advocates a 'non-punitive model of victims' rights' that would be based around principles of restorative justice and crime prevention. Rather than specify a safety net on the lines of Cavadino and Dignan, Roach simply expresses the belief that due process rights for defendants would be respected in a non-punitive system.

A new way: the 'freedom' approach

Clearly we need a model of criminal justice that systematically combines the insights of all the approaches discussed in the previous section. This is what Richard Young and I have attempted to do (Sanders *et al.* 2010: ch. 1), as I summarize and elaborate in this section.

The foundations of a new approach: human rights and resources

All the approaches discussed so far have value. They also all have an instinctive appeal to anyone concerned about criminal justice, whatever their particular viewpoint may be. So the problem is not whether or not we agree that this multiplicity of goals and values is important – in the main, we all do – but in deciding how to prioritize one over another when, as is usually the case, not all are equally achievable together.

Let us begin with Gearty's (2006) analysis of human rights. We discussed earlier what a commitment to human rights should *not* lead to. But what, if anything, does the concept of 'human rights' mean in a positive sense for Gearty, and what is the point of 'human rights' from Gearty's perspective? He argues that a key feature of a civilized society is equality of esteem to all, and from this it follows that we should respect human dignity. Dignity involves three elements: autonomy (the ability to choose one's options), real choice (which requires a certain minimum level of education, health, resources, etc.) and the liberty to pursue these choices.

Gearty argues that respect for 'human rights' means both not eroding these elements, and actively pursuing them.[18]

However, to put my own gloss on Gearty's argument, these are *policies* (in the sense that Dworkin (1981) might use the term) rather than *principles*. In other words they should inform political discourse and political choice, rather than being the basis in and of themselves of legal rules of which there are 'right' and 'wrong' answers. Gearty identifies three threats to the survival of the idea of human rights, of which two concern me here. The first threat is the 'crisis of authority' (Gearty 2006: ch. 2) where he sets out the foundation set out above, making no claim as to any fixed meaning for any particular human right. For in attempting to pin human rights down too concretely the way is open to destructive critique on the lines set out (above, pp. 49–55) against Ashworth and Redmayne. The second threat is the 'crisis of legalism', discussed earlier.

Thus, as Gearty says, 'Legal rights are the servant of the political, changing with the ebb and flow of political debate' (2006: 68). It is true that democracy might be characterized as tyrannical majoritarianism that allows the oppression of minorities. However, Gearty argues, this would be inconsistent with the principles of respect for human dignity and equality of esteem, and for legality (i.e. the rule of law). Thus Gearty refers to dignity, legality and democracy as 'the DNA of human rights'.

Human rights policies should be part of the foundation for a coherent set of criminal justice goals, but Gearty's formulation is almost entirely abstract. It exists in a world free of resource constraints. In the real world, it is not just that prudent policy-makers should be concerned not to overburden the tax payer; nor even that, whether or not they should be concerned, they will be anyway. Far more important is the fact that criminal justice is a matter of social justice. As such, criminal justice, and all other aspects of the legal system, must compete for resources with other aspects of the welfare state – health, education, housing, social security, environmental protection, etc. We therefore need to know how to balance social justice priorities.

Further, we also need a way of balancing different criminal justice priorities in terms of resource expenditure. While it is taken for granted (by Ogus, this book, Chapter 2, for example) that 'regulatory' agencies should 'balance' the use of resources and cost of enforcement on one hand, against the significance of particular regulatory crimes on the other, it

[18] For more discussion of Gearty's argument, and his response to it, see Economides (2007).

should be equally obvious (though this is rarely acknowledged) that the police do the same. We have seen that legal challenges attempting to force the police to enforce the law have always failed when the reason for less-than-full enforcement is a calculation about where and how to deploy scarce resources. Another example would the rationing of police surveillance teams in response to information received about drug and other conspiracies (Sanders *et al.* 2010: ch. 6). Not only should resource allocation within the police, within other 'criminal justice' agencies, and within 'regulatory' agencies be rational, but resource allocation *between* all these agencies should be equally rational.

Thus if we add 'effective use of resources' to Gearty's 'DNA' the building blocks of a new approach become equality of esteem (from which he derives the importance of 'dignity' and liberty), legality (or, as we might alternatively call it, 'justice'), democracy and effective use of resources.[19]

An overriding goal: enhancement of freedom

We have seen that in recent years many governments have claimed to 'rebalance' the criminal justice system in favour of victims and away from the accused. Underlying this rhetoric there is, usually, an unspoken assumption that victims should be held in more esteem than the accused. The rhetoric generally conflates the accused with the convicted, treats all crimes and thus all crime victims alike, and does not differentiate between different ways of giving esteem.

Let us tackle the problem from a different angle and ask what is the point of protecting victims, offenders and, indeed, anyone affected by crime and the criminal justice system. We could say that it is primarily to protect and enhance freedom (in Gearty's terminology, 'liberty'). We make it a crime to thieve or assault because the losses and hurts they cause are (among other things) losses of freedom: to enjoy one's possessions, to walk the streets without fear, and so forth. We seek to convict thieves and violent offenders in the hope that the punishment or treatment they receive will reduce their reoffending, and reinforce everyone else's law-abiding instincts and behaviour. In the same way, we can ask what the point is of protecting suspects and defendants, innocent or guilty. Again, protection is not a goal in itself, but a means to the end of promoting their freedom. We insist that the police must obey the rule of law because

[19] I argued some years ago that the last three of these four building blocks should be seen as 'core values' of criminal justice: Sanders (2002a).

when they do not do so we no longer feel that we live in a free society. The idea of 'freedom' used here is the same as that of 'dominion' as used by Braithwaite and Petitt (1990).

This means that, in theory at least, the problem of allocating priority to conflicting goals is solved. All we have to do, in relation to any one incident or problem, is to prioritize the goal that is likely to enhance freedom the most. This is, in my opinion, utilitarian, and so what is most likely to enhance freedom will vary from circumstance to circumstance.[20] Under this model, the freedom of victims as well as the freedom of people accused of crime is valued: Gearty's principle of equality of esteem applies. To argue for these two measures of freedom to be balanced is one thing, but knowing how to do so is quite another. Crime control adherents and government rhetoric tends to the view that suspects and offenders should have fewer rights than victims and that their freedoms should have a low weighting. This would be a mistake.

Once a crime is committed the harm it causes is usually irreversible, so the application of state power to apprehend and sanction the alleged offender may do nothing to redress the balance. Indeed, less than one-tenth of all stop–searches lead to arrest, and less than one-half of all arrests lead to caution or prosecution (Povey *et al.* 2009). Unless the use of these stop–searches and arrests have a net deterrent effect in themselves, these are applications of power which reduce freedom for suspects in exchange for virtually no gain, even if those who are apprehended but not prosecuted are guilty of offences. If they are innocent (and most will be) the loss of freedom will be even greater. State power through criminal justice should only be used if it is likely to enhance more freedom than it erodes. Moreover, by doing nothing and not exercising criminal justice power there is the potential to use the money saved to enhance the lives (indeed, the positive freedom) of everyone through improved health, education, housing, and so forth. Not only would this be freedom enhancing in itself, but these welfare improvements could do more to reduce crime – i.e. to enhance the freedom of potential victims – than arrest and prosecution.

The freedom approach can also be used to inform the way in which law enforcement and criminal justice processes are carried out. This is partly a matter of approach: the manner in which arrest, search and questioning is a matter of dignity, but it can also be cast in terms of an

[20] This is easier to argue than to demonstrate. But the argument is fleshed out in the context of prosecutor behaviour in Young and Sanders (2005), and further examples are discussed in the next section (pp. 65–8). My collaborator, Richard Young, insists that this position is not simply utilitarian, but is 'distribution-sensitive rule consequentialism'.

effect on freedom: we all know the difference, for example, when being security-checked at an airport or prison, between treated with and without respect. Again, the human rights perspective is inferior to the freedom perspective, for while 'dignity' is important for Gearty, human rights only protect and constrain when dignity is grossly undermined. Not even the most enthusiastic human rights advocate would say that the rudeness and disdain so often shown by police to marginalized sections of the population breaches human rights. But if low-level disrespect is frequent and systemic, it is hugely corrosive. This may be difficult for middle-class white readers to understand. Consider, then, the American case of a black professor who was arrested because a passer-by saw him struggling with the front door of his (middle-class) home and thought he was a burglar. He was handcuffed, fingerprinted and locked up for several hours, but the indignity stemmed equally from his belief that had he been white he would not have been treated this way. He said of his arrest: 'It's one thing to write about it, but altogether another to experience it.'[21]

Approach to victims is as important as approach to the accused. Much of the impetus behind victim-centred approaches is recognition of the secondary victimization all too often caused by criminal justice processes. The freedom approach clearly endorses this (for secondary victimization inevitably erodes freedom) but pushes reform in the direction (a) of less resource-intensive measures (services for victims, not monetary compensation); and (b) measures that do not simultaneously erode the freedom of the accused. Thus, again, services for victims, plus better information about progress of cases, involvement in restorative processes – not involvement in decision-making, victim impact statements, etc. which tend to be retributive in effect (Sarat 1997; Sanders 2002b).

It is also a matter of the level of enforcement: take Ayres and Braithwaite's (1992) 'pyramid' of sanctions, whereby the least intrusive sanctions are at the base, while the most intrusive are at the apex, and sanctions move up a level only in response to failure to comply and repeated offending. Prosecution both uses more resources than do alternatives, and encroaches more on the freedom of the suspect than do alternatives. Unless there are obvious gains to freedom by moving up the pyramid, there is no good reason to do it. This is the 'compliance' approach by another name – and, as Braithwaite (2002) argues – police-enforced crime should be approached in the same way as every other type of crime.

[21] *Guardian*, 22 July 2009. See discussion of the experience of stop–search and arrest in Sanders *et al.* (2010: chs. 2 and 3), including that of the (black) Bishop of Stepney.

But the approach has to be applied sensitively. Some 'alternatives' to prosecution, for example, are actually more freedom-reducing than prosecution. As Cohen (1985) observed many years ago, apparently 'soft' alternatives are sometimes more coercive and controlling than a swift punitive sanction. Modern examples include Penalty Notices for Disorder (Young 2008), and others offered by Crawford (2009). Frequently, 'alternatives' are actually additions. Less obviously, measures against companies that lead to shut down, removal to other jurisdictions or reduced activity might be as hugely harmful to the freedom of innocent people as it is for the offenders for whom we may have less sympathy. But these examples show the need to (a) be clear about what elements in the pyramid are genuinely 'higher' and 'lower' than others; and (b) develop alternatives that are proportionately intrusive and do not harm innocent people (e.g. state takeover of offending companies instead of shut down). Neither of these examples, nor Grabosky's development of the pyramid idea on three dimensions (this book, Chapter 4) undermine the *idea* of the pyramid. But the freedom approach shows us how it is sometimes abused, and should be used.

Concretizing the freedom approach

It could be said that the freedom approach set out here is too vague to be useful; but that as soon as one tries to make it more concrete one will end up with an arbitrary 'freedom calculus' about which we could never agree. It is true that the approach needs to be worked out in more detail to be applied concretely. One way of doing this may be to adapt Maslow's (1998) hierarchy of needs by creating a 'hierarchy of criminal justice (and other social) needs'.[22] It is also true that, in contrast to the cruder 'universalist' strand of human rights thinking, 'freedom' will not mean the same in all contexts and at all times in history. Taking my cue from Gearty, my concept of 'freedom' is a political matter that will change as the political terrain changes. Whether fear of crime and fear of apprehension by the police should be included will always be a matter for debate. But at least with the freedom approach we can insist that the latter be given the same weight as the former.

Even with these concessions to the vague and contingent nature of the freedom approach, we can see its concrete value if we take a few examples. First, at the level of law making, jury trial has frequently been a hotly

[22] Thanks to Hannah Quirk for this suggestion.

contested issue, and there has been a steady erosion of jury trial. None of the models discussed above (pp. 46–60) have anything to say about it, but for many people it is central to justice and democracy. This is recognized in the freedom model, as legality, democracy and the effective use of resources require that juries, and jury-like summary justice, remains central to criminal justice (Sanders 2002a).

To take a different example, how is it that the vast majority of deaths at work are subject to no prosecution at all, let alone homicide prosecutions (Tombs and Whyte 2008), while the prisons are full of petty offenders, many non-violent and many mentally ill? Victim perspectives would identify the deaths as more deserving of prosecution, though only if such deaths are considered to be criminal. This is a problem if one accepts Ogus's (this book, Chapter 2) viewpoint. To say, as Ogus does, that regulatory crime is fundamentally different from 'real' crime because the former involves socially valuable work is of no consolation to bereaved families. However, victim perspectives do not take account of wider freedom losses that would result from changes in law enforcement patterns (e.g. the impact on firms and their employees). And none of the other traditional models have anything to say about this. The freedom approach would start from the assumption that such deaths should be treated more severely than non-violent crime, but would seek to do so in ways that minimize adverse effects (e.g. taking recidivist enterprises into state or cooperative ownership). The relatively new Corporate Manslaughter and Corporate Homicide Act 2007 is unlikely to do much about the former (Gobert 2008) – partly because it does absolutely nothing about the latter. Thus the freedom approach provides a way of reconciling the concerns of victims and radicals such as Whyte with those of Ogus (both this book, Chapters 7 and 2, respectively).

At the level of court decisions, let us take again as examples the speeding cases of *O'Halloran and Francis* v. *UK*. It will be recalled that these cases illustrate one reason why the human rights approach cannot be the basis for a coherent approach. The freedom approach asks how much freedom is gained by enforcing the road traffic laws in question (a large amount, in terms of lives saved and injuries avoided), what is lost by requiring the owners of speeding cars to say who was driving (almost nothing) and whether or not a more resource efficient way can be found of achieving the same benefits (almost certainly no). A court applying the freedom approach would have no difficulty reaching the same conclusion reached by both the ECtHR and Ashworth, but without making exceptions based on mere expediency and without abandoning logical reasoning.

But if we take some other cases we can see how different results would be reached. Take the policing of demonstrations, for example. In recent years the police have developed the tactics of cordoning, 'kettling', restraining and searching demonstrators, often with no reasonable suspicion that any of these people were, or were about to, breach the peace or behave criminally. This has even been criticized by official reports, into the Kingsnorth environmental protest in August 2008, for example.[23] But only the freedom approach would require police tactics to change considerably. In *Austin and another* v. *Commissioner of Police for the Metropolis* ([2009] UKHL 5), for example, the courts upheld earlier similar police actions (the 2001 May Day protest in London). In other cases the protection of human rights is far more concerned with form than substance. For example, the ECHR requires that everyone has a right to bail, unless there is evidence that warrants pre-trial detention. Attempts to remove the right to bail for people charged with homicide and rape cases were thwarted for this reason (even though very few people in this position would be granted bail anyway), but the fact that less than one-half of all people who are denied bail are subsequently given custodial sentences is not regarded as significant by the courts.[24]

At the level of law enforcement decisions we know from commentators on the compliance approach – both advocates and critics – that the 'crisis of under-enforcement' (as Tombs and Whyte (2008) see it) is not just a matter of inadequate law. Even Establishment figures are concerned. Thus an independent report into the loss of life on building sites, for instance, recently identified policy, culture and resources as equally important, and recommended stronger action (Donaghy 2009). But the problem goes far beyond loss of life to a level of illness and injury far exceeding that caused by 'normal' violent criminals (Whyte, this book, Chapter 7). As with debates about the content of the law, victim perspectives can lock onto the unjustified disparity of enforcement strategies between 'normal' and 'regulatory' laws (though with the caveats identified earlier) but only the freedom perspective can deal with it adequately. Similarly, we have seen that police enforcement strategies tend to favour crime control approaches, both in volume (numbers of people stopped and arrested in general and at demonstrations, for example) and style (disrespecting

[23] See *Guardian*, 23 July 2009 report on two official investigations into Kent police's handling of this event. The reports are, however, secret: Ames (2009). This secrecy is another offence against the freedom approach that other models are not able to deal with.

[24] The key case was *Caballero* v. *UK* (2000) 30 EHRR 643. See generally Sanders *et al.* (2007) ch. 9.4 and Law Commission (2001).

certain social groups, use of force, etc.). Only the freedom perspective can provide a principled and coherent way of establishing more appropriate strategies.

Conclusion

Without an approach that prioritizes goals coherently, crime control goals dominate over other concerns; human rights get reduced to minimal safety nets and/or become political footballs; and economic and political forces are allowed to shape rationales for differential enforcement that make no sense in moral or human terms.

The freedom approach allows us to incorporate a fluid notion of human rights, to prioritize constitutionally agreed goals and to integrate the way 'normal' and 'regulatory' crime and other social problems are dealt with. No longer will we have to argue about whether or not victims of health and safety offences, for example, should benefit under the Code of Practice for Victims of Crime (currently, and scandalously, they do not – under New Labour only certain victims were put at the centre of the system). All victims of serious misfortune would be given consideration, according to the scale of their suffering and in view of what is needed to ensure they retain genuine freedom, not according to whether they fall into one politically motivated category or another. In short, criminal justice agencies (defined broadly) should have mutually consistent policies and practices, and they should be required to treat everyone equally. However, this does not mean treating as equal those who are unequal: it is a fallacy to think that formal justice can ignore substantive injustice (Sanders and Young 1994). Treating everyone equally means taking account of inequality, so the freedom approach attempts, as far as is possible, to do justice by taking account of our fundamentally unjust society – recognizing, for example, that coercive police action against ethnic minorities is more harmful than against middle-class people because of the history and meaning lying behind such action.

Adopting this approach enables us – indeed, requires us – to view 'criminal justice' and 'regulation' as all part of the same enterprise. Policies and practices characteristic of one should be used, where appropriate, in the other. This might lead to more use of coercive law enforcement in 'regulatory' crimes, but the greater change might be in the 'criminal justice' sphere, where respect would be given greater prominence, and coercion would be used more sparingly. Earlier I referred to the idea of the criminal justice system as a 'toolkit' (p. 44). We could see this as a potentially benevolent idea, wherein the least damaging and most freedom-creating 'tools' are used to deal with crime, antisocial behaviour and social harm.

Finally, this approach, like that of Braithwaite and Pettit (1990), is naturally decremental. This is because every application of power is freedom removing. State power has therefore to be justified by positive effects on freedom (rather than appeals to retribution or the 'rights' of victims). Not only would this restrict state power, and reduce the use of the most coercive (i.e. the most freedom-reducing) state power, it would also push the state into using its powers – all other things being equal – less coercively and more effectively. Thus genuinely intelligence-led policing would gradually supplant mass stop, search and detention. The middle classes may dislike the increased surveillance and record keeping and more invasion of privacy and more extensive DNA databanks that would result. But the poor, marginalized and socially excluded – those who currently suffer most both as victims and as those against whom coercive powers are most used – would benefit disproportionately from, say, fewer strip-searches. So don't expect the change to happen soon.

References

Abbot, C. (2009) *Enforcing Pollution Control Regulation*. Oxford: Hart.

Ames, C. (2009) 'The Truth about Kingsnorth' (*Guardian*, 29 May, 'comment is free' – accessed 30 July).

Ashworth, A. (1998) *The Criminal Process*, 2nd edn. Oxford University Press.

Ashworth, A. and Redmayne, M. (2005) *The Criminal Process*, 3rd edn. Oxford University Press.

Ayres, R. and Braithwaite, J. (1992) *Responsive Regulation*. Oxford University Press.

Becker, G. (1968) 'Crime and Punishment – An Economic Approach', *Journal of Political Economy*, **76**, 169.

Beloof, J. (1999) 'The 3rd Model of Criminal Process: The Victim Participation Model', *Utah Law Review*, **2**, 289–330.

Birdling, M. (2008) 'Self-incrimination Goes to Strasbourg: *O'Halloran and Francis* v. *United Kingdom*', *International Journal of Evidence and Proof*, **12**, 58–63.

Braithwaite J. (2002) *Restorative Justice and Responsive Regulation*. Oxford University Press.

Braithwaite, J. and Petitt, P. (1990) *Not Just Deserts*. Oxford University Press.

Campbell, D. (2009) 'The Threat of Terror and the Plausibility of Positivism', *Public Law*, 501.

Cavadino, M. and Dignan, J. (1996) 'Towards a Conceptual Framework for Conceptualising and Evaluating Models of Criminal Justice from a Victim's Perspective', *International Review of Victimology*, **4**, 153.

(1997) 'Reparation, Retribution and Rights', *International Review of Victimology*, **4**, 233.

Cohen, S. (1985) *Visions of Social Control*. Cambridge: Polity.

Cook, D. (2006) *Criminal and Social Justice*. London: Sage.

Crawford, A. (2009) 'Governing through Anti-Social Behaviour: Regulatory Challenges to Criminal Justice', *British Journal of Criminology*, **49**(6), 810–31.

Doak, J. (2008) *Victims' Rights, Human Rights and Criminal Justice*. Oxford: Hart.

Donaghy, R. (2009) *One Death Too Many* (Cm. 7654). London: Department for Work and Pensions, TSO, Norwich.

Downes, D. and Morgan, R. (2007) 'No Turning Back: The Politics of Law and Order into the Millennium', in M. Maguire, R. Morgan and Reiner (eds.), *Oxford Handbook of Criminology*. Oxford University Press, ch. 9, pp. 201–40.

Dworkin, R. (1981) 'Principle, Policy, Procedure', in C. Tapper (ed.) *Crime, Proof and Punishment*. London: Butterworths, pp. 193–225.

Economides, K. *et al.* (2007) 'Can Human Rights Survive? A Symposium on the 2005 Hamlyn Lectures', *Public Law*, 209.

Environment Agency (1998) *Enforcement and Prosecution Policy*. London.

(2006) NW Region page on the Agency website, as at 6 February 2006.

Ewing, K. and Tham, J.-C., (2008) 'The Continuing Futility of the Human Rights Act', *Public Law*, 668.

Garland, D. (2001a) *The Culture of Control*. Oxford University Press.

(2001b) *Mass Imprisonment: Social Causes and Consequences*. London: Sage.

Gearty, C. (2006) *Can Human Rights Survive?* Cambridge University Press.

Gobert, J. (2008) 'The Corporate Manslaughter and Corporate Homicide Act 2007: Thirteen Years in the Making But Was It Worth the Wait?', *Modern Law Review*, **71**, 413.

Hawkins, K. (2003) *Law as Last Resort*. Oxford University Press.

Hillyard, P., Pantazis, C. and Tombs, S. (2004) *Beyond Criminology – Taking Harm Seriously*. London: Pluto Press.

Home Office (2002) *Justice for All* (Cm. 5563). London: TSO.

Hudson, B. (2007) 'Diversity, Crime and Criminal Justice', in M. Maguire, R. Morgan and R. Reiner (eds.), *Oxford Handbook of Criminology*. Oxford University Press, ch. 7, pp. 158–75.

Jackson, J. (2003) 'Justice for All: Putting Victims at the Heart of Criminal Justice?', *Journal of Law and Society*, **30**, 309.

Law Commission (2001) *Bail and the HRA* 1998 (Report no. 269). London: TSO.

Maslow, A. (1998) *Towards a Psychology of Being*. New York, NY: Wiley.

Matthews, R. (2005) 'The Myth of Punitiveness', *Theoretical Criminology*, **9**, 175.

McBarnet, D. (1981) *Conviction*. London: Macmillan.
McEwan, J. (2005) 'Proving Consent in Sexual Cases: Legislative Change and Cultural Evolution', *International Journal of Evidence and Proof*, **9**, 1.
Ormerod, D. (2003) 'The ECHR and the Exclusion of Evidence', *Criminal Law Review*, **61.**
Packer, H. (1968) *Limits of the Criminal Sanction*. Stanford University Press.
Padfield, N. (2008) *Criminal Justice Process*. Oxford University Press.
Povey, D., Smith, K., Hand, T. and Dodd, L. (eds.) (2009) *Police Powers and Procedures England and Wales 2007/08*, Home Office Statistical Bulletin 07/09. London: Home Office.
Pratt, J. *et al.* (eds.) (2005) *The New Punitiveness: Trends, Theories, Perspectives*. Cullompton, Devon: Willan.
Roach, K. (1999) *Due Process and Victims' Rights*. University of Toronto Press.
Sanders, A. (2002a) 'Core Values, the Magistracy and the Auld Report', *Journal of Law and Society*, **29**, 324.
(2002b) 'Victim Participation in an Exclusionary Criminal Justice System', in C. Hoyle and R. Young (eds.), *New Visions of Crime Victims*. Oxford: Hart.
Sanders, A. and Young, R. (1994) 'The Rule of Law, Due Process and Pre-trial Criminal Justice', *Current Legal Problems*, **47**, 125.
Sanders, A., Young, R. and Burton, M. (2010) *Criminal Justice*, 4th edn. Oxford University Press.
Sarat, A. (1997) 'Vengeance, Victims and the Identities of Law', *Social and Legal Studies*, **6**, 163.
Smith, D. (1997) 'Case Construction and Goals of the Criminal Process', *British Journal of Criminology*, **37**, 319.
Tombs, S. and Whyte, D. (2007) *Safety Crimes*. Cullompton, Devon: Willan.
(2008) *A Crisis of Enforcement: The Decriminalisation of Death and Injury at Work* (CCJS Briefing No. 6).
Whyte, D. (2007) 'Victims of Corporate Crime', in S. Walklate (ed.), *Handbook of Victims and Victimology*. Cullompton, Devon: Willan, pp. 149–90.
(2007/8) 'Gordon Brown's charter for corporate criminals' (2007/8) *Criminal Justice Matters*, **70**, 31.
Yeung, K. (2004) *Securing Compliance: A Principled Approach*. Oxford: Hart.
Young, R. (2008) 'Street Policing after PACE: The Drift to Summary Justice', in E. Cape and R. Young (eds.), *Regulating Policing*. Oxford: Hart, ch. 7, pp. 149–90.
Young, R. and Sanders, A. (2005) 'The Ethics of Prosecution Lawyers', *Legal Ethics*, **7**, 90.
Zedner, L. (2007) 'From Pre-Crime to Post-Conviction', *Theoretical Criminology*, **11**(2), 261–81.

4

On the interface of criminal justice and regulation

PETER GRABOSKY*

At first glance, one might be tempted to regard systems of regulation and of criminal justice as essentially unrelated. But like humans compared to other primates, regulation and criminal justice have much in common. The theorists and practitioners of each have learned a great deal, and have a great deal yet to learn, from each other. This chapter will explore the interface of regulation and criminal justice. It will identify how principles and strategies of each have been used, with varying success, by devotees of the other. First, it will discuss criminal justice as an instrument of regulation. Criminal justice is, in fact, one component of a regulatory system; the most egregious examples of regulatory non-compliance may incur criminal liability. Then, the chapter will discuss regulation as an instrument of criminal justice. There are many regulatory activities that are incidental to criminal justice. When functioning properly, these may preclude the necessity for mobilizing the criminal process. A great deal of crime prevention, for example, is based on regulation. The chapter will then explore some common theoretical bases. Both regulation more generally, and criminal justice as a subset, can entail similar techniques, such as contracting out, or the use of coercive powers. Their relative efficiency and effectiveness within and between regulatory and criminal justice domains is an important question. Finally, the chapter will discuss normative principles that might govern the various measures that might be brought to bear in regulatory and criminal justice domains.

* The author wishes to thank Carolyn Abbot, Charles Loft and participants in the Manchester Seminars on Regulation and Criminal Justice for comments on an earlier draft.

Criminal justice as an instrument of regulation

Regulation is a mansion with many rooms. Within the Regulatory Institutions Network (RegNet), we define regulation as any activity, legal, political, social, economic or psychological, the purpose of which is to steer the flow of events. Much of what constitutes the regulatory craft (Sparrow 2000), at least as performed by government agencies, are practices that can best be described as gentle (Grabosky and Braithwaite 1986). They entail the provision of information to enable regulated entities to know what their responsibilities are, and how to fulfil them. They may also entail positive or negative feedback, often communicated informally.

Negotiation, persuasion and the provision of information constitute the basic tools of regulators. The first condition of regulatory compliance is the regulated entity's awareness and understanding of the rules in question (Abbot 2007, 2009). Most regulators will be quick to state that they resort to the criminal process only as a last resort. There are circumstances, however, in which behaviour of a regulated entity deviates to such an extent from prevailing norms that the criminal sanction is mobilized. It is this point at which the criminal justice system becomes an instrument of regulation. The mobilization of the criminal process by regulatory authorities usually arises from the most egregious regulatory violations, particularly those resulting in death, serious injury, or significant financial loss or property damage. Alternatively, wilful, persistent non-compliance may also invite criminal prosecution.

Resort to the criminal process is not undertaken lightly, because it can be slow, costly and the outcome may be unpredictable. A large corporate defendant may command resources vastly in excess of a state regulator. Public sector agencies are now required to manage their finite resources responsibly. It is not difficult to imagine how a regulatory agency may forego the expensive path of prosecution in favour of lesser, more certain outcomes.

To place criminal sanctions within a wider regulatory context, it is instructive to use the heuristic developed by John Braithwaite: the regulatory pyramid (see Figure 4.1 below). This was discussed in Ayres and Braithwaite's *Responsive Regulation: Transcending the Deregulation Debate* (Ayres and Braithwaite 1992), arguably the most important work on the regulatory process published during the 1990s.

According to Ayres and Braithwaite, government response should be commensurate with the compliance behaviour of the regulated entity.

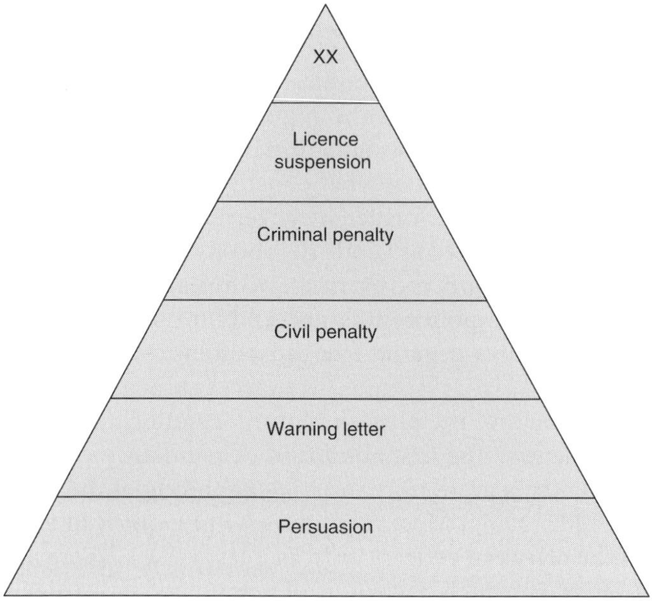

Figure 4.1 The regulatory pyramid (adapted from Ayres and Braithwaite 1992)

Severity of response should reflect the gravity of the offender's transgression. Simple persuasion and the provision of information are mobilized against initial minor contraventions. Persistent non-compliance is met with escalating severity of response, through warning letters, civil penalties, criminal penalties and, ultimately, licence suspension and revocation; the latter representing what might be described as corporate capital punishment.

Ayres and Braithwaite used a simple, but elegant graphical depiction, the pyramid, to represent the circumstances of interaction between regulator–regulatee. Based on ideas developed in Braithwaite's earlier work on the regulation of coal mine safety (Braithwaite 1985), the pyramid represents the range of sanctions available to a regulatory agency to encourage compliance, and to respond to non-compliance when this occurs. The vertical dimension of the pyramid represents severity of regulatory response. Negotiation and persuasion, non-coercive responses, take place at the base of the pyramid. Persistent non-compliance will lead to an escalation of response through administrative penalties, civil sanctions and ultimately criminal prosecution.

The triangular shape of the pyramid, that is the relative width of its base and sharpness of its apex, implies that most regulatory interventions are relatively benign, and coercive instruments are mobilized only when lesser interventions prove insufficient to secure compliance. In other words, there is a range of regulatory responses that can be mobilized in response to the behaviour of the harm doer. These include negotiation and persuasion, the provision of information and the use of incentives, among other things.

The concept of a pyramid depicting a range of regulatory instruments is a compelling one, as it illustrates the basis for much greater regulatory flexibility than would accompany the existence of but a single enforcement option. One can readily envisage how a regulatory posture tailored to a particular context of non-compliance, and adaptable to improvements or deterioration in compliance performance, can be superior in terms of both justice and efficiency to a single standardized response. The latter situation contains a substantial risk of under-regulation, on the one hand, or of regulatory overkill on the other. Moreover, Charles Loft (2007) reminds us that 'the state' is often not a single entity, and that regulatory responsibility may be shared between agencies and with subordinate jurisdictions such as provincial and local governments.

To summarize, resort to the criminal process is but one instrument in the regulator's toolkit. It is best used sparingly and strategically, when more benign instruments fail to elicit the requisite degree of compliance.

But there is more to regulation than the work of governments. Ayres and Braithwaite's analysis advocated wider participation in the regulatory process, to include not only government agencies and regulated entities, but also third parties representing public interests (public interest groups, or PIGs).

Pluralistic responsive regulation

Despite its elegance and usefulness as a heuristic, the Ayres–Braithwaite pyramid suffers from oversimplification. It reflects state regulatory action and state regulatory action alone, and thereby fails to represent the activity of both regulated entities and third parties. Indeed, one of the significant contributions of Ayres and Braithwaite's book is the support that they give to the concept of regulatory tripartism,[1] and the constructive

[1] The concept of regulatory tripartism, embracing the possibility of constructive collaboration between the three main institutional forms, is already manifest in a variety of

role that they envisage for non-governmental actors, particularly PIGs, in the regulatory process. Ayres and Braithwaite themselves recognize that there is much more to the regulatory process than the activities of governments.

For example, PIGs engage in education and persuasion of both cooperative and recalcitrant corporate actors, often in a manner more convincing than do state agents (Alston and Roberts 1999). Should this not suffice to improve corporate compliance, interest groups can engage in public denunciation, often quite strident.

Consumer campaigns in favour of 'dolphin-friendly' tuna or clothing made in non-exploitative settings can reward socially responsible business and financially punish the unconcerned. When the consumer is a national or global organization with massive buying power, such as Sainsbury's supermarket or the Body Shop, the impact can be that much greater.

Banks may refuse to lend to a prospective borrower with a poor record of health, safety or environmental performance; insurers may refuse to insure them against loss (Richardson 2001).

Industry associations can withdraw accreditation or certification from a member who does not conform to required performance standards. In industries such as organic agriculture or meat export, certification may give a producer a competitive edge. Indeed, where certification is a *sine qua non* of access to a market, denial of such certification by an industry self regulatory regime may contribute to the demise of the enterprise.

Moreover, the two-dimensional pyramid fails to represent the interactive nature of regulatory life; the fact that many regulatory components are not unilateral phenomena, but rather hybrid instruments or institutions, combining elements of state, regulated entity and third-party activity (Gunningham and Grabosky 1998). These various instruments in turn, may impact upon each other, enhancing or lessening the influence of a given component or set of components (Grabosky 1994). The spectre of state intervention can inspire strong self-regulatory initiatives; or, the state may require a corporate actor to engage the services of a rigorous gatekeeper. Such services can be as diverse as required financial audits for public companies, or required health examinations for airline pilots or sex workers.

settings such as tripartite regimes for the regulation of occupational health and safety, and at a more general level, corporatist governance (Grabosky and Braithwaite 1986: 66; Streeck and Schmitter 1985; Schmitter and Lembruch 1979).

Ayres and Braithwaite, in their chapter on tripartism, demonstrate how an active public interest sector can energize state regulatory authorities and thereby reduce the likelihood of capture by the private sector. Third parties can also bring influence directly to bear upon companies, by mobilizing adverse publicity in the aftermath of a significant violation or by dealing in a constructive manner with the firm, beyond the regulatory gaze of government (Smith 2001).

Towards a three-dimensional pyramid

One can build upon the work of Ayres and Braithwaite by adding another dimension to their pyramid. The model presented here goes beyond the depiction of instruments available to state regulatory authorities, to include the other institutions which comprise a regulatory system: regulated entities themselves and their industry associations; and third parties, both public interest institutions and commercial actors.

To depict this wider conception of a regulatory system we shall use a graphical representation of a three-dimensional pyramid, or more precisely, a tetrahedron (Figure 4.2). This object has a triangular base, and three triangular faces. One face represents the government; it is, in fact, the Ayres–Braithwaite pyramid. A second face represents the regulated entity, whether individual firm or industry association. The third face represents third parties, including not only public interest actors, but also commercial third parties such as institutions of finance and insurance.

The vertical dimension, that is, the altitude of a point in the tetrahedron, represents coerciveness. The higher the location in regulatory space, the more coercive the regulatory instrument. One should bear in mind that the dimensions of the tetrahedron represent theoretical limits; the fact that the state possesses the power to close down an enterprise does not imply that such power is occasionally, or ever, invoked. The actual configuration of a regulatory system 'in action' can be depicted by a form, or more likely, a set of forms, located inside the tetrahedron.

It is also important to note that the exercise of regulatory coercion is by no means a monopoly of the state. Each of the three main institutional actors, state, industry and third parties, have extremely coercive instruments at their disposal. In the case of the non-governmental institutions, industry and third parties, these in practice may even exceed the coercive capacity of the state. Market forces may bring about the demise of a company in a way that regulators cannot.

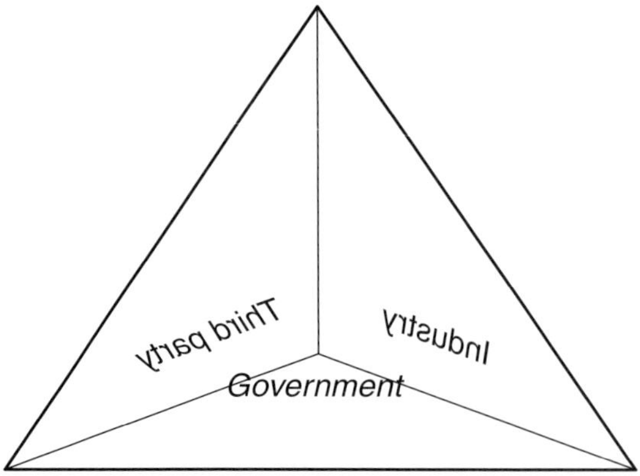

Figure 4.2 The regulatory tetrahedron

For example, an industry association may suspend or expel a member. Thus, disciplinary boards of medical societies and of the Financial Industry Regulatory Authority (FINRA) may put their members out of business (Gittleman and Sacks 2008).[2] This is the self-regulatory manifestation of corporate capital punishment, and can be represented by a point at the top of the tetrahedron, on the self-regulatory face. Societies for the prevention of cruelty to animals undertake investigation and prosecution of animal rights violators. Such action would be represented by a point towards the top of the tetrahedron on the third-party face.

Massive damages in tort by an injured third party can be catastrophic to a corporate defendant. So too could foreclosure on a loan to a corporate entity by a bank or other financial institution. These can be tantamount to corporate capital punishment, and may be represented by a point at the apex of the third-party face.

But there is more to a tetrahedron than its external surfaces. Unlike the Ayres–Braithwaite pyramid, which is two dimensional, this is a three-dimensional space. To the extent that a given regulatory instrument combines elements of state, self-regulatory or third-party activity, it can be depicted as a form within the tetrahedron (see Figure 4.3). Theoretically, any regulatory instrument can be located within the

[2] FINRA (www.finra.org) is a non-governmental entity created in 2007 with the consolidation of the National Association of Securities Dealers and elements of the New York Stock Exchange.

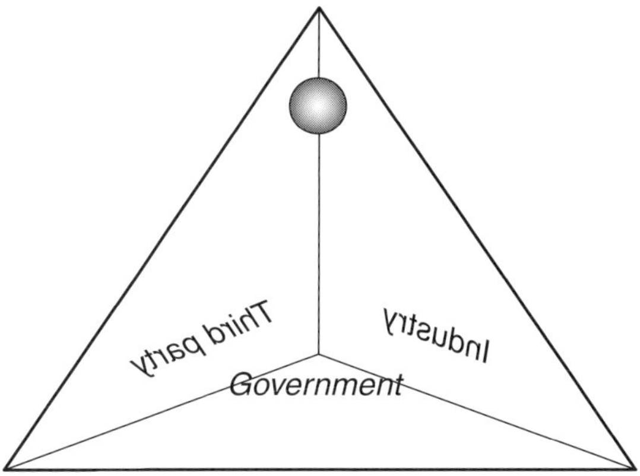

Figure 4.3 A coercive regulatory instrument wielded unilaterally by government

space, depending upon its institutional sponsor (or sponsors) and its coerciveness.

For example, the power of a government agency to withdraw the licence of a nuclear power generator, thereby shutting it down, is a regulatory instrument which is wielded unilaterally. As such, it would be located on the government surface of the tetrahedron, at or near the apex.

By contrast, a hybrid instrument such as a prize for the revegetation of former mine sites jointly awarded by the government and the mining industry, would be located towards the base of the tetrahedron between government and industry faces (see Figure 4.4).

The actions of a bank in requiring certification with ISO 14000 (environmental management standards developed by the International Organization for Standardization) as a condition of finance would be represented by a plane located between third party and regulated industry, midway to the apex of the tetrahedron. A decision of the lending institution to cancel the loan could elevate the plane closer to the apex.

Regulatory systems, in theory and in practice, will vary depending upon context. Some instruments will be more effective when applied to certain types of firms in certain situations. Others, ironically, may impede compliance rather than facilitate it (Abbot 2007, 2009). Braithwaite and his colleagues have observed that a trusting approach by regulatory authorities, by fostering the internalization of regulatory objectives, is more conducive to compliance (Braithwaite and Makkai 1994). By contrast, an antagonistic approach, where regulatory disapproval is articulated in

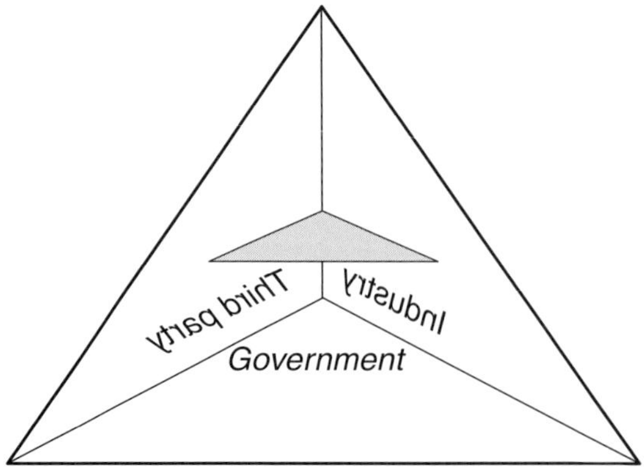

Figure 4.4 A hybrid instrument wielded jointly by industry and a third party

such a manner as to denigrate the professionalism of the recipient, may lead to the development of a defiant, calculating identity and corresponding regulatory response.[3]

All of these regulatory mechanisms, whether state, private or hybrid, are amenable to graphic representation in three-dimensional space. Their vertical location within the tetrahedron will reflect the degree of coerciveness with which they impact on the organizational life of the regulatee; their horizontal location will reflect their institutional (or inter-institutional) form.

The heuristic value of our three-dimensional conceptualization of regulatory space should be obvious. It permits a graphical representation of entire regulatory systems, enabling one to visualize their coercive properties, as well as to visualize the mix of their constituent institutional forms (see Figure 4.5). It also permits comparison of systems in terms both of coerciveness and institutional composition (or lack thereof).

Any location on or within the tetrahedron can be represented by precise coordinates, and is thus amenable to formal (i.e. quantitative) representation. Although current scholarship on regulatory systems may not have attained the sophistication in conceptualization and measurement that this would require, the next generation of regulatory scholars may include those who might wish to undertake more precise description or modelling of regulatory systems. This could permit a degree of hypothesis testing

[3] To quote one respondent of Makkai and Braithwaite (1994: 16) 'When they keep treating you as unprofessional, untrustworthy, you end up deciding if they want to treat me like a businessman who only cares about the bottom line, then I'll be a businessman.'

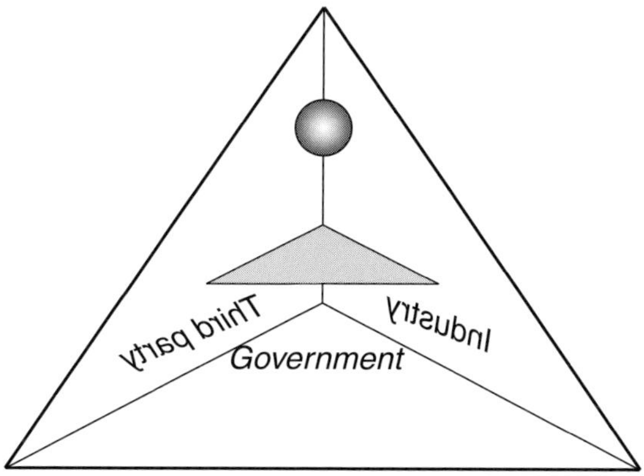

Figure 4.5 Depiction of multiple instruments operating independently

and theory building which has thus far been largely absent from the literature on regulation. Much as aeronautical engineers or molecular biologists are able to visualize the systems with which they deal, so too could future 'regulatory systems engineers' explore alternative institutional forms.

Regulation as an instrument of criminal justice

In everyday regulatory life, not all harmful or otherwise antisocial behaviour is subject to criminal sanction. Some misconduct is simply tolerated. Other bad behaviour may lead merely to disapproval, gossip, avoidance or civil litigation. Indeed, the criminal process is increasingly used as a last resort, to be mobilized only when other means of social control and conflict resolution fail.

The process of criminalizing regulatory non-compliance entails first, recognizing the behaviour in question as harmful to the extent that it is worthy of criminal prohibition, then, formally defining it as a crime. The next step is to detect the harm in question when it occurs, and then to identify it as proscribed behaviour.

The fourth step is to investigate the case and assemble evidence sufficient to support a prosecution. This can be challenging indeed, particularly in those countries whose legal systems value the rights of the accused, and whose rules of evidence are strict.

The fifth step is to prosecute. The decision to prosecute is not always easy. Prosecutorial authorities do not have unlimited resources. Often they must weigh a number of considerations. These may include:

- the degree of harm to persons and property caused by the behaviour in question;
- the degree of criminal intent on the part of the alleged perpetrator (malice/recklessness/carelessness; ignorance);
- the prior record of the alleged perpetrator;
- the extent to which the accused cooperated with the investigation;
- the cost of prosecution;
- the probability of conviction;
- the likelihood of a significant sentence in the event of conviction;
- the public interest in prosecution: e.g. would a successful prosecution close down the city's major employer? Would a successful prosecution deter future wrongdoing?; and
- media attention accorded to *both* the harm in question *and* the government's response.

The sixth and final step, in the event that a prosecution succeeds, is to fix a penalty appropriate to the offence in question. This can vary from a simple reprimand, to imprisonment in the case of individuals, to terminating the organization in the case of a corporate offender.

These suggest that impediments to mobilizing the criminal process in response to non-compliance can be formidable indeed. The good news, however, is that regulation can make a positive contribution to criminal justice by reducing criminal motivations and reducing criminal opportunities, without incurring the cost and imposing the stigma of criminal sanction.

The best current thinking in policing has its application to regulation. Perhaps the most significant theoretical development in policing during the last quarter of the twentieth century was problem-oriented policing (Goldstein 1990). Criminological research began to demonstrate that crime was not randomly distributed across time and space, and that both offending and victimization were not randomly distributed across members of the public. Rather, crime tended to concentrate at certain places and at certain times. Moreover, a small proportion of offenders was responsible for a large proportion of offences, and a small proportion of individuals was disproportionately vulnerable to victimization. This gave rise to a movement in policing devoted to the identification of hot spots, repeat offenders and repeat victims with a view towards neutralizing the underlying driver, rather than reacting to individual incidents.

One of the more innovative scholars of regulation, himself a former police officer, applied the logic of problem-oriented policing to the challenge of winning regulatory compliance (Sparrow 2000). His classic, *The Regulatory Craft*, could as easily be entitled *Problem-oriented Regulation*.

It has long been acknowledged that the criminal justice system is a very imperfect instrument of social control. Indeed, it is only when traditional institutions such as family, school, church and neighbourhood fail, that the criminal justice system is called into play. There is, of course, a myriad of other institutions in the public, private and non-profit sectors, which, in the course of their normal operations, perform a social control function.

The increasingly complex nature of crime, and the fiscal constraints that prevail in advanced industrial societies, are such that conventional law enforcement responses are often no longer adequate to the task of crime control. Crime is becoming more sophisticated, and is increasingly recognized as being interlinked with economic and social systems. The existence and normal operation of a wide variety of institutions (in both the public and private sectors) generally unrelated to criminal justice can facilitate or inhibit criminal activity. For example, the location, design and management of public housing facilities can generate more, or less, business for police. So too can the policies of education authorities regarding truancy. The location of a drug treatment facility, or planning approval for a fast-food outlet, can also impact on surrounding street life, legal and illegal (Felson 2006).

It should come as no surprise that institutions outside the criminal justice system and indeed, outside the public sector, can be harnessed, or nurtured, in a manner that can enhance the capacity of criminal justice institutions. Perhaps because of the unique role and customary insularity of the police, the basic idea of 'steering' in addition to 'rowing' (Osborne and Gaebler 1992) did not spread rapidly in the law enforcement community. These new ideas point towards a more expansive, entrepreneurial role for police in controlling crime, if they are up to the task (Wood *et al.* 2008). Unfortunately, the traditional reactive posture of police, and their self-image as 'catchers of crooks', may have inhibited the development of a more expansive entrepreneurial role, involving strategic planning, policy development and policy coordination in areas far afield from traditional policing.[4]

Nevertheless, the intersection of licit and illicit markets, and the dependence of illicit markets on the former, have invited regulatory intervention

[4] In an ideal world, this expansive role would be performed with sensitivity to human rights as well.

in furtherance of crime control. Some of this is not new. Legitimate financial institutions are now required to scrutinize cash transactions and to report those which appear to be suspicious (Reuter and Truman 2004). Second-hand goods dealers are required to maintain records of transactions (Weatherburn and Grabosky 1999). In many places, chemical manufacturers and retail pharmacists are now required to take steps to reduce the likelihood that certain precursor chemicals will not be diverted for the illegal manufacture of methamphetamines (Cherney *et al.* 2006a). Proprietors of licensed premises are subject to regulations designed to inhibit irresponsible consumption of alcohol, and the antisocial behaviour that often accompanies binge drinking (King and Richards 2003).

The organized crime strategy of Victoria Police explicitly includes engaging with the regulatory environment as one of its six key areas. It envisages networked arrangements for the exchange of intelligence and information between police and regulatory agencies (Victoria Police 2005).

From the configuration of computer systems to the design of public housing facilities, decisions outside the normal purview of police can have profound impacts on the challenges that police will eventually face (Lessig 2006; Katyal 2002). The ability of the police to influence these external business and policy decisions, either directly or through more traditional regulatory institutions, will determine the nature of the police workload down the track.

One can easily envisage the application of a regulatory tetrahedron to criminal justice. Informal institutions of social control will be represented closer to the base of the tetrahedron, at some distance from the state façade. So too will crime prevention measures of a less coercive nature. Private civil remedies such as those discussed by Mazerolle and Ransley (2005) will be located closer to the apex, as will such measures as Anti-Social Behaviour Orders. Private prosecutions, rare though they may be, will be higher still.

Theoretical convergences

Readers at this point will have noted that criminal prosecution is a very imperfect instrument of regulation, and of social control more generally. That is not to suggest that the apex of the pyramid in either the domain of regulation or of conventional crime control, is devoid of merit or of use. But it is at best complementary to less dramatic activities. Of greater interest are institutional arrangements that can be achieved towards the base of the tetrahedron to preclude the necessity of catching crooks, or lesser regulatory offenders, after the fact. The design and implementation of these arrangements has been described as 'meta-regulation' (Cherney *et al.* 2006b).

There are various basic forms by which state activity, whether it involves regulatory or law enforcement agencies, can be shared with or devolved upon private interests. This applies equally to regulation and to criminal justice. Some are already quite familiar; each may have the potential for wider applicability. The following section, based on a previous overview of nine complementary regulatory instruments (Grabosky 1995), presents an application of these principles to the crime control process, in descending order of what might be described as state intrusion or coerciveness:

- conscription;
- required private interface;
- required record keeping and disclosure;
- cooptation of private interests;
- conferring entitlements;
- incentives;
- contracting out;
- delegation or deference to private parties; and
- abdication.

Perhaps the most direct of these is conscription. Governments may simply command third parties to assist with one or more processes of law enforcement or regulation. Cash transaction reporting requirements have become increasingly common in western democracies over the past quarter century. In essence, these mandate that banks and other defined cash dealers systematically report transactions in excess of a certain amount, and other transactions which might appear suspect, to regulatory authorities.

In some jurisdictions, members of certain professions are required by law to report suspected cases of child abuse or neglect to the appropriate authorities. As is the case with other forms of conscription, this dramatically enhances the surveillance capacity of the state (Ayling and Grabosky 2006a). The USA Patriot Act empowered the FBI to issue 'national security letters', forcing telephone and Internet providers to turn over customer records without court authorization, and to prohibit the companies from disclosing this to anyone (Donohue 2008: 240).

In contrast to conscription, where commands are directed at third parties, the required private interface approach entails governments requiring that targets of crime control engage the machinery of private institutions.

Social security authorities and other agencies that bestow public benefits increasingly require that recipients maintain a bank account into which the benefits may be paid directly. Not only does this reduce the agency's clerical expenses, and the risk to the beneficiary of loss or theft, but it significantly reduces opportunities for fraud.

Governments may require independent certification of some aspect of a private actor's conduct. The idea that departures from law-abiding behaviour can only be monitored by public servants is, in many areas of law enforcement, no longer realistic. Accordingly, governments have begun to rely increasingly on independent certification by third parties. Shapiro (1987: 205) refers to 'private social control entrepreneurs for hire'.

Members of certain professions, in the course of delivering services to their clients, are in a position to facilitate (or to impede) illegal conduct. Because of their strategic situation and unique knowledge, some professionals are often ideally situated to prevent, detect and disclose illegality on the part of their clients. For this reason, such actors have been called 'gatekeepers' (Kraakman 1986).

The classic model for this form of coproduction is the requirement that the financial accounts of public companies be audited on a regular basis by formally accredited professionals. This exposes such accounts to a degree of scrutiny that arguably would not occur if audits were left up to public agencies to perform. The very existence of such surveillance by independent professionals is an important deterrent to illegality.

In addition, regulatory authorities can make it obligatory that regulated entities hold liability insurance as a condition of doing business. Conditions of a private insurance contract may equal or exceed government-licensing conditions in terms of stringency, and surveillance on the part of the insurer may surpass that of government (Richardson 2001).

In order to encourage introspection, or with a view to informing markets or other private institutions in a position to foster compliance, governments may require disclosure of certain aspects of a regulatee's activities. The simple process of enumeration and record keeping has a regulatory function. When subject to disclosure, these accounts increase a subject's visibility to the world. They provide a record of conduct that regulators and criminal justice authorities can scrutinize. So it is that physicians' prescriptions for pharmaceutical opioids and amphetamines are compulsorily reported and rigorously monitored. Enumeration can also lead to a degree of self-awareness and peer awareness, which can have a significant impact on compliance. When the phenomenon enumerated is undesirable, as, for example, workplace injuries, CO_2 emissions, or related party transactions involving the directors of public companies, the necessity of enumeration focuses managerial attention on the underlying phenomenon (Fung *et al.* 2007).

In some settings, public agencies may actively seek the cooperation of private interests in furtherance of surveillance and detection. Airline staff are encouraged to report suspicious passengers to customs or drug enforcement authorities. Operators of taxis and other forms of public transport may be invited to assist law enforcement. The formality of these arrangements can vary from the relatively casual, to detailed contractual specification. In addition to the role of organized interests, diffuse interests can also contribute to crime control. The very idea of community policing itself embodies collaboration with the public to identify issues of grassroots concern, and to identify appropriate remedial strategies (Tarr *et al.* 2005).

There are two basic avenues by which governments can empower private interests to enforce the law. The first entails the creation of certain specified rights, conferring them upon private parties, and leaving it up to those private parties to enforce. Many systems of patent, trade mark and copyright rely on such private enforcement. In Australia, the vast majority of actions brought under the Trade Practices Act are brought by private parties. Company and securities regulators also encourage private actions on the part of aggrieved parties. Successful private litigation may result in damage awards that exceed penalties available to the state; the deterrent effect posed by many potential private enforcers should not be underestimated. Thus can the pursuit of private interest serve the public.

A second avenue of private enforcement entails empowering third parties to undertake enforcement actions on behalf of the state. The principle is by no means a modern one. A fourteenth-century English statute specified that 25 per cent of fines imposed on stallholders engaged in trade after the close of a fair be paid to citizens intervening on behalf of the King (5 Edw III, ch.5 (1331)).

Private enforcement in the public interest is alive and well in many jurisdictions, most notably in the United States, where federal environmental laws contain provisions for private enforcement (Langpap 2008). Regimes for the control of fraud against the US federal government also provide for citizen litigation. In the UK, the generally available right of private prosecution has been exercised in the public interest by third parties. Each year, the Royal Society for the Prevention of Cruelty to Animals investigates tens of thousands of complaints and successfully prosecutes about 2,000 cases. The vigilance exercised by these private individuals and institutions far exceeds that wielded by the state.

In their book, *Third Party Policing*, Mazerolle and Ransley (2005) discuss how citizens are empowered and encouraged to seek civil remedies against activities conducive to criminality. Nuisance suits against owners of premises used for illegal activity such as drug sales are the classic example.

Governments may offer incentives directly to targets of regulation to induce compliance, or to engage in a desired course of conduct. This could include the engagement of professional services that would foster compliance. Many systems of taxation provide that costs incurred in furtherance of compliance are tax deductible. Alternatively, in various regulatory regimes companies which have an approved compliance programme in place, or which subject themselves to a regular compliance audit by an independent assessor, may qualify for licence fee rebates, or may be subject to less scrutiny by regulatory authorities.

Other incentive systems may be structured in a manner to facilitate crime control. Consider, for example, how a system of deposit refunds for irreparably damaged or unserviceable motor vehicles would, if priced appropriately, reduce the number of abandoned vehicles and render more difficult the 'rebirthing' of stolen cars.

Governments may also offer incentives to third parties for the co-production of law enforcement services. Rewards and bounties for surveillance and enforcement activity are common in many regulatory and law enforcement settings. Most prominently, the US government is offering a reward of $25 million for information leading to the capture of Osama bin Laden. In the United States, more routinely, private citizens may receive rewards for information leading to the successful prosecution of tax evasion and insider trading (Ventry 2008). In Australia, the Financial Management and Accountability Act contains provisions for rewards. Such mechanisms can significantly enhance the surveillance capacity of government authorities.

There are times at which governments, for one reason or another, might seek to engage private consultants rather than rely upon in-house resources. They may be driven by ideology. They might seek to achieve the appearance or the reality of disinterested independence. They may seek to control or to influence the product in a manner not available through normal institutional channels. They may seek to access skills and other resources not available 'in-house', or they may simply seek to save money

(Ayling and Grabosky 2006b). Governments may also contract out one or more regulatory functions, from specialized testing to an entire regulatory regime.

Police already purchase a myriad of services, including training, traffic control, audiotape transcription, some forensic investigations and prisoner transport (Ayling and Grabosky 2006b: 667). The increasing sophistication of crime will require the enlistment of very specialized skills by law enforcement agencies. Certain forms of fraud investigation are now routinely outsourced to private investigators. One imagines that as telecommunications-related crime becomes increasingly refined, the role of private computer security professionals and 'forensic systems analysts' will become that much greater, with their specialized knowledge hired on a case-by-case basis by law enforcement authorities.

In some instances, governments may become aware that certain functions relating to regulatory compliance or to conventional crime control are already being performed or could be performed by private parties. In such cases, governments may be content to rely upon this activity rather than duplicate it with public sector resources.

Standards developed in the private sector are often accepted and given official status by public agencies. In some regulatory systems, the task of developing rules is delegated to private interests (Mahoney 1997). The US Securities and Exchange Commission has delegated considerable rule-making functions to professional self-regulatory organizations. Galanter (1981) refers to such technologies as 'regulatory endowments'.

Other professional roles may be encouraged by special accreditation or other considerations accorded their practitioners by regulatory authorities. One example is tax advisers who are formally accredited by taxation authorities (Braithwaite 2009). Professions may be created and invested with legitimacy by the state in order to facilitate just such a role.

The role of volunteers in criminal justice has a long history. Indeed, it pre-dates the development of criminal justice (Grabosky 1992). Today, from victim assistance and support services, to night patrols that help look after public inebriates in Australian indigenous communities, they provide services that might normally lie beyond the resources and the capacity of police to deliver.

Finally, the state may simply abdicate some regulatory or policing functions, and leave allocative and ordering decisions to the market.

Private interests, left to their own devices, can market services in furtherance of crime control. The private security industry, broadly defined, represents a familiar example. In most advanced industrial societies, private security employees outnumber sworn police by a factor of two or three. Police, aware that many commercial premises have engaged private security services may focus their patrols elsewhere. At another level, holders of home contents insurance are often required to have a certain degree of security hardware as a condition of insurance. The pricing of policies may depend upon the level of security measures in place.

Markets are also arenas of surveillance. In addition to the surveillance normally exercised in the market by competitors, the scrutiny accorded compliance behaviour by banks, insurers and institutional investors can be formidable. The solution to the availability of objectionable material on the Internet, for example, may lie not in censorship, but in the development of software to screen out offensive content. While this might not please those fundamentalists who object to any communication of material that they deem offensive, at the very least it can protect individuals from personal intrusion.

The criminal risks faced by a country's enterprises doing business abroad may lie beyond the jurisdiction of the government at home to address. Authorities in the host nation may be preoccupied with their own concerns, or indeed, may even be part of the problem, whether it entails industrial espionage or other activity directed against foreign business. Thus entire markets in specialized loss prevention services are becoming available to private industry.

One of the virtues of abdicating a regulatory role in deference to markets is that market-based orderings tend to be perceived as non-coercive, or in any event, as less coercive than government commands. Thus market signals, no matter how dictatorial they may be in reality, create less resentment than government direction.

To conclude, it is boldly apparent that both 'regulatory space' (Shearing 1993) and 'crime space' are pluralistic in nature. These pluralistic spaces have a common basis. Beginning with the Thatcher–Reagan ascendancy of the 1980s, and long before the current global financial crisis, governments in most parts of the world have been under great fiscal pressure. Whether driven by ideology, voter resistance to higher taxes, or the influence of world financial markets, governments have been inclined to reduce public expenditure unless their very survival in office depends on it.

At the same time, citizens in many countries have continuing, if not increasing expectations of government services. Demands for improved health services, a cleaner environment, safer products and safer streets, are a feature of western industrial societies. What this means is that governments are seeking creative solutions to achieve more with less. Some of the strategies outlined above are means to this end.

Normative considerations

Relaxing one's hold upon the reins of law enforcement (or of regulation), or releasing them altogether, is not without risk. The following section discusses some of the problems that might arise when governments seek to use leverage to achieve crime control or regulatory objectives.

Perhaps the greatest risk in devolving law enforcement or regulatory functions to private interests is the potential loss of accountability. Even for those who may be unconcerned with the legitimacy of handing certain powers of the state over to private actors, tracking the exercise of that power may become problematic. At least in theory, private institutions and actions, one step removed from the democratic process, are less accessible to public scrutiny. The decentralized, dispersed nature of law enforcement and regulatory activity may be less visible and less amenable to control. When government contractors hide behind the veil of commercial confidentiality to conceal the business they conduct on behalf of the public, it is the public that suffers (Freiberg 1999).

One should not overlook the fact that many law enforcement and regulatory problems arise from market failures in the first place. The global financial crisis of 2009 is one example. From tainted food, to anti-competitive conduct, to foul air and water, to depleted fisheries, to professional misconduct, entire new fields of regulation have sprung from the flawed operation of unrestrained, or insufficiently restrained, market forces. To the extent that governments rely upon market mechanisms to foster compliance, there still exists the risk of market failure. Not all markets punish poor performers. Illicit markets can richly reward the unscrupulous player. Some of the more common market failures acting to the detriment of regulatory compliance occur in markets for professional services. The private security sector has received its share of criticisms.

Market failures can also arise from undersupply. The challenge of contracting out can be made extremely difficult when the number of available vendors is limited. When choice of supplier is really no choice at all, the purchaser becomes a captive of the market, and risks being stuck with an inferior product. For all their potential virtues, markets require oversight.

The requirement that one engage the services of gatekeeping professionals is by no means a failsafe bulwark against illegality (Coffee 2004).

Gatekeepers may be 'captured' by their clients, in the sense that they come to view reality not through a lens of professional detachment, but from the client's perspective. Professionals may be financially dependent upon a continuing engagement, and may thus bend over backward to accommodate a client. Professional services can thereby foster non-compliance.

Market forces themselves may contribute to professional failure. Not all professions can be relied upon to inform their membership of regulatory responsibilities or to police compliance. Nor can all gatekeepers be trusted to prevent, detect or disclose illegality on the part of their clients. Many corporate collapses that took place during the 1980s occurred in the aftermath of 'clean' audits. The Enron debacle is a more recent example. Accountants have long insisted that they are 'watchdogs' not 'bloodhounds'. Cynics may be forgiven for insisting that many of them are really 'lapdogs'.

There is also the risk that the policy process may be captured if too much responsibility is delegated or contracted to private institutions. At the extreme, government agencies can exist as hollow shells, with the real work of enforcement being performed by private interests. To the extent that these private interests dominate the public agenda, there is a problem. Even in settings which may be designed to further the public interest, third parties can have their own priorities. Well-resourced and shrill interests may not always act in furtherance of the wider public good.

The behaviour of private actors may at times diverge from that which may be desirable from the standpoint of the general public. Reliance on contractors for enforcement may lead to conflicts of interest.

Contractors may also engage in 'rent seeking', to the detriment of the public interest. In other words, many contractors seek to generate a continued or, better yet, an increased demand for their services. In a sense, they have an incentive to accentuate the magnitude of the task for which they have been engaged, or worse, to fabricate new and larger problems that they would be available to address in the course of a return engagement. Opportunism remains an essential element of commercial success. This can apply to IT consultants as well as to paid informants.

The extent to which professions or other mediating institutions are conscripted or co-opted by the state may force a change in the relationship between them and the citizen (Ayling *et al.* 2009). Professional–client relations, traditionally based on an atmosphere of trust and confidentiality, may be significantly transformed. Under regimes which require a degree of disclosure or notification, the professional, previously more or less a servant of the client, becomes to some degree an agent of the state. Once the client's champion, the professional may become more of an adversary.

Thus, the role of the banker or cash dealer is transformed from that of serving the consumer, to one of exercising regulatory vigilance on behalf of government. The impact of such a change on the willingness of the client to be candid or forthcoming may be substantial. Similar reservations have been voiced against mandatory disclosure of suspected child abuse by health professionals.

Excessive reliance on rewards, bounties and other incentives to private individuals for the co-production of regulatory services may have its dark side. A society in which any person may be a spy for the government is in danger of being blighted by mistrust and suspicion. The risk that such intrusive devices will be applied against relatively minor offenders rather than the sharks of this world is all too real.

With the devolution of so many public functions to private interests, there exists the real risk that a sense of public duty or civic obligation will be lost. Commercial activity may not encourage self-sacrifice for the greater good.

The idea embodied in the words 'public service' is at risk of becoming significantly tainted when the activity is undertaken by a private contractor. To the extent to which public service becomes commodified, it may lose its public meaning and become nothing more than a contractual relationship. To the extent that market relationships predominate, the bonds of community are weakened. There may be a real risk that cultural values will move away from the spirit of voluntarism and civic obligation towards those suited to a society of mercenaries as citizens. Few would favour any system of social control which is largely driven by opportunistic bounty hunters or profiteers.

When governments loosen the reins of enforcement, relying instead on decentralized and independent interests, there may be a loss of policy coherence or an imbalance in enforcement activity. Critics of private enforcement under the US Clean Water Act, for example, have argued that enforcement targets are selected on the basis of convenience and potential damage award, rather than the actual harm they may be causing to the environment (Greve 1989). Others would contend that private actions in furtherance of public agenda setting might be misplaced, that intense minorities might distort priorities, and that weak minorities may suffer.

All of the above risks point to one broader issue; that of the public interest. A shift from the exercise of state authority to a crime control process based on exchange and collaboration will significantly reduce the government's ability to manage results. When the public sector engages the private sector to perform certain regulatory functions, or when the state withdraws altogether in deference to private orderings, who looks out for the interests of the public? Who ensures the rule of law? I now suggest some of the means by which the remaining officials of the shrinking state may oversee and guide decentralized processes of crime control.

One can, in fact, envisage a set of normative principles that may suit both regulation and criminal justice. Beyond the bedrock principles of procedural justice and equality before the law, one must look first to Braithwaite and Pettit's dictum that restrictions on liberty should be used only when they enhance overall freedom.

But subsidiary principles are also worth noting. Whether wielded by criminal justice or regulatory agencies, interventions should abide by the principle of coercive parsimony. That is, coercion should be used no more than necessary to achieve the task, and should be proportionate to the task at hand. Another principle might be called the principle of financial parsimony. Interventions should be as inexpensive as possible. In furtherance of both principles of parsimony, regulatory and criminal justice authorities should be mindful of cost–benefit considerations, including unintended consequences.

Other principles that should apply to both regulation and criminal justice are transparency and democracy. The processes by which criminal justice and regulatory systems operate should be as transparent as they can be. One might also suggest that the public should be consulted and accorded the opportunity to comment on major policy matters in both domains.

Another principle shared by regulation and criminal justice is that of multiple instruments. As the pyramid and tetrahedron models suggest, regulation is a pluralistic endeavour. So too is criminal justice.

Rarely if ever will one enforcement strategy or regulatory technique work at all times and for all cases. A combination of methods is likely to achieve the most appropriate outcome. Braithwaite has used the metaphor of the web to illustrate this principle. A web is made of many strands, no one of which may be expected to bear a load. But collectively, they will suffice. Regulatory and criminal justice webs function in a comparable manner. State regulatory enforcement alone may not achieve a desired degree of compliance. But state regulatory enforcement backed up by a vigilant public interest movement and strong market forces may fill the bill. Families, schools and neighbourhoods are the most potent institutions of social control in modern society. The shortcomings of one may be compensated for by the strengths of others. Institutions of private security may compensate for the lack of public institutions. As Braithwaite would argue, layered webs of control are superior to a single strand.

Conclusions

Regulation and criminal justice are but two forms of social control. Both rely on each other. But recent developments in each raise significant issues of transparency and accountability. Nevertheless, the potential for more effective, more efficient control is promising indeed. To the extent that either system relies on third parties or other external institutions, it is inappropriate for the state to rely on non-state actors to do its 'dirty work'.

We are currently in the middle of a drastic change in the nature of criminal justice and in regulation more generally. Governments are becoming increasingly reliant upon private forms for the conduct of both law enforcement and regulation, as for other public business. The concern which this has caused among some observers is not misplaced; the risk of failure and erosion of accountability was noted above. But with these risks come new potentials and opportunities: the possibility of achieving more efficient, effective and democratic outcomes.

Governments may achieve greater law enforcement and regulatory leverage by engineering systems in which they themselves play a less dominant role, facilitating the constructive participation of private interests, and relying on more or less naturally occurring institutional orderings. These private institutions and orderings will vary in terms of their distance from governmental influence. Outside of direct state command, there are those institutions that might be described as hybrid forms, combining elements of state and non-governmental resources. Beyond these are naturally occurring orderings, arising more or less spontaneously; orderings for which governments establish a basic legal foundation and little else.

Rather than merely implementing their own programs and monitoring their impact, the role of law enforcement and regulatory agencies will become one of oversight, and the management of contracts. While it may appear at first glance that police and other regulatory officials will be relinquishing certain functions, it is more likely that their capacity will be enhanced. In addition, a degree of strategic surveillance will be important to observe the operation of new relational forms and natural orderings which operate beyond the immediate ambit of government.

What will be the role of the twenty-first century police or regulatory agency? The need to anticipate emerging policy issues will be greater than ever. So too will the need to oversee all of the activity, public sector and private, which occurs in a given policy space.

The role of law enforcement and regulatory agencies will be one of monitoring the overall spaces in which they operate, broadly defined, and one of 'fine-tuning': manipulating incentives, accrediting private competencies and auditing third-party performance in order to facilitate the constructive contributions of non-government interests. Traditional law enforcement and regulatory agencies will be less prominent on centre stage, but rather will remain authoritative and be unobtrusively influential from a position offstage.

Governments may also exert subtle influence on elements of citizen co-production. Governments can vary the degree of incentives they offer for citizen co-production of surveillance and enforcement. At one extreme, they can actively discourage officious intermeddlers, or ignore them. Alternatively, they may accept surveillance and enforcement assistance passively, offering no incentives. Beyond this, they may reward unobtrusively, or at the other extreme, offer highly publicized rewards and bounties for enforcement co-production.

In both regulatory and policing domains, governments can act as facilitators and brokers, rather than commanders. Through the judicious use of incentives, or by wielding their own purchasing power, governments are often able to structure a marketplace so that market outcomes fulfil public purpose (Osborne and Gaebler 1992: 280–1).

The risk that criminal justice or regulation will become 'commodified' can be lessened by emphasizing the public nature of private activity. Most professions already have codes of ethics which invoke the public interest as a fundamental principle; all but the most aggressive capitalists recognize a sense of civic obligation and social responsibility. Indeed, this ethos may be fostered more successfully from within the private sector than by government.

The issue of whether law enforcement or regulation should be done by government agencies on the one hand, or by some private alternative, has become a misplaced question. One must now inquire what institutional form, or even more appropriately, what blend of institutional forms, is best suited to a given task. The design and guidance of hybrid law enforcement and regulatory systems will be an essential activity of government in the twenty-first century.

This invites two ironic observations. One may speculate whether the fiscal constraints which have contributed to the shrinking state will nevertheless permit investment in the new and more sophisticated forms of managerial capacity which will be required to oversee and guide these hybrid systems.

Indeed, Kettl (1993: 14) has remarked that some of these new relational forms entail not the privatizing of public sector activity, but rather the governmentalizing of activity which to date has been largely private. Changes wrought to private relationships as a result of emerging policing and regulatory control forms are even more dramatic. There has always been more to law enforcement than the activity of police, and much more to regulation than the activity of regulators; there is likely to be even more still.

References

Abbot, C. (2007) personal communication, 6 November.

(2009) *Enforcing Pollution Control Regulation*. Oxford: Hart.

Alston, K. and J. P. Roberts (1999) 'Partners in New Product Development: SC Johnson and the Alliance for Environmental Innovation', *Corporate Environmental Strategy*, **6**, 110–28.

Ayling, J. and Grabosky, P. (2006a) 'Policing By Command: Enhancing Law Enforcement Capacity Through Coercion', *Law and Policy*, **28**(4), 420–43.

(2006b) 'When Police Go Shopping', *Policing: An International Journal of Police Strategies and Management*, **29**(4), 665–90.

Ayling, J., Grabosky, P. and Shearing, C. (2009) *Lengthening the Arm of the Law: Enhancing Police Resources in the Twenty-first Century*. Cambridge University Press.

Ayres, I. and Braithwaite, J. (1992) *Responsive Regulation: Transcending the Deregulation Debate*. New York, NY: Oxford University Press.

Braithwaite, J. (1985) *To Punish or Persuade: Enforcement of Coal Mine Safety*. Albany, NY: State University of New York Press.

Braithwaite, J. and Makkai, T. (1994) 'Trust and Compliance', *Policing and Society*, **4**(1), 1–12.

Braithwaite, J. and Pettit, P. (1990) *Not Just Deserts: A Republican Theory of Criminal Justice*. Oxford University Press.

Braithwaite, V. (2009) 'Tax Evasion', in M. Tonry (ed.), *The Oxford Handbook of Crime and Public Policy*. New York, NY: Oxford University Press, pp. 381–405.

Cherney, A., O'Reilly J. and Grabosky, P. (2006a) 'The Multilateralization of Policing: The Case of Illicit Synthetic Drug Control', *Police Practice and Research*, **7**(3), 177–94.

(2006b) 'Networks and Meta-Regulation: Strategies Aimed at Governing Illicit Synthetic Drugs', *Policing and Society*, **16**(4), 370–85.

Coffee, John C. (2004) 'Gatekeeper Failure and Reform: The Challenge of Fashioning Relevant Reforms' University of California, Berkeley, Law and Economics Workshop, paper no. 9.

Donohue, L. K. (2008) *The Cost of Counterterrorism: Power, Politics and Liberty*. Cambridge University Press.

Felson, Marcus (2006) *Crime and Nature*. Thousand Oaks, CA: Sage.

Freiberg, A. (1999) 'Commercial Confidentiality and Public Accountability for the Provision of Correctional Services', *Current Issues in Criminal Justice*, **11**, 119–34.

Fung, A., Graham, M. and Weil, D. (2007) *Full Disclosure: The Perils and Promise of Transparency*. Cambridge University Press.

Galanter, M. (1981) 'Justice in Many Rooms', *Journal of Legal Pluralism*, **19**, 1–47.

Gittleman, C. and Sacks, R. D. (2008) 'The Development of US Regulation of Broker–Dealer Research', *Journal of Investment Compliance*, **9**(2), 12–25.

Goldstein, H. (1990) *Problem Oriented Policing*. New York, NY: McGraw Hill.

Grabosky, P. N. (1992) 'Law Enforcement and the Citizen: Non-Governmental Participants in Crime Prevention and Control', *Policing and Society*, **2**, 249–71.

(1994) 'Green Markets: Environmental Regulation by the Private Sector', *Law and Policy*, **16**(4), 420–48.

(1995) 'Using Non-governmental Resources to Foster Regulatory Compliance', *Governance*, **8**(4), 527–50.

(1995) 'Regulation by Reward: On the Use of Incentives as Regulatory Instruments', *Law and Policy*, **17**(3), 256–81.

Grabosky, P. and Braithwaite, J. (1986) *Of Manners Gentle: Enforcement Strategies of Australian Business Regulatory Agencies*. Melbourne: Oxford University Press.

Greve, M. (1989) 'Environmentalism and Bounty Hunting', *Public Interest*, **97**, 15–29.

Gunningham, N. and Grabosky, P. (1998) *Smart Regulation*. Oxford University Press.

Katyal, N. (2002) 'Architecture as Crime Control', *Yale Law Journal*, **111**(5), 1039–139.

Kettl, D. (1993) *Sharing Power: Public Governance and Private Markets*. Washington, DC: Brookings Institution.

King, T. and Richards, J. (2003) *Australian Local Government: Alcohol Harm Minimization Projects – A Good Practice Guide*. Report prepared by Turning Point.

www.alcohol.gov.au/internet/alcohol/publishing.nsf/Content/resources-harm-minimisation/$FILE/alc_harm.pdf (visited 16 April 2009).

Kraakman, R. H. (1986) 'Gatekeepers: The Anatomy of a Third-Party Enforcement Strategy', *Journal of Law, Economics and Organization*, **2**, 53–104.

Langpap, C. (2008) 'Self-reporting and Private Enforcement in Environmental Regulation', *Environmental and Resource Economics*, **40**(4), 489–506.

Lessig, L. (2006) *Code: Version 2.0*. New York, NY: Basic Books.

Lester, A. (2001) 'Crime Reduction Through Product Design', *Trends and Issues in Crime and Criminal Justice*, 206. Canberra: Australian Institute of Criminology.

Loft, C. (2007) personal communication, 5 November.

Mahoney, P. G. (1997) 'The Exchange as Regulator', *Virginia Law Review*, **83**(7), Symposium: The Allocation of Government Authority (Oct. 1997), 1453–500.

Makkai, T. and Braithwaite, J. (1994b) 'The Dialectics of Corporate Deterrence', *Journal of Research in Crime and Delinquency*, **31**(4), 347–73.

Mazerolle, L. and Ransley, J. (2005) *Third Party Policing*. Cambridge University Press.

Osborne, D. and Gaebler, T. (1992) *Reinventing Government*. Boston, MA: Addison-Wesley.

Regan, P. (2004) 'Old Issues, New Context: Privacy, Information Collection, and Homeland Security', *Government Information Quarterly*, **21**(4), 481–97.

Reuter, P. and Truman, E. M. (2004) *Chasing Dirty Money: The Fight Against Money Laundering*. Washington, DC: Institute for International Economics.

Richardson, B. J. (2001) 'Mandating Environmental Liability Insurance', *Duke Environmental Law and Policy Forum*, **12**, 293–329.

Schmitter, P. and Lehmbruch, G. (eds.) (1979) *Trends Towards Corporatist Intermediation*. Beverly Hills, CA: Sage.

Shapiro, S. (1987) 'Policing Trust', in C. Shearing and P. Stenning (eds.), *Private Policing*. Beverly Hills, CA: Sage, pp. 194–220.

Shearing, C. (2003) 'A Constitutive Conception of Regulation', in P. Grabosky and J. Braithwaite (eds.), *Business Regulation and Australia's Future*. Canberra: Australian Institute of Criminology, 1993, pp. 67–80.

Smith, N. C. (2001) 'Changes in Corporate Practices in Response to Public Interest Advocacy and Actions', in Paul N. Bloom and Gregory Thomas Gundlach (eds.), *Handbook of Marketing and Society*. Beverly Hills, CA: Sage, pp. 140–61.

Sparrow, M. (2000) *The Regulatory Craft: Controlling Risks, Solving Problems, and Managing Compliance*. Washington, DC: Brookings Institution Press.

Streeck, W. and Schmitter, P. (1985) 'Community, Market, State and Association? The Prospective Contribution of Interest Governance to Social Order', in Streeck and Schmitter (eds.), *Private Interest Government: Beyond Market and State*. Beverly Hills, CA: Sage, pp. 1–29.

Tarr, R. W., McGurk, V. and Jones, C. (2005) 'Intermodal Transportation Safety and Security Issues: Training against "Terrorism"', *Journal of Public Transportation*, **8**(4), 87–100.

Ventry, D. J. (2008) 'Whistleblowers and Qui Tam for Tax', *Tax Lawyer*, **61**(2), 357–406.

Victoria Police (2005) *Victoria Police Organized Crime Strategy, 2005–2009*. Melbourne: Victoria Police.

Weatherburn, D. and Grabosky, P. (1999) 'Strategic Approaches to Property Crime Control', *Policing and Society*, **9**, 77–96.

Wood, J., Fleming, J. and Marks, M. (2008) 'Building the Capacity of Police Change Agents: The Nexus Policing Project', *Policing and Society*, **18**(1), 72–87.

PART II

Criminal justice as regulation: responsivity, alternatives and expansion

5

Nodal governance and the Zwelethemba Model

CLIFFORD SHEARING AND JAN FROESTAD

Our brief for the workshop paper in the Manchester seminar series was to consider two related issues. First, the idea of 'nodal governance' as a conceptual framework and, second, what has come to be known as the Zwelethemba Model; a specific set of arrangements for governing security in poor urban communities which is an example of nodal governance.

A considerable amount has already been written about the Zwelethemba Model as a dispute resolution mechanism for doing security governance in ways that mobilize local, and often marginalized, knowledges and capacities (Shearing 2001; Roche 2002; 2003; Johnston and Shearing 2003; Dupont *et al.* 2003; Gerits 2004; Gordon 2006; Froestad and Shearing 2005, 2007a, 2007b, 2007c, 2007d). This chapter adds to the literature by exploring the Model's history and situating it within current debates on the nature of nodal governance and, in particular, on the role of the state.

'Zwelethemba' is the name of the community where this Model was initially developed. Fortuitously, the Xhosa word 'zwelethemba' means 'country or place of hope'. At the time of its early development the Zwelethemba Model was intended to explore the political hope – which had been an important feature of the struggle for a new South Africa – for more participatory forms of governance that would accord poor communities a greater voice in their governance. The Model seeks to constitute a set of processes (institutional arrangements), guiding values to be enacted through these processes, and a regulatory framework intended to ensure that these processes do, in practice, realize these values. The Model's objective is to effectively, efficiently and accountably mobilize and integrate a variety of knowledges and capacities (especially local) so as to promote good (effective and legitimate) security governance.

There is also is a growing body of literature on nodal governance. 'Nodal governance' refers to an analytic framework to be used in describing and thinking about polycentric forms of governance. It is intended to provide conceptual tools for comprehending the diversity of governance mentalities, institutions, technologies and practices that characterize contemporary governance.

While the logical place to start in linking these two topics would perhaps be with the nodal governance framework, and then to move from there to Zwelethemba, we propose for pragmatic reasons to start with the Zwelethemba Model and then move to an explication of nodal governance.

A brief history

There is a longer history to the evolution of the Zwelethemba Model than we will present here. The ideas associated with it have a long lineage and selecting a particular time and place to locate the beginning of this history is arbitrary. For pragmatic reasons we will begin in Toronto with a security governance project supported by the Metropolitan Toronto Housing Authority.

What prompted this project was a 1987 lunch between Shearing and John Sewell – the Chairperson of the housing authority and an ex-mayor of Toronto. Sewell knew of the work Shearing had been undertaking with colleagues (in particular Philip Stenning) at the Centre of Criminology at the University of Toronto since the mid-1970s on the pluralization of security governance.

Sewell spoke about the insecure conditions that several of the residential complexes within the Authority were experiencing and enquired whether Shearing would be interested in suggesting ways of governing security in these arenas more effectively. Shearing agreed and with Sewell selected several pilot sites for what they thought of as 'experiments' in urban security within a form of 'mass private property'.

Using the Deweyan-inspired language that Dorf, Fung and others (Cohen and Sabel 1997; Dorf and Sabel 1998; Fung 2001, 2004; Fung and Wright 2001, 2003) have used more recently, one might think of what they set out to do as 'democratic experimentalism'.

Sewell and Shearing agreed to several conditions for these experiments. Two are relevant for this discussion. First, that Shearing and his team would be able to short-cut existing bureaucratic requirements in getting things done. Second, that Sewell would make available to the project a security governance budget – what they thought of at the time as a 'policing budget' (a term incidentally used in the Patten Commission report) (Independent Commission on Policing for Northern Ireland 1999).

The team's principal *modus operandi* as it went about this work was to gather together people in small groups (what the Zwelethemba Model terms 'gatherings') made up of the Authority staff and tenants, to think about and propose solutions for security issues. The team did not use a single group of individuals but rather brought together different sets of people depending on the issue at hand. Similarly, the mix of staff and tenants varied depending on the issue. These groups were asked to consider what could be done to improve security governance with respect to the issues they were discussing and to come up with suggestions that relied on capacities that were already available locally, which could then be 'trialled' in a series of initiatives/experiments.

The idea underlying this was to tap into what the team thought of as 'local knowledge and capacity' in order to reimagine how security at the Authority might be governed. The intention was to deliberately bring together sets of knowledge and capacity (staff and tenants) that were usually kept distinct and that were usually not mobilized around security issues, which until this point had been deemed to fall exclusively within the professional knowledge and capacity of the Authority's security personnel.

While the team did not engage in any formal evaluation of what was done (in the way in which this might be thought of today), the team and the groups met regularly to consider how these experiments were going and how they could be improved. For those involved, this was a crude form of evidence-based thinking. In thinking about this process they borrowed an idea from the management thinking of Tom Peters and Robert Waterman in Pursuit of Excellence 'do it, fix it, try it' (2004: 134) which was expressed as a TTI process – 'Try it, Test it, and Improve it'.

In group 'brainstorming' sessions designed to elicit local knowledge the team learned early on that there were several impediments to innovative and imaginative thinking of the sort it was trying to promote. Two are perhaps worth mentioning here. The first was 'force of habit', in particular 'habits of mind' (Dewey 1927: 160–2) – these had the effect of moving groups very quickly to a solution in ways that short-circuited the problem–analysis phase.

The team developed an antidote to such habits by treating brainstorming as a game where players were encouraged to deliberately put 'established' answers out of play. This compelled thinking to go in new directions: after all, most of the established solutions were already being used and had not proved to be particularly useful.

The second, pervasive impediment the team encountered was the 'put others down' habit. What tended to happen in brainstorming sessions was that the people acted as if a 'good' discussion required that participants should find flaws with the ideas of others – this was regarded as critical thinking. The result was a spiral of criticism, as people criticized previously 'got their own back' by criticizing others when their turn came around in the discussion. The team developed a simple set of rules to counter this habit. Every idea presented was put up on the wall and before the end of the session the best idea was selected to be tested.

The process nicely illustrates Dewey's perception of an experimental process as one in which the definition of a problem as well as the construction of its solution are created in and through the practice by which a situation is experimentally reformed (Dewey 1938; Kaufman-Osborn 1985: 836).

What resulted was very often the 'discovery' of knowledge and capacity that existing arrangements had systematically (though not necessarily intentionally or knowingly) marginalized. This discovery sometimes led to the constitution of new governing 'nodes' – understood as institutional sites of knowledge and capacity that could be routinely mobilized.

The result of the team's 'gatherings' was a series of innovative governance initiatives. Some of these were not developed, but many were developed and extended through its TTI process. After a few months the security environment within the Authority had become very different, as incident reports and the day-to-day experience of the staff and tenants made clear. Areas that had been regarded as unsafe now came to be regarded as safe. Very soon what might be thought of as a 'tipping point' (Gladwell 2002: 7) occurred. A new set of practices in terms of tenant, visitors and staff activities – that took security rather than insecurity for granted – became the order of the day. Soon the downward, negative spirals that had characterized the Authority were replaced by upward, positive spirals (Wood 1996).

An intended, but nonetheless remarkable, feature of the initiatives developed within the pilot sites was that they, for the most part, used very different sets of resources from those that are normally used to govern security. An example was the provision by the Authority of free barbecues on summer evenings in open spaces. This proved to be a useful 'tipper' in moving from one spiral to another. Another example was encouraging older women to play bridge in foyer areas of buildings. Yet another example was the use of beautification as a security initiative. For instance, the use of flower gardens to create real and virtual boundaries. It is in examples such as these that the wisdom of having an open 'security budget' that was not pre-allocated to security personnel, became very evident.

As a consequence of these developments, security governance within the Authority was deliberately pluralized, in the sense that a variety of 'new' and different sets of resources and knowledge were mobilized and integrated as part of a diverse and integrated security programme that involved police, private security and a host of other nodes and nodal practices. Nodes were identified, created, mobilized and integrated into a new policing assemblage. What was previously a nodally 'thin' security governance environment was transformed into a nodally 'thick' environment (Walzer 1994). The normative implication here was that nodally thick environments tend to be more effective and legitimate than nodally thin ones (Shearing and Stenning 1985).

In summary, the normative conclusion reached by the Authority's research team was that a critical determinant of effective, efficient and legitimate security governance proved to be the thickening of security governance through the identification, mobilization and integration of appropriate sets of knowledges and capacities. Some of the nodes included in this nodal mix had been 'occupationalized' as security resources – for example, contracted security firms – while others had not. The security governance problem within the Housing Authority before the project began, the team concluded, was that there were inadequate institutional arrangements for mobilizing non-occupationalized knowledges and capacities so that they could be actively engaged in security governance.

The next phase in this history occurred when Shearing was a member of the Goldstone Commission's Panel on the Prevention of Public Violence and Intimidation that was tasked with proposing a policy for policing demonstrations in the run-up to South Africa's first democratic elections in 1994 (Heymann 1992). In much the same way as the Toronto Housing Authority research team had done the Panel concluded that the organizers of demonstrations were likely to be a critically important source of knowledge about how best to govern demonstrations, and an important source of capacity for doing so.

The Panel found themselves face to face with a nodal governance problem: namely, how to take cognizance of the Foucaultian point that 'power comes from everywhere' (Foucault 1990: 93) in ways that would enhance the likelihood that the 1994 South African elections would be peaceful. In light of this analysis, the Panel directed its attention to figuring out an alternative set of institutional arrangements – thicker arrangements that would depart from thin police-focused ones that had dominated the governance of demonstrations in South Africa for decades. This would enable the mobilization and coordination of the knowledge and capacity of demonstration organizers and the police.

The essence of the Panel's proposals was as follows. Everyone had a right to demonstrate, but no one had a right to demonstrate in a non-peaceful manner. This premise gave rise to the argument that a licence to demonstrate should be required. To obtain a licence, demonstrators would be required to show that their proposed demonstration would be peaceful because they had developed a practical and reliable policing plan.

Although no formal evidence was collected, there is widespread agreement that these alternative nodal arrangements were a great success. The election period was remarkably peaceful, and the police could play the role envisaged for them because the self-policing that took place was by and large well-planned and effective (Shearing and Foster 2007).

Zwelethemba

The next step in this sequence of experiments was initiated after a conversation Shearing had with the then South African Minister of Justice, Dullah Omar, about communities that had been neglected under apartheid and were particularly insecure places, as they still are. Minister Omar said, essentially:

> Why don't we adopt the same approach as was adopted in the elections in thinking about governing security within poor South African communities? Create a model that we, the government, can implement and then we will take it forward.

Omar and Shearing proceeded to secure support from the Raoul Wallenberg Foundation in Lund, Sweden, to explore an iterative model-building process in Zwelethemba.

Again the focus was on developing institutional arrangements. In thinking about these arrangements the project team – a small group of researchers based at the School of Government at the University of the Western Cape – argued, that they must be robust, sustainable and legitimate. This thinking was in part based on the lessons learned from the nodal governance initiatives just outlined.

By robust, the team meant that arrangements must be easy to implement and low cost. This in turn meant that the role of professionals would need to be minimal – for reasons both of expense and availability. By sustainability the team meant that the procedures must be easy to scale up and easy to maintain. Legitimacy was vital, as many of the local initiatives that had developed in response to apartheid had become violent and were not accountable to either local communities or to the law – indeed many of these initiatives were clearly illegal. In thinking of legitimacy, the team was also cognizant of developing processes that resonated with established cultural practices.

The process was initiated through a number of 'community meetings' – all well attended. These were preceded by contacts with community members who could help set up and advertise these meetings. The meetings led to the emergence of a small group of people who were keen to be involved in taking the process forward. The research team and this group agreed that they were looking to discover a process that met the above criteria of being robust, sustainable and legitimate. A process that could be used to assist in the governance of security in Zwelethemba: a community of some 20,000 persons with formal housing that had been built over years with government assistance and a sizable sector of informally constructed housing (commonly termed 'shacks' in a South African context).

Initially, it was thought that a similar approach to that taken in Toronto could be adopted. The team soon found, however, that it was difficult to get busy people out to these discussions and to implement ideas. In Toronto there had been a Housing Authority with a committed staff to facilitate these sorts of discussions and to engage in the implementation of the ideas proposed. In the South African context although there was a very active civil society there were constant meetings that people were invited to attend. An additional set of meetings without an immediate and pressing reason for attending them was not something that most people wanted to engage in. The team quickly discovered that as soon as there was some really pressing matter related to security – typically an argument or a dispute of some kind – people affected by this were more than willing to engage in finding a solution to it. Two of the most frequent disputes that people began to bring forward were arguments over money-lending and domestic quarrels – these disputes were often very energetic and at times led to violence of one sort or another if not resolved.

At this stage it was decided to invite a small group of academics interested in the governance of security to visit South Africa and assist in the model-building process by reflecting on what had been taking place. Three scholars accepted the team's invitation: David Bayley from the United States, John Braithwaite from Australia and Enrique Font from Argentina. A little later in a separate visit the project hosted two Canadians: Barry Stewart, a judge from the Yukon, and Mark Ridge, a First Nations member who had worked with Judge Stewart to develop 'healing circles' within criminal justice. Soon after formal reflection meetings had concluded Braithwaite and Shearing visited a community of poor people who had been building their own formal houses using government subsidies when what was identified as a 'rape' was brought to them. Quite suddenly, Braithwaite found himself facilitating an informal 'conference' along the lines of the family group conferencing that he had been involved with in Australia and had written extensively about.

The team's own experiences before and in light of the reflection process, and Braithwaite's unexpected recruitment as a facilitator in a quickly organized conference, convinced the Zwelethemba team of two things. First, that dealing with somewhat abstract security issues, of the sort that had been addressed in Toronto, was not something around which it was going to be possible to build a process that met the three governing criteria that had been decided upon. Second, that it would be much more useful to build the process around pressing problems that people were facing in particular disputes. The team concluded that, while it could learn much from processes developed elsewhere it could not simply borrow them. This was for two particularly important reasons. First, professionally focused processes were too costly and, second, they were too past focused, when what was required in the South African context of poor communities was to move forward quickly. What was particularly attractive about the Toronto process and other similar ones, however, was that they were 'gathering' focused – something that had very strong cultural resonances.

This period of critical reflection provided the impetus for a period of trial-and-error engagements that culminated in the Zwelethemba Model. The Model has a strong family resemblance to family group conferencing and healing circles, but is fundamentally different. The Zwelethemba Model is sharply and strongly focused on 'creating a better tomorrow', to use a phrase that was increasingly used as the Model emerged.

From this discussion it will be evident that an essential feature of the Zwelethemba Model is its focus on disputes. Beside the urgency and mobilizing impetus that these provided, another key reason for focusing on disputes was that it was due to failure to deal with such matters that prompted the escalation of relatively minor incidents into more difficult security challenges. At the core of the Zwelethemba process was the idea that disputes required a future-focused approach that asked the question, 'what could be done easily and simply to reduce the likelihood of disputes continuing'. To answer this question gatherings of people were convened at which plans of action (including monitoring the implementation) were agreed by participants. A routine outcome of these gatherings and agreements was that persons who had been involved in disputes and interactions became active players in crafting and implementing peaceful resolutions – troublemakers became peacemakers. The critical condition in fostering this turnaround was the future orientation that the process encouraged. Within a future-focused context, cooperation became possible, and was elicited. Gatherings were often concluded with gestures of reconciliation such as handshaking or hugs, often accompanied by tears. Within the Model these gestures, and the emotions they expressed, were regarded as useful to the extent that they helped create a better tomorrow.

Incentives designed to encourage people to give up their time to facilitate the Zwelethemba process were incorporated into the Model. Persons willing to facilitate gatherings were organized into Peace Committees comprising a group of any number of people from a handful to twenty. Monetary incentives were provided to members who ran gatherings in accordance with the process. In an attempt to reinforce the forward-focused outcomes approach described above (which came to be called 'the Steps'), compliance with a Code of Good Practice was required.

A crucial feature of the Code was the direction that in organizing or facilitating a gathering Peace Committees should not resort to physical coercion, which had become a notorious feature of other informal processes, especially those known as 'street committees'. Theoretically, an important intention of this rule was endorsement of the Hobbesian/Weberian position that states should monopolize authorizations with respect to the use of force. While Peace Committee members did enjoy limited authorizations to use force as citizens (for example, citizen's arrest and self-defence) this element of the Code discouraged any use of force in relation to members' work as Peace Committee members. At a more practical level this direction was seen as essential if Peace Committees were to be trusted and seen as legitimate within communities. In addition the Code explicitly constrained Peace Committee members to act within the law and the South African Constitution. One of the implications of this was that Peace Committees were viewed by their members and others as supporting state institutions such as the South African police service.

An essential feature of the Zwelethemba process, and thus a central feature of the mentality the Code and Steps sought to embed in Peace Committee practices, was the future/risk focus noted above. The intention was to establish security governance nodes (Peace Committees) that worked explicitly to promote different and more peaceful sets of practices. The rationale for this was not that blaming processes were not useful and appropriate at times, but that they needed to be complemented by preventive future-focused technologies that conceived of prevention in terms other than simply deterrence.

The key features of the Zwelethemba process are as follows. Disputants bring a dispute to a Peace Committee. The Committee, after consulting with the disputants, convenes a gathering to which persons thought to be able to contribute to a forward-focused outcome are invited. At gatherings each disputant tells their side of the story so as to inform those present of the nature of the issues. No attempt is made to come to a single accepted account. The focus of gatherings then turns to consider the root cause of the dispute, and the issue of how to reduce the likelihood of it continuing. A plan of action to achieve this is then formulated. This plan – which typically includes a monitoring process – is then agreed to, and those present commit themselves to facilitating its realization by signing it. This often means agreeing to specific actions by particular people. Data have been collected on each gathering: of the more than 15,000 analysed, plans of action were agreed to in over 98 per cent of them.

Implied in much of the above is that Peace Committees were established to fill a preventive niche within a wider network of policing nodes. Central to this network was, of course, the police. As part of the model-building process, and in collaboration with the district commanders of the South African police service, a process was established whereby police and Peace Committees could formalize a relationship that would enabling a shifting of 'cases' between them. This meant that disputants were able to choose a police or Peace Committee process and to change their mind if they wished. In some instances, both were chosen to run concurrently. This, however, was rare.

The accountability mechanisms embedded in the Zwelethemba Model emerged through a conscious attempt to combine a range of accountability mechanisms situated along both horizontal and vertical axes (O'Donnell 1994). Within the Model the 'Code of Good Practice' operates as a 'constitutional framework' that, alongside the Peace-Making Steps, sets out how gatherings should be run. A key intention of insisting that Zwelethemba Model values and processes are followed is in recognition that if Peace Committees are to contribute effectively to local security governance they have to be recognized as legitimate and trustworthy.

Committee members are rewarded, in the payment system noted above, for following the Steps and for acting within the dictates of the Code. Records of cases are kept, and with audits of gatherings constitute a vertical accountability axis. Members are paid a small amount for facilitating a gathering in compliance with rules and values rather than for successfully resolving disputes through a plan of action. The Model requires the Code of Good Practice to be read aloud at the beginning of all gatherings and the Steps to be followed are also outlined. The intention in requiring this is to enable those present at the gathering to hold Peace Committee members accountable to the requirements of the Model through a process of horizontal accountability.

In the development of the Model the issue of sustainability has proved difficult. Participants in Peace Gatherings, during the pilot phase, often raised the 'free rider' problem, saying: 'We do all of this work from which the community benefits; but we get no compensation and the members of our households would prefer us to spend the time earning some money instead.' This sentiment and the pressures associated with it prompted a relatively high turnover of members, which the payment system was developed to reduce. The payment arrangements – which serve as the foundation of its vertical accountability – are based on a 'no compliance, no payment' rationale.

The audit features of the accountability mechanism were designed to trigger remedial responses on the part of the agency responsible for overseeing the processes the Model advocates. At the time the Model was developed this was the Community Peace Programme located in the University of the Western Cape. In addition to the review of cases mentioned, data were assembled on the basis of case reports, audit visits to gatherings and regular community surveys. These data were analysed in order to direct remedial engagements in the form of coaching, both through Committee exchanges and coaching by the Programme's staff. The Community Peace Programme, which now exists as an independent NGO, continues to carry out these audit and coaching activities. At the time of writing, Peace Committees operate in over 100 different schools and associated communities within South Africa's Western Cape Province.

A crucial intention of the Model is to deepen local involvement in security governance and engage a wide range of knowledge and capacity in ways that enhance South Africa's emerging democracy. In particular, the aim is to deepen democracy through proliferating appropriately regulated problem-solving deliberative forums that encourage citizens to participate in nodal governance networks. The Model thus seeks to give effect to a central value of democracy, namely, the right of every citizen to contribute to effective governance. This is motivated by the need to explore ways of enhancing the voice of poor and marginalized South Africans within governance processes (Wood and Shearing 2007).

In thinking about this Model, those of us who have been developing and researching it have borne in mind a distinction between what we think are its design principles and the way they are implemented. The crucial underlying design principle of the Zwelethemba Model is that a significant contribution can be made to security governance at the local level by creating institutional arrangements that mobilize local knowledge and capacity in order to provide forward-looking solutions to problems through a process that is recognized as legitimate (Wood and Shearing 2007). What the Zwelethemba Model seeks to accomplish is a template for the establishment of a simple, low cost and easily replicable set of institutional arrangements that will realize this design aspiration within particular South African contexts.

The nodal policing arrangements that the Zwelethemba Model seeks to promote resonate with institutional arrangements in many other contexts – especially in other parts of Africa (Baker 2002, 2004, 2008; Marenin 2005; OECD 2006; Dupont *et al.* 2003). Zwelethemba's particular contribution to these ongoing explorations in security governance is to find ways of routinizing and extending robust and sustainable nodal forms of governance that enhance the voice of marginalized constituencies in highly regulated and accountable ways.

The fact that the funding for the Model has now shifted from international donors to the South African government is testament to its success in achieving at least a modicum of sustainability. Whether this continues will depend on the willingness of governments to build the necessary funding into their budgets as well as the extent to which the Model's processes become a widespread feature of security governance in South Africa.

Normative experimentation and exploration of the potential of nodal or polycentric policing does not end with development of the Zwelethemba Model. The Northern Ireland Patten Commission (Independent Commission for Policing in Northern Ireland 1999), which developed proposals for the renewal of policing, was directly influenced by the Zwelethemba experiment. The Commission's proposals included recommendations for a policing rather than a police board, and a policing rather than a police budget, with a remit that included but was not limited to police. The Dutch police have been actively exploring mechanisms (as part of what they call a *nodale orientatie*) that pay particular attention to flows of people and information and developing a programme of 'neighborhood directing' that focuses attention on identifying, mobilizing and integrating nodal resources (Project Group Vision on Policing 2006).

More recently the Victoria police in Australia have been exploring how to reimagine the police, not simply as the deliverers of policing services but as nodal coordinators, in a series of bottom-up experiments of just what this would mean in different policing arenas (Police Act Review Team 2007).

Nodal governance

Alongside the expanding body of normative engagements which seek to promote effective and legitimate polycentric governance, there has been a growing body of thinking and research about the nature of polycentric governance, some of it under the sign of 'nodal governance'. These engagements constitute an iterative process of 'research–theory–engagement–research–theory–engagement–', some of which has taken place among a loose network of 'nodal scholars'. Reference has already been made to some of their work and we now turn to this developing body of research in an examination of nodal governance ideas.

Polycentric governance

Increasingly research is making clear that taken-for-granted state-centred claims about the structure of security governance are empirically false. There is a now well-established consensus in many academic milieus that governance is no longer the sole province of the state, it has become polycentric – involving public and private sectors, civil society and international institutions. This transition from state-centric analysis to more polycentric ones can be found within a range of disciplines.

By way of example, contemporary international relations scholarship has recently begun to focus on relationships between a variety of state and non-state political entities (Palan 2004). The established view of 'states-as-billiard balls' is, in Hobson's words, 'being transformed into a global co-web of transactions that cuts across the increasingly porous boundaries of nation-states' (Hobson 2000: 2).

The same trend can be seen within development studies, poverty research and peace studies. Within each of these domains scholars have moved away from paradigms that identify states as the primary sources of governance. Taylor and Jennings (2004: 32–3), for example, argue that a state focus makes it difficult to conceive of the wide plurality of issues that affect human security. Focus on the governance of security rather than the government of security shifts empirical and theoretical attention to a complex array of nodes that act as both auspices and providers of governance (Marenin 2005: 17).

Similarly, again in the domain of security, the 'New Security' studies literature (associated with the 'Copenhagen School' of Buzan and associates) has expanded the concept of security, both horizontally and vertically, to include political and military aspects of state security and 'communitarian aspects' that cross borders (Buzan *et al.* 1997). One consequence of this and similar developments is that previously obscured insecurities of marginalized groups, within and between states, have been moved to the centre of the conceptual stage.

This attempt to broaden the understanding of governance has, however, been hampered by the state-focused habits of mind. One consequence of this is failure to appreciate fully the varied array of interests being pursued within polycentric governance arrangements. A focus on this variety has been central to the critique of state-centric understandings developed by the 'Critical Security' approach of the 'Aberystwyth School'. A central normative query of this body of work has been whether states are the most appropriate sources of security governance (Booth and Vale 1997).

Yet another related domain of polycentric governance thinking has been the 'New Regionalism'. This body of work has conceptualized contemporary forms of regionalization and security governance as being plural and informal. These scholars conceive of security governance, especially urban security governance, as multilayered (state, market, society) and cross-cutting (Grant 2000; Grant and Söderbaum 2003). Like other literatures that conceive of governance as fundamentally polycentric, they advocate 'a theoretical framework that does not privilege the state and avoids assumptions a priori of who is the "driving actor"' (Grant and Söderbaum 2003: 197). This argument that the state is one governance player among many has also been a feature of some of the criminological literature on governance (Wood and Shearing 2007; Bayley and Shearing 2001).

These arguments for a 'nodal' (Johnston and Shearing 2003), 'polycentric' (McGinnis 1999) or 'multi-choice' (Baker 2004) conception of governance have been echoed in a variety of policy reports. For example the 2006 report on a 'vision for policing' within the Netherlands (Project Group Vision on Policing 2006: 500) argues for a 'nodal orientation' in policing. The British organization Demos in its 2006 report *A Force for Change: Policing in 2020* argues that 'government should develop a market in policing' and that 'police should invest in networking and collaboration' (Edwards and Skidmore 2006: 36–7). Similarly, the Law

Commission of Canada, in its 2006 report to the Canadian Parliament, *In Search of Security: The Future of Policing in Canada*, talks of a 'new era of pluralized policing' that 'raises questions concerning the existing legal and regulatory environment' within which security governance operates (Law Commission of Canada 2006: vii). This polycentric conception of governance is also a pervasive term found in the US 9/11 Commission Report.

Maps and ties

Given this polycentric or nodal understanding of governance, a key governance question becomes the mapping of nodes and their engagements with other nodes as they cooperate and compete with each other to shape the flow of events in ways that will promote different visions of order. Dupont (2006) and Dupont and Wood (2006) have been active in exploring methodological tools for mapping nodal governance. In doing this they have focused on issues such as the structure of nodes and the nature of nodal networks. This has involved exploring questions such as network density, connectivity, clusters of exchange, existence of cliques and sub-groups, and so on.

The development of methodological techniques that describe nodal governance arrangements is important for a variety of reasons, which include explorations of the distribution of authority and power – which might assist in the identification of 'missing links' in governance networks (Burris 2004; Wood 2006) – and accountability or meta-regulatory arrangements and possibilities (Dupont 2006).

A much debated issue within these literatures concerns the significance of weak and strong ties in systems of governance. The social capital approach has tended to assume that collective capacity depends upon strong bonds of mutual identity and trust (Putnam 1993). Charles Tilly's (2005) work on 'trust networks' emphasizes the capacity of such networks to carry out major long-term enterprises and to insulate themselves from political control by a variety of strategies. Other contributions, however, suggest that a plurality of weak ties is essential for collective capacity, facilitating formations of strategic partnerships and search for useful knowledge, learning and innovation (Granovetter 1973, 1983; Hansen 1999). An advantage of embeddedness in many weak ties, it is argued, is that knowledge is acquired about the logic of thinking and patterns of action in other nodes, clusters of nodes and networks (Heclo 1978).

Guilhot (2005) observes how nodes that acquire such knowledge and experience develop an ability to move among and between nodes and networks in the heterogeneous landscape of polycentric governance, which increases their power and capacity to influence the course of events within nodal assemblages. Actors in weak positions often have access to many weak resources, both directly and through enrolment, that can be brought together to provide considerable strength (Wood and Shearing 2007). As documented by Hutchens (2007) in her study of the Fair Trade movement, one crucial resource is often strength in numbers, provided that these numbers can be made to count. She demonstrates how the mobilization of many weak bonds among loosely connected networks committed to a variety of different projects – as a strategy of 'networking networks for scale' – was a key mechanism that has enabled Fair Trade to become an international movement with significant influence. Hutchens also observed that a smaller network of policy entrepreneurs bound together by stronger bonds of identity and commitment, and who were aware of the dangers of co-option while constantly looking for new opportunities, played a significant role in maintaining the vitality of the movement.

A key coordinating mechanism observed in many governance systems is the existence of 'superstructural nodes'. These bring together representatives of different nodal organizations in a nodal site to concentrate the members' resources and technologies for a common purpose without integrating the various networks (Burris *et al.* 2005). Superstructural nodes can be conceived of as the command centres of networked governance that enable the mobilization of resources in particular nodal sites to produce action by other nodes in the network and thereby increase the ability of nodes or alliances of nodes to govern the course of events in the system.

Nodes and networks

Auspices and providers of governance can be thought of as nodes. Nodes within this context are not simply points where 'flows' intersect; they may or may not be networked. Nodes, in this context, are institutional sites of knowledge and capacity engaged in governing. A key analytic question within security governance is to create a framework for describing nodes and their engagement in security. The nodal governance perspective builds on, but differs from that of network theory in placing greater emphasis on the internal characteristics of nodes that allow them to exert influence across networks. Theories of governance should, from this perspective, focus on the ways nodes are constituted and related. By focusing on nodes, a nodal framework provides a fuller theoretical platform for conceiving how networks and configurations of nodal assemblages operate (Burris *et al.* 2005). A node is conceived of as a site where knowledge, capacity and resources are mobilized to shape the flow of events exhibiting four essential characteristics (Burris *et al.* 2005: 37–8):

- a way of thinking (mentalities) about governance;
- a set of methods (technologies) for exerting influence over the flow of events;
- resources to support a node's operations; and
- institutional structure that enables the directed mobilization of resources, mentalities and technologies over time.

A 'mentality' can be understood as 'the culture of the node, its way of thinking about itself, its objects of governance and the world around it (operating) to bring coherence and thus enable longevity and collective action within a node. Such a culture is not a blueprint for specific action, but is a narrative of the world that guides the ongoing processes of adaptive improvisation in a node' (Burris 2004: 341; on this conception of organizational culture see also Shearing and Ericson 1991). Interventions in the world always presuppose that problems and governmental objects are conceived of in particular ways. When we intervene we 'make up the world' in ways that make it measurable and governable. Such 'mentalities' both facilitate and limit reflections on how to intervene in an efficient and proper manner. In developing the Zwelethemba Model, for instance, an early emphasis was to avoid a 'crime' construction of the disputes attended to at the Gatherings. According to the Model, individuals directly involved in the conflict are understood as participants, parties or disputants rather than 'victims' and 'offenders'. The victim–offender binary is viewed within the Model as serving to separate, exclude and prejudge. In practice it is commonplace for a 'case' brought to the attention of local peacemakers to be regarded as no more than a single slice in time that should be located within a history of conflict between the parties. Within this context the 'offending' party and the 'harmed' party may, and probably do, change place over time. In other words, today's offender may have been yesterday's 'victim'. The Model is based on the argument that the language of 'victim' and 'offender' structure the meaning of what happened in the past in ways that make it difficult for the parties involved to understand and articulate their own reality of lived experience. Avoiding this binary is seen as important in changing local practices of conflict resolution from a past-oriented 'blaming practice' to a problem-solving activity focusing on the prospects for future peace.

New mentalities often lead to new ways of thinking and doing. An example in security governance is the idea that we live in a 'risk society'. We might be sceptical about accepting the most totalizing version of this theory, but it is evident that risk and its management now occupy a central place in many human affairs. The risk society, as pictured by authors like Giddens (1991) and Beck (1992), gives rise to increasing instabilities, breaks, disruptions and, most probably, greater disparities and inequalities. It also points to new opportunities to take part in future-focused negotiations and processes which aim to construct new understandings and ways of conducting governance.

Shearing and Johnston (2005) have explored the implications of the spread of risk mentalities for the management of security. The major difference, as they conceive it, between the conventional way of managing conflicts and crimes through retribution and punishment and managing securities through risk, is the priority each mentality gives to the past or the future. The punishment paradigm is essentially a backward-looking experience that distributes punishment according to the degree of the blameworthiness of the past offences, because this is 'justly deserved'. With risk, the whole logic turns away from moral and past concerns to a concern with how to manage the future in terms of minimizing loss and maximizing the likelihood of desired outcomes. In this way risk and its management points to new opportunities for actors that are embedded in plural security landscapes to escape a 'blaming logic' and to take part, instead, in a more future-focused and preventive governance of mutual risks and insecurities.

As we have seen, an underlying assumption in the Zwelethemba experiment was that the logic of risk was under-utilized in many governance programmes that sought to bring security problems back under the control of lay people and local communities (Shearing and Johnston 2005; Froestad and Shearing 2007a, 2007b and 2007c). A focal point of the experiment was how to move people from the habit of blaming to a habit of risk management and future-focused problem solving.

The technologies – the means of intervention – by which mentalities are sought to be implemented, have distinct significance. Sometimes, as observed by Miller and Rose (1990), the technologies that seek to operate on activities and processes may produce their own difficulties, fail to function as intended or intersect poorly with the emerging mentalities in terms of which their role is conceived.

Resources come in many forms, quantities and combinations. As Rhodes (1997) and other scholars have documented, governing nodes participate in networks because other nodes have resources they need to acquire. Exchange of resources, to reduce insecurity by increasing access to information and other kinds of resources, is a key aspect of polycentric governance. The importance of resources in networked governance is tied to the particular need in such environments for a node to enroll or enlist other nodes to take part in their own projects and agendas. To be able to persuade others and gaining access to a resource base is essential. As we explore below, the way this resource base is structured, as either functional or institutional budgets, is often critical.

Governing nodes have different degrees of formality. Formal structure enables and facilitates a conscious alignment and mobilization of resources, mentalities and technologies. To the extent that formal nodal structures become 'infused with values' over time (Selznick 1957), enhances their legitimacy and capacity to resist change and external pressures. Nodal actors might prefer, however, to organize and work in loose personal networks instead of through formal organizational structures. Informality has the advantage (or disadvantage) of remaining, to a large extent, invisible and outside the control of state bureaucracy. This is often a strategy preferred by poor and vulnerable groups, as it is with groups at the other end of this spectrum.

The nodal governance perspective embraces the study of informal 'organised practices' (Nuijten 1999: 1) as well as more formally organized governance auspices and providers. The approach allows for identification and analysis of complex dynamics of governing practices and governing regimes – both actual nodal arrangements as well as normative preferences about desirable arrangements (Johnston and Shearing 2003). The approach challenges a priori assumptions about nodal arrangements that conflate normative preferences with what is the case empirically. This has occurred most clearly with respect to states where the normative aspiration that states (and their nodal assemblages) should monopolize governance has been assumed to describe what actually happens. This may be the case in some space–time locations but it is often not the case.

Nodal contests

The outcomes of contests between governing nodes across space and time are uneven and success or failure are major determinants of networked governance structures. A key observation from the various literatures on polycentric forms of governance has been that the benefits have been varied and unequal. Some constituencies have done better than others in polycentric governance contests. By and large, well-to-do populations have benefited more from these developments than marginalized populations. A growing governance disparity, it is argued, now parallels the wealth disparity across the globe (Haas 2004). Thus while polycentric governance, in theory, holds out a promise for greater democratic direction and control for all, opportunities to develop poor people's self-direction, rights and access to services have typically not been enhanced (Held *et al.* 1999). A critical normative question for polycentric governance is therefore how to address the inequalities that pervade governance, both at the delivery level and at the level of governance direction.

The dominant proposals have long been ones based on established mechanisms of aggregating and representing interests. Within this context, strong interest groups have been able to create parallel organizational structures to public bureaucracies. This has enabled them to influence political and administrative decisions at each governmental level (Eckstein 1971). But scholars have repeatedly pointed to problems associated with these developments, especially for the weak and the marginalized (Braithwaite and Drahos 2000; Drahos and Braithwaite 2002). Hierarchical organization, combined with a centralized and state-focused strategy of political mobilization, has tended to produce oligarchic relations internally and elite integration within the state externally (Piven and Cloward 1979). Dryzek (1996) has reconceptualized this argument. He claims that a focus on influencing the agenda of the state might be an appropriate strategy when the values or the interests of a group are strongly aligned with the state's own imperatives for survival, internal order or resource extraction. Otherwise cooption without power, he argues, is a likely outcome.

This suggests the need to reimagine strategies of participation so that they might strengthen the position of the poor and the marginalized, as citizens, receivers and co-producers of services. Contemporary state-centred approaches, which conceive of participation fundamentally as the mobilization of poor communities to monitor, evaluate and advise on public service delivery, have not led to viable strategies. Evidence strongly suggests that participatory forums under such conditions are sidelined by policy processes that engage other stakeholders, such as powerful politicians and bureaucrats, corporate interests and international institutions and donors (Cooke and Kothari 2001; Froestad 2005). A state-focused strategy of participation does not enable poor communities to combine resources and become 'players' in governance systems consisting of a plurality of networked actors. The global governance deficit cannot be countered by relying on the state alone.

Two questions that have emerged in responding to this challenge are: first, how to identify and mobilize local capacities and knowledges that are not regularly included in networked governance and, second, how to reimagine weak groups' strategies of power in nodal environments.

One idea that can be used to explore these questions is that of 'missing or absent nodes' – this refers to marginalized constituencies who are excluded from participating in governing processes even though their capacities and resources might improve governance outcomes. Wood (2006) reports on a 'youth safety' project in a border town in Victoria, Australia, where a range of representatives working with youths, along with academics, came to the conclusion that the youth groups were often 'missing nodes' in the governance of their own safety. In response, a decision was jointly taken to begin designing an institutional structure that would allow youths to mobilize their own knowledge and capacities in acting on their own 'problematisations' of security (Wood 2006: 236–7).

In Zwelethemba, as we have already pointed out, the intention was to build a robust, sustainable and legitimate model of governing security that mobilized local knowledge and capacity to direct and provide security services. By mobilizing such knowledge and capacity within institutional arrangements (nodes) controlled by the poor themselves, and embedding it within a wider network of policing nodes – including a routinized relationship with the public police – a new assemblage of security 'auspices' and 'providers' (Bayley and Shearing 2001) was established that enabled marginalized constituencies to respond to and play a central role in the governing of their security.

Braithwaite (2004), building on his work with Drahos in exploring global business regulation (Braithwaite and Drahos 2000), has articulated a series of 'methods of power for development'. Drawing upon understandings of the ways in which strong players have secured and maintained their positions of strength, he elaborates on the possibility of using these insights as a guide for weak actors to build more effective 'methods of power' conceived as 'weapons of the weak'. Wood and Shearing (2007) build upon Braithwaite to fine-tune his guiding principles. The Zwelethemba Model provides one illustration of how people within marginalized constituencies have created governing nodes – Peace Committees – through which they concentrate their knowledge and resources to govern their security. For Braithwaite, and Wood and Shearing, this is a critical guiding principle within the series of 'methods for power'. By engaging in a partnership with the police in a process of mutual enrolment poor constituencies have increased their ability to become players who participate in the steering of governance. The superstructural nodes developed to achieve this are the 'Community Peace Centres' consisting of the police and the local Peace Committee. Polycentric governing arrangements present new challenges and new opportunities for weak players, but as Wood and Shearing conclude, 'Within a nodally governed world, effective nodal access is a prerequisite for bargaining' (2007: 113).

Resources

A key factor structuring nodal governance is access to resources within nodal assemblages and understanding the particular ways in which these resources flow. This makes budgets, and the way they are structured and allocated, critical in understanding nodal governance. An important feature of how budgets are allocated is whether they are organized along functional or institutional lines. For example, it matters whether a budget is a policing budget or a police budget. The way budgets are structured varies across the nodal terrain. Evidence on security governance suggests that private sector budgets are more likely to be functional budgets, while within the public sector they are more likely to be institutional. Functional budgets facilitate the distribution of resources across nodal assemblages, whereas institutional budgets restrict resources to a particular set of predefined institutions.

In Zwelethemba a key problem of acquiring resources to scale up and maintain the Model arises from the fact that security budgets, especially line budgets, are 'owned' by state institutions. In Northern Ireland, the Patten Commission, in recognizing this, argued for the establishment of policing rather than conventional police budgets. Not unexpectedly, proposals such as this are typically met with strong opposition from institutions that have established budget ownership.

Normative claims

The governance terrain is shot through with normative claims and competing claims about good governance. These claims constitute an important empirical feature of the governance terrain. Typically, normative claims express sets of socio-political assumptions about what conditions are necessary for realizing effective and legitimate governance. The orthodox answer to questions of this type is that the best conditions are achieved when states play a central and a dominant role in nodal arrangements. Accordingly, the appropriateness or accuracy of claims made by the state about its role and those of other nodes in nodal assemblages is a critical empirical question in nodal governance explorations.

Scholars interested in polycentric governance, of course, engage with these normative issues and they are a major source of controversy in a variety of disciplines. The two related normative questions that have principally engaged scholars are: what assemblages of nodes in particular contexts will most likely produce just and democratic outcomes; and what should the state's role be within these assemblages?

Within criminology, for example, Loader and Walker (2007) have developed a strong argument that polycentric systems of governance need to be state anchored. They regard states as the only node that can provide democratic direction and accountability within nodal assemblages. Their argument is based, as Kempa (2008) has noted, on two premises. First, only states have the required managerial and regulatory capacities to properly pool, manage and distribute public resources and services as well as regulate and compensate for market failures. Second, only states can direct and provide security in a way that will enhance the symbolic dimensions to governance necessary to build a political community. As Kempa observes, this position adopts a 'social capital' argument that claims security will be most effective and legitimate when governance auspices are constructed around strong bonds of solidarity and shared identity within a political community.

The nodal governance approach has remained decidedly eclectic with respect to normative arguments about good governance. Where nodal theorists tend to differ from state-centric theorists is their tendency to leave space for governance arrangements that are not state anchored. Accordingly, while nodal scholars tend to agree with Loader and Walker on the importance of collective constraints and accountability in nodal governance, they tend to be more open-minded about just how this might be achieved in different contexts. For example, in countries where police are a major source of insecurity as perpetrators of human rights abuses it might be more appropriate to look for alternatives to state anchoring (Dupont *et al.* 2003; Wood and Dupont 2006) in favour of more horizontal, and less vertical, accountability mechanisms (Braithwaite 2006).

In these and similar contexts a more appropriate way of building legitimate 'collective efficacy' (Sampson *et al.* 1999) might be to forge 'weak bonds' across individuals and social groups. In such circumstances an appropriate role for the state might be to facilitate horizontal forms of accountability that favour weak ties. For example, Dupont *et al.* (2003) proposed delivery and accountability arrangements for weak and failing states that draw on the particular resources of states, domestic civil society, international civil society, interstate organizations, multinational business and hybrid non-governmental auspices. They propose that a legitimacy-resource test of each of the principal auspices and providers might give some guidance as to the assemblage of security nodes in a particular context that might be best suited to foster democratic and effective practice. Similarly, for many nodal theorists the globalized character of many governance challenges requires looking for less state-centred ways of promoting effective and legitimate governance (Kempa 2008).

The question of how to develop effective nodal governance is, as we have just suggested, closely related to the question of how to promote accountable governance. Policy studies conducted in many parts of the world have attributed successful governance arrangements to the presence of strong accountability systems (Paul 1994; Putnam 1993). A nodal governance approach argues that in promoting both effective and accountable governance it is necessary to acknowledge the polycentric realities of most contemporary systems of governance. This, nodal scholars argue, requires finding ways of reimagining governance and accountability within a polycentric world. This requires accepting that there are likely to be a range of mechanisms for promoting effective and accountable governance. The challenge is to identify mechanisms and blends of mechanisms that support democratic values.

Scott has identified two potential mechanisms of what he terms 'extended accountability'. The first mechanism focuses on interdependency. Accountability through interdependency is applicable within a polycentric governance context as many actors rely on the resources and capacities of each other. The central idea in this Model is of a plurality of actors (nodes) accounting for their actions to one another within a common discursive space (Scott 2000, 2006). The second extended accountability model identified by Scott is redundancy. This model is applicable in plural contexts where there are overlapping accountability mechanisms. This redundancy reduces the centrality of any particular mechanism and thereby reduces the risks involved should any particular accountability mechanism break down.

A range of empirical and theoretical studies have recently been published analysing and debating the realities of accountability mechanisms in polycentric governance arrangements. What they have in common is the attention they pay to hybrid accountability mechanisms (Black 2008; Dowdle 2006 and Considine 2002, who related accountability to organizational learning theory). A common argument is that plural accountability modalities offer the best approach to regulating plural governance (Scott 2000).

These arguments resonate with the intentions we outlined earlier in discussing Zwelethemba and the regulatory arrangements embedded in the Model. The Zwelethemba Model emerged through a conscious attempt to combine a range of accountability options and modalities that utilized elements of 'direct deliberation', 'community', 'hierarchy' and 'market', in ways that built upon both horizontal and vertical lines of accountability. While interferences between the various mechanisms have been observed, the overall experience is that this use of a plurality of mechanisms serves to foster accountability.

All the regulatory ideas we have canvassed confront problems and challenges to do specifically with the dispersed nature of nodal governance arrangements. What is required are careful empirical studies, like those briefly canvassed above, that explore the development of accountability mechanisms within nodal contexts and the ways in which nodal governors seek to manage the problems that emerge.

Conclusion

These comments on nodal governance are intended to be illustrative rather than definitive and provide a sense of the richness and breadth of the emerging literature on nodal governance.

By way of conclusion we return now to where we began – the process that led to the emergence of the Zwelethemba Model. This process can in hindsight be understood as an iterative series of attempts to construct institutional mechanisms that provide an opportunity for marginalized constituencies to play a role in nodal governance arrangements, as auspices and providers of security. In the course of these experiments those involved were confronted with many of the issues we have canvassed, and sought to find workable solutions to them. In reflecting on these processes – the decisions that were taken and the outcomes they generated – we have sought to highlight some of the key features of the Model that was developed and to place it within a broader theoretical context. We have attempted to show that the questions facing those involved in the history we have outlined are general questions that lie at the centre of security governance scholarship.

References

Baker, B. (2002) 'Living with Non-State Policing in South Africa: The Issues and Dilemmas', *Journal of Modern African Studies*, **40**(1), 29–53.

(2004) 'Protection from Crime: What is on Offer for Africans?', *Journal of Contemporary African Studies*, **22**(2), 165–88.
(2008) *Multi-choice Policing in Africa*. Uppsala: Nordic Africa Institute.
Bayley, D. and Shearing, C. (2001) *The New Structure of Policing*. Washington, DC: National Institute of Justice, US Department of Justice.
Beck, U. (1992) *Risk Society: Towards a New Modernity*. London: Sage.
Black, J. (2008) 'Constructing and Contesting Legitimacy and Accountability in Polycentric Regulatory Regimes', *Regulation and Governance*, **2**, 137–64.
Booth, K. and Vale, P. (1997) 'Critical Security Studies and Regional Insecurity: The Case of Southern Africa', in K. Krause and M. Williams (eds.), *Critical Security Studies: Concepts and Cases*. London: UCL Press, pp. 329–58.
Braithwaite, J. (2004) 'Methods of Power for Development: Weapons of the Weak, Weapons of the Strong', *Michigan Journal of International Law*, **26**(1), 297–330.
(2006) 'Accountability and Responsibility through Restorative Justice', in M. W. Dowdle (ed.), *Public Accountability: Designs, Dilemmas and Experiences*. Cambridge Studies in Law and Society, Cambridge University Press, pp. 33–51.
Braithwaite, J. and Drahos, P. (2000) *Global Business Regulation*. Cambridge University Press.
Burris, S. (2004) 'Governance, Microgovernance and Health', *Temple Law Review*, **77**, 335–59.
Burris, S., Drahos, P. and Shearing, C. (2005) 'Nodal Governance', *Australian Journal of Legal Philosophy*, **30**, 30–58.
Buzan, B., Waever, O. and de Wilde, J. (1997) *Security: A New Framework for Analysis*. Boulder, CO: Lynne Rienner Publishers.
Cohen, J. and Sabel, C. (1997) 'Directly-Deliberative Polyarchy', *European Law Journal* **3**(4), 313–42.
Considine, M. (2002) 'The End of the Line? Accountable Governance in the Age of Networks: Partnerships and Joined-Up Services', *Governance: An International Journal of Policy, Administration and Institutions*, **15**(1), 21–40.
Cooke, B. and Kothari, U. (2001) *Participation: The New Tyranny?* New York, NY: Zed Books.
Dewey, J. (1927) *The Public and its Problems*. Chicago, IL: Swallow Press.
(1938) *Logic: The Theory of Inquiry*. New York, NY: Henry Holt & Co.
Dorf, M. and Sabel, C. F. (1998) 'A Constitution of Democratic Experimentalism', *Columbia Law Review* **98**, 267–463.
Dowdle, M. W. (2006) 'Public Accountability: Conceptual, Historical, and Epistemic Mappings', in M. W. Dowdle (ed.), *Public Accountability: Designs, Dilemmas and Experiences*. Cambridge Studies in Law and Society, Cambridge University Press, pp. 1–29.

Drahos, P. and Braithwaite, J. (2002) *Information Feudalism*. London: Earth Scan Publications Ltd.

Dryzek, J. S. (1996) 'Political Inclusion and the Dynamics of Democratization', *American Political Science Review*, **90**(1), 475–87.

Dupont, B. (2006) 'Delivering Security through Networks: Studying the Relations Landscape of Security Managers in an Urban Setting', *Law and Legal Change*, **45**, 165–84.

Dupont, B., Grabosky, P. and Shearing, C. (2003) 'The Governance of Security in Weak and Failing States', *Criminal Justice*, **3**, 331–49.

Eckstein, H. (1971) 'The Determinants of Pressure Group Politics', in M. Dogan and R. Rose (eds.), *European Politics: A Reader.* Boston, MA: Little, Brown and Co.

Edwards, C. and Skidmore, P. (2006) *A Force of Change: Policing 2020*. London: Demos Final Report (at: www.demos.co.uk/files/aforceforchange.pdf; accessed 18 March 2009).

Foucault, M. (1990) *The History of Sexuality: An Introduction*, vol. 1. New York, NY: Random House.

Froestad, J. (2005) 'Environmental Health Problems in Hout Bay: The Challenge of Generalising Trust in South Africa', *Journal of Southern African Studies*, **31**(2), 333–56.

Froestad, J. and Shearing, C. (2007a) 'Conflict Resolution in South Africa: A Case Study', in G. Johnstone and D. W. van Ness (eds.), *Handbook of Restorative Justice*. Cullompton, Devon: Willan, pp. 534–56.

(2007b) 'The Zwelethemba Model: Practicing Human Rights through Dispute Resolution', in S. Parmentier and E. G. M. Weitekamp (eds.), *Crime and Human Rights, Sociology of Crime*. Law and Deviance Series 9. London: Elsevier. pp. 193–214.

(2007c) 'Beyond Restorative Justice – Zwelethemba: a Future-focused Model Using Local Capacity Conflict Resolution', in R. Mackay, M. Bosnjak, J. Deklerck, C. Pelikan, B. van Stokkom and M. Wright (eds.), *Images of Restorative Justice Theory, Frankfurt am Main*. Frankfurt: Verlag für Polizeiwissenschaft, pp.16–34.

(2007d) 'Effecting Security and Deepening Democracy through Peacemaking and Peacebuilding Forums: A South African Rural Experiment', in R. Southall (ed.), *Conflict and Governance in South Africa: Moving towards a More Just and Peaceful Society*. Lyttelton, NZ: Conflict and Governance Facility, pp. 312–33.

Fung, A. (2001) 'Accountable Autonomy: Towards Empowered Deliberation in Chicago Schools and Policing', *Politics and Society*, **29**(1), 73–103.

(2004) *Empowered Participation: Reinventing Urban Democracy*. Princeton University Press.

Fung, A. and Wright, E. O. (2001) 'Deepening Democracy: Innovations in Empowered Participatory Governance', *Politics and Society*, **29**(1), 5–41.

(eds.) (2003) *Deepening Democracy: Institutional Innovations in Empowered Participatory Governance*. Real Utopias Project IV. London: Verso.

Gerits, R. (2004) *Restorative Justice in South African Townships: In Search of the Possibilities and Limits of the Zwelethemba Model*. Faculty of Law, Catholic University of Leuven.

Giddens, A. (1991) *Modernity and Self-identity: Self and Society in the Late Modern Age*. Stanford University Press.

Gladwell, M. (2002) *The Tipping Point: How Little Things Can Make a Big Difference*. Boston, MA: Little, Brown and Co.

Granovetter, M. (1973) 'The Strength of Weak Ties', *American Journal of Sociology*, **78**(6), 1360–80.

(1983) 'The Strength of Weak Ties: A Network Theory Revisited', *Sociological Theory*, **1**, 201–33.

Grant, J. A. (2000) 'Special Issue: Globalizations/New Regionalism/Development', *International Insights*, **15**(3), 1–131.

Grant, J. A. and Söderbaum, A. (2003) *New Regionalism in Africa*. Aldershot: Ashgate.

Guilhot, N. (2005) *The Democracy Makers: Human Rights and International Order*. New York, NY: Columbia University Press.

Haas, P. M. (2004) 'Addressing the Global Governance Deficit', *Global Environmental Politics*, **4**(4), 1–15.

Hansen, T. H. (1999) 'The Search–Transfer Problem: The Role of Weak Ties in Sharing Knowledge across Organization Subunits', *Administrative Science Quarterly*, **44**, 82–111.

Heclo, H. H. (1978) 'Issue Networks and the Executive Establishment', in A. King (ed.), *The New American System*. Washington, DC: American Enterprise Institute for Public Policy Research, pp. 87–124.

Held, D. A., McGrew, D. and Goldblatt, Perraton, J. (1999) *Global Transformations: Politics, Economics and Culture*. Cambridge: Polity Press.

Heymann, P. (ed.) 1992. *Towards Peaceful Protest in South Africa: Testimony of Multinational Panel Regarding Lawful Control of Demonstrations in the Republic of South Africa before The Commission of Inquiry Regarding the Prevention of Public Violence and Intimidation*. Pretoria, SA: HSRC.

Hobson, J. M. (2000) *State and International Relations*. Cambridge University Press.

Hutchens, A. (2007) 'Entrepreneurship, power and defiance: the globalisation of the Fair Trade movement', Ph.D. thesis, Australian National University, Canberra.

Independent Commission on Policing for Northern Ireland (1999). *A New Beginning: Policing in Northern Ireland*. Report of the Independent Commission on Policing for Northern Ireland. Norwich: HMSO (at: www.

nio.gov.uk/a_new_beginning_in_policing_in_northern_ireland.pdf; accessed 18 March 2009).

Johnston, L. and Shearing, C. (2003) *Governing Security: Explorations in Policing and Justice*. London: Routledge.

Kaufman-Osborn, T. V. (1985) 'Pragmatism, Policy Science and the State', *American Journal of Political Science*, **29**(4), 827–49.

Kempa, K. (2008) 'Conceptualisation et réforme des processus policiers à l'ère de la mondialisation:l'économiepolitiquedelasécuritéhumaine[Conceptualizing and Reforming Policing in the Context of Globalisation: The Political Economy of Human security]', *Revue Criminologie*, **41**(1), 153–75.

Law Commission of Canada (2006) *In Search of Security: The Future of Policing in Canada*. Ottawa: Law Commission of Canada (at: http://dsp-psd.pwgsc.gc.ca/Collection/JL2-26-2006E.pdf; accessed 18 March 2009).

Loader, I. and Walker, N. (2007) *Civilizing Security*. Cambridge University Press.

Marenin, O. (2005) 'Restoring Policing Systems in Conflict Torn Nations: Processes, Problems, Prospects'. Occasional Paper No. 7, Geneva Centre for Democratic Control of Armed Forces, Geneva.

McGinnis, M. D. (1999) *Polycentric Governance and Development: Readings from the Workshop in Political Theory and Policy Analysis*. Michigan University Press.

Miller, P. and Rose, N. (1990) 'Governing Economic Life', *Economy and Society*, **19**(1), 1–31.

New Zealand Police Act Review Team 2007. *Police Act Review: Building for a Modern New Zealand Police*. Public Views on Policing: An overview of submissions to 'Policing Directions in New Zealand for the 21st Century'. Wellington, New Zealand Police.

Nuijten, M. (1999) *Institutions and Organising Practices: Conceptual Discussion*. Sustainable Development Department, Food and Agriculture Organization (FAO) (at: www.fao.org/sd/ROdirect/ROan0020.htm; accessed 18 March 2009).

O'Donnell, G. (1994) 'Delegative Democracy', *Journal of Democracy*, **5**(1), 55–69.

OECD (2006) 'Enhancing the Delivery of Justice and Security in Fragile States. Contribution by the DAC Network on Conflict, Peace and Development Co-operation (CPDC) to the Fragile States Group (FSG) Workstream on Service Delivery', *OECD Journal on Development*, vol. 3.

Palan, R. (2004) 'Constructivism and Globalisation: From Units to Encounters in International Affairs', *Cambridge Review of International Affairs*, **17**(1), 11–23.

Paul, S. (1994) 'Does Voice Matter?: For Public Accountability, Yes'. Policy Research Working Paper 1388. Washington, DC: World Bank (at: http://ideas.repec.org/p/wbk/wbrwps/1388.html; accessed 18 March 2009).

Piven, F. F. and Cloward, R. A. (1979) *Poor People's Movements: How They Succeed, How they Fail.* New York, NY: Pantheons Books.

Project Group Vision on Policing (2006) *The Police in Evolution. Vision on Policing.* The Hague: Board of Chief Commissioners.

Putnam, R. D. (1993) *Making Democracy Work: Civic Traditions in Modern Italy.* Princeton University Press.

Rhodes, R. A. W. (1997) *Understanding Governance: Policy Networks, Governance, Reflexivity and Accountability.* Buckingham: Open University Press.

Roche, D. (2002) 'Restorative Justice and the Regulatory State in South African Townships', *British Journal of Criminology*, **42**, 514–33.

(2003) *Accountability in Restorative Justice.* Oxford University Press.

Sampson, R. J., Morenoff, J. D. and Earls, F. (1999) 'Beyond Social Capital: Spatial Dynamics of Collective Efficacy for Children', *American Sociological Review*, **64**, 633–60.

Scott, C. (2000) 'Accountability in the Regulatory State', *Journal of Law and Society*, **21**(1), 38–60.

(2006) 'Spontaneous Accountability', in M. W. Dowdle (ed.), *Public Accountability: Designs, Dilemmas and Experiences.* Cambridge Studies in Law and Society, Cambridge University Press, pp. 174–91.

Selznick, P. (1957) *Leadership in Administration.* New York, NY: Harper & Row.

Shearing, C. (2001) 'Transforming Security: A South African Experiment', in H. Strang and J. Braithwaite (eds.), *Restorative Justice and Civil Society.* Cambridge University Press.

Shearing, C. and Ericson, R. V. (1991) 'Culture as Figurative Action', *British Journal of Sociology*, **42**, 481–506.

Shearing, C. and Foster, D. (2007) 'Back to the Future in South African Security: From Intentions to Effective Mechanisms', *Acta Juridica*, 156–70.

Shearing, C. and Johnston, L. (2005) 'Justice in Risk Society', *Australian and New Zealand Journal of Criminology*, **38**(1), 25–38.

Shearing, C. and Stenning, P. C. (1985) 'From the Panopticon to Disney World: The Development of Discipline', in A. N. Doob and E. L. Greenspan (eds.), *Perspectives in Criminal Law: Essays in Honour of John Ll. J. Edwards.* Toronto: Canada Law Book, pp. 335–49.

Taylor, M. B. and Jennings, K. M. (2004) *In Search of Strategy. An Agenda for Applied Research on Transitions from Conflict.* Oslo: FAFO Report 480.

Tilly, C. (2005) *Trust and Rule.* Cambridge University Press.

Walzer, M. (1994) *Thick and Thin: Moral Argument at Home and Abroad.* Loyola Lectures in Political Analysis. University of Notre Dame Press.

Wood, J. (1996) *Historical Milestones, Trends and Challenges in the Delivery of Security: 1970–1996.* Report submitted under contract to the Metropolitan Toronto Housing Authority, Security Services Branch.

(2006) 'Research and Innovation in the Field of Security: A Nodal Governance View', in J. Wood and B. Dupont (eds.), *Democracy, Society and the Governance of Security*. Cambridge University Press.

Wood, J. and Dupont, B. (2006) 'Conclusion: The Future of Democracy', in J. Wood and D. Dupont (eds.), *Democracy, Society and the Governance of Security*. Cambridge University Press.

Wood, J. and Shearing, C. (2007) *Imagining Security*. Cullompton, Devon: Willan.

6

Regulatory compliance: organizational capacities and regulatory strategies for environmental protection

GARY LYNCH-WOOD AND DAVID WILLIAMSON

Introduction

In this chapter we argue that forms of regulation vary in their capacity to influence behaviour. This is because the receptive capacity to particular forms of regulation varies between different actors. As a consequence, the successful application of regulatory approaches will only be secured if they are correctly aligned to these receptive capacities. This is a critical issue, particularly as the focus within the literature on regulatory compliance has tended to be on the relative effectiveness of different regulatory strategies and tools, without considering in any depth this question of differential capacity to respond. In a sense, our argument constitutes an extension and elaboration of the idea of responsive regulation (Ayres and Braithwaite 1992; Grabosky, Chapter 4, this book): we argue, in effect, that regulators should be responsive not only to the conduct of those they seek to regulate but also to their capacities to comply and internalize different approaches. This has some important implications for regulatory strategies.

To develop this argument and substantiate our claims, we focus on one specific substantive area, namely, environmental regulation directed at private sector businesses. This is, of course, an important area in its own right but we suggest that our argument has wider implications, including for the criminal justice arena, and we return to consider these in our conclusion.

We begin by showing first that these firms vary in how they respond to regulatory pressures, with some firms going beyond what is required in law while others purposely disregard what is demanded of them. This variation is associated with important differences in the firms themselves, to the extent that it is posited that differences in organizational response materially affect the strategies we should use to regulate firms. In practice, this means that firms which go beyond compliance will respond more deeply to civil regulatory pressures and reflexive laws, while deviant firms are more likely to respond to traditional command-and-control approaches. Although this observation is in some ways obvious, it nevertheless has important implications for how we should devise regulatory strategies for environmental improvement.

The basis for reconsidering regulatory strategies starts with the observation that all firms have environmental impacts and that regulators have neither the resources nor the capabilities to improve the environmental performance of all types of firms. Given this context it is perhaps to be expected that regulators have tended to focus their efforts on firms with the greatest potential impacts. Typically, this translates to the targeting of large firms in environmentally sensitive industries (e.g. chemical manufacturers) using conventional command-and-control measures (e.g. emission limits, standards). The inevitable outcome of this approach is that most firms are overlooked, or at any rate are not given sufficient consideration, from a regulatory point of view. In practice this equates to that group of firms classified as small and medium enterprises (SMEs).[1] This is important because SMEs comprise 99 per cent of all firms and are estimated to produce 60 per cent of all business carbon dioxide emissions (Marshall Report 1998), 70 per cent of business pollution (Smith and Kemp 1998), 60 per cent of commercial waste and 43 per cent of serious pollution incidents (NetRegs 2006). It is also indicative of a broader failure of regulation in the sense that the constraints that produce this situation continue to be overlooked. One way of addressing this shortfall is to consider how all firms can be made more environmentally responsible, such that large polluters show improvements in environmental performance and there is a collective reduction in the environmental impact of SMEs. However, it is unlikely that this is achievable unless we are bold enough to accommodate more sophisticated views on how firms can and should be

[1] In the EU an SME is a firm employing fewer than 250 people and which has a turnover of less than €50m or a balance sheet total below €43m. This definition has within it the subcategories of *micro*, *small* and *medium* firms. Micro firms have fewer than 10 employees and a turnover or balance sheet total of less than €2m. Small firms have between 10 and 49 employees and a turnover or balance sheet total of less than €10m, with medium-sized firms having between 50 and 249 employees and a turnover of less than €50m or a balance sheet total of less than €43m. Over 95 per cent of SMEs are micro firms.

regulated. This, in turn, requires us to have a better understanding of how firms actually behave, and in particular of how critical factors such as resource availability, visibility and moral orientation combine to produce different compliance orientations.

The chapter approaches this task by first considering why many people feel regulation has to change if concerns for future well-being are to be addressed. Following this brief review of the dynamics of regulatory change and critical discourses on regulation, the chapter analyses how the compliance orientations of firms can vary and how these orientations can then influence the effectiveness of regulatory approaches. This provides the backdrop for the development of a more responsive model of environmental regulation – a model based on receptive capacity. By seeking to make regulation more responsive to the predispositions of firms the analysis acknowledges and develops the view that groups of firms possess sufficient commonality that they constitute distinct regulatory 'systems'. Recognizing the existence of these systems has important implications for how regulatory resources are distributed and how strategies can be formulated to secure – and encourage behaviour that exceeds – compliance. In our conclusion, we look at some of the wider implications of this argument, including for criminal justice.

Dynamics of regulatory change

It is an inescapable fact that corporate activity has an environmental impact and that this can be a complex externality to manage due to the many ways it can manifest itself. Policy-makers have responded by developing a sophisticated portfolio of regulatory measures, the forms of which represent the view that regulation should both contain and reduce the impacts of pollution – to the extent that it actually induces deeper levels of change so that innovative solutions, including cleaner production and consumption methods, are stimulated. This latter view, that regulation can stimulate innovation, is a relatively modern development and is significant because it represents a departure from the mantra that retrospective command-and-control approaches, through the application of neutral external scientific expertise, can deal with environmental harm (Weale 1992; Fiorino 2006). Indeed, disquiet with this traditional approach continues into the present with criticisms that it cannot manage small and less identifiable pollution sources and is excessively costly, bureaucratic and inflexible. As such, it is incapable of delivering the degree of change required for a sustainable level of development.

Alongside – and perhaps as a consequence of – these criticisms, there has arisen the view that environmental solutions are only really addressable if they are integrated into the capitalist system itself. This requires a process of 'ecological modernization' in the sense that there has to be a harmonization of environmental and economic objectives, which from a policy perspective requires that frameworks support and are compatible with the inherent urge within market economies to modernize themselves (Hajer 1995; Mol 1997; Jänicke 2008). Thus, ecological modernization stresses the need for modernization through innovation, particularly through the use of a wider range of instruments and the incorporation of state and non-state actors in order to facilitate appropriate and supportive participatory practices (Hajer 1995; Gunningham and Sinclair 2002; Jänicke 2008). In promoting these pluralist approaches, ecological modernization clearly incorporates contemporary debates on the roles and functions of 'state', 'civil society' and 'industry' domains in the formulation and enforcement of regulatory rules (Hajer 1995; Gunningham and Grabosky 1998; Hutter and Jones 2007; Gunningham 2009). The aggregate effect of this has been to push the emphasis of regulation away from centralized and hierarchical 'government' towards a more decentralized and self-organizing form of 'governance'.

When we look at the domains of government and governance more closely it is clear that government-type measures primarily focus on instruments to curb pollution (e.g. rules, permits, standards, etc.). A critical issue for this approach is getting firms to comply with the rules, with much debate over whether this should be achieved using deterrence (e.g. sanctions) or compliance (e.g. negotiation and persuasion) approaches. Taking this discussion forward, Ayres and Braithwaite (1992) argue that both approaches should be accommodated using a 'tit-for-tat' – or responsive – compliance strategy. This approach is portrayed as a 'pyramid' of sanctions, with the regulator applying a progressively more punitive set of deterrence responses should firms fail to respond. Accompanying the pyramid of sanctions is a pyramid of regulatory strategies where, at the industry level, governments seek a self-regulatory solution in the first instance. When this fails it can be replaced by enforced self-regulation, and in the final instance by command-and-control strategies.

The concept of responsiveness has been taken up by Baldwin and Black (2008) when they claim that regulation can only be truly responsive when it properly accommodates the cultures and understandings of regulated organizations. This suggests that regulation should take cognizance of all factors affecting compliance and as such can include a broader range of governance mechanisms. Surrogate pressure of this kind can manifest itself as civil regulation, where customers, trade associations and others such as consumers can exert considerable regulatory pressure (Vogel 2005; Gunningham *et al.* 2004; Gunningham and Rees 1997; Hutter and Jones 2007). Taking the idea of governance even further is the concept of reflexive law. Although space precludes a detailed analysis of the ideas that underpin reflexive law theory, it describes the view that there are factors internal and external to law that necessitate the installation and refinement of self-regulatory mechanisms so that actors can be empowered to manage (i.e. regulate) on behalf of the state. Originally articulated by Teubner (1983), it builds on the work of Nonet and Selznick (1978), Habermas (1979: see also 1984, 1987, 1996) and Luhmann (1982: see also 1989, 1993, 1995). Teubner contends that reflexive law evolves from, and overlaps with, previous versions of formal and substantive law, that it enables social development through communicative agreement on the validity of competing norms, and that it is necessary due to functional systems (e.g. business) becoming increasingly differentiated and closed. This latter point suggests that systems have their own inner world-views and discourse and, accordingly, can be most effectively catered for by integrating the management of the system within the system itself. By doing this, we make the system reflexive in the sense that incoming information can be assessed in light of the practices of the system and where changes are deemed necessary for the system to then be best placed to make the most appropriate changes. From this perspective, reflexive instruments encourage organizations to learn from, and modify behaviour based on, experiences and received information. Consequently, instruments should focus on enhancing the self-referential capacities of social systems and institutions outside the legal system, rather than on direct interventions using detailed rules (Orts 1995). Reflexive environmental policies should therefore promote the design of self-regulating social systems such that the lighter the regulatory touch, the greater the regulatory outcome. An example of an instrument that inculcates responsible environmental behaviour is the European Eco-Management and Auditing Scheme (EMAS). Although voluntary, EMAS requires firms to have procedures for maintaining compliance, that they produce a register of significant environmental impacts, that they carry out periodic audits, and that they disclose performance data.

In briefly reviewing the dynamics of regulatory change it is clear that the scale of required change brought about by modernity has provoked a radical reassessment of regulatory forms and strategies. We will argue, however, that for these to be successfully applied they must be properly aligned to firms' receptive capacities. This has implications for reflexive law as it means that it can only function effectively when the necessary preconditions are in place. Equally, too strict an adherence to the pyramid of regulatory strategies cannot be justified when we take a more contingent view of regulation. In practice, this means that government and governance mechanisms are both separately required – but not as separateness through a hierarchical ordering of strategies. Rather, it is strategies based on differentiated systems of regulatory receptivity that determine their suitability. To justify this claim, we will now look at how size and environmental orientation influence organizational receptivity to different forms of regulation.

Environmental orientation of firms

Many descriptions of organizational greening, the process by which firms become more active, are based on classifications that involve 'stages' of development or 'typologies' of ideal types. Both approaches tend to present a spread of organizational behaviour typically ranging from non-compliant or reactive through to leading-edge or proactive. What is important for our analysis is that the shift from non-compliance to leading-edge reflects the tendency of firms to respond to different regulatory forms. To support this claim, the factors that shape different greening positions are examined to show why they also equate to different regulatory pressures and propensities to different types of regulation. We do this by looking at the available evidence using an amended version of the Bansal and Roth (2000) model of organizational greening. The following analysis uses the basic framework of Bansal and Roth to look at the differences between large and small firms as manifested through variations in their drivers and mediating context, and how this then affects organizational motivations.

Drivers

The main drivers of environmental behaviour are 'legislation', 'stakeholders', 'economic opportunity' and 'ethical motives'. These are the internal and external factors that influence corporate behaviour. As we will now try to show, their intensity is heavily affected by firm size.

Compliance with environmental legislation is often cited as the main driver of SME behaviour, particularly when environmental improvements cannot be justified on economic grounds (Worthington and Patton 2003, 2005; Baylis *et al.* 1998). SMEs tend to be instrumental and pragmatic, which is consistent with the finding that their positive environmental attitudes are often not converted into beyond compliance behaviour (Worthington and Patton 2005). By comparison, although compliance is essential for large firms due to the potential impact on legitimacy, it is not, of itself, the primary driver of compliance or beyond compliance behaviour (Gunningham *et al.* 2004). For example, in an examination of the US Environmental Protection Agency's voluntary 33/50 programme, which sought to reduce the release and transfer of key toxic chemicals by encouraging firms to develop less toxic substitutes, the largest firms with the greatest toxic releases were the most likely participants – for public recognition rather than compliance reasons (Arora and Cason 1996).

The need for recognition and legitimacy suggests stakeholders, defined as individuals or groups that can affect and be affected by firms' actions (Freeman 1984), have a huge potential to influence organizational behaviour. Sources of environmental stakeholder pressure include non-governmental organizations (NGOs), neighbours, communities, customers and investors. Critically, the size of the impact of stakeholders varies across different types of firms. For example, research indicates that external stakeholders have little interest in, and insufficient power to influence, the environmental practices of SMEs (Rowe and Enticott 1998; Williamson and Lynch-Wood 2001; Lynch-Wood and Williamson 2007). The result, which again is linked to instrumentality, is that the environment becomes a relatively low priority for smaller firms (Revell and Blackburn 2004), which may also explain why SMEs have little to gain from developing their environmental reputations (Graafland and Smid 2004). However, since larger firms are more visible and have more prominent brand identities to safeguard, their stakeholders are more active and powerful (Lynch-Wood and Williamson 2007). Evidence that the stakeholders of large firms do exert more pressure than those of smaller firms is provided by Weber and Wasieleski (2003), and it supports our view that visibility increases as firm size increases, which makes large firms more vulnerable to attention from interested parties and augmented institutional pressures.

The link between firm size and variable effect also manifests itself economically, with the perceived economic opportunity from being green tending to increase as firm size increases. There is evidence, for example, that many SME owner-managers see their firms as lean, which can generate a view that green economic opportunities are negligible since they must have already secured potential green efficiencies – which then gets reinforced by, as well as produces, the view that they have negligible environmental impacts (Williamson *et al.* 2006). It is therefore hardly surprising that the economic rationality of SMEs translates itself as seeing environmental benefits in terms of small-scale cost reductions and efficiency gains (Baylis *et al.* 1998). Such a minimalist mentality also manifests itself in a reduced likelihood that SMEs will capitalize on green opportunities if it entails significant capital outlay – as reflected in their reluctance to incur debt and preference for short payback periods (Petersen and Rajan 1994, Michaelas *et al.* 1999). Associated with this minimalist and instrumental mindset is a lack of resources, a combination that reinforces a tendency to see the environment as a marginal concern. This is why environmental improvement is not generally perceived to be an economic opportunity and why SMEs tend not to participate in environmental improvement programmes (Petts *et al.* 1999; Hitchens *et al.* 2005). Again, and by way of contrast, the ability of larger firms to make large-scale investments, to reduce costs, and to exploit emerging market opportunities, can be attributed to a greater willingness and capacity to invest on account of their different perceptions of what they can do, and what they may need to do, to be competitive (Porter and van der Linde 1995; Russo and Fouts 1997; Judge and Douglas 1998).

When we look at ethical motives, which include social legitimacy expectations and management values (Di Maggio and Powel 1991; Wood 1991; Greening and Gray 1994; Marshall *et al.* 2005), there is evidence that social legitimacy expectations have a greater impact on large firms due to them being more visible to the pressures that induce ethical behaviour. This, together with their greater capacity to exploit green market opportunities, makes it, from a strategic perspective, more rational for them to adopt beyond compliance and good practice measures. SMEs, on the other hand, are more likely to be influenced by the ethics of their owner-managers, which in turn are influenced by market values that diminish the worth of the natural environment. Indeed, the decision-making frames of owner-managers can cause them to exhibit certain types of behaviour while ignoring others (Lewicki *et al.* 1999). This may also explain why the positive environmental values frequently exhibited by owner-managers rarely translate into good environmental performance (Smith and Kemp 1998; Hitchens *et al.* 2004). More generally, the predominance of market values in the decision-making frames of owner-managers takes a priority over other ethical considerations (Williamson *et al.* 2006).

Mediating context

The factors that influence the degree to which drivers are interpreted and acted upon include 'issue salience', 'field cohesion', 'individual concern' and 'resource endowments'. Issue salience is the level of importance a particular ecological issue has for firm constituents, and is determined by certainty, transparency and emotivity (Bansal and Roth 2000). Certainty relates to the measurability of environmental issues, with toxic waste disposal, for example, having a high degree of certainty since people generally appreciate the impact associated with unsafe disposal. Global warming, however, would tend to have a low level of certainty because the impact of a firm's activity is less obvious or direct. Transparency concerns how environmental issues are attributed to firms' activities. Noise pollution is thus more transparent than air pollution since it is easier to link noise to specific sources. Emotivity relates to the emotional responses induced by environment issues. A major oil spillage that leads to significant destruction of wildlife will inevitably elicit a more emotional reaction than waste going to landfill. With these examples in mind, we would hypothesize that each determinant becomes more intense as firm size increases. A single major pollution incident is much more measurable than many frequent but small impacts. Consequently, certainty and transparency are much stronger for the activities of large firms. If certainty and transparency are more apparent in large firms, it follows that emotivity is also likely to be stronger.

Field cohesion refers to the intensity and density of formal and informal network ties between constituents in an organizational field – the organizational field being a recognized area of institutional life (e.g. key suppliers, product customers, regulatory agencies). Although field cohesion will vary across firms of all sizes, there will be significant differences between small and large firms. Large firms are often associated with powerful elites, institutional decision-making, supply chain control, financial power and dominant products (Pettigrew 1992). Since they are more likely to interact with powerful stakeholders (e.g. environmental regulators and NGOs) their field cohesion strengthens the drivers of green behaviour. In contrast, smaller firms have been associated with the lower middle class, a lack of financial power and local markets (Owens 2002). Consequently, they tend not to interact with major stakeholders and their field cohesion is generally less intense with regard to the mediation of green drivers.

Individual concern is the degree to which organizational members value the environment coupled with the degree of discretion they have to act. With respect to discretion, this is likely to increase as firm size decreases since the key influence in smaller firms is owner-managers. That individual discretion decreases as firm size increases is due to the growing power of other stakeholders, particularly shareholders. Nonetheless, while owner-managers of smaller firms may have more discretion than employees of large firms, it is unlikely this discretion will be associated with increasing concern for the environment or improved environmental performance. The reason for this, as we showed previously, is that the decision-making frames of SME owner-managers tend to be dominated by market values that emphasize and prioritize revenue-based activities over environmental activities (Williamson *et al.* 2006). The market reinforces this by providing greater rewards for competitiveness and price than it does for environmental behaviour (Spence *et al.* 2000). For large firms, it is managers – who do not own the business – who make and implement decisions. In doing so, they are accountable to a far wider range of stakeholders; some of whom will have environmental expectations (e.g. NGOs). Managers who share these values can therefore use these stakeholder expectations to justify their own preferences for how the firm should behave and develop. Likewise, managers who do not have environmental values may find they have to follow the values of wider stakeholders. This, of course, is not to suggest that profit maximization is not a key influence in large firms, just that it can be offset by other stakeholder expectations. Smaller firms are also driven by profit maximization, but are less likely to have stakeholders that can offset such behaviour. We thus hypothesize that the mediating factor of individual concern is generally more important in large firms than it is in small firms. What is more, since the literature suggests that individual concerns are enduring, we would expect these differences to be long-lasting.

Finally, the resource endowments of firms can influence how they respond to opportunities and threats (Barney 1991; Peteraf 1993). Resources refer to assets, knowledge, capabilities and processes. In a resource-based analysis of environmental performance, Russo and Fouts (1997) demonstrate that firms which tend towards compliance will differ in their resources than those that tend towards prevention. This concurs with evidence that scarce resources underpin a lack of environmental activity in SMEs (Hutchison and Chaston 1994). It is well documented, for example, that smaller firms do not possess the human and financial capital to enable them to make sustained environmental improvements (Gerstenfeld and Roberts 2000; Hitchens *et al.* 2004). Further evidence of how the resource profile affects behaviour has been provided by Nooteboom's (1994) study of innovation. This shows that differences in resources results in small firms having comparative advantage in the earlier stages of innovation because it is less expensive, while large firms have advantage in the later stages because they have resources to scale up innovative ideas.

Motivations

Firms are motivated, to differing degrees, by 'competitiveness', 'legitimation' and 'ecological responsibility' (Bansal and Roth 2000). These influence how firms perceive and react to, and yet are also a consequence of, the drivers and mediating contexts outlined above.[2] Although firms can possess all three motivations, we argue that SMEs are more likely to be motivated by competitiveness and legitimation, and large firms by competitiveness, legitimation and ecological responsibility. As we now discuss, this arises from the way the strengths and intensities of these motivations vary as a consequence of the association that firm size has to the factors that produce these intensities and motivations.

Large firms which are motivated by competitiveness tend to perceive ecological responsiveness as a means of improving long-term profitability (Bansal and Roth 2000). Examples of competitive responses include energy and waste management savings, material input reductions to produce more with less and the development of eco-products. In comparison, small firms that are motivated by competitiveness tend to be more inactive environmentally (Petts *et al.* 1999; Worthington and Patton 2003, 2005). They perceive ecological responsiveness in terms of basic compliance (Williamson *et al.* 2006; Worthington and Patton 2003, 2005), which is a rational competitive response given their lack of resources to exploit capital dependent savings and longer-term market opportunities. For example, Scherer and Ross (1990) show that, unlike most large firms, who will seek to develop longer-term green product/market positions due to their greater capacity for long-term research and availability of resources, smaller firms tend to focus on process intensification-type measures to reduce costs.

A similar picture emerges when we look at legitimacy. This derives from the relationship that an organization has with its operating environment

[2] An extensive management literature argues that organizational culture strongly influences the 'world-view' of firms and that this affects how strategy is formulated and acted upon (see Mintzberg and Waters 1985; Johnson 1988).

(Suchman 1995) and involves firms justifying their existence to a peer or superordinate system (Maurer 1971). For example, the need for legitimacy is evident in how firms respond to societal pressures by publishing environmental and social reports, as the reporting mechanism enables firms to identify with legitimacy-enhancing symbols, values and institutions (Dowling and Pfeffer 1975). In general, large firms are more likely to report on their environmental behaviour than small firms because their need for legitimacy is greater (Lynch-Wood and Williamson 2007). This derives from the fact that legitimacy – or perceived illegitimate activities – can affect a firm's reputation, which for large firms is a significant asset that can directly affect stock market valuations. Since larger firms have a proportionally greater need to protect their reputation, they are more likely to attempt to legitimize themselves by going beyond compliance (i.e. superior corporate performance can safeguard and improve the value of a core corporate asset). That reputation capital is a less significant asset for SMEs can therefore be ascribed, at least in part, to them not being listed and their share capital residing in the management of the company. This, together with the preceding analysis, suggests that legitimation for smaller firms is quite specific (e.g. they will want to avoid fines) and less about reputational loss more generally.

When we look at ecological responsibility, which is corporate concern for the environment as manifested in actions such as the provision of less profitable green product lines and donations to environmental interest groups, it can be argued that firms adopt these practices out of a sense of responsibility or self-interest. The preceding analysis would suggest that large firms are proportionally more likely to act responsibly than SMEs because there are greater institutional and social pressures requiring such behaviour – although it is, of course, in their self-interest to do so. Likewise, smaller firms are less likely to act altruistically, but when they do so it will be more likely that this is not out of self-interest.

In outlining the factors that influence the environmental orientation of firms it is clear that size-related issues that are external and internal to the firm do affect world-views and practices. The analysis would suggest that this is due to size being a proxy for that bundle of factors that broadly influence environmental behaviour. Explanations that suggest otherwise (see Bowen 2002) are not wrong in the sense that visibility and slack resources rather than firm size explain variations in environmental performance and that small firms may therefore be more environmentally proactive than larger firms. But they are incorrect in suggesting that the aggregate effect of these variations does not make firm size an appropriate measure for approximating environmental behaviour. This is because the elements of a firm's visibility and resource availability that promote environmental responsiveness may not result from size alone, but they are nevertheless likely to be associated with size differences. As the following section demonstrates, this is important when examining the ability of firms to respond to different regulatory controls

A resource-based model

Policy-makers and regulators have traditionally taken a sector-based approach to pollution control. This has led to a prioritization of environmental issues, resulting in regulatory effort being targeted at larger installations producing significant impacts. The Environment Agency of England and Wales, for example, devotes a significant share of its pollution control resources to firms with Part A1 permits under the environmental permitting regulations, a regime for controlling certain industrial activities.[3] These permitted firms are typically large on account of the size of the thresholds used. Indeed, around four-fifths of affected firms are large – one-fifth of them FTSE350 companies (Environment Agency 2007). Only 700 of the 3,500 Part A1 sites belong to SMEs.

This approach seems logical from the perspective of individual risk, but becomes less so when considering firms' capacities and propensities to comply. Generally speaking, large firms have more awareness of environmental issues, and have the resources, systems, expertise and pressures to go beyond compliance. By way of contrast, SMEs have less well-developed systems, expertise and awareness, and face fewer pressures. Consequently, there should be less danger of large firms being non-compliant, particularly when suitable regulatory strategies are in place. As it stands, incidents of non-compliance are far higher for SMEs. Moreover, the cumulative impact of these incidents is significant. The implication of this, as shown in Figure 6.1, is that the risk of non-compliance increases as firm size decreases. On this basis it can be argued that present strategies fail to maximize regulatory effectiveness because controls are largely applied to where they are least needed from a 'risk of breach' and an 'ability to comply' perspective.

The inverted relationship outlined above, and the underpinning relationship to the capacity to respond to different environmental drivers that

[3] The provisions of the Pollution Prevention and Control (England and Wales) Regulations 2000 were replaced by the Environmental Permitting Regulations 2007 which came into force in England and Wales on 6 April 2008.

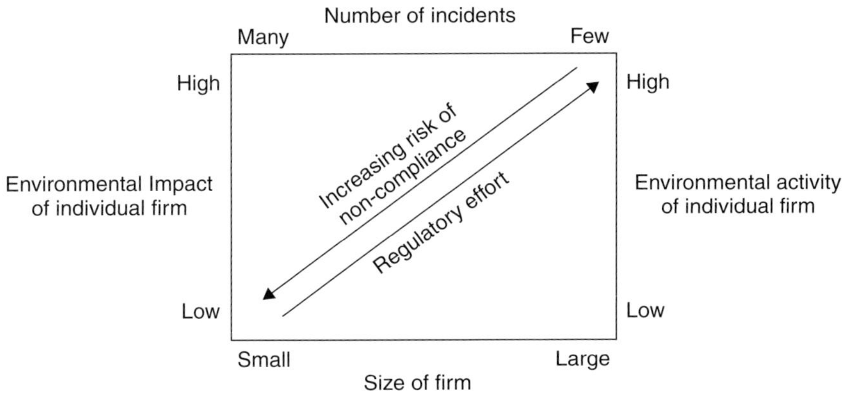

Figure 6.1 Risk of non-compliance and regulatory effort

have been identified in the previous sections, provides a basis for a proposed realignment of regulatory resources shown in Figure 6.2. This involves, among other things, redirecting resources to where they are needed for improved aggregate compliance and performance. While it may appear counter-intuitive to redirect resources to smaller firms because they individually pollute less and are more difficult to manage, the adoption of a resource-based view is predicated on the view that it is both rational and feasible. The resource-based model shown in Figure 6.2 accommodates the fact that compliance behaviour ranges from non-compliance to beyond compliance, and that the ability of firms to respond to regulatory strategies that are aligned to this range of compliance behaviours is affected by the capability profiles of firms – a composite measure that incorporates size-related visibility and resource availability factors. The axes combine to produce eight organizational systems with distinct compliance orientations. These are 'delinquents', 'vulnerable satisfiers', 'minor strategic players', 'altruistic citizens', 'ogres', 'safe satisfiers', 'major strategic players' and 'benevolent giants'. As might be expected these systems are not evenly populated. Most firms are SMEs that are classed as vulnerable satisfiers, and there will be very few altruistic citizens or benevolent giants.

The resource-based model provides a framework for understanding how groups of firms behave and how regulatory resources can be targeted accordingly. It therefore allows resources to be used more effectively by directing approaches to where they can be most appropriately applied to achieve maximum environmental effect. Before these compliance orientations and associated regulatory approaches are briefly outlined it is important to emphasize that the model increases the available

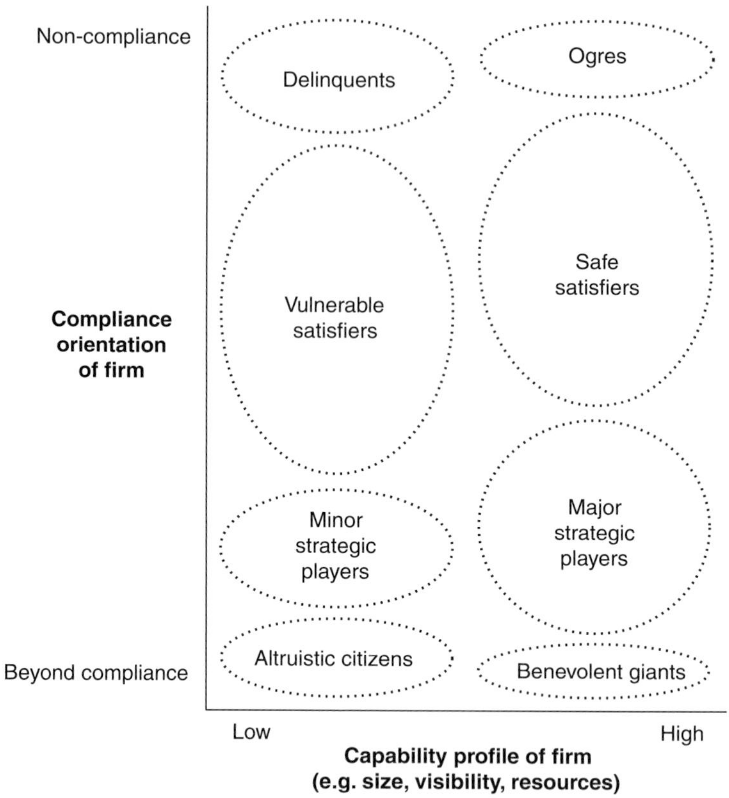

Figure 6.2 Resource-based model of regulatory behaviour

regulatory resource and as such should not be construed as a methodology for deregulating large firms. Rather, it accommodates differences in organizational capabilities so that regulatory resources can be directed to where they are most needed. By doing so, it builds on the fact that different types of firms can, and will, react to different things.

Compliance systems

The systems on the left of the model in Figure 6.2 are inhabited by smaller firms that generally lack visibility and spare resources. Delinquents tend to be very small and may be transitory in that they reconstitute themselves when circumstances require it (e.g. to continue trading when previous misdemeanours render this difficult). A further and essential distinguishing feature of delinquents is that they deliberately or recklessly pollute, making them indifferent to some sanctions, such as small fines or warnings. They also typically engage in low-level activities such as fly-tipping and are frequently overrepresented in industries such as construction and demolition waste (Webb and Marshall 2004). It is equally the case they may engage in wider criminal activities (e.g. tax evasion) and can even be part of organized gangs. As amoral calculators (Kagan and Scholz 1984), delinquents are problematic because they function underneath the regulator's normal focus of activity, thus making them difficult to find, control and reform. Possible regulatory approaches include intelligence-led policing so that delinquent firms can be effectively targeted, and rehabilitation to facilitate moral reinstatement. Sanctions, however, must be tough since their normal behaviour is to avoid compliance due to their imperviousness to societal pressure for change. Broadly speaking, delinquents can therefore be described as having neither the resources nor interest to reflect on their environmental actions unless forced to do so.

The largest system of firms is vulnerable satisfiers. Although these firms are naturally compliant in that they wish to comply, they are at the same time vulnerably compliant due to constraints imposed by having limited resources and a laissez-faire orientation. The effect is to produce a position that tends towards basic compliance with sufficient but minimal resources being allocated for legitimacy and peace of mind. Vulnerable satisfiers therefore operate with a risk of being non-compliant, although breaches would probably lack intention or recklessness. However, being naturally compliant they will seek compliance when they know what is required of them – which is likely to require support given their limited resources. This point is important as the opportunity to facilitate compliance using multiple agencies is financially and practically attractive when the regulator is constrained in what they can do. A regulatory strategy that focuses on achieving compliance for this system of firms can therefore incorporate handholding and guidance with the backup of a strong incentive to participate (e.g. latent threat of large civil or criminal sanctions and increased inspections for suspected non-compliance). The rationale for adopting this approach also provides the basis for a rejection of reflexive practices that focus on self-regulation through the use of environmental management systems and disclosure strategies, and so forth on account of the necessary preconditions not being in place.

The distinguishing feature of minor strategic players is that, unlike vulnerable satisfiers, they seek to identify with market opportunities for good environmental behaviour in order to exploit emerging market opportunities or to safeguard their strategic position by reducing risk through the protection of their legitimacy. Thus they are responsible because it is in their interests to be so. A firm, for example, may work towards the accreditation of an environmental management system (e.g. ISO 14001) if required to do so by an influential customer. While this is not an altruistic act, accreditation demonstrates positive environmental behaviour and allows the regulator to adopt a different compliance approach. For example, the regulator may take a more arm's-length approach by allowing them to self-report, an act which may further encourage responsible practices. Since compliance with this approach is in the interests of minor strategic players – as it demonstrates good practice – their characteristics make them receptive to more reflexive strategies.

In comparison to the previous categories of firms, the environmental behaviour of altruistic citizens is motivated by ethical concerns. Indeed, ethical or ecological responsibility, rather than business success as measured through profits, is likely to be a primary motive. For example, Traidcraft is a trading company that is also a development charity. It was established as a Christian response to poverty, and promotes approaches to trade that help poor people in developing countries. Its ethical principles extend to the environment itself (e.g. use of 100 per cent renewable electricity and a planned reduction in the use of air freight). Given this ethical orientation and the concomitant desire to go beyond compliance, it seems appropriate that the regulator should adopt an arm's-length approach based on observed behaviour and that it should actually reward such behaviour through positive actions (e.g. positive publicity by bestowing labels of excellence, relaxation of formal compliance requirements, reduced statutory payments). As such, altruistic citizens are clearly receptive to reflexive approaches.

The compliance systems on the right of Figure 6.2 are populated by a smaller number of larger firms. Ogres are firms that intentionally or recklessly function outside legal rules and accepted norms. Prominent examples include acts of purposeful fraud by firms such as Enron, Worldcom and Palmalat, and wilful environmental risk-taking as exemplified by Union Carbide in Bhopal, India. A recent example includes BP's 2009 settlement of $179m with the US government over air pollution breaches at its Texas City refinery following an explosion in 2005 which killed fifteen people – the size of the settlement reflected the additional requirement that pollution offences were addressed through the installation of pollution abatement equipment and restriction of air pollution emissions at its other refineries (ENDS Report 2009). We should also stress that ogres may and often do engage in reckless or intentionally damaging activities in developing nations, even in situations where they demonstrate compliance or good practice in their home state. The mines and smelter operated by the Southern Peru Copper Corporation, which is owned by Grupo Mexico, caused severe environmental degradation through riverine disposal (i.e. dumping mine waste into rivers) in contravention of Peruvian law (Earthworks and Oxfam America 2004). This, however, cannot be justified since the firm should have the resources and technical knowledge to manage its impacts regardless of where it operates. Due to their intentional and reckless behaviour, and given their large resource base, ogres should be heavily penalized, both financially and publicly and, where appropriate, criminally.

Firms classified as safe satisfiers have the capacity to develop sophisticated environmental strategies, but generally fail to do so. A reason for this is their lack of exposure to the types of civil pressures that can encourage beyond compliance behaviour. This lack of civic pressure may stem from the products and services they are involved in (e.g. finance), their position within the supply chain (e.g. not supplying to consumers), the structure of the company (e.g. conglomerate with many unrelated business units), or the fact that they can offset criticism by satisfying minimum compliance requirements. But since they do have the capacity to go beyond compliance, the task of the regulator is to provide the necessary incentives for this to occur. One way of doing this is to increase their visibility so that civil society pressure is engaged (e.g. through performance disclosure strategies). This can be augmented by raising the profile of the environment to the firm itself (e.g. introduce mandatory self-auditing) and by then reinforcing this through the latent threat of large civil or criminal sanctions and increased inspections. A strategy of positive criticism may also be appropriate – although they comply, they can do better by going beyond compliance.

Large firms can also be major strategic players, which although similar to safe satisfiers in terms of resource availability are different on account of their desire to exploit green market opportunities and/or to protect their market position. This arises from the fact that they are more likely to be visible to, or perhaps would like to be visible to, a wider range of influential stakeholders. Both situations require them to protect or enhance their legitimacy, typically through a willingness to incorporate sophisticated environmental strategies and demonstrate environmental leadership. Accordingly, major strategic players are receptive to reflexive mechanisms that demonstrate good practice. Since they will readily adopt environmental management systems and participate in voluntary disclosure strategies to demonstrate compliance, it seems inappropriate and wasteful to allocate scarce regulatory resources to this task. A more appropriate regulatory strategy is to acknowledge and incentivize such behaviour by using these types of activities to demonstrate compliance, and simultaneously to reinforce the behaviour through positive feedback in the form of awards and positive publicity. To safeguard the trust inherent to the approach, and to reinforce the appropriateness of the approach, the strategy must be supported using the latent threat of large civil or criminal sanctions. Publicity strategies would be highly effective too since poor publicity would be particularly damaging to these firms.

The final system of firms is benevolent giants whose business model is driven by ethics. A good example is Grameen Bank, an organization that has reversed conventional banking practice and which adopts the premise that credit is a human right and not a privilege and in doing so has facilitated the lifting of poverty for many people. That there are very few benevolent giants suggests they find it difficult to compete in many markets due to cost disparities and the ability of competitors to mimic their approach. Where they do operate the regulator should reward such behaviour through the use of reflexive mechanisms. This is likely to include the acceptance of compliance conformance using self-reporting mechanisms and, where appropriate, a reduction of the business burden more generally.

In summary, the resource-based model of responsive regulation seeks to reallocate resources to where they are most required. By linking strategies to the orientations of firms we can make regulation more responsive in many ways. The most obvious way is to move scarce inspection resources from those firms with the resources to be most compliant to those that are deliberately non-compliant or find compliance demanding. It also enables society to reward positive behaviour through incentive schemes such as self-reporting, reduced business burdens and positive publicity. Although space limits a fuller exploration of these compliance systems, the intention has been to show that it is possible to target regulatory instruments and the mechanisms for their delivery to improve the regulatory compliance of all firms.

Discussion

The argument that regulatory strategies can be more effective if properly aligned to the response capacity of firms is challenging because it undermines contemporary practices. Yet if we accept that the state has limited resources and lacks the capacity to regulate in all contexts, and that the enormity of modern-day environmental challenges requires us to rethink how we can improve the environmental performance of firms, then it is incumbent on us to do so. To do this we need to understand the contexts in which different forms of regulation will work since there is no basis to assume that regulation will work the same way in different settings. In demonstrating this it was shown that the way a firm responds to regulation is influenced by a complex set of factors that are associated with the compliance capacity and compliance orientation of the firm. Thus the resource and visibility differences between large firms and SMEs were shown to materially affect their ability and willingness to respond to different forms of regulation – even with the caveat that firm size is a blunt measure of organizational differences.

Notwithstanding the potential problems of using the composite measure that firm size represents, there is ample evidence that it can help determine appropriate strategies. For instance, there is little doubt that larger firms have greater incentives and capacities than smaller firms to comply with and go beyond legal requirements. By recognizing this and amending regulatory strategies accordingly we are simply contextualizing regulation to relevant circumstances. The proposed approach also has the advantage of increasing the totality of the regulatory resource by channelling state, civil society and industry resources to the most suitable regulatory output, rather than as now which is largely to the same regulatory object. Given the potential benefit of this approach it is important that disquiet over claims that large firms would be treated more leniently than smaller firms are addressed. Therefore – and at the expense of being repetitive – we reiterate that the resource-based model does not in any way seek deregulation. In reality the opposite is true since the intention is to improve the compliance profiles of all firms by correctly aligning regulatory strategies.

This intention builds upon the view that there are different types of firms but that groups of firms share sufficient commonality to comprise distinct systems of firms with system-specific compliance orientations and response capacities. So, to operationalize the resource-based approach we must individualize regulation to the extent that system-level strategies *build on* universal rules and, where appropriate, specific risk-based requirements. By this we mean that it is appropriate for all firms to meet certain key minimum requirements such as a 'duty of care' (e.g. simple and general obligations that specify common and minimum standards), and that there need to be targeted obligations which affect those firms that pose a specific risk (e.g. permitting requirements for chemical firms). The strategies shown in Figure 6.3 incorporate these approaches

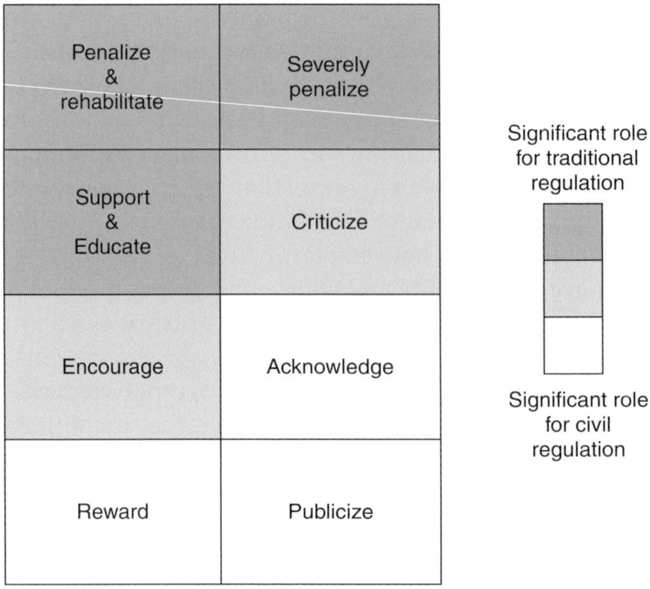

Figure 6.3 Regulatory strategies

and at the same time show how rules can be most appropriately enforced and 'beyond compliance' behaviour most appropriately encouraged.

Although these regulatory strategies can only be sketched out in this chapter, it is important to note that they require consideration of three issues: the regulatory instruments firms need to comply with, the methods for supporting compliance with these mechanisms, and the enforcement approaches should non-compliance occur. Before these are briefly outlined it is however necessary that we consider the implications arising from the need for universal rules (e.g. the waste duty of care) and risk-based approaches (e.g. integrated permitting). The waste duty of care provision, a measure for ensuring safe and proper disposal of waste, is relatively uncomplicated and applies across firms. For delinquent firms, the response to this requirement is likely to involve evading the costs and procedures associated with safe disposal by fly-tipping. In contrast, vulnerable satisfiers will try to comply but will minimize their compliance effort by using a designated waste contractor. It is likely that neither delinquents nor vulnerable satisfiers will have a total appreciation of the full nature of the duty, but the act of purposely disregarding the measure compared to using a legitimate contractor is unquestionably material. It demonstrates that although the same rules apply to both systems of firms, the approach for ensuring compliance should be differentiated. For delinquents, this may require them to be watched, penalized and, it is hoped, rehabilitated while for vulnerable satisfiers it may involve support and education to ensure continued compliance. Equally, if major strategic players recklessly fail to comply with the duty, then we would expect a more severe sanction than if they had genuinely tried to comply. This illustrates that, notwithstanding the need to particularize regulatory strategies as shown in Figure 6.3, there is a further need to particularize the methods used to support compliance and enforcement when there are breaches of universal rules, and on the basis of the same logic, for rules based on risk. Thus universal environmental permitting regimes should remain but the regulatory compliance strategy should be different for different systems of firms (e.g. for smaller firms the support strategy may need to be different than that for larger firms).

With this in mind it is clear that different systems of firms require different approaches. Extending this line of thinking for each of the eight systems enables us to construct a picture of how a resource-based model of responsive regulation would work in practice. For larger firms at the top right-hand side of Figure 6.3 this may include mandatory self-reporting, while for large firms at the bottom right side it may focus on encouraged self-reporting. Both approaches are reflexive in character and can be operationalized through the requirements of accredited environmental management systems. Importantly, this is a viable strategy as large firms have the resources to implement such systems. Also, if the information from self-reports is made available to the widest possible audience, then there is the added possibility that we can enhance the power and effectiveness of civil society oversight. If large firms decide to abuse the trust embodied in self-reporting, then they should, as previously discussed, be heavily penalized.

For smaller firms on the left-hand side of Figure 6.3 there is a general need for simple rules. This facilitates compliance because it takes account of the fact that they possess fewer resources than larger firms and that the compliance requirement should therefore be proportionally easier to demonstrate. On this basis it makes little sense to require smaller firms to implement an environmental management system. If they voluntarily do adopt such systems – minor strategic players and altruistic citizens may do – then this should of course be acknowledged and used to demonstrate compliance. However, for most small firms the lack of available resources is compounded by the lack of stakeholder (and wider civil society) pressure for reflexive behaviour, which itself further undermines the case for using reflexive instruments. This dependency on context applies to enforcement too, since it makes no sense to treat systems as equivalent in all respects.

The view that there are systems of firms and that these systems are distinct, and that they are required to comply with common and different rules, is the essential point being made in this chapter. In doing so, the aim has been to accommodate differences in regulatory response capabilities through a better alignment of regulatory tools and compliance strategies. This demonstrates that extant policy approaches, and indeed responsive regulatory theory, does not take full or proper cognizance of the differences between firms and of regulatory mechanisms. By doing so it is possible to show that substantive law can underpin reflexive approaches and that government can underpin civil regulatory approaches. The model therefore supports both the idea that the state is not the sole locus of authority (Black 2008) and that there is a place for tit-for-tat responsive regulation (Ayres and Braithwaite 1992). Yet it also shows that we should not adopt a self-regulatory strategy for all systems of firms or that we should assume a common receptivity to regulation and compliance across firms. Fortunately, the world we inhabit is more interesting and complicated than this.

We have developed and illustrated our argument in relation to environmental regulation targeted at private sector business but it clearly has wider implications, including for criminal justice matters. For example, questions concerning differential capacity to respond to regulation lie at the heart of current debates about strategies for tackling antisocial behaviour, where efforts to (re-)build the capacity of individuals or families to behave 'properly' are central to some of the new initiatives (see Flint and Hunter, this book, Chapter 8). The issue of 'visibility', and the consequences for regulatory compliance, is also relevant when thinking about the regulation of criminal justice agencies such as the police and prisons, where the fear of 'bad publicity' can be a powerful motivator for compliance (see: Owers, this book, Chapter 10; Seddon, this book, Chapter 11). We believe, then, that our extension of the idea of responsiveness and receptivity has significant implications for regulatory strategies across many different sites and fields far beyond environmental protection. Indeed, it opens up a challenging new research agenda for both regulation and criminal justice scholars.

References

Arora, S. and Cason, T. (1996) 'Why Do Firms Volunteer to Exceed Environmental Regulations? Understanding Participation in EPA's 3/50 Program', *Land Economics*, **72**(4), 413–32.

Ayres, I. and Braithwaite, J. (1992) *Responsive Regulation*. Oxford University Press.

Baldwin, R. and Black, J. (2008) 'Really Responsive Regulation', *Modern Law Review*, **71**(1), 59–94.

Bansal, P. and Roth, K. (2000) 'Why Companies Go Green: A Model of Ecological Responsiveness', *Academy of Management Journal*, **43**(4), 717–36.

Barney, J. (1991) 'Firm Resources and Sustained Competitive Advantage', *Journal of Management*, **17**(1), 33–46.

Baylis, R., Connell, L. and Flynn, A. (1998) 'Company Size, Environmental Regulation and Ecological Modernization: Further Analysis at the Level of the Firm', *Business Strategy and the Environment*, **7**(5), 285–96.

Black, J. (2008) 'Constructing and Contesting Legitimacy and Accountability in Polycentric Regulatory Regimes', *Regulation and Governance*, **2**, 137–64.

Bowen, F. (2002) 'Does Size Matter? Organizational Slack and Visibility as Alternative Explanations for Environmental Responsiveness', *Business and Society*, **41**(1), 118–24.

DiMaggio, P. and Powell, W. (1991) 'The Iron Cage Revisited: Institutional Isomorphism and Collective Rationality', in W. Powell and P. DiMaggio (eds.), *The Institutionalism in Organizational Analysis*. University of Chicago Press, pp. 63–82.

Dowling, J. and Pfeffer, J. (1975) 'Organizational Legitimacy: Social Values and Organizational Behavior', *Pacific Sociological Review*, **18**(1), 122–36.

Earthworks and Oxfam America (2004) *Dirty Metals: Mining, Communities and the Environment*.

ENDS Report (2009) 'BP to Pay $179m to settle Texas Pollution Case'. Report 410, March, pp. 67–8.

Environment Agency (2007) 'Spotlight on Business: Environmental Performance in 2006' (at: http://publications.environment-agency.gov.uk/pdf/GEHO0707BMMX-e-e.pdf).

Fiorino, D. (2006) *The New Environmental Regulation*. Cambridge, MA: MIT Press.

Freeman, R. (1984) *Strategic Management: A Stakeholder Approach*. Boston, MA: Pitman.

Gerstenfeld, A. and Roberts, H. (2000) 'Size Matters: Barriers and Prospects for Environmental Management in Small and Medium-Sized Enterprises', in R. Hillary (ed.), *Small and Medium-sized Enterprises and the Environment: Business Imperatives*. Sheffield: Greenleaf Publishing Limited.

Graafland, J. and Smid, H. (2004) 'Reputation, Corporate Social Responsibility and Market Regulation', *Tijdchrift voor Economie en Management*, **49**(2), 271–308.

Greening, D. and Gray, B. (1994) 'Testing a Model of Organizational Response to Social and Political Issues', *Academy of Management Journal*, **37**(3), 467–98.

Gunningham, N. (2009) 'Environment Law, Regulation and Governance: Shifting Architectures', *Journal of Environmental Law*, **21**(2), 179–212.

Gunningham, N. and Grabosky P. (1998) *Smart Regulation: Designing Environmental Policy*. Oxford University Press.

Gunningham, N., Kagan, R. and Thornton, D. (2004) 'Social License and Environmental Protection: Why Businesses Go Beyond Compliance', *Law and Social Inquiry*, 29(4), 307–41.

Gunningham, N. and Rees, J. (1997) 'Industry Self-regulation: An Institutional Perspective', *Law and Policy*, **19**, 363–414.

Gunningham, N. and Sinclair, D. (2002) *Leaders and Laggards: Next Generation Environmental Regulation*. Sheffield: Greenleaf Publishing Limited.

Habermas, J. (1979) *Communication and the Evolution of Society*. London: Heinemann.

(1984) *The Theory of Communicative Action. Vol. 1, Reason and the Rationalization of Society*, trans. T. McCarthy. Boston, MA: Beacon.

(1987). *The Theory of Communicative Action. Vol. 2, Lifeworld and System: A Critique of Functionalist Reason*, trans. T. McCarthy. Boston, MA: Beacon.

(1996). *Between Facts and Norms*. Cambridge: Polity Press.

Hajer, M. (1995) *The Politics of Environmental Discourse: Ecological Modernisation and the Policy Process*. Oxford: Clarendon Press.

Hitchens, D., Clausen, J., Trainor, M. and Thankappan, S. (2004) 'Competitiveness, Environmental Performance and Management of SMEs', *Greener Management International*, **44**, 45–57.

Hitchens, D., Thankappan, S., Trainor, M., Clausen, J. and de Marchi, B. (2005) 'Environmental Performance, Competitiveness and Management of Small Businesses in Europe', *Tijdschrift voor Economische en Sociale Geografie*, **96**(5), 541–57.

Hutchinson, A. and Chaston, I. (1994) 'Environmental Management in Devon and Cornwall's Small and Medium Sized Enterprise Sector', *Business Strategy and the Environment*, **3**(1), 15–22.

Hutter, B. and Jones, C. (2007) 'From Government to Governance: External Influences on Business Risk Management', *Regulation and Governance*, **1**, 27–45.

Jänicke, M. (2008) 'Ecological Modernisation: New Perspective', *Journal of Cleaner Production*, **16**, 557–65.

Johnson, G. (1988) 'Re-thinking Incrementalism', *Strategic Management Journal* **9**, 75–91.

Judge, W. and Douglas, T. (1998) 'Performance Implications of Incorporating Natural Environmental Issues into the Strategic Planning Process: An Empirical Assessment', *Journal of Management Studies*, **35**(2), 241–62.

Kagan, R. and Scholz, J. (1984) 'The "Criminology of the Corporation" and Regulatory Enforcement Strategies', in K. Hawkins and J. Thomas (eds.), *Enforcing Regulation*. Boston, MA: Kluwer-Nijhoff.

Lewicki, R., Saunders, D. and Minton, J. (1999) *Negotiation*. New York, NY: McGraw-Hill.

Luhmann, N. (1982). *The Differentiation of Society*. New York, NY: Columbia University Press.

(1989) *Ecological Communication*. Cambridge: Polity Press.

(1993) *Risk – A Sociological Theory*. New York, NY: De Gruyter.

(1995) *Social Systems*. Stanford University Press.

Lynch-Wood, G. and Williamson, D. (2007) 'The Social Licence as a Form of Regulation for Small and Medium Enterprises', *Journal of Law and Society*, **34**(3), 321–41.

Marshall, R., Cordano, M. and Silverman, M. (2005) 'Exploring Individual and Institutional Drivers of Proactive Environmentalism in the US Wine Industry', *Business Strategy and the Environment*, **14**(2), 92–109.

Marshall Report (1998) 'Economic Instruments and the Business Use of Energy'. Report to Chancellor of the Exchequer. London: HM Treasury.

Maurer, J. (1971) *Readings in Organization Theory: Open-System Approaches*. New York, NY: Random House.

Michaelas, M., Chittenden, F. and Poutziouris, P. (1999) 'Financial Policy and Capital Structure Choice in UK SMEs: Empirical Evidence from Company Panel Data', *Small Business Economics*, **12**(2), 113–30.

Mintzberg, H. and Waters, J. (1985) 'Of Strategies, Deliberate and Emergent', *Strategic Management Journal*, **6**(3), 257–72.

Mol, A. (1997) 'Ecological Modernisation: Industrial Transformations and Environmental Reform', in M. Redclift and G. Woodgate (eds.), *The International Handbook of Environmental Sociology*. Cheltenham, Glos: Edward Elgar Publishing Ltd, pp. 138–49.

NetRegs (2006) *SME-nvironment 2006*. Bristol: Environment Agency.

Nonet, P. and Selznick, P. (1978) *Towards Responsive Law: Law and Society in Transition*, repr. 2001. New Brunswick, NJ: Transaction Publishers.

Nooteboom, B. (1994) 'Innovation and Diffusion in Small Firms: Theories and Evidence', *Small Business Economics*, **6**(5), 327–47.

Orts, E. (1995) 'Reflexive Environmental Law', *Northwestern University Law Review*, **89**(4), 1227.

Owens, A. (2002) 'Inheritance and the Life-Cycle of Family Firms in the Early Industrial Revolution', *Business History*, **44**(1), 21–46.

Peteraf, M. (1993) 'The Cornerstones of Competitive Advantage: A Resource-Based View', *Strategic Management Journal*, **14**, 179–88.

Petersen, M. and Rajan, R. (1994) 'The Benefits of Lending Relationships: Evidence from Small Business Data', *Journal of Finance*, **49**(1), 3–37.

Pettigrew, A. (1992) 'Fundamental Themes in Strategy Process Research', *Strategic Management Journal*, **13**, 163–82.

Petts, J., Herd, A., Gerrard, S. and Horne, C. (1999) 'The Climate and Culture of Environmental Compliance within SMEs', *Business Strategy and the Environment*, **8**, 14–30.

Porter, M. and van der Linde, C. (1995) 'Green and Competitive', *Harvard Business Review*, September–October, 120–34.

Revell, A. and Blackburn, R. (2004) 'SMEs and Their Response to Environmental Issues in the UK'. Kingston University, London: Small Business Research Centre.

Rowe, J. and Enticott, R. (1998) 'Evaluating the Links between Locality and Environmental Performance of SMEs: Some Observations from Survey and Partnership Programmes in the Greater Bristol Area', *Eco-Management and Auditing*, **5**(3), 112–25.

Russo, M and Fouts, P. (1997) 'A Resource-Based Perspective on Corporate Environmental Performance and Profitability', *Academy of Management Journal* **40**(3), 534–59.

Scherer, F. and Ross, D. (1990) *Industrial Market Structure and Economic Performance*. Boston, MA: Houghton Mifflin.

Smith, M. and Kemp, R. (1998) *Small Firms and the Environment 1998: A Groundwork Report*. Birmingham: Groundwork.

Spence, L., Jeurissen, R. and Rutherfoord, R. (2000) 'Small Business and the Environment in the UK and the Netherlands: Towards Stakeholder Co-operation', *Business Ethics Quarterly*, **10**(4), 945–66.

Suchman, M. (1995) 'Managing Legitimacy: Strategic and Institutional Approaches', *Academy of Management Review*, **20**(3), 571–610.

Teubner, G. (1983) 'Substantive and Reflexive Elements in Modern Law', *Law and Society Review* **17**, 253–4.

Vogel, D. (2005) *The Market for Virtue: The Potential and Limits of Corporate Social Responsibility*. Washington, DC: Brookings Institution Press.

Weale, A. (1992) *The New Politics of the Environment*. Manchester University Press.

Webb, B. and Marshall, B. (2004) *A Problem-Oriented Approach to Fly-Tipping*. London: Jill Dando Institute of Crime Science, University College London.

Weber, J. and Wasieleski, D. (2003) 'Managing Corporate Stakeholders: Subjecting Miles's 1987 Data-Collection Framework to Tests of Validation', *Journal of Corporate Citizenship*, **9**(1), 133–53.

Williamson, D. and Lynch-Wood, G. (2001) 'A New Paradigm for SME Environmental Practice', *International Journal of Total Quality Management*, **13**(6), 424–32.

Williamson, D., Lynch-Wood, G. and Ramsay, J. (2006) 'Drivers of Environmental Behaviour in Manufacturing SMEs and the Implications for CSR', *Journal of Business Ethics* **67**, 317–30.

Wood, D. (1991) 'Corporate Social Performance Revisited', *Academy of Management Review*, **16**(4), 691–718.

Worthington, I. and Patton, D. (2003) 'Researching the Drivers of SME Environmental Behaviour: A Study of the UK Screen-printing Sector', *Business Strategy and the Environment*, **12**(5), 352–62.

(2005) 'Strategic Intent in the Management of the Green Environment within SMEs: An Analysis of the UK Screen-printing Sector', *Long Range Planning*, **38**, 197–212.

7

An intoxicated politics of regulation

DAVID WHYTE*

Introduction

The preceding chapter by Lynch-Wood and Williamson presents a case for something that has become known as 'responsive' regulation. On one hand, their chapter rehearses a series of well-worn arguments that connect to an established hegemony of thought around regulation. On the other hand, the chapter represents an attempt to explore how 'responsive' regulatory strategies might be modified to take account of Small and Medium Enterprises (SMEs). In doing so, the authors raise some key and under-explored issues, particularly in relation to how the law-abiding tendencies of firms are mediated by size. In so far as those arguments appear on the face of things to offer a corrective to business-lobby driven appeals for regulatory withdrawal from SMEs, this is an interesting contribution. Moreover, the size of a firm has a crucially important bearing upon the visibility of its offending and the ability of regulators to respond, and therefore the authors open up some important territory here. This chapter argues that however well intentioned their analysis is in terms of its attempt to place SMEs under greater scrutiny, at best it ends up presenting a naive and oversimplified understanding of the regulatory process, and at worst, is likely to provide support to the intensification of regulatory disengagement that has characterized UK government policy in recent years.

This chapter begins by theoretically locating their analysis. It then explores how their theoretical approach leads them to make some major

* I am grateful to the participants in the ESRC seminar series from which this book was produced for critical discussion of some of the arguments set out here. This chapter owes a particular debt to Steve Tombs, drawing as it does upon my ongoing research collaborations with him on the politics of regulation. I also owe a debt of gratitude to Joel Stern and Nick Johnston at the Environment Agency who responded to my requests for unpublished data with the utmost courtesy and professionalism.

assumptions about the nature of corporations and shapes their conservative cynicism about the potential for regulatory intervention. The chapter then explores how the pluralist position that we find in their work – and more generally in the mainstream of academic discourse – is derived from, and reinforces, the politics of regulation that we find at the heart of government. The chapter then argues that the pluralist approach of Lynch-Wood and Williamson is both compatible with, and easily translates as an intellectual support for, the neo-liberal regulatory strategy that it purports to critique.

Theoretical approaches to regulation

Pluralist approaches to the problem of regulation dominate the academic literature. The pluralist model is based upon the idea that power in modern social orders is dispersed rather than concentrated and that a variety of interests can be mobilized to influence the formal political agenda. It is through the mobilization of those interests that changes in the social order are made possible (see Pearce 1976: 38–41). Pluralist approaches support 'compliance' (Pearce and Tombs 1991) or 'consensus' (Whyte 2004) models which advocate regulation by mutual agreement between and within competing interests. Thus, pluralists seek to reconcile opposed interests (for example the interests of polluters and polluted communities) by negotiation, or a process of bargaining between those interests. This process of consensus building is normally achieved through a combination of institutional mechanisms, formal and informal political channels and/or regulatory agencies.

A key feature of pluralist approaches to regulation in recent years has been the consolidation of the idea that corporations can potentially act as good citizens; that it is possible for corporations to act with a *moral* rationale, rather than an economic or operational rationale. On one hand, this assumption depends upon the idea of corporate social responsibility; that it is possible for corporations to construct a set of goals that are distinct from organizational goals of survival or success. On the other hand, it depends upon the idea that corporations are capable of acting according to human values – and that corporations are capable of using those human values to suppress other organizational, political and legal responsibilities. Once those assumptions are accepted, it then becomes feasible to differentiate between different corporations or businesses based upon their ability to act as 'good' citizens or not. It is this, pluralist, perspective, then, that allows us to differentiate between 'good' and 'bad' business; or, put differently, businesses that are compliance-oriented and those that are not. Indeed separating the 'good' from the 'bad' using ever more sophisticated risk assessment techniques and compliance indicators is increasingly viewed, from a pluralist perspective, as the core purpose of regulation (Tombs and Whyte 2006). It is the search for the corporate good citizen that enables pluralist theorists to promote the voluntary compliance of business (or 'self-regulation') as a utopian outcome of regulatory systems.

The utopian concept of the 'citizen corporation' is rejected by neo-liberal theorists who seek to remove all moral content from the realm of the economy. Thus, the seminal neo-liberal position is that the only responsibility of business is to make profits (Friedman 1973). Despite this key difference, variations of regulatory pluralism have in recent years found some common ground with neo-liberal approaches to the study of the regulatory process. The neo-liberal perspective generally draws upon the assumption that we are over-regulated, and that this is a negative consequence of overbearing government since regulation ultimately stifles business performance and efficiency. For neo-liberals, 'red tape' and 'burdens on business' are symbolic terms that represent the obstacles to profit accumulation. Market mechanisms are more appropriate – and certainly more efficient – for allocating resources and exerting control on participants in markets than governments. Neo-liberals are in principle opposed to legal interventions by the state. In practice, however, few neo-liberals would argue for a *complete* withdrawal of regulatory functions in respect of minimal levels of worker and public protection, not least since it is clear that no economic system can function without various forms of state support (Tombs and Whyte 2007, 2009a).

Where pluralist and neo-liberal approaches converge is in their acceptance of market mechanisms of regulation. For pluralists, the potential of resolution through the locating of common interests is always within grasp while at the same time reserving for egregious if rare cases of non-compliance a capacity for law enforcement. Pluralists favour market-based systems of regulation because they view capitalist social orders as based upon competing interests that can be mutually satisfied through a range of mechanisms. For neo-liberals, optimal regulatory outcomes are achieved through the market, so that the sanctions for non-compliant firms should emanate not from the criminal law but from the laws of supply and demand. Thus, instead of a system of inspection and investigation leading to a range of punitive and non-punitive regulatory resorts, firms which perform poorly in respect of occupational safety experience are likely to suffer problems of labour supply, or consumer demand via reputation loss. Third-party regulation is to be achieved by a mix of 'invisible hand' market mechanisms and civil legal systems of compensation where it is down to private individuals themselves (or groups of private individuals) to seek redress for corporate wrongs in the courts.

From those different perspectives, pluralists and neo-liberals promote 'self-regulation' or 'voluntarism' as a panacea to the range of dilemmas posed by regulating corporations in neo-liberal economies. Thus, whether wittingly or not, both pluralist and neo-liberal approaches to regulation provide a closely coherent theoretical justification for self-regulatory or voluntarist strategies of regulation that currently dominate in capitalist economies. Self-regulation approaches seek to ensure that businesses regulate their own level of legal compliance, and often make claims to being able to encourage businesses to move beyond compliance with a set of legal minima and to develop proactively higher environmental standards. This is to be achieved not through proscriptive regulation and enforcement, but through a range of 'mechanisms' and 'levers' that cohere closely to other organizational goals (long-term success, sustainability, and so on).

The potential of self-regulation, is explored on the bases that state regulators will never have the resources to enforce regulatory law effectively, and that internal regulators enjoy certain technical and social advantages over those on the outside (Braithwaite and Fisse 1987). In most accounts, self-regulation is represented as a process that moves through a series of 'trial and error' stages. Where self-regulation proves ineffective, the next preferred regulatory tactic is to move to 'enforced self-regulation', a more invasive approach which requires a firm to develop a tailored set of rules by which it intends to comply with law. Once this set of rules is approved by external regulators, they can then be 'enforced' internally; where evidence of non-compliance emerges, the potential of (punitive) intervention by an external regulator remains (Ayres and Braithwaite 1992: 102–16).

Counter-arguments to 'self-regulation' and 'voluntarism' propose that making regulated parties responsible for their own compliance, no matter how sophisticated the levers or mechanisms, heightens the potential for regulatory degradation. If government withdraws from regulatory enforcement – making it less likely that workplaces will be inspected, less likely that inspections will result in enforcement, less likely that enforcement is of the more rather than less punitive type – then this creates greater opportunities for non-compliance. This is not by any means to argue that intervention by regulatory agencies is the only guarantor of compliance, but it is to recognize that regulatory intervention remains key to incentivizing compliance.

Few would disagree that in capitalist societies, governments tend to act in ways that promote dominant business interests above other interests. Indeed, this point is recognized to some extent by both pluralists and neo-liberals. The pluralist position tends to recognize that regulatory settlements often favour larger business concerns. But for pluralists, instances of this tendency are explained by corruption of regulatory systems, or by a pathological flaw in the normal function of liberal democracies, rather than being understood as a systematic feature of capitalist societies. In neo-liberal theory, over-concentration of power in the hands of (monopoly) business elites is a problem that can be blamed upon overbearing state intervention in market activity; the product of this corruption, the monopoly corporation, also represents a fundamental threat to market democracy. Although there is no consensus about the origins of this embedded bias or the extent to which it can be treated as some kind of iron law of regulation, one point that most analyses of regulation recognize (albeit to varying degrees) is that *state regulation has a tendency to favour big-business interests.*

The starting point for critical legal and neo-Marxist approaches to understanding this embedded bias in law is a recognition that regulation is shaped by *antagonistic* struggles within interest groups (for example, struggles between different sections of business) and between interest groups (for example, between polluters and polluted communities). Theorists adopting a critical perspective argue that those antagonistic interests cannot be easily resolved by consensual agreement; indeed, one feature of capitalist social orders is that such conflicts of interest can never be fully resolved. In contradistinction to the perspectives outlined above, then, it is more accurate to think about *dissensus* rather than *consensus* as the driving force behind the politics of regulation (Snider 1991: 211).

Legal arenas are, from this perspective, always conceived of as sites of struggle and conflict. This is an important point for understanding the function of regulatory agencies. For, regulatory agencies do not determine regulatory outcomes in an instrumental or mechanistic fashion; regulation is not something that regulatory agencies 'do' to regulated parties. Rather, they act in ways that mediate ongoing conflict and dissensus. In comparison to other government institutions, regulatory agencies are 'special cases' (Mahon 1979) that are charged with absorbing and dissipating those struggles between and within social groups. The role of regulatory agencies is to arrange 'compromises which reflect the specific combinations of the demands of "rebels", the "regulated" and the hegemonic fraction' (*ibid.*: 159). In contrast to the pluralist approach, regulatory agencies are not sites where competing interests can be mutually resolved, but are '*unequal* structures of representation' (*ibid.*: 154, my emphasis). For Mahon, the function of regulatory agencies is clear: to reach a form of compromise which does not undermine the basic structure of unequal representation that we find in the institutional arrangements that govern late capitalist states.

This section has mapped out some of the commonalities and differences across differing perspectives on regulation. It has done this in order to show that there are a range of theoretical starting points that researchers take when embarking upon research into regulation, and that researchers make choices about the theoretical perspectives they adopt (even if generally they are not explicit about the perspectives that underpin their work). For the purposes of the critique that follows, we can use this theoretical frame to locate the orientation of the contribution by Lynch-Wood and Williamson.

The hegemony of pluralist analysis

It is clear from a series of statements they make at the outset of the chapter that Lynch-Wood and Williamson's approach has resonance with the pluralist tradition. Thus, they make the assertion that the 'moral orientation' of a firm combines with its resources and the visibility of its activities to produce compliance. Indeed this process of securing compliance must be understood within a system of regulation that should not only be seeking to reduce impacts of pollution but, at the same time, can stimulate innovation to create 'cleaner' production techniques. Here, regulation is seen as a rational process to reduce the harms created by a range of autonomous businesses. Environmental regulation is thus understood essentially as a reactionary process: an 'impact' arises from a particular set of business activities and then an appropriate regulatory response follows. At the same time, regulation is asserted as a means of securing, seamlessly, and without conflict, economic development on one hand, and the 'greening' of business on the other. Thus, according to Lynch-Wood and Williamson, consensus styles of regulation need to encourage 'deep' organizational change that is compatible with the profit-oriented goals of firms: 'there has arisen the view that environmental solutions are only really addressable if they are integrated into the capitalist system itself'. However laudable this view may be, there are two key problems here. First, there is no indication of exactly how those hitherto contradictory (but now compatible) aims might be secured. Second, although this is presented as a 'new' claim, in fact it is precisely the same claim that has been made for some time by the corporate social responsibility movement and has been convincingly discredited by commentators from a range of theoretical and political positions (see for example, Friedman 1973; Glasbeek 1988; Lubbers 2002; Fauset 2006, Christian Aid n.d.).

Locating their analysis in a Luhmann-influenced legal systems theory, the authors assume a mutually reinforcing relationship between self-regulation and an autopoietic concept of reflexive law, although they leave this assumption undeveloped and unexplained. We can surmise, however, that this way of thinking projects a view of regulation as a relatively self-referential system which is sustained by the logics and practices that exist in the regulatory relationship between regulator and regulated, and by the logics and practices of law and institutional enforcement mechanisms. Thus, regulatory systems are understood as having an autonomous, self-referential capacity to reach regulatory settlements. This is an interesting point in itself, and one which powerfully explains the extent to which regulation has been institutionally delineated and the extent to which regulatory logics and practices are self-perpetuating and self-fulfilling. Yet in their haste to reduce Luhmann's theory of autopoiesis to a principle of regulatory autonomy, those complex features of the regulatory landscape are too easily oversimplified by the authors. The concept of autopoiesis ends up being used rather crudely to support an argument for self-regulation.

The self-referential capacities alluded to by Lynch-Wood and Williamson, essentially a combination of self-regulation mechanisms, and regulation by third-party stakeholder groups, are crudely juxtaposed with regulation by 'rules' and 'law'. Thus, civil society groups (such as consumer groups and NGOs) are very easily delineated from the world of 'law' and 'regulation' and seen merely as competing sources of regulation. This (pluralist) position paints a highly idealized picture of the relationship between the regulated party and the regulator. From this perspective, both 'regulation' and the 'impacts' of pollution are seen as external to each other, existing in separate worlds, with an independent (as opposed to an interdependent) existence.

If, however, we see regulation as a broader process that sets the parameters and develops rules, practices and norms for organizing regimes of production and consumption – both inside and outside the factory gate – then we have to view the regulatory process and the 'impacts' of production as inextricably linked. The impacts of pollution, just as every other feature of production, are generated within sets of parameters set by the regulatory regime. When government agencies license businesses to pollute at a particular level, they set the regulatory parameters that allow business to generate environmental impacts; and when governments give planning permission and provide transport and communications infrastructure to allow production facilities to locate in particular places, they also set the regulatory parameters that allow business to generate environmental impacts. In this sense, then, 'regulation' is an ongoing relationship that both creates the potential for harm to be produced and acts to set limits on the harms that are produced out of the regulatory relationship. Civil society groups – trade unions and workers organizations, local residents groups, environmental NGOs and trade associations – have an ongoing role in struggling for, and seeking resolution through precisely the same regulatory process. In other words, it makes no sense to present systems of 'government regulation' on one hand and 'self-referential' as ontologically distinct on the other.

The importance of seeing regulation as part of a broader process that involves mobilizing the efforts and resources of government to support business activity is that it prevents us foreclosing questions about the possibility of regulatory intervention. Regulation is not the sum total of its 'command and control' capacities. Neither is 'regulation' a linear, 'power-over' mechanism that involves an autonomous government agency acting to limit the activities of a set of (external) autonomous business actors. Viewed as the sum total of the administrative remit of a given regulatory agency, its physical resources, and the political constraints imposed upon the agency, the possibilities for regulation appear highly limited. Viewed as an ongoing relationship that both creates the potential for harm to be produced and acts to set limits on the harms that are produced from the regulatory relationship, 'regulation' appear as a much more open-ended and contingent field in which the possibilities for changing the basis of regulation are expansive.

It is this feature of pluralist analyses – a concept of regulation that is practically limited by the particular form that a given regulatory agency takes – that forecloses questions that a less self-constrained academic investigation might ask. A wider set of questions that is not delineated by administrative remit or available regulatory resources might include: what is it about the policing of environmental offences (most of which fall squarely within the criminal law) that makes them 'different' from other types of offending? Why do we 'regulate' and not 'police' environmental crimes? Why are crimes against the environment rarely prosecuted in comparison to interpersonal crimes? Now some of those questions are clearly related to the historical development of different bodies of law, and some are related to the historical development of administrative bureaucracies in different contexts.

To ask such questions is to raise broader possibilities about how we approach regulation. To ignore such questions is to allow academic inquiry to be structured by whatever political or administrative arrangements are in place at any given time. Its containment within this limited ontological terrain – combined with a preoccupation on the formal, visible, liberal political mechanisms – is why research based upon a pluralist approach is unable to offer a critique of the form that regulation takes in a given social formation. It also allows us to understand how pluralist analyses are inclined to provide hegemonic support to the political formation from which they derive their organizing categories.

Regulatory defeatism

A measure of the hegemonic 'capture' that shapes the analysis by Lynch-Wood and Williamson is their unquestioning acceptance of the administrative status quo. Thus, their starting point in the chapter is that regulators have only limited resources to address the environmental performance of firms. Now this point cannot be disputed. But what is important is where the argument leads from taking this as the starting point.

A critical approach to the administrative arrangements that are established for dealing with environmental offences in the UK does not have to go far in its analysis to uncover some undeniably stark contrasts. The Environment Agency (EA) in England and Wales has a wider remit than perhaps any other regulatory agency and yet has barely more than 1,550 front-line officers involved in regulatory enforcement.[1] This compares to approximately 15,000 new Police Community Safety Officers introduced in England and Wales in the past six years. Now, there clearly is an imbalance of resources here.

[1] There are currently approximately 1550 warrant holders undertaking enforcement activity. Staff who carry a warrant have powers of entry and are authorized under the various Acts governing environmental enforcement (personal correspondence with Environment Agency Planning and Performance Team, 30th September 2009).

The EA barely prosecutes more than 700 offences a year. In the current political climate, there is downward pressure on all regulatory resources, but particularly on resources for enforcement. In this political context, the chances of the EA maintaining existing levels of enforcement are slim. As Walters (2009: 7) notes, 'The ratio of licensed sites to Environment Agency inspectors is such that regulation relies upon operators to report incidents that breach or affect authorisation.' Yet at no point do Lynch-Wood and Williamson raise the possibility that the paltry resources available to the EA might be insufficient to ensure compliance in any meaningful sense, no matter how it is targeted. Or that when understood in the context of the wider criminal justice system, a doubling or tripling of EA front-line inspectors would actually represent a relatively small shift in resources (as the figure on Police Community Safety Officers cited above indicates). It is this failure to question the administrative status quo that, as we will see below, leads them to advocate a particular form of targeted intervention.

A recognition of the 'realities' of regulatory enforcement that does not ask wider questions about the way that we prioritize particular forms of offending for state intervention, or about the resources that are readily available for other forms of policing forecloses the questions raised on the previous page. Regulatory agencies have always had to work within a framework of resources that is not remotely comparable with other law enforcement agencies. And resignation by academics and other commentators to this position has certainly been made more likely by the concerted attack on the regulation of environmental offending, and other forms of corporate crime that has unfolded in recent years (Tombs and Whyte 2008).

Regulatory degradation

It is not the intention of this chapter to suggest that Lynch-Wood and Williamson are politically motivated in their analysis, rather that there is a point of convergence here between their analysis and the unfolding regulatory climate. If for a moment we pause to examine what has been going on in regulatory policy in the past decade or so, it becomes very clear that this political climate bears directly upon the questions that are being asked by researchers and the starting point for exploring the dilemma of 'regulation'.

A key moment in recent UK regulatory politics came in March 2004, when the Treasury under Gordon Brown established the Hampton

Review to 'consider the scope for reducing administrative burdens on business by promoting more efficient approaches to regulatory inspection and enforcement without reducing regulatory outcomes' (Hampton 2005). The report – *Reducing Administrative Burdens: Effective Inspection and Enforcement* – called for more focused inspections, greater emphasis on advice and education and, in general, for removing the 'burden' of inspection from most premises. Specifically, Hampton called for the reduction of inspections by up to one-third – across all regulatory agencies, this would equate to one million fewer inspections – and instead recommended that regulators make much more 'use of advice' to business. A key practical way that the Hampton agenda proposes to achieve all this without creating a regulatory collapse is to withdraw regulatory scrutiny from those that, in the terms used in the Hampton report, have 'earned' their 'autonomy'. The Hampton report represents an enthusiastic endorsement of twin-track regulation whereby regulatory interventions are 'targeted at the worst offenders'.

The Hampton reforms have at their heart a very carefully constructed rationale which defines regulation first and foremost in terms of its *economic* burden on business. Thus, section 1 of the Legislative and Regulatory Reform Act 2005, which implemented Hampton's recommendations aims to 'enable delivery of swift and efficient regulatory reform to cut red tape' (Cabinet Office 2006). In order to achieve this, the Act creates a remarkable new power for a Minister of the Crown to make an order that removes from government a 'regulatory burden', defined in the Act as a 'financial cost', an 'administrative inconvenience' or 'an obstacle to efficiency, productivity or profitability'. The Act itself therefore is framed by 'burdens on business' rhetoric, a rhetoric that juxtaposes economic health and success as a counterbalance to overbearing investigation and enforcement. There is a very unashamed and open honesty about the language being used here; we now find in legislation and in policy a very open promotion of self-regulation as part of a neo-liberal business-led agenda.

If we look at the case of health and safety regulation, reductions in resources, combined with political pressures from government have led to a spectacular collapse in regulatory activity equivalent to a halving of the number of prosecutions taken by the inspectorate for safety offences between 1999–2000 and 2007–8 (Tombs and Whyte 2009b). This collapse in prosecutions is mirrored by declines in other enforcement and front-line interventions. Thus, as a report by the Centre for Corporate Accountability noted, investigations of major injuries fell by 43 per cent between 2001–2 and 2006–7 and investigations of injuries requiring an absence of three days or more was reduced by two-thirds in the same period (UNITE/CCA 2008). Those are major shifts that indicate the Health and Safety Executive (HSE) has been particularly quick – and perhaps quicker than the EA – to adopt the Hampton agenda, but it is also an indicator of the degree to which the Hampton agenda has the potential to undermine enforcement strategies.

If we explore the detail of the collapse in health and safety enforcement, clear trends can be discerned in Figure 7.1 below between three periods: first, a period of gradually rising prosecutions between 1997–8 and 1999–2000; second, a gradual decline between 1999–2000 and 2003–4; and third a much steeper decline between 2003–4 and 2007–8.

A rather different trend discernible in the pattern of enforcement activity is set out in Figure 7.2. Here we see a steady rise in the use of enforcement action (and this category includes cautions, enforcement notices and prosecutions) between the EA's inception in 1999 and 2005 (although this rise is interrupted in 2002 and 2003). Following 2005, there appears to be a steep decline in enforcement action. If this trend is disaggregated into two forms of enforcement action (prosecution and enforcement notices), we find the same trend discernible in enforcement notices and prosecutions.

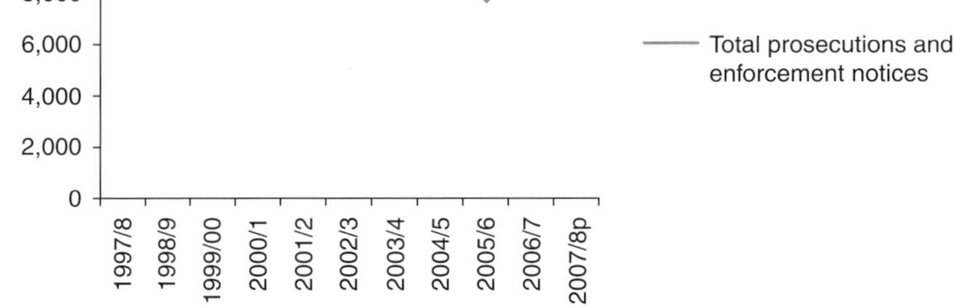

Figure 7.1 HSE enforcement action (HSE published enforcement statistics; at: www.hse.gov.uk/statistics/enforce/index.htm, downloaded 17/02/09; 2007–8 figures are provisional)

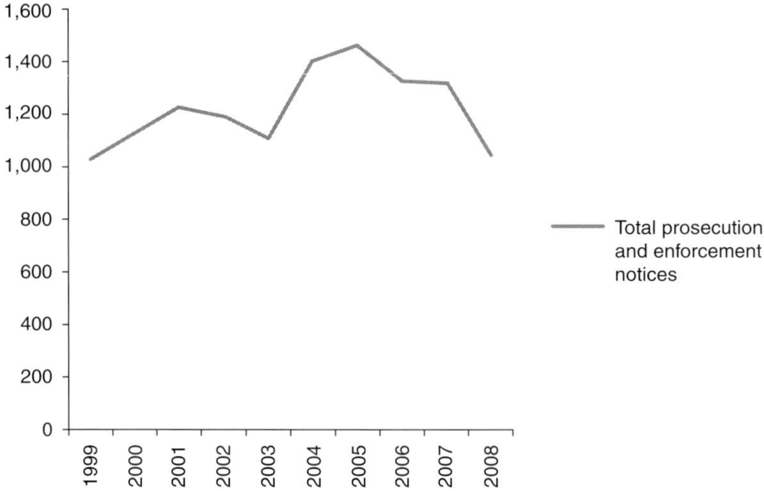

Figure 7.2 EA enforcement action (data supplied in personal communication with EA, 11/08/09)

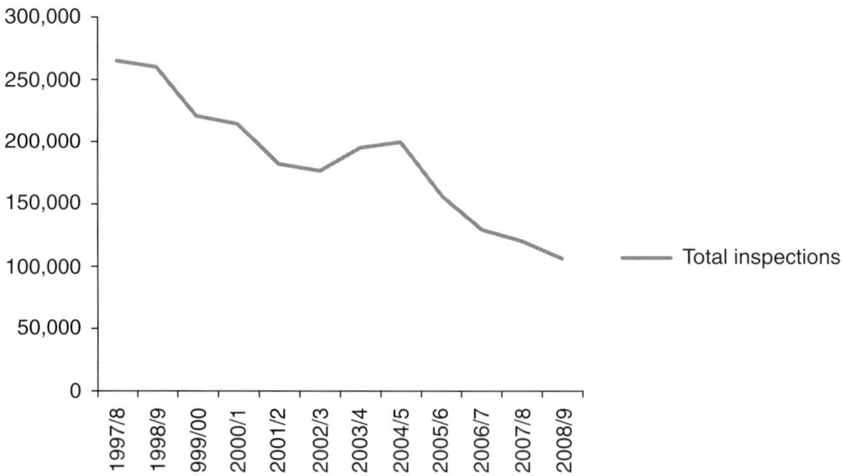

Figure 7.3 EA inspections (data supplied in personal correspondence with EA Planning and Performance Team, 05/11/09)

A more insightful understanding of shifts in the work of the EA can be discerned from an analysis of trends in inspection activity. As Figures 7.3 and 7.4 indicate, there has been an explicit shift away from the use of inspections towards the use of audits. We see from Figures 7.3 and 7.4 a

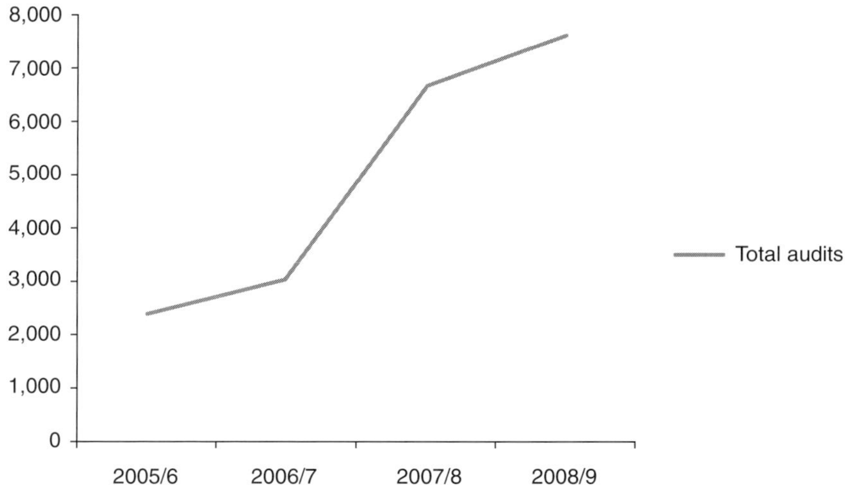

Figure 7.4 EA audits (data supplied in personal correspondence with EA Planning and Performance Team, 05/11/09)

clear shift towards a targeted system of intervention. There are two trends revealed by these Figures that are significant. First, there is a fall-off in inspections (of 33 per cent) from 1997–8 to 2002–3. There follows a slight rise in the next two years (of 13 per cent), before falling steeply again (46 per cent) between 2004–5 and 2008–9. In this latter period, the number of audits conducted by the EA has increased from just over 2,000 to 8,000 audits, as inspections have fallen by around 92,000.

To take a long view over the period of the data represented in Figures 7.3 and 7.4, around 8,000 audits have effectively replaced more than 150,000 onsite inspections between 1997–8 and 2008–9.

Without going into the complex political and technical reasons that lie behind the shift away from inspections, it is important to note that this shift implies a move away from what has been called 'command and control' form of regulation, towards a model of self-regulation. Broadly speaking, an inspection is a 'snapshot' assessment of whether the activities onsite are compliant with the permit conditions at that time, conducted by an inspector onsite. An audit is a typically more comprehensive, detailed and thorough analysis of the permitted operation at the site and would typically take more time, would involve a number of EA officers and require greater collaboration from the operator or site manager. It is through this collaborative role, whereby duty holders are required to provide their own data and documentation to verify the audit. The consequence of this shift in regulatory style, then, is a deepening of reliance upon duty holders both to construct the basis for their own compliance as well as to increase reliance greatly of the regulator on the honesty and willingness of the duty holder to own up to offences and breaches. Without entering into a full discussion about the merits or dangers of such a strategy, it is clear that this represents a major shift in EA activity.

The data set out above indicate that a shift away from inspections (and more recently) away from punitive interventions is related directly to the Hampton-led consolidation of a pluralist consensus or compliance approach to regulation in government and in regulatory agencies. This is the context – the emergence of a new politics of regulatory consensus – within which the proposals by Lynch-Wood and Williamson must be understood. Yet it is a context that is not mentioned even in passing in their work. The seismic changes in EA activity indicated in this section are part of a move to targeted intervention which is unacknowledged by the authors. Their proposal to withdraw resources from the largest companies and allocate them to the smallest does not take account of the major shifts in the withdrawal and redeployment of inspection resources that are currently gathering momentum. But more significantly, Lynch-Wood and Williamson fail to ask questions about the general effects of the shift towards an audit regime: what happens when over 100,000 duty holders simply disappear from an inspection regime? What does this mean for the EA's ability to secure compliance; and what does it mean for the EA's ability to assess the real extent of legal non-compliance and environmental crime?

Targeted intervention

Those are precisely the questions that Hampton failed to ask. And in this context, we are perhaps asking too much of Lynch-Wood and Williamson to raise such questions, for they offer a set of proposals for 'targeted intervention' that corresponds almost exactly to the exigencies of the Hampton report. Their chapter argues that we can differentiate between the troublesome firms that require to be regulated externally on one hand, and, on the other, those firms that are more likely to be controlled by market-based regulatory pressures or more likely to be compliant as a result of their relationship with stakeholders. And in doing so, the analysis follows closely the rationale that supports a risk-based or 'twin-track' regulatory strategy that is emerging in government, that reduces the business world to a linear spectrum of good corporate citizenship upon which businesses can be assessed and placed on a point somewhere between 'good' and 'bad', or between 'responsible' and 'irresponsible'. Of course, the model Lynch-Wood and Williamson develop is more sophisticated than this, in the sense that it offers a schema of eight types of firms, based upon a 'capacity profile'. Those profiles allow firms to be located on a scale that slides from the 'bad' non-compliers ('delinquents' and 'ogres') through the mid-range compliers ('vulnerable satisfiers', 'safe satisfiers', and 'major' and 'minor' strategic players) to those that perform beyond the terms of their legal obligation ('altruistic citizens' and 'benevolent giants').

Now there is a striking naivety about this model. It assumes that a firm can, at any one time, be placed on a fixed point on this model. Firms are assumed to have the fixed properties of one type or the other – delinquents, ogres or altruistic citizens, and so on. There are clear similarities here with the positivist tradition in criminology that has been concerned with the prediction of criminality. In its modern guises, this mode of research can be found in various types of administrative criminology which emphasize the closely observed interaction between 'criminal', the 'environmental' features of the 'crime' and the 'target'. Importantly, these interactions are located around a small set of very specific 'crime events'. Those events typically exist in isolation from the ongoing, ever-present power relationships that structure the criminal event, its definition and the criminal justice interventions that such events legitimize. A key critique of positivist criminology is made consistently in feminist analyses of male violence which is conceived of as a form of violence that can only be understood as part of an ongoing state of *gendered* power relations (Walklate 2003: 127–9). In corporate crimes, a concept of an unfortunate 'event' or 'disaster' is also of limited value precisely because this focus on a particular moment, fixed in time, with very particular circumstances, does not allow us to view regulatory 'failures' as rooted in more ongoing and ever-present social conditions of unequal power.

A focus upon the 'event' is based upon an acceptance that the various conditions that lead to the event can be isolated and controlled. Thus, the focus is upon the criminogenic aspects of the 'offender' or 'victim', or the isolated features of the operating environment that can be controlled. The control of corporate offending becomes a technical exercise of acting upon the 'criminogenic' business or the 'accident-prone' victim (Tombs 1991). From this perspective, then, a system of targeted intervention, based upon the prior identification of risk factors makes sense. But to most other intents and purposes it makes little sense at all. We know that the corporations that are represented as the most environmentally aware corporations – the most benevolent or altruistic – can also be the same corporations that routinely break the law.

There are some obvious suspects here, such as BP (fined £1m in the Scottish courts following a series of incidents at its Grangemouth plant in 2000; and fined $373m by US authorities in September 2007 for environmental violations and restitution after an explosion at their Texas refinery in March 2005). It is worth noting in this respect that BP is the paradigm 'greenwashing' firm, having changed its name from British Petroleum to 'Beyond Petroleum', a move which was, in part, aimed at establishing its eco-aware credentials. It is also not coincidental that BP now claims to be a firm that has moved 'beyond compliance'. Now there is no doubt that in some areas of process pollution and the development of clean technologies, BP is a key driver of innovation. But the company also remains a serious repeat offender. In this context, any attempt to fit BP into one category of a 'capability profile' appears at best wishful thinking, and at worst little more than an exercise in symbolic pseudoscience.

Recently, regulatory systems in the UK have moved closer to a twin- or two-track regulation model in which regulatory interventions are targeted at the worst offenders. In the most widely cited version of this model (Gunningham and Johnstone 1999) firms are offered a choice – between 'traditional' (track-one) regulation, or the adoption of a safety management system (track two). The latter in particular focuses upon performance and principle-based rather than specification-based standards, and places the onus for determining compliance and how to achieve it upon employers and workers. The right to track-two regulation is often 'earned' by demonstrating a good record of compliance. The Hampton review recommended a system of targeted intervention, incorporating a principle of earned autonomy that ensures that 'good performers are visited less often, or have less onerous reporting requirements' (Hampton 2005: 4).

Now this model is interesting and develops some important arguments about how a risk-based approach might work in practice and indeed the pitfalls of such an approach. But the general effect of advocating such an approach can only be clearly understood if we examine how risk-based and twin-track strategies cohere with current political agendas. The first point to make is that the debate in the Hampton report is framed by the same resignation to the low level of existing resources that we find underpinning the analysis by Lynch-Wood and Williamson. Second, the twin-track approach has considerable support from business associations. As Courtney Davis (2004) has noted, the CBI has long been an enthusiastic proponent of a 'twin-track' strategy from a perspective that promotes its membership as generally responsible, caring citizens, with only a small minority of offenders that need to be rooted out.

The promotion of a business-friendly strategy of targeted intervention is perhaps the most significant current contribution to policy development made by the pluralist academic literature. Yet this influence has been achieved as a result of the political convenience of the approach, rather than the presence of empirical evidence supporting its likely success. Arguments in favour of targeted intervention are generally made on the basis of conjecture or a series of untested empirical assumptions. Unsupported as twin-track strategies generally are, their speculativeness makes them a dangerous set of assumptions to mess around with. Apart from the very obvious point that we should be wary of following advice on crime control from organizations such as the CBI which represents a large number of offenders, the effects of a system of regulation where the majority of players – in this context the largest firms – know they are in for even lighter-touch regulation is likely to impact profoundly not only on patterns of compliance, but on the ability of regulators to *know* whether businesses are complying or not. Inspections are conducted at very low levels at the moment, leaving regulators largely in the dark about who can be said to have earned autonomy in the first place. Further incursions on regulators' capacity to 'know' about levels of compliance on the part of individual firms post-Hampton will curb this capacity even further. There is a great deal being blindly put down to trust here – and at the same time a great deal of obfuscation of the evidence we have of routine offending in companies of all sizes.

The point is not that we should not think seriously about developing 'risk' factors per se, but that in the current climate, risk-based approaches are easily reduced to self-regulation and regulatory withdrawal from particular firms (Tombs and Whyte 2006, 2009b). And this is where the argument by Lynch-Wood and Williamson is interesting. For it is one of the first to attempt to develop a universal principle for achieving this aim. At the heart of this, is their linking of firm size to the likelihood of offending and it is to this critical question that this chapter now turns.

The reification of size

Essentially, the proposal from Lynch-Wood and Williamson is that regulatory resources should target SMEs. A shift in focus away from large firms is justified on the basis that groups of firms are sufficiently similar to constitute distinct regulatory 'systems'. Now the rationale is based on two broad arguments: first, that scarce regulatory resources can be distributed more efficiently if they are focused on SMEs; and second, that this strategy is justifiable since large organizations are vulnerable to regulatory pressure from civil society groups such as NGOs and to forms of public and political pressure that are more significant as compliance levers than the government-centred domain of command and control. Lynch-Wood and Williamson base this argument on the premise that regulators have tended to target larger firms, firms that are believed to cause the most environmental damage. Indeed, they argue that the EA has tended to apply disproportionately conventional command-and-control measures to larger firms.

This focus on larger firms may be the case in some aspects of the EA's work, but it is certainly not reflected in its prosecution practice. Indeed, the opposite is indicated when we do explore the empirical evidence that is available to us.

Most EA prosecutions are for waste offences. While there is no breakdown available to analyse the date precisely by *size* of company, prosecutions for those types of offences typically involve individuals or small firms; the bulk of prosecutions laid by the EA are prosecutions of individuals for waste offences. A large number of those prosecutions are for fly-tipping and other forms of illegal dumping. Thus, the focus of prosecution activity indicated in Table 7.1 appears to be disproportionately upon the type of offending characterized by relatively small duty holders and offenders. Figure 7.5 below presents data that allow us to compare the levels of enforcement action (including prosecutions, enforcement notices and cautions) taken against individuals (and in this category, sole traders are included) and registered companies.

Figure 7.5 shows that individuals are as likely to be the targets of enforcement action taken by the EA as companies. Now, this does not tell us anything about the proportion of SMEs that are targets of formal enforcement action, but it does indicate that the EA's enforcement resources are not concentrated on large firms operating in the most environmentally sensitive areas.[2]

[2] There is no way of disaggregating sole traders from other, non-trading individuals, but the former category – who represent a substantial proportion of SMEs – are included in this

Table 7.1 *Charges laid by EA, by offence type, 2000–7 (data supplied in personal communication with EA, 22/03/08)*

Offence type	No. of charges
Waste	10,602
Water quality	2,542
Fisheries	772
Navigation	213
Water resources	207
Process industry regulation	99
IPPC	68
Flood defence	63
Radioactive substances	52

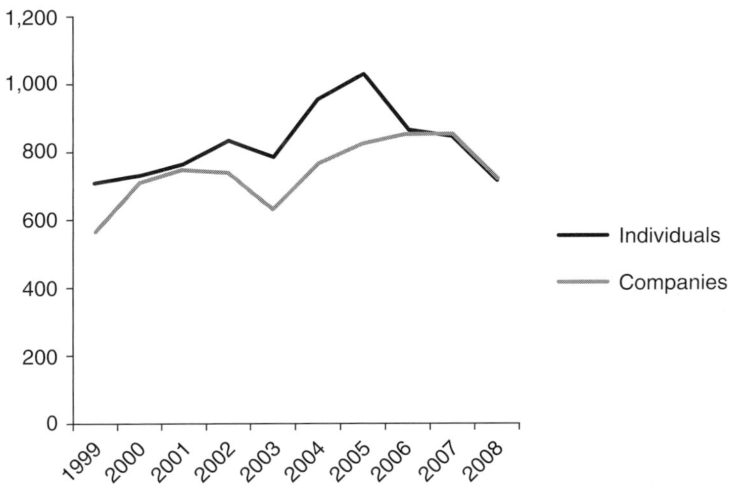

Figure 7.5 Total enforcement action taken by EA against individuals and companies, 1999–08 (data supplied in personal communication with EA, 11/08/09)

If this evidence raises some preliminary empirical questions about the assumptions Lynch-Wood and Williamson make about current regulatory targeting strategies, some more fundamental issues of contention are raised by the theoretical case. In order to construct their case,

data as 'individuals'. At the very least, these data appear to indicate that most enforcement *action* is not focused upon relatively large companies.

Lynch-Wood and Williamson are led into a set of assumptions about the structure and nature of large corporations in relation to a series of compliance levers (stakeholder pressure, economic opportunity and ethical motives). In sum, the argument is that the visibility of the activities of large firms renders them more amenable to what they describe as processes of governance. The basic claim being made here is that large firms are more likely to respond to reputational pressures than legislation. This is partly because environmental stakeholders (NGOs, communities, employees, customers and investors) exert more pressure on large firms in comparison with SMEs. The visibility of the activities of large firms to those groups and the public provides more of an incentive to comply and to move 'beyond compliance'. Moreover, larger firms more readily recognize the economic and business benefits of moving 'beyond compliance'.

We have already seen how the analysis by Lynch-Wood and Williamson is based upon the ontological separation of 'government regulation' on one hand, and a 'self-referential' system on the other. The process of ontological separation assumes that 'stakeholder pressure' is disconnected from broader legislative processes and indeed from the process of regulatory enforcement. If we consider that stakeholders already play an active role in struggling for particular legislative and regulatory outcomes, and often are locked in struggles with governments and regulatory agencies over questions of regulation as they apply in particular contexts, and in terms of struggles for broader sets of reforms, then it makes little sense theoretically to sustain this ontological separation. In what are characterized as traditional command-and-control systems, often no action would be taken by regulators if no 'stakeholder' pressure was applied by workers' organizations or communities. Moreover, the involvement of those stakeholder groups and of businesses, lawyers and investors in lobbying governments for regulatory change is crucial to understanding the complex balance of regulatory politics (Snider 1991). This is by no means a new phenomenon, nor is it a new point for analysts of regulatory reform. It was, after all, Karl Marx's key contribution to understanding the complex politics that shaped the passage and subsequent enforcement of the nineteenth-century Factory Acts (Marx 1887/1954; Tombs and Whyte 2008). Indeed, an understanding of social movements and organizations that mobilize around regulatory problems is now established as an analytical principle in the critical literature on regulation (Whyte 2004: 143–4)

But the system of external 'governance', or of the role played by NGOs and other civil society groups in relation to the size of the regulated firm is, as Lynch-Wood and Williamson propose, best answered with reference to the mediating contexts for regulatory systems. Let us revisit their discussion of those key mediating contexts in outline:

1 Issue salience – the impact of an issue becomes more intense for large firms because they are more likely to cause big, visible incidents involving issues of high public salience.
2 Field cohesion – the institutional and stakeholder networks surrounding large companies are more likely to comprise powerful actors.
3 Individual concern – where there are owner/managers, they are as individuals, more vulnerable to market pressures and less likely to develop environmental values, partly because they are less likely to be in an ongoing relationship with NGOs and other stakeholders.
4 Firm resources – the scarcity of resources affects 'environmental activity'.

Now those mediating contexts are used to present convincing arguments no doubt. But those arguments also have equally powerful counterpoints. The rest of this section will set out those counter-point arguments in turn.

1 While it has become apparent that large firms are certainly more visible and are likely to provoke some measure of *issue salience*, what is equally important is that they have the resources to develop 'greenwashing' strategies to present their activities to the public using resources that are beyond the means of SMEs. Issue salience is therefore mediated crucially by the public relations machinery deployed by the largest corporations. This is also significant in relation to 'field cohesion', since while it is true that some stakeholder networks surrounding large companies may be more likely to comprise powerful actors, if this is the case, then those stakeholder networks can be met with the greater resources and connections into powerful networks that are available to larger corporations. Power, in this sense, must be understood as relational. Moreover, the argument made by Lynch-Wood and Williamson assumes that the fact that institutional and stakeholder networks surrounding large companies are more likely to comprise powerful actors will have a positive impact upon compliance. Given the current political climate, why would network ties between regulators and regulated be more likely to facilitate higher standards of compliance as opposed to collusion?
2 The pluralist concept of *field cohesion* set out by the authors oversimplifies the organization and operational imperatives that structure

business organizations. As Frank Pearce (2001) has argued, the dominant features of corporations (their autocratic and strictly hierarchical command structure, their tightly constructed goals, the fiduciary duties of directors to maximize profits for a distant constituency of shareholders, and the rules of incorporation that grant it limited liability) combine to produce 'structures of irresponsibility'. Given this combination of incentives, impunity and fractured division of function, it is indeed difficult to see how corporations could ever act responsibly. Indeed, in this context, the size of the firm magnifies the ability of managers to remain distant from the real conditions of production, to blur lines of accountability for decisions, and ultimately to eradicate the incentives necessary to remain law abiding. In the context of large corporations, organizational structures mask responsibility more easily, allowing decisions to be buried in layers of bureaucracy and committees. It is those structures that make it virtually impossible to attribute regulatory accountability (especially in systems of self-regulation) to individuals within the largest corporations, never mind to the corporation itself.

3 On the issue the authors call '*individual concern*', and following the previous point, it is equally important to note that the *separation* of ownership and control creates a division of function and labour that depersonalizes and bureaucratizes the most powerful decision makers in companies, and which, in classical organizational sociology implies a process of organizational dehumanization (cf. Max Weber, C. Wright Mills and Adolf Bearle). The consequence of this is, as Sutherland's seminal (1949/1983) study found, that the capacity of large firms to produce criminal acts is enhanced.

4 If the argument that *firm resources* affect ability to comply is self-evident, that does not guarantee that the largest firms are likely to be legally compliant. A list published in the EA's 2007 *Spotlight on Business* report sets out the ten companies with highest fines that year. The list also noted how many fines of £5,000 or more had been levied against those companies previously. Table 7.2 below reproduces this data, alongside figures indicating the size of the firm and the size of the fine in relation to the firm's annual turnover in the year of the conviction.

The first thing to note about this data is that it was compiled using the largest fines imposed by the courts. If the courts are taking into account the ability of firms to pay as they are supposed to within current sentencing guidelines, then this data therefore is likely disproportionately to include the largest firms. Therefore we cannot use this table as an

Table 7.2 *Ten highest fines in EA prosecutions, 2006*

Company	No of employees[3]	Size of fine (£)	Fines as % of annual turnover, 2006–7[4]	Previous fines of £5,000 or more
1 Thames Water Utilities Ltd	5,285	191,600	0.01	2000–5
2 United Utilities Water Plc	3,490	137,300	0.01	2000–5
3 Van Dalen UK Ltd	73	100,000	0.24	2005
4 Castle Cement Ltd	969	99,000	0.05	2000
5 Anglian Water Services	3,611	75,000	0.008	2000–5
6 Wiggins Transport Ltd	n/a	63,000	n/a	
7 Wessex Water Services	1,661	56,250	0.01	2000–5
8 Agresol	n/a	54,000	n/a	
9 Southern Water Services	1,898	52,625	0.009	2000–5
10 Coe of Ilford	67	48,000	n/a	
10 Erith Haulage Company	100	48,000	0.23	2000–3

indication of a relationship between offending and size per se. To this we might add that only a small subset of cases end up in the courts. Prosecution by the EA, as is the norm for regulatory agencies in the UK, is used as a last resort. In other words, just because large companies feature in this table, this does not necessarily mean that large companies are more likely to offend. But what is interesting here is that five of the

[3] Those figures are derived from reportable data held at Companies House and compiled in the FAME database, accessed 03/04/08.

[4] As above note.

six large firms (i.e. to follow the definition of more than 250 employees) that appear on this table are serial offenders. Those firms, all of them water providers, are routinely convicted in the courts for breaches that cause serious water pollution. The habitual offending that we find in those large monopoly water companies is remarkable. Now clearly this is not just about their size – it is most likely also related to their monopoly position and the significance of their role in water supply in a particular area (if there is a pollution offence or breach of licence in water supply, then more often than not it is the supplier that is responsible). But having made this point, it is also their dominant position in those markets that magnifies opportunities to offend. The visibility of those large companies and the importance of their reputation in terms of consumer and client markets do not in this case appear to act as controls on their habitual offending.

Another striking feature of the table above is that the fines appear to have little measurable economic impact on those firms. This is important if it is the case that there appears to be little reputational pressure arising from those prosecutions. Indeed when measured in this way, it is clear that small firms will be much more affected by fines when measured as a proportion of turnover. Thus, it is the case that the deterrence value of a fine to small firms may be more likely given the relative weight of such fines. And this is perhaps the most interesting observation to be drawn about the specific conditions of deterrence that apply to smaller firms. Smaller firms perhaps are less likely to be future oriented, and less likely to approximate the ideal rational-choice decision maker simply because they are often by necessity short-term, reactive and focused upon income generation. But the picture is, at the same time, much more complex than this. Family-owned small businesses, for example, are much more future oriented and concerned about their long-term success than large companies simply because they are rooted in particular communities or have long histories and reputations that are embedded in those communities.

Conclusion

Just as consensus analysts of regulation have previously done, Lynch-Wood and Williamson allow the political rhetoric and normative prescriptions that dominate contemporary government discourse to establish the foundations for their argument. Without convincing empirical evidence or a convincing theoretical case, they present an approach to a debate which is nuanced but occupies a definitional terrain that is delineated by policy formulations that are, in all but name, neo-liberal. In other words, the perspective they adopt is conceptually limited by the parameters of the regulatory debate as set by the current political climate. Thus, their perspective is structured around an appeal to new forms of regulation that propose a mix of 'social licence', voluntary and reflexive instruments as a panacea to derisory EA resources.

Lynch-Wood and Williamson provide a paradigm example of how the conceptual shift between consensus and neo-liberal perspectives is achieved (for a detailed discussion of this process in the context of health and safety, see Tombs and Whyte 2009b). Their chapter invokes a range of standard compliance levers to achieve a new type of regulatory settlement (stakeholder pressure, economic opportunity and ethical motives) that is organized around market principles of self-regulation at its core. While they are clear that tough sanctions, and in particular wider use of publicity sanctions, are the bedrock of any regulatory system, their analysis generally recognizes a reduced role for formal regulation and a shift towards, an 'ecological modernization' that is located in market relationships. 'Reflexive regulation' is offered as a means of drawing in institutions outside of the legal sphere to act as compliance levers. This, however, is not a particularly new solution, but a shift to a familiar pattern of voluntarism and self-regulation.

Proposals for regulatory reform, if they are to have any political appeal in government – or indeed to regulators themselves – must, in the current political climate, be consistent with the Hampton agenda. The proposals put forward by Lynch-Wood and Williamson clearly succeed in this respect, for they deliver a targeted intervention rationale for a regulatory regime that is moving towards twin-track regulation.

So what does this all mean for how we should approach the development of regulatory 'tools' and 'levers'? Of course, we need to start somewhere. And it is axiomatic that all public authorities are always going to have resource limits. But the criminal justice–regulatory asymmetries that we find in all liberal democracies, in which regulatory agencies are dwarfed by the agencies charged with controlling 'street' or conventional crime, are truly astounding. If we simply take those gross asymmetries for granted – as fixed, political 'realities' – then we will fail to problematize the particularly corrosive political moment that we now find ourselves in.

Instead of a speculative science of risk assessment which claims to be able to differentiate the 'good' from the 'bad' and the 'ugly', what is required is a system that gives good reason for *all* businesses not to offend. If we are to begin to take corporate offending seriously, then we need a regulatory system that is properly resourced and given the full range of regulatory options in the 'toolbox'– rather than one that is continually undermined by a partisan, pro-business assault led by government. We need inspectors who are properly empowered to monitor duty holders and to take the appropriate action when there are serious legal breaches, rather than inspectors who are constantly reminded in guidance and legislation of the costs to business of upholding the law.

Size, in this context – and for all of the other reasons I have offered here – is a deviation from the real issue: how do we most effectively control corporate offending across the board? A bigger and much more fundamental question is: how do we use regulatory mechanisms to encourage genuine economic sustainability and to minimize the greater set of harms posed by polluting businesses (including those which are *legalized*)? We can only ask this question when we reject the intoxicated politics of targeted intervention that permeates contemporary debates on business regulation.

Postscript

The circumstances surrounding the explosion of the Deepwater Horizon platform in the Gulf of Mexico, which killed eleven workers and caused a major environmental catastrophe were beginning to emerge as this book went to press. One thing is certain at this stage: that the disaster was a consequence of a crisis in regulation. The three companies that are responsible (BP, Transocean and Halliburton) were given a high degree of autonomy in the management of their safety. Their self-referential capacities had been significantly enhanced by a light-touch regulatory regime. All of those companies are, at the same time, high-profile household names. They all operate on a global stage, are highly visible and are all the subject of a high degree of scrutiny by civil society groups. Indeed, they were also subject to a range of responsive compliance tools used by the former regulator, the Mineral Management Service (MMS). In 2009, BP asked for and was granted a 'categorical exclusion' from the National Environmental Policy Act in exchange for assurances that the necessary safety management systems were in place. This exempted the company from preparing a detailed environmental assessment for the well. US Department of Interior Secretary Salazar gave testimony in the US Senate in which he recognized the failure of his agency to scrutinize BP and to give proper consideration to offshore safety in the Gulf of Mexico.

An earlier Interior Department investigation found that MMS staff did consultancy work for energy companies, accepted gifts and steered contracts towards favoured clients. It also found that MMS personnel were involved in sexual liaisons with oil company management. The very same staff had discouraged the MMS in 2003 from demanding better systems to prevent explosions such as the Deepwater Horizon. In this case, responsive regulation has meant, quite literally, a soft touch.

In the UK, the Health and Safety Executive (HSE) had also used copybook responsive regulation techniques. Despite the fact that it had a long criminal record (BP had the distinction of having been given Britain's first £1 million fine at its Grangemouth refinery for safety crimes, and was served with 21 enforcement notices for 54 different offences between 2006 and early 2010), the company was selected for a 'Director Leadership' case study. The HSE was forced to withdraw this case study. In the wake of the Texas City Oil Refinery explosion which killed fifteen workers, the glaring contradictions of the company's claims could not be reconciled with its criminal record.

Yet the Deepwater Horizon disaster has done nothing to break the deep solidarity between government and business that permeates British politics and the regulatory system. Lord Browne, the architect of the much criticized BP cost- and safety-cutting strategy implicated in the Texas City disaster and a sequence of other safety and environmental crimes, was appointed to oversee the government's initiative to make Whitehall 'more businesslike'. As Rory O'Neill of *Hazards* magazine has pointed out, the scope of the peer's shake-up of government will include all ministries, including those responsible for workplace and environmental safety.

References

Ayres, I. and Braithwaite, J. (1992) *Responsive Regulation: Transcending The Deregulation Debate*. Oxford University Press.

Braithwaite, J. and Fisse, B. (1987) 'Self-Regulation and the Control of Corporate Crime', in C. Shearing and P. Stenning (eds.), *Private Policing*. Beverly Hills, CA: Sage.

Cabinet Office (2007) 'New Bill to enable delivery of swift and efficient regulatory reform to cut red tape', Jim Murphy, Cabinet Office news release, 11 January 2007. London: Cabinet Office Press Office.

Christian Aid (n.d.) *Behind the Mask: The Real Face of Corporate Social Responsibility*. London: Christian Aid.

Davis, C. (2004) *Making Companies Safe: What Works?* London: Centre for Corporate Accountability.

Fauset, C. (2006) 'What's Wrong with Corporate Responsibility'. Oxford: Corporate Watch.

Friedman, M. (1973) 'The Social Responsibility of Business is to Increase its Profits', *New York Times Magazine* (13 September).

Glasbeek, H. (1988) 'The Corporate Social Responsibility Movement – The Latest in Maginot. Lines to Save Capitalism', *Dalhousie Law Journal*, 363–402.

Gunningham, N. and Johnstone, R. (1999) *Regulating Workplace Safety: Systems and Sanctions*. Oxford University Press.

Hampton, P. (2005) *Reducing Administrative Burdens: Effective Inspection and Enforcement*. London: HM Treasury/HMSO.

Lubbers, E. (ed.) (2002) *Battling Big Business: Countering Greenwash, Infiltration and Other Forms of Corporate Bullying*. Monroe, ME: Common Courage Press.

Mahon, R. (1979) 'Regulatory Agencies: Captive Agents or Hegemonic Apparatuses?', *Studies in Political Economy*, 1(1), 154–68.

Marx, K. (1887/1954) *Capital: A Critical Analysis of Capitalist Production, Volume 1*. London: Lawrence & Wishart.

Pearce, F. (1976) *Crimes of the Powerful: Marxism, Crime and Deviance*. London: Pluto Press.

(2001) 'Crime and Capitalist Business Organisations', in N. Shover and J. P. Wright (eds.), *Crimes of Privilege: Readings in White Collar Crime*. Oxford University Press.

Snider, L. (1991) 'The Regulatory Dance: Understanding Reform Processes in Corporate Crime', *International Journal of the Sociology of Law*, **19**(2), 209–36.

Sutherland, E. (1949/1983) *White-Collar Crime: The Uncut Version*. New Haven, CT: Yale University Press.

Tombs, S. (1991) 'Injury and Ill Health in the Chemical Industry: Decentring the Accident-Prone Victim', *Industrial Crisis Quarterly*, **5**(Jan.), 59–75.

Tombs, S. and Whyte, D. (2006) 'Work and Risk', in G. Mythen and S. Walklate (eds.), *Beyond the Risk Society*. London: McGraw Hill.

(2007) *Safety Crimes*. Collumpton, Devon: Willan.

(2008) *The Crisis in Enforcement: The Decriminalisation of Death and Injury at Work*. London: Crime and Society Foundation.

(2009a) 'Corporate Crime? Theft, Violence and Harm', in J. Muncie, D. Talbot and R. Walters (eds.), *Crime: Local and Global*. Milton Keynes: Open University Press.

(2009b) 'A Deadly Consensus: Worker Safety and Regulatory Degradation under New Labour', *British Journal of Criminology*, **50**(1), 44–65.

UNITE/CCA (2008) *Lack of Investigation 2001/2007*, London: UNITE (at: www.corporateaccountability.org/dl/HSE/investig/unite.pdf).

Walklate, S. (2003) *Understanding Criminology: Current Theoretical Debates*, 2nd edn. Buckingham: Open University Press.

Walters, R. (2009) *Crime Is in the Air: Air Pollution and Regulation in the UK.* London: Crime and Society Foundation.

Whyte, D. (2004) 'Regulation and Corporate Crime', in J. Muncie and D. Wilson (eds.), *Student Handbook of Criminal Justice and Criminology.* London: Cavendish.

8

Governing by civil order: towards new frameworks of support, coercion and sanction?

JOHN FLINT AND CAROLINE HUNTER

Introduction

This chapter examines new forms of regulating the 'antisocial' conduct of individuals in the United Kingdom which have emerged over the last fifteen years. These forms of contemporary regulation have been characterized by a greater emphasis on directive, supervisory and punitive policy tools, including a reliance on sanctions (Schram *et al.* 2008). What has emerged is a move away from a purely criminal law model to an increasing reliance on other forms of legal regulation of conduct, including hybrid models where criminal and civil law increasingly overlap (Ashworth 2000). There has been a move away from simply increasing sanctions for past 'bad' behaviour (whether criminal or civil), towards requiring subjects to submit to programmes which seek to reform their behaviour into the future. While it may be argued that in criminal legal punishment there has always been an element which seeks to reform the offender, what is unique about these new forms of governance is that they are not linked to criminal law sanctions following from conviction by the court, but rather to the civil law (though in some cases criminal sanctions may eventually result for failure to comply).

These developments may be located within a historical tradition of managing marginalized populations and the use of the welfare state and welfare sanctions to reform the behaviour of problematized populations dating back to the late 1800s (Deacon 2004; O'Malley 2009). Many of these developments have identified the family as a key site of intervention and although 'successive generations have experienced a web of policies and practices designed to steer families in the desired direction and control those who do not conform' (Burney and Gelsthorpe 2008), it is apparent that the duties and obligations of parents have come under the gaze of the state in new ways (Cleland and Tisdall 2005).

Within these developments there is a particular targeting of what the government terms the 'selfish minority' of 'problem families' (Respect Task Force 2006). Government policies are premised on the belief that the public service response to these families could be improved and that the government should support those individuals who want to take responsibility and challenge more robustly, intensively and universally 'those who will not' (Respect Task Force 2006: 1). Fundamentally the government argues that 'Everyone can change' and indicates its determination that 'if people who need help will not take it, we will make them' (Respect Task Force 2006: 1).

The primary mechanisms through which individuals or households will be 'made' to take up support are new forms of legal or financial sanction. We consider in particular two civil orders which require participation in support programmes: Individual Support Orders and Parenting Orders. We then turn to two mechanisms which link support to the provision of and payment for housing: Anti-social Behaviour Housing Benefit sanctions and Family Intervention Tenancies. In this chapter, we argue that although some of these measures have been subject to considerable academic critique and debate (Burney and Gelsthorpe 2008; Cleland and Tisdall 2005; Deacon 2004; Garrett 2007; Kay and Tisdall 2006; McInytre-Bhatty 2008; Rodger 2006; Walters and Woodward 2008) there are a number of important issues that require further exploration. We begin by charting recent developments of legal sanctions to control conduct and examining these particular mechanisms whereby support has emerged as an important site through which conditionality and sanctions are applied. These mechanisms reveal how coercion to undertake support has been added to the forward-looking civil order, to create a new type of criminal offence and new forms of punitive financial sanction and threat of loss of the home. The chapter suggests that these measures raise important questions about how compliance through the take-up of support is conceptualized and about the capacity of the state. In the final part of the chapter we argue that these measures represent a problematic reliance on 'rational', legal and financial imperatives to reforming behaviour.

The development of legal mechanisms to control behaviour

The contemporary regulation of conduct has been marked by new and developing legal forms. Zedner (2007: 262) notes how:

> In a post-crime society there are crimes, offenders and victims, crime control, policing, investigation, trial and punishment, all of which are

> staples of present criminological enquiry. Pre-crime, by contrast, shifts the temporal perspective to anticipate and forestall that which has not yet occurred and may never do so.

In this 'pre-crime' society we see an increasing use of civil forms of law to control behaviour. Simester and von Hirsch (2006: 174) describe the development of 'two step prohibitions' which move away from the protective safeguards built into the criminal justice system, to the use of civil mechanisms. An initial civil prohibitory order is obtained 'against persons who have been found engaged in … undesired conduct'. If that order is breached a criminal offence is committed. Criminal sanction occurs as the second stage of breach of the civil order (see also Crawford 2003; Ashworth 2000). The most prominent example in the UK is the Antisocial Behaviour Order (ASBO) which although predicated on proof of antisocial behaviour is forward looking in its control of future behaviour. Interestingly, a two-step process was evident in earlier initiatives aimed at regulating the behaviour of tenants of social housing.[1] Such tenants have, since 1980, been given extensive tenancy rights which prevent removal except on proven grounds, and then generally in the case of fault by the tenant, only where the court considers that it is reasonable to make such an order. However, in a mirror of two-step prohibition, the two-step tenancy was introduced in 1996. This was formally called an introductory or starter tenancy, and put tenants on a twelve-month probationary period, before they were able to gain full security. None of these developments in the mid-1990s included any element of support to the targeted individuals which would assist them in ensuring that they would be able to comply with the forward-looking requirements.

In addition to ASBOs, over 20,000 Acceptable Behaviour Contracts (ABCs) have now been issued. These are voluntary agreements whereby an individual (and their parents in the case of children) sign up to a negotiated and agreed mix of codified prohibited conduct and required actions (see Bullock and Jones 2004). Although ABCs have no technical legal standing (in this sense sitting much lower in the enforcement pyramid of Ayres and Braithwaite (1992)), their quasi-legality arises from their potential use as evidence in any future applications for ASBOs or eviction proceedings. Their use can be seen as adding yet further steps to

[1] We use this phrase to denote rented housing provided directly or indirectly through the state. Historically the primary source of such housing has been local authorities, however over the last twenty years there has been a significant shift to not-for-profit providers, who are generally referred to as 'registered social landlords'.

the process of criminalization. The Home Office Guidance indicates how ABCs are enmeshed with the legal process:

> Legal action (such as an application for an anti-social behaviour order or a possession order, if the perpetrator is in social housing) should be stated on the contract where this is the potential consequence of breaking the agreement. The prospect of a more formal, legal intervention can provide an added incentive to adhere to the contract.
>
> (Home Office 2007: 2)

Current Home Office Guidance (Home Office 2007) suggests that in cases of more serious or problematic behaviour, support should be offered in parallel with the contract. Support is not, however essential to the contract, but ABCs' flexible non-statutory form makes it possible for them to be tailored to local circumstances and to include such provisions.

The ASBO has been subject to frequent statutory amendment, but for our purposes a key change came in the introduction of the Individual Support Order (ISO) by the Criminal Justice Act 2003. Until this point the ASBO could only be prohibitory in nature and could not include a positive requirement to take part in activities designed to change the behaviour of the defendant. The ISO applies only to 10–17-year-olds and was a government response to the criticism that ASBOs were negative and offered no support (Wain 2007).

While the development of the ABC indicates some of the local frustration with the statutory form of sanction, there is little evidence that the ISO was picked up to reflect local developments. This may account for the very low take-up of the scheme (Wain 2007) and the government's disappointment that they have not been taken up more widely was expressed by the government spokesman Lord Bassam in a debate on amendments to the legislation in 2008 (Hansard, 10 March 2008, col. 1327).

What though is the consequence of failing to take up the support offered? Here again the individual is criminalized. As with breach of the ASBO, breach of the ISO is a criminal offence, giving us potentially three steps to criminalization: the ASBO is made, the ISO is added, and breach of either can lead to criminal prosecution. In general, the criminal law does not require us to act positively to avoid criminal prosecution. In the case of the ISO, however, it is the failure to undertake a positive act of attending the support (i.e. 'a failure without reasonable excuse to comply with any requirement included in the order': Crime and Disorder Act 1998, s. 1AB(3)) that is then criminalized. Note, too, that as with other offences created by these hybrid orders (Ashworth 2000), the offence does not require any degree of fault. Although there is a defence of reasonable excuse, the offence is otherwise one of strict liability.

Parenting Orders and Contracts

Parenting Orders were introduced in the Crime and Disorder Act 1998 and rolled out in 2000. When initially introduced, they applied in cases where one of a number of orders (including an ASBO) had been made in relation to a child, or a child had been convicted of a criminal offence. As with the ISO they could be conceived of as a three-step prohibition, in that there had to be an order or conviction against the child before the application for the Parenting Order could be made. They were amended however by the Anti-social Behaviour Act 2003, enabling their use for parents whose children had been engaged in antisocial behaviour where the order was 'in the interest of preventing the child or young person from engaging in further criminal conduct or anti social behaviour'. As Holt (2008: 204) points out 'parents who have not committed any crime can receive a Parenting Order in response to their children who have not committed any crime'. In cases of antisocial behaviour, the Parenting Order is a two-step prohibition which is based on qualifying behaviour of a person other than the defendant. Further, like the ISO it criminalizes a failure to take action, rather than a failure to refrain from an action.

Parenting Orders include an explicit focus on the offer and take-up of support, requiring parents to comply with the provisions of the Order and to attend counselling or guidance sessions as required. The Order may also specify any additional requirements that the parent or carer must comply with. The Parenting Order is a Civil Order, but, as with ASBOs, failure to comply without a reasonable excuse is a criminal offence. As with ISOs, the penalty is a fine (up to £1,000).

In terms of the support that was offered as part of the Order, an initial evaluation of Parenting Orders in England (Ghate and Ramella 2002: 8) found that 'few, if any, "tried and tested" models existed for service delivery before the Parenting Programme, and most Youth Offending Teams were entering uncharted territory when they wrote their initial bids for funding'. There were many different models of support, although with some shared themes, which Holt (2008) suggests may account for the variety of experiences found in the various evaluations of parenting programmes. What emerges in this context is how local programmes did not take on board the correctional, punitive function of the scheme:

> It is particularly important to note that whilst the legislation surrounding Parenting Orders may be interpreted in punitive terms (as has been perceived as such by many parents, service providers and by the Courts), projects themselves had no stated objectives that related to 'chastising' errant parents. The closest that any came to using this correctional language was one project that aimed '*to help parents address deviant attitudes*', and most projects saw their function as predominantly supportive.
>
> (Ghate and Ramella 2002: 10)

Many schemes that were set up directly to respond to Parenting Orders, were 'uncomfortable with the idea of "support by compulsion" and many projects have interpreted this to mean that referrals by Order should be a last resort' (Ghate and Ramella 2002: 14). That this variety in the nature of the support and preference for voluntarism continues is confirmed by Burney and Gelsthorpe (2008). To a certain extent this preference was recognized in amendments to the legislation made in 2004 which gave statutory recognition to Parenting Contracts, which enable access to parenting support without the threat of coercion.

The development of support in the housing context

The UK government's strategy towards the regulation of conduct has been particularly targeted at residents of social housing. In legal terms this has taken the form of a number of developments, including broadening of the grounds for possession, reductions in security of tenure (introductory, starter and demoted tenancies) and specific injunction powers (Hunter 2006).

The introductory and starter tenancies can be seen as closely linked to ideas of conditionality – full security of tenure is conditional on twelve months' good behaviour. These tenancies did not have any explicit requirement of support built into the legislative structures. In practice, however many social landlords used such tenancies in combination with a package of tools, including additional support to new tenants (Ruggieri and Levinson 1998; Rowan Associates 2004). In Scotland, use of the Scottish short tenancy was specifically tied to support to families who had been found to be intentionally homeless, in order to enable the families to gain full security.

Parr and Nixon (2009) note that 'despite the lack of empirical evidence on the efficacy of enforcement action, the language used by the Government to exhort local authorities to increase their use of such measures was both confident and unequivocal'. Nonetheless they point to a rejection of the approach at a local level. One of the most significant developments for a more supportive approach was the growth of Family Intervention Projects, to which we now turn.

Family Intervention Projects

Although Family Intervention Projects (FIPs) are not an example of a direct relationship between support and sanction, they are important, both as mechanisms through which other measures discussed in this chapter are situated and applied and as arenas around which many of the debates about the contemporary regulation of conduct coalesce. The contemporary interest in FIPs arose from the positive evaluation of the Dundee Families Project (Dillane *et al.* 2001) where families at risk of eviction on the grounds of antisocial behaviour were subject to intensive surveillance and intervention with the aim of enabling them to sustain a social housing tenancy (see Welshman 2008 for a historical precedent). Parr and Nixon (2009) illustrate how these projects did not initially represent the local implementation of a central policy, but rather provided an alternative discourse 'where the issue of anti-social behaviour was placed within the broader context of social exclusion and aligned with other policy agendas such as homelessness and child protection'. As with the providers of parenting programmes in relation to Parenting Orders or Parenting Contracts, the FIPs were not conceptualized by the providers as disciplining antisocial families, but rather as supporting vulnerable families.

It is important to note that there are different models of project, including outreach services to families who have not been evicted from their home and dispersed tenancies (where the project is able to allocate to social housing stock over a wide geographical area), but those projects that have a core residential accommodation component have been subject to the fiercest debate. It is clear that these types of project most closely resemble Foucault's notion of the panopticon (Foucault 1977; Bentham 1995) with intensive 24-hour surveillance of families, strict rules of conduct and extensive programmes of intervention addressing many fields of family life. Some commentators such as Garrett (2007) refer to these residential units as 'sinbins' and emphasize their punitive, disciplinary and segregation effects and highlight how the voluntary engagement of families is located within the wider coercive effects of the loss of their tenancy if they do not comply. However, they also represent ambitious attempts by local agencies to reintegrate families into local neighbourhoods, improve their opportunities and are an alternative to the punitive ASBO or eviction, which often lack any form of accompanying support package.

Despite localized interpretations and differential development, 'the rationalities and technologies associated with intensive family support were adopted and effectively redistributed by the central state as national policy as part of the Respect Action Plan published in 2006' (Parr and Nixon 2009). The Respect Action Plan facilitated a national roll-out of FIPs and indicated that every local authority should consider providing some form of intensive family support. Thus, in addition to funding for their roll-out they have also been embedded in the provision of support in relation to Parenting Orders and worklessness regimes. The Youth Crime Action Plan will also link into intensive family support, with families 'encouraged and challenged' by key workers with 'non-negotiable elements of support and sanctions for failure to engage' (HM Government, 2008: 5). One mechanism for enacting this sanction is the housing benefit regime.

Housing benefit sanctions in relation to antisocial behaviour

The Respect Action Plan detailed how the government was considering how to encourage those involved in persistent antisocial behaviour to engage with intensive family support. Despite rejection of earlier similar proposals (Deacon 2004), one option would be to introduce sanctions for those people who have been evicted for antisocial behaviour and then refuse to take up offers of help. Sanctions could include financial penalties or housing benefit measures.[2] 'This would provide a very strong incentive to encourage those households to undertake rehabilitation when they have refused other offers of help' (Respect Task Force 2006: 23).

The Welfare Reform Act 2007 set out the circumstances under which a local authority could apply a sanction of housing benefit linked to antisocial behaviour. These were threefold: (a) the household had been subject to a relevant order of possession related to grounds of antisocial behaviour and subsequently left the property; (b) members of the household identified as being responsible for the antisocial behaviour are offered a package of support and refuse to engage with this support; and (c) the individuals concerned do not comply with conditions issued in a written warning notice. Eight local authorities in England were engaged in a pilot of the Housing Benefit Sanction from October 2007 to October 2009 (see Flint *et al.* 2008a and 2008b).

[2] Housing benefit is a means-tested benefit which is paid to those on low incomes to cover some or all of their rent. It many cases the payment will go directly from the local authority who administers the benefit to the landlord.

The sanction scheme operates where orders of possession linked to antisocial behaviour have been granted by courts in the pilot local authority areas and where individuals responsible for the antisocial behaviour make a subsequent claim for housing benefit from a new property within a pilot local authority area. Those households potentially eligible for sanction are to be identified by the Department for Work and Pensions (DWP) by matching court records with scans of future housing benefit claims. Where a match is made, the DWP should inform the sanction coordinator in the relevant pilot local authority area. A multi-agency panel then assesses whether the individual or household are potentially eligible for sanction (for example those with mental health conditions should not be included), the likely impact of a sanction and the appropriate package of support that should be offered. The individual or household receives a written offer of this support and, if satisfactory engagement with this support is not forthcoming (subject to a review period likely to last two months) then a sanction of housing benefit may be considered. The financial sanction is applied in stages of an initial 10 per cent reduction in housing benefit, rising to a 20 per cent reduction and then full deduction of 100 per cent if the individual or household continue to fail to engage adequately with the support package offered to them. Households meeting financial hardship criteria are subject to a maximum 30 per cent reduction.

The DWP guidance (Department for Work and Pensions 2007a, 2007b) is explicit that the support package offered to individuals should be available, tailored to their needs and appropriate to addressing the underlying causes of the antisocial behaviour. The DWP guidance also emphasizes that the primary aim of the sanction is to encourage individuals and households to engage with the support offered to them, and envisaged that a very small number of households would be subject to an actual housing benefit sanction.

Family intervention tenancies

Another legal measure which has also emerged in relation to family intervention projects is a particular new form of tenancy without security. These only come into play where FIPs have a core unit or use dispersed tenancies. In such cases they can grant a family intervention tenancy which prevents the tenant having any security of tenure. The tenancy is not conditional like an introductory or starter tenancy which will at least convert automatically to security if the tenant is 'properly' behaved. In this case, the families are insecure throughout the tenancy.

The basis of the family intervention tenancy, like that of the housing benefit sanction, is the agreement struck with the family. Such a tenancy can only be entered into where there is an 'identified behaviour support agreement'. Guidance on the Family Intervention Tenancy (Communities and Local Government 2009: para. 35) states that the agreement should 'clearly outline the changes in behaviour that are expected; clearly outline the behaviour support that will be provided; and clearly outline what sanctions would be applied for non-compliance with the agreement'.

The Guidance then makes it clear that termination of the tenancy is to be linked to non-cooperation (para. 37):

> Where eviction is sought we would expect this would normally be justified on the basis that a family had wilfully refused to accept support as defined through the Behaviour Support Agreement (having been given opportunities to address any breaches) and that there was no significant improvement in their behaviour.

So here we have another form of coercion to ensure compliance, that of threat of loss of home. In contrast to the ISO, the Guidance at least suggests that it should only be exercised for 'wilful' refusal, thus including some element of fault.

Coercion and support

Family intervention tenancies and housing benefit sanctions symbolize how the local initiatives of support can influence and be taken up at a national level, but how in so doing the (punitive and coercive) discourse of central government becomes imprinted upon them. While the regulatory strategies of the local agencies may not be enforcement led, at a central level, initiatives emerging from those strategies become transformed into those based on enforcement. Thus support is placed within a framework in which people will be forced to accept help and be punished for their failure so to do:

> *Everyone can change* – if people who need help will not take it, *we will make them.*
>
> (Tony Blair, foreword to the Respect Action Plan, Respect Task Force 2006: 1, our emphasis)

> We will take a new approach to tackle the behaviour of 'problem families' by challenging them to accept support to change their behaviour, *backed up by enforcement measures.*
>
> (Respect Task Force 2006: 3, our emphasis)

> It is in the interest of all of us to ensure that the small minority of families who are responsible for a high proportion of problems radically change their behaviour. It is also in the interests of the households themselves to be helped *or forced to take help* so that they, and especially their children, can take up opportunities that others enjoy.
>
> (Respect Task Force 2006: 21, our emphasis)

A number of key elements are apparent in these statements. First, this approach is premised on the belief that individuals are able to change and that this is primarily an issue of choice which may be addressed by aligning the correct regime of incentives and sanctions with the inherent (forward-thinking) rationality of these households. It is targeted therefore at 'individuals who could cope but simply chose not to…wilful neglect by parents of their responsibilities' (Home Office Minister John Patten, quoted in Burney and Gelsthorpe 2008).

Second, it implies the capacity of the state to rectify non-compliance through coercion ('we will make them') and enforcement mechanisms. This bullish statement is not embedded within a wider discussion of the mechanisms and dynamics through which households may be forced to comply. The statements also highlight the growing conceptualization within government that the policy agenda is one of targeting a small number of households, which marks a shift from more generic concerns with an 'underclass' or criminogenic neighbourhoods or communities. It is also important to note that such targeting, intensive support and coercion are located within a wider social justice paradigm of reconnecting individuals to the 'wider opportunities' available to the general populace.

The basis of these conceptualizations lies in the prominence given to the power of contractual relations between households and state agencies and the reciprocity inherent within them (see Crawford 2003). This agenda is about posing greater challenges to households, negotiating a contractual form of engagement and enacting more robust methods of compliance. The Respect Task Force (2006: 22) therefore identify key success factors in managing the most problematic households as including: 'Great persistence and assertiveness by [support] project workers to ensure families stick to agreements and changes in behaviour' and 'brokering and ensuring the adherence to a "contract" between the household and agencies'.

Following Bottoms (1983), these conceptualizations filter and classify particular households or individuals in need of correction, rather than mere regulation. The measures examined in this chapter represent what O'Malley (2009: 72) calls a 'domain of penality' that is disciplinary and correctional, rather than one concerned with the regulation of wider populations. These measures thus become uniquely personalized and specific, reflecting wider welfare reforms as set out in *No One Written Off* (Department for Work and Pensions 2008: 39–41) which are explicitly conceptualized as a form of 'personalised conditionality … designed to influence behaviour', and this 'conditionality regime' will be facilitated by a stronger 'sanctions regime', including specific forms of conditionality for lone parents.

Regulating compliance

If the key arena for application of a sanction is the 'compliance' of an individual in engaging with a package of support, a key issue becomes how this compliance and engagement is defined, monitored and assessed. Clearly, some individuals have been subject to sanction for breaching the conditions of Parenting Orders or have not had introductory tenancies converted into full tenancies. But how are these decisions arrived at? Ghate and Ramella (2002) observed a number of difficulties relating to the assessment of compliance and also reluctance to initiate proceedings for breaches of Parenting Orders. Our research into the housing benefit sanctions has raised a number of important dilemmas in this regard. First, how is 'adequate' engagement and compliance defined? Is it the attendance of an individual at sessions or classes? Is it their actions and statements while attending these support services? Can individuals be said to be complying through their attendance and active engagement with support services even if there is no demonstrable improvement in their behaviour, at least in the short term? What period of time should be given for individuals to demonstrate engagement (the rather arbitrary period of two months appears to be in place for the housing benefit sanction pilots)?

Of equal importance is the question of which actors or agencies will be involved in assessing and determining compliance. In the case of housing benefit sanctions, each case is overseen by a multi-agency review panel which will take the ultimate decision over whether engagement has been sufficient or whether a sanction should be applied. But this decision will be based on the assessment of the staff delivering support services such as FIPs. Many stakeholders have voiced concern that linking project workers to decisions about sanctions will fundamentally alter the relations of trust (and demarcation and distinction from statutory agencies) that are essential to the success of these interventions. The criteria for measuring compliance and the roles of actors within the assessment process remain uncertain (Flint *et al.* 2008a and 2008b).

The other side of the coin is defining whether the package of support offered to individuals is itself appropriate. In the case of housing benefit sanctions, the package of support will be devised by a multi-agency case review panel and should be negotiated and agreed by the individuals subject to a potential sanction. However, there remain questions about the comprehensiveness and quality of the services provided. For example, alcohol and drug counselling services are often oversubscribed, smaller local authorities are not able to provide the same resources as larger urban localities and, in general, support tailored to families tends to be more developed and more robustly linked into enforcement measures than those available to single or childless couple households.

This raises a wider issue about the actual capacities of the state to enact measures that reform the most vulnerable households. Although the government's confident rhetoric and academic accounts of the growth of surveillance and the punitive state ascribe 'awesome' power to state intervention, the reality is somewhat more prosaic. Technical problems in establishing the centralized database within the DWP has meant that, at the time of writing, no individual has been identified as meeting the criteria for potential housing benefit sanction in any of the eight pilot local authorities. There is also variable practice, and active resistance at the local level demonstrated by the variation in the use of Parenting Orders and the reluctance to use Parenting Orders in relation to school attendance and exclusion (see Burney and Gelsthorpe 2008). Similar differences in the willingness to use housing benefit sanctions are evident, and research in the United States illustrates that the use of sanctions linked to unemployment are mediated by the attitudes of benefit managers (Schram *et al.* 2008). The positive evaluations of FIPs (Dillane *et al.* 2001; Nixon *et al.* 2006) and the concerns about the impacts of Parenting Orders on vulnerable families (Walters and Woodward 2008) need to be set alongside the fact that all the state's interventions have not reduced truancy levels in the last ten years (McInytre-Bhatty 2008) and that local authorities looking after young people appear to have little impact on their levels of offending (Darker *et al.* 2008).

The flawed regulation of contract and sanction

Measures such as Parenting Orders have been subject to critique in their conflation of voluntary contract (and the important basis of mutuality and commitment this engenders amongst parties) with coercion (Burney and Gelsthorpe 2008; McInytre-Bhatty 2008). These critics correctly identify that the basis of a voluntary Parenting Contract or ABC is radically different to the compulsory conditions of Parenting Orders or ASBOs, so that the government's conceptualization of one being a tiered stepping stone to the other is flawed. However, more fundamentally, contractual forms of governance (Crawford 2003) have as their basis a form of rationality based on ordering future conduct in a 'logical' response to a series of obligations, incentives and sanctions. Following Cruikshank (1999: 47–8), these measures seek to establish a relationship of governance that conceptualizes individuals as 'acting subjects' who are to be 'made to act.' However, as Stephen (2009) argues, these 'contracts' are not voluntary or a process of negotiation but rather an exercise in power which may serve to remove the sense of agency on the part of their subjects.

Mechanisms such as ABCs, ASBOs, Parenting Contracts and social housing tenancies are premised upon the codification of required conduct and the belief that embedding individuals in contractual relations with agencies, based on a series of rights and responsibilities, will bring about change. Each of the measures discussed in this chapter are future oriented (see Crawford 2003, for a fuller discussion of this point) and this temporal dimension not only maps out a programme or action plan in the form of a succession of interventions aimed at a final goal but also assumes rationalities at each stage of the process.

These measures are characterized by the assumption that financial penalties offer some traction with those subject to them, so that Individual Support Orders, Parenting Orders (both through fines) or housing benefit sanctions suppose that, ultimately the loss of income offers a lever to ensure engagement and the taking up of support. The rationality of subjects is also inherent to the tiered nature of the sanctions, so that the extent of the sanction increases over time in the expectation that, at some point, subjects will reach a threshold where the financial burden will become so severe that they will make the active decision to engage. (It is worth noting that financial incentives linked to behaviour are also increasingly prevalent in the more general regulation of conduct, including tenant reward schemes where tenants receive some form of rent rebate if they are not in arrears and have not behaved antisocially.)

However, as Lister (2004) has pointed out, a rational/economic/legal model of regulation, as epitomized in tenancy agreements, is seldom sufficient to manage the conduct of vulnerable households. There are a number of flaws in the key assumptions and mechanisms in the concept of financial sanction. For example, in relation to housing benefit sanctions related to antisocial behaviour, housing benefit (although subject to reform to increase direct payment to tenants) is usually paid direct to a landlord. Therefore, individuals subject to the sanction will not experience a visible and immediate loss to their personal income, the deficit will arise in the rent received by the landlord. This has the perverse outcome of some local authorities penalizing their own Housing Revenue Accounts and risks private landlords refusing to take households at risk of future sanction. More fundamentally, the fact that those individuals potentially liable to housing benefit sanctions in relation to antisocial behaviour will already have lost their previous home as a result of their conduct suggests that rationality based on future loss of income is unlikely to provide effective leverage to their engagement with support.

The limitations of legal or financial sanctions as influences on conduct are mirrored in the flawed conceptualization and ambiguity in government rationales underpinning their attempts to regulate the most vulnerable households. The contractual and conditional regime is based on the agency, choice and rationality of its subjects. That is, as demonstrated above, it assumes that individuals or parents wilfully choose to be irresponsible and not to take up support and that, in the lack of any moral sense of obligation to their children, their neighbours or the state, they are likely, ultimately, to respond to financial incentives or legal coercion. However, this is contrary to the growing recognition of the pressures faced by these households and their 'chaotic' lifestyles which mitigate the use of rational agency in the way supposed by these mechanisms of sanction. The evidence also suggests that the reframing of imperatives away from a moral sense of respect, duty or obligation is misplaced in terms of the actual value orientations of these households. The research into FIPs consistently reveals that parents are aware of their problems and 'inadequacies' and are therefore keen to take up support when it is packaged in such a way as to represent a break from their previous negative relationships with state agencies. The Respect Action Plan acknowledges that 'Many [parents] say they would value some help with parenting' (Respect Task Force 2006: 17). This is, however, an understatement. The large majority of parents take up the support offered through Parenting Contracts and Orders (Burney and Gelsthorpe 2008) and FIPs. Indeed, this is officially recognized in the housing benefit sanction pilots, where it was always envisaged that very low numbers of individuals would be subject to an actual sanction.

Conclusions

In his foreword to the Respect Action Plan, Tony Blair referred to 'intractable problems with the behaviour of some individuals and families'

(Respect Task Force 2006). One explanation for the emergence of the new mechanisms discussed in this chapter is the recognition of the failure of state agencies to have 'traction' with the most vulnerable households, hence the focus upon 'gripping' families (Respect Task Force 2006: 21). In part then, these measures are an attempt to demonstrate the capacity of state power and to ensure that 'every child matters' and 'no-one is written off' apply to every household, with none being beyond the reach of state intervention. As Vaughan (2000) points out, there is an 'inclusionary pulse' running through modern governance and punishment and, in Foucault's notion of bio-politics, a determination to construct a universal population in which all may be subject to the gaze of the state, whether or not the state then imposes forms of conditionality and exclusion on specific groups within this population. The social justice connotations of 'no one written off', 'every child matters' and 'wider, deeper, broader' anti-social behaviour interventions should not simplistically be dismissed in a wider critique of a disciplinary and punitive turn in social policy.

Regulation becomes more intensive and more personalized and links across more and more dimensions of individuals' lives. These measures are critiqued for imposing 'draconian sanctions' (Moran *et al.* 2004; see also Garrett 2007). However, the elements of inclusion and exclusion involved here are more complex than many critics of such measures have acknowledged to date. This is not merely the silencing, punishment or exclusion of marginalized populations, but rather an attempt to 'open up' their lives for assessment and intervention (Foucault 1978). Although this does indeed represent the increasing 'intrusion' of the state into the realm of private family relations (Cleland and Tisdall 2005; Garrett 2007), it also represents efforts to find transforming mechanisms through which marginalized populations may be reintegrated as 'full citizens'. This is the ambiguity of sanction regimes: they increase the conditionality of the social rights of citizenship within what is, at least in part, an 'inclusionary project' (Vaughan 2000: 26) of rehabilitation. Far from an exclusion of marginalized populations, these new mechanisms of conduct regulation are actually ambitious (and often resource intensive) attempts to 'transform human subjectivities' (Schram *et al.* 2008). This is not to deny significant negative consequences for some households subject to these measures, or the flawed conceptual basis upon which some of these measures are premised, but rather to make the point that marginalized populations are not merely subject to punitive discipline and sanction, but rather, they are 'located in the twilight space between inclusion and exclusion, normalcy and deviance, compliance and disruption' (Schram *et al.* 2008: 18).

In this chapter we have argued that new mechanisms for regulating conduct within a wider regime of conditionality have created engagement with support as a site for governance and the assessment of behaviour. Support has been brought within a coercive regime of sanction which includes criminal, financial and 'loss of home' punishments in which the failure to act (the take-up of the offer of support) has become criminalized. Although these new mechanisms may be located within an increasingly linked and conditional nexus between housing, education, worklessness and crime which spans across social policy, the extent to which this represents a totalizing achievement of reach by the state is cast into doubt by its limited capacities, which challenge both governmental rhetoric and academic criticisms of the panopticon society. The capability of these attempts to force individuals to change their behaviour and 'make' subjects take up support is limited primarily by the fundamental conceptual flaws which prioritize rational models of human conduct based on future-oriented responses to the threat of sanction. In critiquing these developments in regulatory apparatus within the United Kingdom, it is important that the supportive and inclusionary impulses inherent to these new measures are acknowledged alongside their disciplinary, punitive and populist dimensions.

References

Ashworth, A. (2000) 'Is the Criminal Law a Lost Cause?', *Law Quarterly Review*, **116**(Apr.), 225–56.

Ayres, I. and Braithwaite, J. (1992) *Responsive Regulation: Transcending the Regulation Debate*. New York, NY: Oxford University Press.

Bentham, J. (1995) *The Panopticon Writings*. London: Verso.

Bottoms, A. (1983) 'Some Neglected Features of Contemporary Penal Systems', in D. Garland and P. Young (eds.), *The Power to Punish*. London: Heinemann, pp. 84–100.

Bullock, K. and Jones, B. (2004) *Acceptable Behaviour Contracts Addressing Antisocial Behaviour in the London Borough of Islington*. London: Home Office.

Burney, E. and Gelsthorpe, L. (2008) 'Do We Need a "Naughty Step"? Rethinking the Parenting Order after Ten Years', *Howard Journal*, **47**(5), 470–85.

Cleland, A. and Tisdall, K. (2005) 'The Challenge of Anti-social Behaviour: New Relationships Between the State, Children and Parents', *International Journal of Law, Policy and the Family*, **19**(3), 395–420.

Communities and Local Government (2009) *Guidance on the Use of Family Interventional Tenancies*. London: Communities and Local Government.

Crawford, A. (2003) '"Contractual Governance" of Deviant Behaviour', *Journal of Law and Society*, **30**(4), 479–505.

Cruikshank, B. (1999) *The Will to Empower: Democratic Citizens and Other Subjects*. Ithaca, NY: Cornell University Press.

Darker, I., Ward, H. and Caulfield, L. (2008) 'An Analysis of Offending by Young People Looked after by Local Authorities', *Youth Justice*, **8**(2), 134–48.

Deacon, A. (2004) 'Justifying Conditionality: The Case of Anti-social Tenants', *Housing Studies*, **19**(6), 911–26.

Department for Work and Pensions (2007a) *Sanction of Housing Benefit in Relation to Anti-social Behaviour: Guidance for Pilot Areas*. London: Department for Work and Pensions.

(2007b) *Housing Benefit Guidance on Housing Benefit Anti-social Behaviour Sanction for Local Authorities Participating in the Pilot Scheme*. London: Department for Work and Pensions.

(2008) *No One Written Off: Reforming Welfare to Reward Responsibility*. London: Department for Work and Pensions.

Dillane, J., Hill, M., Bannister, J. and Scott, S. (2001) *Evaluation of the Dundee Families Project*. Edinburgh: Scottish Executive.

Flint, J., Jones, A. and Parr, S. (2008a) *An Evaluation of the Sanction of Housing Benefit: Scoping Report*. London: Department for Work and Pensions.

(2008b) *An Evaluation of the Sanction of Housing Benefit: Progress Update Report*. London: Department for Work and Pensions.

Foucault, M. (1977) *Discipline and Punish: The Birth of the Prison*. London: Penguin.

(1978) *History of Sexuality, Volume 1: The Will to Knowledge*. New York, NY: Pantheon.

Garrett, P. M. (2007) '"Sinbin" Solutions: The "Pioneer" Projects for "Problem Families" and the Forgetfulness of Social Policy Research', *Critical Social Policy*, **27**(2), 203–30.

Ghate, D. and Ramella, M. (2002) *Positive Parenting: The National Evaluation of the Youth Justice Board's Parenting Programme*. London: Youth Justice Board.

HM Government (2008) *Youth Crime Action Plan*. London: Home Office.

Holt, A. (2008) 'Room for Resistance? Parenting Orders, Disciplinary Power and the Production of "the Bad Parent"', in P. Squires (ed.), *ASBO Nation: The Criminalisation of Nuisance*. Bristol: Policy Press, pp. 203–22.

Home Office (2007) *Guidance on the Use of Acceptable Behaviour Contracts and Agreements*. London: Home Office.

Hunter, C. (2006) 'The Changing Legal Framework: From Landlords to Agents of Social Control', in J. Flint (ed.), *Housing and Anti-social Behaviour: Perspectives, Policy and Practice*. Bristol: Policy Press, pp. 137–55.

Kay, E. and Tisdall, M. (2006) 'Antisocial Behaviour Legislation Meets Children's Services: Challenging Perspectives on Children, Parents and the State', *Critical Social Policy*, **26**(1), 101–20.

Lister, D. (2004) 'Controlling Letting Arrangements? Landlords and Surveillance in the Private Rented Sector', *Surveillance and Society*, **2**(4), 513–28.

McInytre-Bhatty, K. (2008) 'Truancy and Coercive Consent; Is There an Alternative?', *Educational Review*, **60**(4), 375–90.

Moran, P., Ghate, D. and van der Merwe, A. (2004) *What Works in Parenting Support? A Review of the International Evidence* (Research Report 574). London: Department for Education and Skills.

Nixon, J., Hunter, C., Parr, S., Myers, S., Whittle, S. and Sanderson, D. (2006) *Anti-social Behaviour Intensive Family Support Projects: An Evaluation of Six Pioneering Projects*. London: Office of the Deputy Prime Minister.

O'Malley, P. (2009) 'Theorizing Fines', *Punishment and Society*, **11**(1), 67–83.

Parr, S. and Nixon, J. (2009) 'Family Intervention Projects – Sites of Subversion and Resilience', in M. Barnes and D. Prior (eds.), *Subversive Citizens: Power, Agency and Resistance in Public Services*. Bristol: Policy Press.

Respect Task Force (2006) *Respect Action Plan*. London: Respect Task Force.

Rodger, J. J. (2006) 'Antisocial Families and Withholding Welfare Support', *Critical Social Policy*, **2**(1), 121–43.

Rowan Associates (2004) *Evaluating the Use of Introductory and Starter Tenancies*. Cardiff: Welsh Assembly Government.

Ruggieri, S. and Levinson, D. (1998) *Starter Tenancies and Introductory Tenancies: An Evaluation*. London: Housing Corporation.

Schram, S. F., Fording, R.C. and Soss, J. (2008) 'Neo-liberal Poverty Governance: Race, Place and the Punitive Turn In US Welfare Policy', *Cambridge Journal of Regions, Economy and Society*, **1**(1), 17–36.

Simester, A. P. and von Hirsch, A. (2006) 'Regulating Offensive Conduct through Two-Step Prohibitions', in A. P. Simester and A. von Hirsch (eds.), *Incivilities: Regulating Offensive Behaviour*. Oxford: Hart Publishing, pp. 173–94.

Stephen, F. (2009) 'Governing by civil order: an economist's perspective', paper (unpublished) presented at the ESRC Regulation and Criminal Justice Seminar, University of Manchester, 11 February 2009.

Vaughan, B. (2000) 'Punishment and Conditional Citizenship', *Punishment and Society*, **2(1)**, 23–39.

Wain, N. with Burney, E. (2007) *The ASBO: Wrong Turning, Dead End*. London: Howard League for Penal Reform.

Walters, A. and Woodward, R. (2008) 'Punishing "Poor Parents": "Respect", "Responsibility" and Parenting Orders in Scotland', *Youth Justice*, **7**(1), 5–20.

Welshman, J. (2008) 'Recuperation and Rehabilitation and the Residential Option: The Brentwood Centre for Mothers and Children', *Twentieth Century British History*, **19**(4), 502–29.

Zedner L. (2007) 'Pre-crime and Post-criminology', *Theoretical Criminology*, **11**(2), 261–81.

9

Counter-terrorism and community relations: anticipatory risk, regulation and justice

GABRIEL MYTHEN AND PALASH KAMRUZZAMAN

Introduction

Since the 9/11 attacks in Washington and New York, national security issues have risen sharply up the political agenda in many western nation states (see Amoore and de Goede 2008; McGhee 2008; Vedby Rasmussen 2008; Zedner 2005). Post-9/11 a cluster of incidents, including bombings in Istanbul, the Madrid train explosions and the 7/7 attacks in London have fixed the terrorist risk as a critical social concern. Despite the fact that political violence is a historically omnipresent phenomenon, the attacks committed by supporters of al-Qaeda have reconfigured not just the perceived level of the threat in the UK but also the scope of legal measures taken to tackle terrorism (see Bonner 2008; Lambert 2008). In recent years, terrorism has become ubiquitous in political and media discourse, being emblematic of the fears and uncertainties that characterize the 'risk society' (see Beck 2009; Mythen 2008). Of course, it is easy to see why 'global' terrorism has become such a focal issue. Not only are international terrorist attacks unpredictable and sizeable in scale, they effectively disrobe the claim that the state is able to secure safety and security for its citizens.

The regulatory responses to 9/11 and 7/7 have had wide-ranging impacts on Muslims living in the UK. Following on from these incidents, Muslim minority groups have been subject to intensified modes of monitoring, surveillance and intervention by crime and security agencies. The introduction of multiple forms of security regulation has been underscored by media and political discourses that have cast British Muslims as suspect and dangerous (see Pantazis and Pemberton 2008: 15). In the light of three of the four men that committed the 7/7 attacks being British-born Muslims, worries have been voiced about the threat presented by 'home-grown' terrorism (Longstaff and Graham 2008: 15). In the media, anxieties about the 'alien within' have shaded into and merged with extant discourses which have problematized Pakistani Britons and earmarked young Pakistanis in particular as risky 'others' (Saeed 2007: 451). More broadly, contemporary discourses connecting Islam with terrorism have segued into existing narratives of Muslims as a problem group in areas such as education, immigration and integration. It is important to note that racism towards Muslims in general and towards the British Pakistani community specifically is temporally rooted (see Frost 2008: 566; Poynting and Mason 2007: 63). While the identification of young Pakistani males as a risky group has generated specific incursions in terms of counter-terrorism strategies, discrimination against the wider Muslim community is historically embedded and expressed through a range of institutional discourses and practices (see Mirza 2007; Said 1997). Although the roots of racism in Britain are deep, the terrorist attacks associated with al-Qaeda have led to young Muslims being treated by sections of the media, judiciary and Parliament as a 'suspect population' (see Hillyard 1993; Mythen *et al.* 2009). Pakistani communities have at best been portrayed in the media as unwilling to integrate, at worst as encouraging religious extremism and supporting terrorist activity. In the mainstream British media, young Asian males are infrequently depicted as contributing positively to society and commonly associated with urban unrest, street crime, terrorism and drug use. Among frequent references to 'active terrorist cells' and 'terror plots' in the UK, allied to tense international relations associated with events unfolding in Pakistan, the political climate of suspicion towards Pakistani Britons appears to be worsening.[1] The claim by the then British Prime Minister Gordon Brown that three-quarters of the most serious terrorism cases investigated by British police have links to al-Qaeda in Pakistan will have done little to improve either domestic community relations or international ties (see Dodd 2009b).

It is evident that the security processes set in train post-9/11 have engendered a series of problems for Muslims around the globe. Internationally, these assaults were used to vindicate pre-emptive military action – not only against those suspected of orchestrating the attacks, but against the peoples of entire countries and regions. Domestically, a range of anxieties have been expressed about the impacts of counter-terrorism legislation on the conduct, rights and liberties of young British Muslims targeted by

[1] Since the 2008 election of Asif Ali Zardawi, British diplomatic relations with Pakistan have become palpably strained (see Department for Communities and Local Government Report 2009: 24).

counter-terrorism regulation (see Abbas 2005, 2007; Spalek 2008a: 211, 2008b). In contemporary society, young Muslims are cohering and navigating their identities in an environment in which they are pitched as a threat to national security, while being simultaneously invited to integrate more readily with 'core British values' (Mythen *et al.* 2009). Set within this context, this chapter documents consequential shifts in terrorism legislation towards the deployment of a future-based logic of risk in shaping contemporary technologies of regulation. We go on to identify salient examples of pre-emptive counter-terrorism practices and evaluate their implications for civil rights and liberties. Finally, drawing upon findings from a qualitative study involving young British Pakistanis we consider some of the consequences of cultural and legal forms of counter-terrorism regulation for Muslim minority groups and wider community relations. Aligning with the theme of this section of the book, our contribution raises many questions about the efficacy and justness of counter-terrorism regulation, both inside and outside the criminal justice system.

'New terrorism', anticipatory risk and the pre-emptive turn

There are a number of factors which are relevant when setting the context for discussions about the regulation of terrorism, including political power, prevailing attitudes towards penalty, public trust in government and contemporary legal values. While we will touch upon each of these in the course of the chapter, our principal focus rests on the emergence of two interrelated trends around the consolidation of a narrative of 'new terrorism' and the drive towards pre-emptive modes of counter-terrorism regulation. It is our contention that the ideological construction of 'new terrorism' in the media, security and political realms has both incited and reinforced the introduction of invasive preventive modes of surveillance, policing and intervention which have produced deleterious ramifications for Muslim minority communities in the UK.

Post-9/11, dominant political discourses around terrorism have tended to emphasize the uniqueness and magnitude of the threat from Islamic fundamentalist groups (see Burnett and Whyte 2005). In the UK, the debate about how best to manage the 'new' terrorist threat came to the fore under the tenure of Tony Blair, who vociferously defended the use of pre-emptive counter-terrorism strategies (see Blair 2005; McCulloch and Pickering 2009: 5). The notion that the novelty of modern terrorism requires exceptional domestic and international policies has been supported not only by politicians and those in the intelligence services, but also by academics working in the area of security studies (see Lacquer 2003; Lesser *et al.* 1999; Morgan 2004). This literature posits that, in contrast to the forms of violence practised by older organizations such as ETA and the IRA, new terrorist groups are seeking to enact visually spectacular attacks, using 'high-lethality' weapons and/or suicide bombers. The professed objective of new terrorist groups is to kill and maim large numbers of civilians by launching attacks with no forewarnings (see Hoffman 1999: 9; ISP/NSC 2005: 3). Rather than having well-defined hierarchies and united ideological goals, new terrorist groups are said to be characterized by their diffuse aims, scattered organization and capacity to strike across different continents. In addition, new terrorist organizations make extensive use of new media technologies to capture data, network, disseminate knowledge about attack planning and recruit new members (see Leitzinger 2004; Weimann 2006). The harmonization of the discourse of 'new terrorism' across the media, politics and intelligence industries has fuelled the formation of exceptional counter-terrorism legislation in the UK which has tested long-standing rights and liberties. By accenting the distinctive features of 'new terrorism', New Labour sought to gain a mandate to push through a raft of counter-terrorism legislation. It is apparent that anticipatory risk became a central feature in the counter-terrorism frameworks developed by New Labour.[2] Attempting to reduce harm by pre-empting terrorist attacks has become integral to terrorism strategy post-9/11. Constructed as a grave and existential danger, 'new terrorism' duly requires an unprecedented and extensive legislative response (see Peters 2004: 5). The declaration by Tony Blair that 'the rules of the game have changed' has been mobilized as a justification for what Agamben (2005) dubbed 'states of exception'. At the thick end of the wedge, these states of exception include military invasions, bombing of civilian areas, unjust modes of incarceration and extraordinary rendition. At the thinner edge, creeping forms of restrictive regulation have materialized, not just under the auspices of counter-terrorism legislation, but also in other areas including immigration, welfare and education (see Amoore and de Goede 2008; Mythen and Walklate 2006a). Despite the ubiquity of the 'new terrorism' narrative, there is little material evidence to support the transference into a new phase of 'new terrorism' (see Mythen 2007;

[2] It should be recognized that the drive towards anticipating risk within the criminal justice system was well established before the events of 9/11. That said, the deployment of risk and threat anticipation have expanded considerably via counter-terrorism measures introduced in the last decade (see McCulloch and Pickering 2009: 2).

Sprinzak 2006: 3). While the political and legislative climate surrounding the terrorist threat has become more acute, we can see many 'old' things in the 'new' terrorism, both in terms of organizational structure, political intent, desire to upset capital accumulation and intent to generate a climate of fear (see also Bonner 2008: 20; Burnett and Whyte 2005).[3] Disregarding its contestability, the discourse of 'new terrorism' has accelerated the motion towards pre-emptive modes of risk management (see Amoore and de Goede 2008; McCulloch and Pickering, 2009). The 9/11 Commission's (2004) description of the American intelligence services' inability to prevent the al-Qaeda attacks as a 'failure of the imagination' is highly prescient in this regard. The constellation of suppositions that constitute 'new terrorism' and the much maligned 'war on terror' invoke a precautionary, future-centric calculus of risk. Since 9/11, methodological tools of imagining the future – such as scenario testing and simulated disasters – have come to prominence and taken on wider political significance (de Goede 2008: 156). The playing out of such fictional scenarios in the media – including the detonation of dirty bombs in cities, intercontinental jets seized by terrorists and flown into nuclear power plants and the deliberate poisoning of public water supplies – merge to form a powerful cultural narrative of insecurity *in extremis* (Lee and Mythen 2008). The immanence of such safety-centric thinking, and the catastrophes that they invoke, ground imagined futures in the present and potentially aggravate public fears and insecurities. While horizon scanning and hypothetical attack scenarios are acceptable – and, indeed useful – strategies in training exercises designed to raise preparedness and alertness within the security sector, it becomes problematic if such imaginings seep into political debates about terrorism and serve as vindications for the introduction of exceptional counter-terrorism legislation. If political vistas are driven by the hypothetical appearance of future dangers, the end point is invariably worst-case scenario thinking. The net result of the creeping 'presence of the future' is that future-imagined events have come to direct contemporary policies (Mythen and Walklate 2008; Vedby Rasmussen 2004). Whereas security risk assessments have traditionally

[3] Many of the features ascribed to new terrorist groups have been common to groups formerly defined as 'terrorist'. For example, during its conflict with the British state, the IRA used weapons specialists, deployed a cell system and targeted areas of civilian use such as shopping centres and public houses. While the philosophies and objectives of 'old' and 'new' terrorist groups are clearly divergent, it is far from clear exactly how and why contemporary fundamentalist terrorism marks a radical rupture from political violence in the past (see McGhee 2008: 36; Mythen 2007).

predicted future outcomes based on previous incidents, a revamped calculus of risk has taken precedence under the penumbra of 'new terrorism'. This calculus does not assess the future by focusing on questions of the past, nor indeed the present. Instead, political evaluations – and subsequent forms of legal regulation – are increasingly being steered by the 'What if?' question, linking catastrophic future scenarios to the securitization of the present.

It needs to be recognized that the incalculability of the terrorist danger means that ensuring security measures are proportionate to harm is a difficult task. Threat assessments are made under conditions of incomplete knowledge, echoing Beck's (1999: 78) classic risk society dilemma:

> The ultimate deadlock of risk society … resides in the gap between knowledge and decision: there is no one who really knows the global outcome – at the level of positive knowledge, the situation is radically 'undecideable' – but we none the less have to decide … risk society is provoking an obscene gamble, a kind of ironic reversal of predestination: I am accountable for decisions which I was forced to make without proper knowledge of the situation.

The condition of not only not-knowing, but also knowing about not knowing has clearly unsettled governments and securocrats. While it would be rash to argue that threat assessments are being deliberately distorted by politicians and intelligence experts, it remains important that the regulation of terrorism does not run out of kilter with the degree of threat. We aver that too much political framing of terrorism and too much counter-terrorism legislation is being based around worst-case imaginings. Such scenarios may be useful in relation to thinking through security strategies, but they do not make a sound basis for modifying and augmenting law. Of course, it is not prudent to have lax laws which may encourage terrorist attacks to occur, but nor is it wise to push through draconian legislation which undermines civil liberties. Insofar as projective thought is necessary in thinking through and developing effective jurisprudence, we should not feel comfortable about introducing exceptional laws on the basis of hypothetical crimes. Laws ought to be made on evidence, not imagination.

Counter-terrorism legislation, rights and justice

Pre-emptive counter-terrorism measures are based on projected risks and seek to criminalize individuals who are believed to be the bearers of future harms. The objective of the preventive framework is to decrease the terrorist threat by wielding a mix of coercive sanctions and criminal justice measures to disrupt and counter risks before they materialize (see McCulloch and Pickering 2009: 4). In the UK, an assemblage of preventive measures have been propagated on the principle of anticipatory risk, including indefinite incarceration, extensions to detention without charge, control orders and enhanced stop, search and seize powers. Of course, the political context in which the legislative process is shaped is germane to the kinds of laws that are proposed. During its tenure the New Labour government strongly favoured legal activism in combating terrorism and this itself fused with a wider hegemonic project founded on the idea that legislation could be exercised as a lever for social regulation (see Hanman 2009). A bank of counter-terrorism legislation has been developed over the last decade, through the Terrorism Act 2000, the Anti-Terrorism, Crime and Security Act 2001, the Prevention of Terrorism Act 2005, the Terrorism Act 2006 and the Counter-Terrorism Act 2008. New Labour also implemented supplementary legislation, such as the Criminal Justice Act 1998 and the Regulation of Investigatory Powers Act 2000. These powers have largely been supported by senior police officers and intelligence agents who have held that precautionary measures are required to prevent attacks before they happen (see Evans 2007; Walker 2008: 1395). Yet a range of objections have been lodged by critics who maintain that new counter-terrorism laws fall outside the norms of criminal justice legislation and detrimentally affect fundamental rights and liberties (see Biglino 2002; Hudson 2009). Here we wish to focus on just three examples, namely control orders, the extension of detention without charge and the right to stop and search individuals without requiring reasonable suspicion.[4]

Prior to the acceptance of control orders, s. 23 of the Anti-Terrorism, Crime and Security Act 2001 granted the Home Secretary the power to incarcerate without charge foreign nationals suspected of being involved in terrorism. In 2004 this practice was adjudged to be in breach of the European Convention on Human Rights and declared illegal. Following on from this, control orders were controversially introduced in the Terrorism Act 2005. Control orders afford the Home Secretary the power to tag, track and contain terrorist suspects without formal charges being

[4] The Conservative–Liberal Democrat coalition government announced on 8 July 2010 that powers to stop and search without reasonable suspicion under the Terrorism Act 2000 would no longer be exercised in light of a ruling by the European Court of Human Rights (*Guardian*, 8 July 2010).

brought. In effect, control orders are akin to keeping a suspect under house arrest for up to 16 hours with basic legal rights such as the privacy, asylum and free movement being curtailed.[5] Control orders are a prime example of the mobilization of anticipatory risk to implement legislation that is exceptional in its capacity to disrupt basic human rights. Control orders can be set in train in circumstances in which a person is suspected of being involved with terrorism but the evidence is such that a case against cannot be made public. In effect, the control order leaves individuals subjected to it ignorant of the charge against them, jeopardizing the democratic right of those accused to defend themselves. Control orders place a string of invasive requirements on the individual which make it impossible for them to live the life of a normal citizen, including strict curfews on association and communication, confinement and complying with monitoring systems which disrupt sleeping patterns (see Saner 2009: 28; Travis 2009).

A further strategy of risk-based counter-terrorism legislation has been the lengthening of the number of days for which a terrorist suspect can be legally detained without formal charges being levelled. In the aftermath of 7/7, Tony Blair campaigned to raise the maximum permissible time for detention without charge to 90 days. Although this motion was eventually dismissed in Parliament, the UK has nonetheless seen an unprecedented growth in the time allowed to detain suspects without charge. The Terrorism Act of 2000 raised the standard 48-hour detention limit to 7 days with the permission of the courts. This period was doubled in 2003 and then raised to 28 days under s. 25 of the Terrorism Act 2006, subject to approval from judicial authorities. The argument made for such extensions is that the extent of human lives lost in future terrorist attacks may be so great that post-crime measures are ineffectual and may allow suspected terrorists to go on to commit atrocities. The case in favour of pre-emptive interventions has been underpinned by the so called 'ticking bomb' scenario, in which a terrorist suspect may possess information that could prevent a large-scale attack from happening. Given that the old modes of post-crime regulation would only allow for limited detention and questioning, the magnitude of the impending catastrophe dictates that exceptional pre-crime measures are called for to extract the relevant information and thwart the attack before it occurs. Under scrutiny, the ticking-bomb scenario does not make a particularly convincing case

[5] At the time of writing, there are 17 Control Orders in operation, 11 of which involve foreign nationals (see Travis 2009).

for the various 'states of exception' that have emerged post 9/11. There is nothing to suggest that a determined terrorist would be willing to impart the information required to prevent an attack regardless of the length of time or the conditions in which they were held. The argument that terrorism plots are more complex to investigate is easily unravelled. On the contrary, one could argue that gathering evidence and intelligence about terrorist activity was far more problematic prior to the use of computers and mobile phones. In a technological society, a much wider and deeper evidence trail is likely to exist than in previous epochs. Further, given that the palette of laws under the 2005 Terrorism Act reduces the threshold for being charged with terrorist offences, it would seem reasonable to posit that if no evidence can be found to charge a person under law, then they ought really to be released from detention. Aside from the unconvincing rationale for these dramatic modifications, British law is anomalous in comparison with other countries that have suffered serious terrorist attacks. The maximum permissible period of detention without charge in the United States is 48 hours, in Turkey it is 7.5 days and in Spain 5. It can only be assumed that the police and security services in such nations face similarly difficult circumstances in extricating terrorist plots. So far as the rights of the individual go, adherence to the logic of anticipatory risk in the setting of law has reduced the need to gather concrete evidence and removed the ancient right of *habeas corpus* (see Zedner 2008: 19). The incremental extension of detention without charge effectively switches presumption of innocence to presumption of guilt. To say that there are presently few cases in which long periods of detention apply does not constitute a firm case for its permanent introduction in law, nor does it recognize the way in which terrorism legislation can and has been deployed against other citizens considered a threat to social order, such as climate change protestors or those campaigning against the use of nuclear power. Strategies of anticipatory risk management – such as control orders and preventive detention – form part of a broader trend of developing pre-crime regulatory methods (see McCulloch and Pickering 2009; Zedner 2007). Feeley (2003: 126) has previously described the embedding of crime as a 'master theme' that has acted as a touchstone for political debate and policy-making. Building on this proposition, the threat of terrorism appears not only to have risen to the surface within political debates around security, but also impacted on areas of social policy previously considered peripheral to crime control, such as immigration and welfare. Working beyond governance through crime, it would appear that a movement can be traced towards 'governing through terrorism' (see Mythen and Walklate 2006a). All of this raises the barbed question of whether it is the level of the terrorist threat that has changed so dramatically or whether recent changes are symptomatic of the drift towards a risk-averse and punitive political climate.

The third controversial form of terrorism regulation that we wish to discuss is the enhancement of police stop and search powers. Part Five of the Terrorism Act 2000 authorizes police stop and searches on a person or a vehicle for items that could be used in connection with terrorism, 'whether or not the constable has grounds for suspecting the presence of articles of that kind'. In effect, s. 44 powers do not require a police officer to have reasonable suspicion of the person. Following on from the 9/11 attacks in New York and Washington, use of these powers was stepped up dramatically in the UK. Stop and searches conducted under s. 44 have been unevenly applied across the population, with young black and Asian males being disproportionately affected.[6] Unsurprisingly, the routine deployment of s. 44 has been challenged by British Muslim community groups and civil rights campaigners. Furthermore, legal challenges raised in the European Court of Human Rights have led to s. 44 powers being reviewed by the Conservative–Liberal Democrat coalition government. Unfortunately, as far as relations between Muslim minority groups and the police are concerned, the damage may already have been done. Despite the unevenness of application causing resentment in minority communities, the police decided to increase strategically the use of s. 44 after the 7/7 bombings (see Dodd 2009a). This produced further spikes in the figures that indicate that black and Asian individuals are disproportionately stop–searched in comparison with white British citizens. Government figures show that black and Asian people have been targeted, with the number of black people stopped under the powers rising by 322 per cent, with a rise among individuals from Asian minority groups of 277 per cent (Dodd 2009a). In practice, excessive and uneven use of stop–search powers has further frustrated and alienated the very communities that the police are dependent upon for cooperation and intelligence around counter-terrorism. As Ryder (2009: 1) points out, 'however tempting it may be to gather information in this way, it is a flawed strategy. The figures reveal that only a small percentage of stops glean meaningful information. At the same

[6] The number of Asian people stopped and searched under anti-terrorism laws in the UK quadrupled in the year after the 9/11 attacks, from 744 in 2001–2 to 2,989 in 2002–3 (Morris 2004). Following the 7/7 London bombings there was a sevenfold increase in the number of Asian people stopped and searched by the British Transport Police (Dodd 2005).

time, each unjustified stop exacts a price in good community relations. It creates a cycle of distrust that makes it even harder to obtain information in the future.' The governmental response to Muslim communities that have rallied against the use of racial profiling in police decisions to utilize s. 44 powers has done little to assuage fears.[7] Furthermore, the actual effectiveness of the practice in reducing the terrorist threat is debatable. In 2006–7 the number of stop–search powers under counter-terrorism legislation was 41,924. In 2007–8 that number trebled, with police officers using such powers to search 124,687 people. Only 1 per cent of those searches ended in an arrest of any sort and only 73 of that number were for terror offences (see Verkaik 2009). The human rights campaign group Liberty estimates that just six in every 10,000 stops results in an arrest.[8] More tellingly, s. 44 powers have not led to a single conviction for terrorist offences (Dodd 2009a). Post-dissemination of the 2007–8 statistics, the Assistant Commissioner of the Metropolitan Police, John Yates, conceded that the intensive use of stop–search powers has produced little benefit in reducing the terrorist threat and has damaged community relations.

The tightening of anti-terrorism legislation in response to 9/11 and 7/7 has impacted negatively on Muslim minorities in general and on the everyday movements and practices of young male Muslims in particular. The point at issue here is not just the law itself, but what, and moreover who, the law gets attached to. While we would clearly want those guilty of committing or planning to commit terrorist offences interrupted and punished, there has been a sequence of disquieting cases of 'proactive' policing that have unsettled Muslim minority communities. In 2006, under faulty intelligence 250 police officers surrounded and stormed a house in Forest Gate in search of a chemical weapon. In the subsequent arrest, Mohammed Kahar was shot in the chest while being arrested with his brother Abdul. After being detained and questioned for eight days, both were subsequently released without charge. More recently, 12 students, 11 of whom were studying on student visas from Pakistan, were arrested at gunpoint and detained for questioning. Seemingly disregarding the

[7] In 2005 then Communities Secretary Hazel Blears stated publicly: 'Muslims will have to accept as a reality that they will be stopped and searched by the police more often than the rest of the public' (cited in Abbas 2007: 294).

[8] According to the lawyer Corinna Ferguson 'a threefold increase in anti-terror stop and search is the clearest signal that these powers are being misused. Only 6 in 10,000 people stopped were arrested for terrorism, let alone charged or convicted. And the disproportionate impact on ethnic minorities is even greater than in previous years' (cited in Dodd 2009a).

perils of prejudicing the legal process, Prime Minister Brown, as he then was, stated: 'We are dealing with a very big terrorist plot ... there were a number of people who are suspected of it who have been arrested' (Laville 2009). At the time of the arrests, the media released details of the apparent 'targets', including the Arndale and Trafford shopping centres in Manchester. At the time of writing, ten of the twelve remain imprisoned and are facing deportation back to Pakistan despite no evidence whatsoever being tabled to implicate them in terrorist activities. The net effect of these kind of high-profile injustices on community relations is difficult to measure. What is highly disturbing is the degree of negative labelling used by the media in its representation of British Pakistani communities and the ways in which governmental discourses have failed to distinguish adequately between the views of a small minority of religious extremists and those of the majority of peaceable Muslims. The continued identification of Muslim minority groups as 'suspect communities' – alongside the criminalization and marginalization of young male Muslims – is serving to alienate an already materially disadvantaged and politically disaffected group (see Poynting *et al.* 2004). From our discussion, it is apparent that modes of counter-terrorism legislation driven by anticipatory risk can generate tensions in terms of civil rights, proportionality and impact on Muslim minority groups. It is the latter issue that we now wish to turn to in more detail.

Listening to young Muslims: counter-terrorism, risk and regulation revisited

In the UK, Pakistanis make up almost half of the British Muslim population and contemporary estimates of the Pakistani Muslim population put the figure at around 900,000 (Department for Communities and Local Government 2009: 6). Recent figures show that 98 per cent of the Pakistani population in the UK are Muslims (Department for Communities and Local Government 2009: 7). There are some sharp disparities in socio-economic opportunities when comparing white British citizens with Pakistani Britons. Relative to their white counterparts, British Pakistanis are more likely to be unemployed, receive a low income, live in inferior housing, suffer poor quality of health and face discrimination in employment and education (see Abbas 2005, 2007; Modood 1997; Peach 2006; Platt 2007). A recent study commissioned by the Joseph Rowntree Foundation reported that the poverty rate for British Pakistanis stands at 55 per cent, compared to 20 per cent among white British people (Palmer and Kenway 2007). Pakistani communities in the UK are geographically dispersed, although there are relatively large populations in London, Yorkshire, the West Midlands and Lancashire. It is within the last of these regions that our study was located.

The findings we draw upon here were generated during a qualitative inquiry conducted in 2007 involving 32 British Muslims aged between 18 and 26.[9] Before we come to our findings it is first necessary to provide a capsule account of our research methods. Given the sensitive nature of the topics that we wished to discuss, we set up our study using first-phase focus group discussions followed by second-phase in-depth interviews with a tranche of the group. The focus group method was selected for the first phase of the study as it enabled frank and open discussion among peers. The focus group method potentially affords socially excluded groups the opportunity to talk and discuss issues relatively informally and autonomously (see Krueger 2003). Previous studies have demonstrated the utility of focus groups when researching sensitive issues and complex situations (see Morgan 1993; Silverman 2002). The participants involved in the study were contacted through local agencies involved in work with young Muslims within the local community and subsequent snowball sampling.[10] We set out with a deliberately open framework rather than a particular hypothesis. As such, we were interested to explore a trio of interlinked issues around media representations of Islam/Muslims; the impacts of counter-terrorism legislation on experiences of victimization and the relationship between discourses of the terrorist risk and identity construction. In harmony with the trajectory of the collection, it is the latter couplet that we wish to unpack here. Our focal research areas were cascaded into questions to be debated within focus groups. While we were

[9] Given the location and size of the sample we do no not purport to have achieved representativeness in our sample, nor are our findings generalizable en bloc to all young British Pakistanis in the UK. Our findings should be treated as reflecting critical moments in the lives of our participants and providing a snapshot of the values and experiences of our sample. Given that our research issues were specific rather than generic, this snapshot is selective and represents particular frames of experience related to our overall research questions rather than the totality of lived experiences.

[10] The research project was sanctioned by the University of Liverpool's Ethics Committee. Confidentiality and anonymity for participants was assured by adherence to the ethical guidelines provided by the British Society of Criminology. Participants were briefed on the purpose of the research and on the topics to be discussed. Freely given and informed consent was attained from all participants engaged in the study. Research participants were informed that they had the right to withdraw from the study at any stage for any reason and without repercussion. The names of all participants have been altered to ensure anonymity.

keen to avoid over-steering discussions by generating discussion around these issues, our framework allowed us to capture a full dataset and to trace intragroup differences through interaction, dialogue and disagreement. After transcribing the focus groups, prescient themes or phenomena were labelled as they arose through axial encoding which enabled the fracturing and reassembly of data in multiple forms. Frequent and discursively prominent issues were identified through thematic analysis and these themes were further excavated in follow-up interviews which permitted us to explore salient issues arising in the focus groups and to subject-specific topics to deeper analysis. In essence, the collective picture built up in first-phase focus groups was complemented by dense individual narratives in the second phase of interviews. As such, the second phase of in-depth interviewing was designed to draw out thick descriptions of lived experiences, particularly through focusing on personal biographies and identities. The interview stage allowed for thorough investigation of central issues arising in the focus group phase and permitted the researchers to cross check ambiguities and contested issues. The individualized format of the interviews was designed to supplement the collective perspectives garnered in the first focus group phase of research to provide a rounded reflection of the experiences, feelings and opinions of participants.[11] We adopted a consciously reflexive approach to the study which entailed analysing and questioning the impact of our own preconceptions and values on the research inquiry. Our findings were validated through a process of triangulation and the data garnered in both project phases was subjected to internal scrutiny and reflection.

During the course of the study we posed a range of open questions about the experiences of our participants within different social institutions and the broader public sphere. The majority of participants claimed to have experienced institutional racism and many of them discussed explicit forms of prejudice in dealings with the police, government, media or within the legal system. This victimization was viewed as operating at two levels, against the individual and against the Muslim community as a collective. At an individual level, narratives of verbal racist intimidation, physical attack, being spat on, damage to property and having clothing forcibly torn or removed were all recounted. At a collective level,

[11] The member of the research team that facilitated the focus groups and conducted the in-depth interviews is a second-generation British Muslim fluent in English, Urdu and Punjabi. Familiarity with the social and civic issues experienced and negotiated by Pakistani communities in the UK enabled us to broach otherwise hard-to-reach issues, allowing us to gather a rich set of data and adding to the integrity of our findings.

victimization was couched more in terms of domestic terrorism legislation, foreign policy, policing and media stereotyping. As we shall discuss, these individual and collective factors were seen as acting in symbiosis in relation to discrimination and victimization. In as much as our inquiry was designed to explore a range of issues around identity, victimization and regulation, we especially wanted to investigate the effects of the current climate of suspicion around terrorism on identity construction and wider community relations. During focus group discussions, we asked our respondents directly about their thoughts and opinions about counter-terrorism legislation in the UK. The overwhelming feeling from the discussions that we facilitated was that the government had pushed through excessive forms of regulation that were having a detrimental impact on community relations with other ethnic groups and on the relationship between Pakistani communities and the police force. The experiential narratives that our participants described – around the surveillance, suspicion and interruption that they encountered on a daily basis – were disconcerting and sobering. Respondents roundly expressed dissatisfaction about the operation of counter-terrorism law. While some took issue with specific aspects of current legislation, others recounted personal testimonies of being put under intensified surveillance and scrutiny by the police. Taken together these discrete and generic concerns fuelled the widely shared view that young Muslims were being suspected and questioned not for their actions at any given moment, but because of their race:

ABID: I got stopped in Manchester once. It was around that whole 9/11 thing. My brother got stopped three times in one day. In one day! Just for a random stop and search, in the end he completely lost the plot with the coppers and, hmm, they threatened to put him in a cell so he had to calm down. Three times in one day!

SAJID: It's more directly an issue for men of our age really. Most us have personally experienced what it's like to be stopped as it happens so frequently. It makes you feel so exposed. So even if you've done nothing and you see the police you start getting paranoid about what you're doing. When I've been stopped I've been so wound up wanting to say something, but you know if you say anything you're going to be the one who loses out. So there's no way of letting that anger and frustration out.

(Focus Group 1)

Although some of our participants responded to what they perceived as unjust legislation by retreating inwards and attempting to keep a low profile in public, the majority expressed infuriation:

AAFREEN: It's pure victimization. Every Muslim I know has friends or family who've been hassled by the police, so people are bound to get angry. When it's happening to people you know for no other reason than how they look it can't be anything other than discrimination. And which Muslims do you know who won't get affected by that?

ZAREENA: I'm angry, what else can you feel? All the legislation they've brought in is used to target Muslims. Like stop and search, they're not using that on white people, it's used against Asians and Muslims. It makes you worry about people you know. They can stop you on the streets; search your property whenever they want. It's a racist's dream come true. Look what happened with the Forest Gate thing. Everyone's asleep then the next minute all hell breaks loose and that guy ends up shot, no charges or anything. That's the reality of what's happening.

(Focus Group 2)

The combination of feeling victimized and treated as suspicious, allied to disgruntlement about counter-terrorism regulation and policing had for most, strengthened their Muslim identities. Feelings of anger and disenchantment often shaded into statements about the reinforcement of religious and political identity, as evidenced in the following exchanges:

FACILITATOR: Has your identity changed following the events of 9/11?

SHAMS: Only that I now feel more Muslim. Yes, it's worked out really bad for us, but it's made me more politically Muslim rather than religiously Muslim, do you see what I mean? But like I said it has strengthened how I identify myself. I feel more Muslim than anything else.

REHMAN: It's the same for me I feel that I'm part of a worldwide community. Before I really dwelt on the negative aspects of Islam, in a way I wanted to get away. Now there are still things I don't agree with in the religion but now I'm proud to be a Muslim.

(Focus Group 1)

ANNIS: I don't know if I've changed. I feel that people have changed towards me because I look Muslim. That makes me feel like saying piss off; you know it makes me angry. So if I've changed it's because they've changed towards me. The only thing I'll say is that before I'd pray *namaaz* and not really think about what it means to me, but now it's made my conviction stronger and I suppose it's made me more Muslim, if you know what I mean?

YASMIN: I personally think that my identity has become, hmm, reinforced. Because since the events, I mean, we've had no choice. Muslims have had to come together. The only thing we've had to unify us is our beliefs, you know, our Islam, and these are the times when we have to really stick by it and be proud of who we are.

(Focus Group 3)

Although our findings cannot be generalized, they reflect the results of larger-scale studies which have shown a retrenchment of Islamic identities among young British Muslims (GFK 2006: 23; Mirza *et al.* 2007). In many respects the identity narratives we listened to chime with Modood's (1997) identification of 'reactive pride' in response to negative labelling and stigmatization. Among young British Muslims, the mobilization of Islam as a primary facet of identity is being expressed as a new-found assertiveness that is 'sometimes a religious revival, sometimes a political identity, sometimes both' (Modood 1997: 386). As the dialogues above suggest, 9/11 and 7/7 have served as critical moments at which religious and political identities have been both challenged and crystallized. In so far as indiscriminate terrorist attacks were condemned, the young people we spoke to collectively believed that the failure of the state to address British Muslims' cultural, political and religious grievances was central in provoking 'home-grown' religious extremism. Furthermore, the military invasions of Iraq and Afghanistan cropped up often in talk alongside the intransigence of the British state in challenging violence enacted on Muslims by the Israeli state:

SHAMS: It is a result of attacking Iraq and Afghanistan. Muslims are just being picked on all over the world and they are powerless. So maybe it's anger. It's hard not to let your feelings get the better of you at times. I don't mean I think about going out and doing something. You just get so angry at what's happening, not just here, but over there, in Iraq and Israel I mean.

(Focus Group 1)

For our participants, then, the revival of Muslim identity is a process catalyzed in defiance of hostility and suspicion. For many of the young people we spoke to, feeling targeted and victimized was serving to solidify the religious and political aspects of their identities. In effect, a widespread experiential feeling of suffering personal injustice was strongly being connected to the wider Pakistani community in the UK and Muslims in other parts of the world. To this end, we detected a trend towards referring to the ummah as a source of union between self and collective identity. This combination of reactive pride and the stranding together of local and global is captured in the following exchanges:

FACILITATOR: So how do you feel about the introduction of recent anti-terrorism legislation?

REHANA: First and foremost, very angry. Very angry. It's an invasion of privacy, stopping and searching, invading your house with no reason, hmm, just because they want to. It makes you feel like you're being bullied.

VIRAF: That's not the point, where does it end? I'm proud to be Muslim. All this sort of thing does is make me want to show I'm Muslim more. It's not Jack Straw's place to tell us what we can and cannot wear. Why doesn't he tell Sikhs not to wear the turban, Jewish people skull caps? Why are they picking on us? They just want to get rid of all our customs. Kill us in Iraq, Afghanistan and Palestine and stop us from wearing what we want in England

ANNIS: Detain us without reason in Guantánamo.
ASAD: Stop and search us without reason wherever and whenever you want.
ZAF: Raid our houses using false intelligence.

(Focus Group 3)

In addition to specific quarrels with domestic and international terrorism strategies, we also found a sense of bewilderment at the pervasive nature of Islamophobia in British society. The young Muslims we spoke to very much felt that 9/11 and 7/7 had reopened a floodgate of racism simmering beneath the surface. Many believed that Islamophobia had become culturally normalized in the UK, citing various examples of public figures who had voiced anti-Muslim sentiments. Mirroring other empirical work in the field, our respondents reported having to frequently explain themselves and their religion to non-Muslims and being pressured into accounting for the behaviour of other Muslims (see Hopkins 2007). This often involved being obligated to distance themselves from the ideas and actions of extremists and to correct misperceptions about Islam as a religion.

The data that we have drawn upon here are intended to offer illustrations of just some of the problems and issues facing young British Pakistanis in the UK and some of the coping strategies being resolved in order to maintain a sense of self and community. While our discussion has been succinct, our findings demonstrate that positive solutions to longstanding inequalities and discrimination affecting the British Pakistani community are urgently required. Post 9/11, existing grievances appear to have been further aggravated by aggressive counter-terrorism policies which have disproportionately targeted British Muslims. What the young Muslims we conversed with called for was a wider political focus that may actually elucidate some of the root causes of tensions within communities, including institutional discrimination, economic and cultural inequalities and the morality of current foreign policies in the Middle East. The all-encompassing nature of the construction of young Muslims as a problematic and risky group has left little space for the development of alternative positive narratives. Our participants felt that the opportunity for them to speak openly and freely about social and political issues has shrunk considerably. Broadening our discussion out, participants expressed lucid narratives about the narrowness of the dominant political focus on what Muslims in the UK should and ought to be doing: about how they should dress, about how they should communicate with white British communities, about how they should practise their religion and about how they should respond to fellow Muslims. This version of 'integration' was described as a one-way process of Muslims fitting in with what is construed as traditional British culture. For the young people in the study, improving community relations requires not just a deeper understanding of Muslim cultures, but also focusing on Muslim–non-Muslim relations as a two-way process that requires effort from all involved.

Conclusion

In this contribution we have surveyed several problems and difficulties stemming from the formation, consolidation and deployment of counter-terrorism regulation in contemporary Britain in the last decade. We began by locking onto the current shift towards the use of pre-emptive and preventive modes of law enforcement and travelled on to problematize specific modes of pre-crime counter-terrorism regulation founded on the logic of anticipatory risk. Under the rubric of the 'What if?' question the range of catastrophic imaginings of terrorist attacks relayed to the public has been sizeable (de Goede 2008; Mythen and Walklate 2008). Such premeditations have been politically marshalled to maximize support for stringent counter-terrorism measures. Of course, law is dynamic not static and new measures may well be necessary to reduce the risk to the public. Yet it is incumbent on government to ensure that terrorism regulation is proportionate to the actual not the imagined threat level. In our later discussions we migrated from the macro to the micro, giving voice to the reflections of a group of young Pakistani Muslims on the consequences of both cultural and legal modes of counter-terrorism regulation. In so doing, we have raised a number of difficult and sensitive issues around the justness and the efficacy of legal interventions geared towards pre-emption. We have also documented some of the deleterious effects of cultural forms of regulation associated with the socio-political construction of terrorist criminality. Finally, we have demonstrated that many aspects of counter-terrorism regulation are vociferously contested by those at the sharp end of such policies and practices. With disputes over the nature and causes of terrorism very much in mind, we need to remember that legal regulation constitutes a diffuse normative and moral attempt to bring people to order: 'regulation appears to suggest the institutionalization of the process by which persons are made regular. Indeed, to refer to regulation in the plural is already to acknowledge those concrete laws, rules and policies that constitute the legal instruments through which people are made regular' (Butler 2004: 40). In this sense, the practice of regulation not only functions to maintain social order, it also regularizes certain groups and ostracizes others. For the young people that we talked to, the dilemmas and contradictions of regulation are not academic. They have real consequences and effects.

The wider questions of what happens to civil and human rights under terrorism law devised under states of exception is clearly connected to the shifting balance in the criminal justice system away from the liberties of minorities and towards the 'security' of majorities. On the evidence presented here, this tipping of the scales brings with it a constellation of risks. While we are living in a labile and, in some respects, a frightening world, it is crucial that we do not allow our minds to become 'factories of fear' (Tillich 1952), susceptible to sanctioning punitive injustices in the pursuit of security. As Bonner (2008: 21) reasons: 'If our response to any significant threat to our security or safety is without proof of a criminal offence to lock away or seriously disrupt the lives of those merely thought to be a threat, this represents a grave danger.' It is critical that British Muslims are afforded the same principles and treatment as individuals from other faith and non-faith groups. That is to say that Muslims have the right to be presumed innocent, unless there is evidence that they are guilty. In order to puncture and disrupt the present climate of pre-emptive delirium, it is beholden on criminologists to ask searching and critical questions of those involved in proposing, sanctioning and implementing counter-terrorism legislation. As Zedner (2005: 525) has argued, with political will exceptional measures brought in to combat terrorism can become socially normalized. Further, what are originally classified as states of exception can, in maturation, act as platforms for subsequent tiers of restrictive legislation (McCulloch and Pickering 2009). It should be remembered too that unjust policies and the unfair application of law can serve to anger and alienate the individual and ratchet up tensions between the police, the state and minority communities. At present, draconian counter-terrorism policies have succeeded in encouraging hostility towards Muslim minority groups and have unjustly criminalized Muslims as a suspect population (Frost 2008: 546). In this sense, in the long term, modes of legal regulation formally designed to decrease the terrorist risk may actually serve as grist to the mill for extremists, reducing rather than enhancing national security. In other words, this is not just unappealing or disliked regulation, it is positively counter-productive. The issue that needs to be foregrounded in the present debate about the management of the terrorist risk is what degree of liberty is worth paying for what degree of security. If the pursuit of security erodes human rights, then not only is the quality of that security questionable, but underlying democratic principles are abused. Attempts to regulate the behaviour of minority groups raise important issues of principle for the whole of society.

References

Abbas, T. (2005) *Muslim Britain: Communities Under Pressure*. London: Zed.

(2007) 'Muslim Minorities in Britain: Integration, Multiculturalism and Radicalism in the Post-7/7 Period', *Journal of Intercultural Studies*, **28**(3), 287–300.

Agamben, G. (2005) *State of Exception*. Chicago University Press.

Amoore, L. and de Goede, M. (2008) *Risk and the War on Terror*. London: Routledge.

Beck, U. (1999) *World Risk Society*. London: Sage.

(2009) *World at Risk*. Cambridge: Polity Press.

Biglino, I. (2002) *Anti-Terrorism Legislation in Britain*. London: Liberty.

Blair, T. (2005) Prime Minister's Press Conference, 5 August (at: www.number10.gov.uk/output/Page8041.asp).

Bonner, D. (2008) 'Have the Rules of the Game Changed?', *Criminal Justice Matters*, **73**(1), 20–1.

Burnett, J. and Whyte, D. (2005) 'Embedded Expertise and the New Terrorism Thesis', *Journal of Crime, Conflict and Media Culture*, **1**(4), 1–18.

Butler, J. (2004) *Undoing Gender*. New York, NY: Routledge.

Department for Communities and Local Government (2009) *The Pakistani Muslim Community in England*. London: Change Institute.

Dodd, V. (2005) 'Asian Men Targeted in Stop and Search', *Guardian* (17 August).

(2009a) 'Police to Severely Curtail Use of Stop and Search Powers', *Guardian* (6 May).

(2009b) 'Pakistan Anger at UK Terror Slurs', *Guardian* (25 April).

Evans, J. (2007) *Intelligence, Counter-terrorism and Trust*. London: Security Service.

Feeley, M. (2003) 'Crime, Social Order and the Rise of Neo-conservative Politics', *Theoretical Criminology*, **7**(1), 111–30.

Frost, D. (2008) 'Islamophobia: Examining Causal Links between the State and "Race Hate" from Below', *International Journal of Sociology and Social Policy*, **28**(11), 546–63.

GFK (2006) *Muslim Views: Foreign Policy and its Effects*. London: 1990 Trust.

Goede, M. de (2008) 'Beyond Risk: Premeditation and Post 9/11 Security Imagination', *Security Dialogue*, **39**(2), 155–76.

Hanman, N. (2009) 'Explainer: Terrorism Legislation', *Guardian* (22 January).

Hillyard, P. (1993) *Suspect Community: People's Experience of the Prevention of Terrorism Acts in Britain*. London: Pluto Press.

Hoffman, B. (1999) 'Introduction', in I. Lesser, B. Hoffman, J. Arquilla, D. Ronfeldt, M. Zanini and B. Jenkins (eds.), *Countering the New Terrorism*. Santa Monica, CA: RAND.

Hopkins, P. (2007) 'Young Muslim Men's Experiences of Local Landscapes after 11th September 2001', in C. Atkinson, P. Hopkins and M. Kwan (eds.), *Geographies of Muslim Identities: Diaspora, Gender and Belonging*. Aldershot: Ashgate.

Hudson, B. (2009) 'Justice in a Time of Terror', *British Journal of Criminology*, advance access archive, doi:10.1093/bjc/azp034.

Krueger, R. (2003) *Doing Qualitative Research*. London: Sage.

Lambert, R. (2008) 'Ignoring the Lessons of the Past', *Criminal Justice Matters*, **73**(1), 22–3.

Laqueur, W. (2003) *No End to War: Terrorism in the 21st Century*. New York, NY: Continuum.

Laville, S. (2009) 'Student Visa Link to Terror Raids as Gordon Brown Points Finger at Pakistan', *Guardian* (10 April).

Lee, M. and Mythen, G. (2008) 'Security, Liberty and Justice: 1984 and the Past–Present', in T. Majoribanks (ed.), *Re-imagining Sociology*. University of Melbourne Press.

Leitzinger, A. (2004) 'Postmodern Terrorism?', *Eurasian Politician*, (Jan.), 1–3.

Lesser, I., Hoffman, B., Arquilla, J., Ronfeldt, D., Zanini, M. and Jenkins, B. M. (1999) *Countering the New Terrorism*. Santa Monica, CA: RAND.

Lint, W. de and Virta, S. (2004) 'Security and Ambiguity: Towards a Radical Security Politics', *Theoretical Criminology*, **8**(4), 465–89.

Longstaff, A. and Graham, J. (2008) 'Anti-terrorism and Police Powers: Should We Be Concerned?', *Criminal Justice Matters*, **73**(1), 15–16.

McCulloch, J. and Pickering, S. (2009) 'Pre-Crime and Counter-terrorism: Imagining Future Crime in the "War on Terror"', *British Journal of Criminology*, advance access archive, doi:10.1093/bjc/azp023.

McGhee, D. (2008) *The End of Multiculturalism? Terrorism, Integration and Human Rights*. Buckingham: Open University Press.

Mirza, M. (2007) 'Being Muslim Is not a Barrier to Being British', *Guardian* (7 February).

Mirza, M., Senthilkumaran, A. and Ja'far, Z. (2007) *Living Apart Together: British Muslims and the Paradox of Multiculturalism*. London: Policy Exchange.

Modood, T. (1997) *The Politics of Multiculturalism in the New Europe: Racism, Identity and Community*. London: Zed.

Morgan, D. (1993) *Successful Focus Groups: Advancing the State-of-the-Art*. London: Sage.

Morgan, M. (2004) 'The Origins of New Terrorism', *Parameters*, spring edition, 29–43.

Morris, N. (2004) 'The Politics of Fear', *The Independent* (23 November).
Mythen, G. (2007) 'The Postmodern Terrorist Risk: Plus Ça Change, Plus C'est la Même Chose?', in T. Owen and J. Powell (eds.), *Reconstructing Postmodernism: Critical Debates*. New York, NY: Nova Science Publications.
(2008) 'Sociology and the Art of Risk', *Sociology Compass*, **2**(1), 299–316.
Mythen, G. and Walklate, S. (2006a) 'Criminology and Terrorism: Which Thesis? Risk Society or Governmentality?', *British Journal of Criminology*, **46**(3), 379–98.
(2006b) 'Communicating the Terrorist Risk: Harnessing a Culture of Fear?', *Crime, Media, Culture: An International Journal*, **2**(2), 123–42.
(2008) 'Terrorism, Risk and International Security: The Perils of Asking What if?', *Security Dialogue*, **39**(2–3), 221–42.
Mythen, G., Walklate, S. and Khan, F. (2009), 'I'm a Muslim, but I'm Not a Terrorist: Victimization, Risky Identities and the Performance of Safety', *British Journal of Criminology*, advance access archive, doi: 10.1093/bjc/azp032.
9/11 Commission Report (2004) Final Report of the National Commission on Terrorist Attacks Upon the United States. Washington, DC: National Commission on Terrorist Attacks.
Palmer, G. and Kenway, P. (2007) *Poverty Rates Among Ethnic Groups in Britain*. London: Joseph Rowntree Foundation.
Pantazis, C. and Pemberton, S. (2008) 'Trading Civil Liberties for Greater Security? The Impact on Minority Communities', *Criminal Justice Matters*, **73**(1), 12–14.
Peach, C. (2006) 'Muslims in the 2001 Census of England and Wales: Gender and Economic Disadvantage', *Ethnic and Racial Studies*, **29**(1), 629–55.
Peters, M. (2004) *Postmodern Terror in a Globalized World*. University of Glasgow.
Platt, L. (2007) *Poverty and Ethnicity in the UK*. York: Joseph Rowntree Foundation.
Poynting, S. and Mason, V. (2007) 'The Resistible Rise of Islamophobia: Anti-Muslim Racism in the UK and Australia before 11 September 2001', *Journal of Sociology*, **43**(1), 61–86.
Poynting, S., Noble, G., Tabar, P. and Collins, J. (2004) *Bin Laden in the Suburbs: Criminalising the Arab Other*. Sydney Institute of Criminology Press.
Ryder, M. (2009) 'The Police Need to Stop and Think about Stop and Search', *Guardian* (3 May).
Saeed, A. (2007) 'Media, Racism and Islamophobia: The Representation of Islam and Muslims in the Media', *Sociology Compass*, (1), 443–62.
Said, E. (1997) *Covering Islam: How the Media and the Experts Determine How We See the Rest of the World*. London: Vintage.
Saner, E. (2009) 'A Day in the Life of a Terror Suspect', *Guardian* (13 June).

Silverman, D. (2002) *Interpreting Qualitative Data: Methods for Analysing Talk, Text and Interaction*. London: Sage.

Spalek, B. (2008a) Muslim Communities Post-9/11 – Citizenship, Security and Social Justice', *International Journal of Crime, Law and Justice*, **36**(4), 211–14.

(2008b) 'Terrorism: Emerging Critiques', *Criminal Justice Matters*, **73**(1), 10–11.

Sprinzak, E. (2006) 'The Great Superterrorism Scare' (at: www.radiobergen.org/terrorism/super-2.html).

Tillich, P. (1952) *The Courage To Be*. Glasgow: Collins.

Travis, A. (2009) 'Law Lords Outlaw Control Orders' Evidence', *Guardian* (11 June).

Vaughan, B. and Kilcommins, S. (2007) *Terrorism, Rights and the Rule of Law*. Cullumpton, Devon: Willan.

Vedby Rasmussen, M. (2004) 'It Sounds Like a Riddle: Security Studies, the War on Terror and Risk', *Millennium: Journal of International Studies*, **30**(2), 381–95.

(2008) *The Risk Society at War*. Cambridge University Press.

Verkaik, R. (2009) 'Muslims Hit by Trebling in Stop and Search', *The Independent* (1 May).

Walker, C. (2008), 'Keeping Control of Terrorists Without Losing Control of Constitutionalism', *Stamford Law Review*, **59**, 1395–98.

Weimann, G. (2006) *Terror on the Internet: The New Challenges, the New Arena*. Israel: Haifa University.

Zedner, L. (2005) 'Securing Liberty in the Face of Terror: Reflections from Criminal Justice', *Journal of Law and Society*, **32**(4), 507–33.

(2007) 'Pre-crime and Post-Criminology?', *Theoretical Criminology*, **11**(2), 261–81.

(2008) 'Terrorism, the Ticking Bomb and Criminal Justice Values', *Criminal Justice Matters*, **73**(1), 18–19.

PART III

Regulation of criminal justice: monitoring, effectiveness and accountability

10

The regulation of criminal justice: inspectorates, ombudsmen and inquiries

ANNE OWERS

This chapter explores the particular difficulties of regulating the criminal justice system. In many ways, it is less a system than a group of overlapping organizations with a common population, but not necessarily congruent goals. These tensions are reflected in the arrangements for regulating the different parts of the system.

This chapter is written entirely from a practitioner's point of view, and focuses on the inspection of places of custody, which is the most extreme sanction the state can impose. It draws strongly from my experiences and perceptions of nearly eight years as HM Chief Inspector of Prisons, and of inspecting a particular, and the most extreme, form of the regulation of behaviour through criminal sanction – imprisonment. I look at that role in the context of the inspection of criminal justice as a whole in England and Wales. I examine recent attempts by the government to create a single inspectorate and explain why I believe that this is inappropriate. I also look at the other mechanisms for redress and monitoring in England and Wales and conclude with some reflections on methods of inspecting and monitoring places of custody in other countries, specifically the United States and France.

There are five criminal justice inspectorates in England and Wales: the Inspectorates of Constabulary, Crown Prosecution Service, Courts Administration, Probation and Prisons. Their areas of responsibility are self-evident but they are differently constituted and have varying functions. In 2006, they were faced with merger into a single Police, Criminal Justice and Custody inspectorate, but the legislation failed to get through Parliament. Instead, the chief inspectors, who had already been working together informally as a criminal justice chief inspectors' group, agreed to more formal cooperation and an expanded programme of joint inspection work across criminal justice, on which reports are made to the three criminal justice ministers (the Justice Minister, the Home Secretary and the Attorney General).

However, for much of the succeeding two years, this activity was still being critically scrutinized by the newly created department of Business Enterprise and Regulatory Reform (BERR),[1] which inherited the objectives and responsibilities of the Better Regulation Executive – a Cabinet Office/Treasury body. That body was set up essentially to regulate regulation: initially to free business and private enterprise from what was seen and described as the 'burden of regulation'. It then assumed that the same principles could and should apply to the public sector, and to all public sector activity equally. Thus, the answer to public sector inspection and regulation was four inspectorates: an inspectorate for local government (essentially an expanded Audit Commission), an inspectorate for children's services, including education (Ofsted),[2] an inspectorate for health and social care (the Care Quality Commission)[3] and a criminal justice inspectorate. BERR remained unconvinced that its regulatory principles and desired outcomes could be achieved in criminal justice by the current loosely federated approach, and continued to dangle the Damoclean sword of legislative merger.

This process, and these assumptions, have been uncontaminated by any clear definitions of what is meant, or desired, by inspection, regulation or indeed criminal justice. First, the criminal justice inspectorate's activity is not confined to criminal justice – nor are they the only inspectors or regulators with powers and interests in criminal justice activity. The police have a crime prevention and public order role, the courts inspectorate covers civil matters, the probation inspectorate inspects the multi-agency youth offending teams, and the prisons inspectorate has responsibility for inspecting places of immigration detention. There are many other players within the criminal justice regulatory field, whether criminal justice is defined broadly or narrowly: the Audit Commission in relation to local authority powers and duties on crime prevention, the transport and health and safety regulators, the Care Quality Commission in relation to those detained for criminal activity under Mental Health

[1] Since May 2009, subsumed into the Department for Business, Innovation and Skills (BIS).

[2] Incorporating the children's social care responsibilities of the Commission for Social Care Inspection (CSCI).

[3] Operative from April 2009 and combining the previous Healthcare Commission, Mental Health Act Commission and the adult social care responsibilities of CSCI.

Act powers, and the revenue inspectors, for example. There is therefore a wide and overlapping field of bodies with inspection or regulatory duties within and across criminal justice boundaries. BERR and its predecessors have tried to control (or indeed regulate) this disparate field by creating statutory gatekeepers: inspectors or regulators who alone can give permission for another body to enter a specific public service area – though there has already been a considerable amount of jostling in the gateway.

Similarly, the criminal justice inspectorates are not the only inspectorates and regulators with an interest in their discrete areas. Within my own area, for example, neither domestic nor international obligations could be fully met without the complementary work of the Independent Monitoring Boards (previously Boards of Visitors) – volunteer monitors who have statutory right of entry into their local prison and certain statutory duties, and who attend there every week – and the Prisons and Probation Ombudsman (see below).

In addition, no inspectorate can carry out its role alone: all operate in partnership with other inspectorates and regulators, at least for part of their business. Some are partnerships within the criminal justice inspectorates: joint offender management inspection by prisons and probation; the recent programme of regular joint inspections of policy custody by the police and prisons inspectorates; joint work between police, courts and CPS inspectorates on the effectiveness of pre-trial procedures, and so on. But some are partnerships outside criminal justice: all full prison inspections are carried out jointly with Ofsted (to look at education and training) and the Care Quality Commission (to look at the commissioning of healthcare, complementing our inspection of its actual delivery). This joint work is important in obtaining a holistic picture; it also prevents what I characterize as the 'Garden of Eden defence' by individual agencies, each pointing the finger of blame at deficient partner agencies. It argues for a cooperative and overlapping approach, and for a recognition that the weaknesses, as well as the conflicts and tensions, occur where the different systems overlap or supposedly join.

It is, however, a far cry from that necessary cooperation to a universal model, and the division of the public sector world into four neat parts. There has been a simplistic assumption that, as inspection is a part of a regulatory framework, it is interchangeable with regulation; and a subsidiary assumption that all inspection is the same, with the same goals and objectives (see Seddon, this book, Chapter 11). Thus, there should be a clear and relatively simple methodology which can be applied to any form of inspection or regulation. This is at the heart of the proposal that there be only four public sector inspectorates. It has led to the development of ten government 'principles of inspection' (OPSR 2003) to be applied to all, and to a theology based on those ten commandments which has outlawed rolling programmes of inspection, called for a focus on value for money, and required a 'light-touch' approach offering 'inspection holidays' to good performers. Indeed, BERR later pressed hard for all public sector inspectorates to be bound by the statutory Regulators' Compliance Code (originally drafted for private sector and business regulation). This includes, *inter alia*, a requirement to have regard to, and not undermine, economic progress. Moreover, underneath this reductionism and regulation of regulators, is another fundamental assumption: that by focusing, rationalizing and joining up inspection, government can focus, rationalize and join up potentially recalcitrant public services. So, inspection is the military wing of the departmental and ministerial public service reform agenda.

I start from the principle that inspection and regulation are not coterminous: that there are different and complementary forms of regulation, and that inspection itself can take a variety of forms which need to reflect the context in which it operates. I also argue that the reductionist principle has been shown to be dangerous, and may be particularly so (and indeed unachievable) in the area of criminal justice and particularly in relation to the inspection of places of detention.

Inspection does not, at least in criminal justice, involve investigating individual complaints or cases. That reactive task – an equally important part of regulation – is undertaken by the Prisons and Probation Ombudsman (PPO), and the Independent Police Complaints Commission (IPCC). Both bodies are now charged with investigating all deaths in custody: whether due to suicide, murder, misadventure or natural causes – a consequence of the requirement in Article 2 of the European Convention on Human Rights that there should be independent investigation of deaths in custody, where the state has acquired a positive duty of care. Both bodies also provide an important form of redress in less serious matters: responding to individual complainants who have been unable to obtain redress through internal complaints mechanisms.

It is important that there is an effective feedback loop not only between these bodies and the relevant agencies, but also between them and inspectorates. For example, the Prisons Inspectorate will look at PPO reports on recent deaths in custody in each prison inspected, and will check whether resulting recommendations from him, or the coroner, have been implemented. Similarly, the PPO's investigators will look at recent inspection reports, to see whether there are gaps or recommendations in relation to safer custody procedures. Ideally, there should be similar cooperation in relation to individual prisoners' complaints, which are an important source of intelligence. Unfortunately, neither the inspectorate nor the PPO at present has resources to do this routinely, though informal cooperation happens regularly. Indeed, the PPO has identified resource constraints as a major problem in delivering his core business sufficiently promptly.[4]

The other and much more serious flaw, particularly in relation to fatal incident investigations, is that the PPO still has no statutory basis or powers, and therefore is entirely reliant on protocols negotiated with the appropriate services in order to be able to carry out investigations. There are no powers to compel either witnesses or documents. Though in practice this has rarely been a problem, it occasionally has, and the absence of statutory powers and independence raises serious questions as to the compliance of the procedures with Article 2 requirements. It also prevents the PPO being able to do what many other ombudsmen do; launch inquiries at his own volition into matters of concern. However, there is no doubt that the combination of the PPO and the Prisons Inspectorate provides a much more effective mechanism than previously for investigating and preventing deaths in prison custody.

Judicial inquiries are at the top end of investigations into major or systemic failures. They are necessarily extremely expensive, and time-consuming. The inquiry[5] into Stephen Lawrence's death cost £4.2 million, and the Mubarek inquiry into the murder of Zahid Mubarek[6] at Feltham £2.5 million. They were, however, cheap compared to the judicial inquiry into the Shipman case, which cost £21 million. Clearly, it is better to get procedures right in the first place. Some of those inquiries – Shipman is a prime example – played an important part in uncovering how systemic and serious failures were able to happen. Others, however, like Mubarek or Lawrence, followed or were preceded by both internal investigations and litigation which exposed many or most of the salient facts. Greater, and

[4] The same information-sharing and cooperation is envisaged with the IPCC in relation to police custody inspection and its investigative and complaints duties.

[5] The inquiry set up in 1997 under a former High Court judge, Sir William Macpherson, to inquire into the racially motivated death of a black teenager and to advise on the investigation and prosecution of such crimes. It reported in July 1999.

[6] The inquiry set up in 2004 under Lord Justice Keith to examine the circumstances of a racist murder in a young offender institution and to recommend action. It reported in 2006.

earlier, use of existing independent bodies – investigatory and/or inspectorate – could arguably produce speedier results; and indeed it is unlikely that the courts would have required either of the latter two inquiries had a properly independent PPO or IPCC existed at the time of those deaths. However, judicial inquiries also fulfil an important public role. With the authority of a senior judge, they are able to mark the importance society attaches to a particular crime or systems failure. They allow detailed and public ventilation of important issues. They should only be needed, and used, sparingly, if other regulatory systems are operating effectively, but they are an important backstop.

Inspection, by contrast, is essentially preventive: it aims to report on, and monitor the operation of, public services to improve performance and maintain appropriate standards. None of the criminal justice inspectorates has regulatory powers. To that extent, they all operate as part of the civil society part of the tetrahedron described in Peter Grabosky's chapter in this book (Chapter 4): with a statutory duty (sometimes, but not always, backed by statutory powers) to inspect and report to ministers, but no coercive powers to back up their findings and recommendations. Their ability to effect change depends on interaction with three separate sets of players: the executive, the inspected service and the public, or civil society. Inspectorates vary in relation to which of these is the more powerful, or more often used. Most use ministerial or departmental clout as their primary leverage: they inspect against the standards set by ministers for the inspected service, sometimes in public service agreements (PSAs), and sometimes in more detailed agency-specific standards. At one end of the spectrum some, like the Inspectorate of Constabulary, have had an even closer advisory or quasi-operational role. At the other end is the Prisons Inspectorate, which has its own human rights-based criteria, referenced against international rights standards. This is because its role does not simply rest on a domestic statute: it also derives from an obligation, in international law, to ensure proper treatment and conditions in places of detention: most explicitly set out in the Optional Protocol to the UN Convention against Torture and Inhuman and Degrading Treatment, which requires states parties to have a national preventive mechanism (NPM) to provide regular and independent inspection of places of detention (see below). This makes it more independent of departments and more reliant on advocacy – though it crucially needs to win the hearts and minds of the executive and the inspected services. The relationship with Parliament, by contrast, is weak for all inspectorates: the relevant minister is usually obliged to lay the chief inspector's annual report before Parliament, but there is no obligation for Parliament to debate it, or for a select committee to examine the chief inspector or the minister on its contents.

The Inspectorate of Constabulary, which has existed for over 150 years, has filled a gap left by the absence of a national police force. It was set up as a mechanism for ensuring the efficiency of (and hence whether there should be central funding towards) the police forces that each county and borough was statutorily required to maintain under the Police Act of 1856. Its focus has remained efficiency and effectiveness. Its chief inspector acts as the Home Secretary's principal adviser on policing; he and three of the four current regional inspectors are ex-chief constables, and they help select chief constables, appraise their annual performance, and recommend performance pay and decorations for them. Most inspectors are serving and warranted police officers. The inspectorate plays a key role in monitoring and enforcing centrally set performance standards across the forty-three locally run police forces in England and Wales. The green paper on policing has changed the emphasis somewhat, requiring 'a strengthened, refocused role for HMIC, as a fierce advocate and more explicit guarantor of the public interest', and with more non-police inspectors. However, it will remain one of the Home Secretary's principal means of ensuring performance and efficiency among and between individual police forces, by criteria that reflect national government priorities.

The Probation Inspectorate fulfilled somewhat the same function before the creation of a National Probation Service in 2001. Its chief inspector, a former chief probation officer, acted as the government's main adviser on probation and indeed developed, and then monitored and inspected, the national standards by which the forty-two separate probation services were to operate. Its operational staff were almost entirely seconded or ex-probation staff. Following 2001, under the first (and so far only) chief inspector who had never worked in probation – Professor Rod Morgan – it developed a new and more independent methodology for assessing and inspecting probation work. Its inspectors and practice assessors now come from a wider range of disciplines (though twenty out of twenty-nine inspectors come from the probation service). It still largely sees its role as independently inspecting against the national standards it first created, and the current objectives of the probation service (now, of course, no longer a separate national probation service, but a part of the National Offender Management Service).

The Courts and Crown Prosecution Service Inspectorates are the newest kids on the criminal justice inspection block, and their creation again reflected a perceived need for some cohesion and consistency in disparate services. Her Majesty's CPS Inspectorate (HMCPSI) arose out of the Glidewell Report, which recommended that the recently established internal CPS inspection arrangements should be formalized, extended and made independent of the CPS itself. It was designed to provide assurance as to the quality of casework and performance in the forty-two CPS areas, and to ensure their effectiveness and efficiency. Because of the technical nature of much of the work, it has fourteen legal inspectors (including the chief inspector and his deputy), but also now has seven business management inspectors from a variety of backgrounds. The chief inspector reports to the government's chief legal officer, the Attorney General, who relies on HMCPSI heavily to provide independent and accurate assessment of the CPS.

The Inspectorate of Courts Administration (HMICA) was formed in 2005, in parallel with the creation of the Court Service. It developed out of the Magistrates' Courts Service Inspectorate, created in 1997 to inspect the organization and administration of the disparate magistrates' courts. In its new role, it acquired CAFCASS (the troubled Children and Family Courts Advisory and Support Service), as well as the administration of the Crown and county courts – but with the very clear proviso that it had no remit to inspect 'persons making judicial decisions or exercising any judicial discretion'. In 2007, it lost CAFCASS to the expanded Ofsted (which has taken over all children's services). HMICA's Chief Inspector is a career civil servant, as are six of its seventeen inspectors: the remainder include lawyers and people with experience of police, prison, education and the voluntary sector. The restriction on inspecting judicial decision-making covers not only the conduct of cases, but also some grey areas where administration and judicial decision-making intersect, such as decisions on listing cases. The judiciary have been deeply suspicious of an inspectorate that they see as potentially able to exert the influence of the executive on the work and priorities of the judiciary. The criminal justice inspectorate's ability to inspect criminal case management is therefore circumscribed and extremely sensitive.

Finally the Prisons Inspectorate. Prisons inspection has a long history. As Sean McConville's (1995) book, *Next Only Unto Death: English Local Prisons 1860–1900*, shows, independent prisons inspection, initially carried out by local magistrates, was subsumed into the new Prisons Commission created in the reforms of the late nineteenth century. An independent inspectorate, in its current form, was recreated in 1981, following the May Inquiry into prison disturbances, and the perception that it was necessary for Home Secretaries to have access to an independent assessment of prison conditions. It is, as far as I know, the only inspectorate which does not have the power or the duty to inspect the service as such. Like the other inspectorates, its statutory remit reflects faithfully its *raison d'être*: it is simply to 'inspect the conditions in prisons and the treatment of prisoners' (subsequently extended to include places of immigration detention and those detained in them). There are indeed no other statutory powers or duties: the right to enter prisons, without warning, to acquire documents, and even to publish reports are all accretions that have developed during the inspectorate's history and are now held to be prerequisites for carrying out the statutory duty. The chief inspector, by established convention, cannot have worked for the Prison Service; around half the inspectors come from the Prison Service, while the other half are from a variety of backgrounds, including probation, social work, health, the law and the civil service.

The looseness of the statutory formulation has, in my view, been a benefit. It has meant that the inspectorate is not tied to inspecting against existing Prison Service standards or instructions, and indeed has developed and published its own inspection criteria, referenced against international human rights standards; and its own methodology, relying on four internationally accepted tests of a 'healthy' custodial environment. The link with human rights is important for all inspectorates, but the Prisons Inspectorate is founded on them – reflecting the extreme nature of and the power relationships within a closed custodial institution, and the positive duties the state acquires when it incarcerates individuals. That difference is also manifested in the form of inspection: it needs to be regular, and must involve being there and assembling and analysing the detail of the running and culture of a closed institution. Both of these prerequisites run counter to the BERR principles.

It is clear that each inspectorate is a product of its history, and in particular, of the circumstances and the reason for which it was created. While there was no shared view among chief inspectors about the merits of a single criminal justice inspectorate, all were agreed that the proposals put forward for this merger were flawed. Essentially, as matters developed, they would have simply stitched together five existing bodies, with reserved powers and duties for police and prisons inspection. What is more, it became apparent in the course of the prolonged discussions that preceded the aborted merger that those in the executive who were most wedded to the idea of a merged inspectorate were also those least sensitive to the notion of independence – or rather defined independence as independently being able to verify that central departmental objectives of the time were rigorously being pursued. This was perhaps most vividly illustrated in the proposition, put forward strongly at one point, that the chief inspector of the merged inspectorate should report to the Office of Criminal Justice Reform (the group of officials responsible to the criminal justice ministers for the effectiveness of the criminal justice system) – despite the fact that, properly understood, this was a body which should itself be subject to inspection. The failure to pursue statutory independence for the PPO, referred to above, four years after it was first promised, is also not indicative of an understanding or commitment to independence, whether perceived or actual.

This was not the only reason for being wary of a single criminal justice inspectorate. There is also my second point: the danger of a reductionist approach to criminal justice inspection, and prisons inspection in particular. This raises the question of what 'effectiveness' is in the context of something which manifestly is not a 'system' and to some extent cannot be, since it necessarily involves balancing conflicting interests and rights. The executive arm of government will always tend towards efficiency (principally speed and value for money) as a measure of effectiveness. But efficiency in the criminal justice system needs always to be set against fairness, due process and human rights. Pause to think, then, about a merged criminal justice inspectorate, reporting to, and to some extent reliant on, the executive, which includes prosecutors and police, but not the defence or judiciary; and which involves oversight of the agencies that punish offenders. Except for the Prisons Inspectorate, none of the constituent parts has a specific focus on the rights and interests of those regulated by the criminal justice system. That is not to say, of course, that other inspectorates have no interest in fairness or human rights – of course they do – but their methodology and focus is on the effectiveness of the agencies of criminal justice, and also, increasingly, on the interests of victims of crime. The Prisons Inspectorate, in many ways, has more in common with the PPO, particularly since it acquired the remit in relation to deaths in custody, and with the local Independent Monitoring Boards.

Joint work across criminal justice agencies can often expose these differences. The governmental response to the Audit Commission's powerful critique of the inefficiency in pre-trial and trial procedures, *Justice for All* (2002), led to a range of initiatives and targets for the relevant criminal justice agencies, known as the offences brought to justice (OBTJ) targets. However, there can be an inherent tension and even conflict between efficient criminal case management and the fundamental requirement of fairness and thoroughness. The aims, objectives and effectiveness measures of the police, CPS and courts administration are not identical – leave alone those of the judiciary. Inspection can and does expose inefficiency in the separate and joined systems and agencies; but it should not sail under the banner of corporate efficiency, by attempting to airbrush out the necessary contradictions, or to assume that efficiency and effectiveness are the same.

Indeed, inspection should and could be more alert at exposing such contradictions. The Inspectorate of Constabulary reports on the performance of each police force in England and Wales against national performance indicators. They include, obviously, the target for bringing offenders to justice (which includes offenders who are cautioned, and offences taken into consideration, as well as those convicted by a court). HMIC annual reports were able to record gratifying increases against this target. Meanwhile, at the other end of the system, the Youth Justice Board and the Prisons Inspectorate were noting the increasing number of children and young people brought to court, and sometimes imprisoned, for relatively minor offences. The two were not unconnected. A system that rewarded a police force (and financially rewarded its chief constable) simply on the volume of cases brought to court, irrespective of seriousness or effort required, carried with it the strong temptation to reach that target by picking low-hanging fruit. This often proved to be young people out on the streets, and could be at the expense of targeting the most serious, and therefore the most work-intensive, criminals and crimes. The Chief Inspector of Constabulary formally alerted government to this effect, and changes were secured: arguably, there should have been a better feedback loop earlier.

At my end of the business, there are also evident tensions. We are the only criminal justice inspectorate specifically charged with protecting the rights of those who are sanctioned or regulated by criminal justice. We have developed over time four tests of a 'healthy' (i.e. effective) prison: that prisoners are safe, are treated with respect for their human dignity, are able to engage in purposeful activity and are prepared for resettlement. Those tests combine two separate objectives for a penal system: that prisons should be safe and decent places, and that they should be part of an effective criminal justice system, by contributing to rehabilitation. The two are, of course, interconnected: dynamic security in prisons depends on activity as well as relationships; prisoners who are treated with humanity are more likely to recognize and respond to it than those who are brutalized. However, it is important to recognize that they also stand alone: prisons should be humane and safe places as a matter of principle, irrespective of whether this directly leads to the reduction of offending. In other words, there is considerable overlap between the protection of prisoners and the protection of the public; but they are separate, and they can be competing, aims.

One such tension is evident within the National Offender Management System (NOMS) – the much-restructured body that was set up in 2003 to join up prisons and probation, with the very challenging target of reducing reoffending by 10 per cent. The instrument for achieving this is a system of 'offender management': involving the individual case management of offenders jointly by the probation and prison services throughout sentence. A community-based 'offender manager' is in overall charge of the process; while the offender is in prison, a prison-based 'offender supervisor' (who may be a prison officer or a prison-based probation officer or probation support officer) is responsible for ensuring that the prescribed interventions are in place, and their effect monitored and reviewed. This is an ambitious and costly programme, and its implementation has followed the Probation Service's approach of targeting resources where risk of harm is greatest. So, its introduction into prisons at first was confined to high risk and persistent and prolific offenders, and was recently extended to those serving indefinite sentences for public protection. This is a combination of risk and necessity, since they are not necessarily the most risky of indeterminate-sentenced prisoners, but they are those that pose the greatest political risk, since the courts have threatened to declare their imprisonment unlawful if they are not managed more effectively through sentence.

The Probation Inspectorate has developed a methodology for inspecting offender management (OMI) which links to the probation imperatives of minimizing risk of harm and protecting the public. When offender management extended to prisons, it was necessary to work jointly with the Prisons Inspectorate, which already had a methodology for inspecting activities (including interventions) and resettlement (including sentence planning). There have, however been tensions. The Probation Inspectorate brings to the table a more sophisticated approach to risk assessment and case management – sometimes sadly lacking in prison management and approach – but also one that is individualized, and targeted at an agreed subset of prisoners. The Prisons Inspectorate looks at outcomes for all prisoners, and is very aware of the dangers of excluding any group of prisoners from access to positive interventions, education programmes or practical resettlement help: in terms of the dynamic security of the prison and the human rights implications, as well as the effects on society of low-level but intrusive offending. Reducing reoffending targets are unlikely to be much affected, for example, by the way that NOMS deals with non-offenders (those on remand), or foreign nationals who will be deported, or indeed life-sentenced prisoners with lengthy tariffs. But those prisoners, too, have the right to decent and humane treatment, and moreover are likely to be a risk to the security of prisons if they do not receive it and have little to lose.

These are tensions which are already emerging within joint inspection, and at a macro-level within NOMS itself. On the one hand is the instrumental view of prison and its regimes: aligned to a prior aim and contingent on that. On the other is a view of a 'healthy' prison, an institution that aims to provide a safe, decent, stable and purposive environment for all prisoners, even the most vulnerable and the least immediately redeemable. Prisons have not always been such places, and are not in some other countries. At a time of increasing prisoners, and decreasing public resources, this is a necessary and important balance.

Holding that balance is something that is now mandated under international human rights law, which recently has acquired more domestic teeth for doing so. The Optional Protocol to the UN Convention against Torture and Inhuman and Degrading Treatment (Opcat) requires states parties to have in place an independent and expert 'national preventive mechanism' (NPM) to carry out regular visits to all places of detention and to report publicly on findings, with the specific purpose of *preventing* torture or mistreatment. The UK was one of the earliest signatories to Opcat, which became operative in June 2006. Its NPM is relatively complex, consisting of all the independent bodies, throughout the four nations in the UK that already have the right of access to, and the task of inspecting or monitoring, places of detention: the various inspectorates for prisons, immigration, police, mental health and secure children's facilities, as well as the independent volunteer monitoring and visiting bodies. The Prisons Inspectorate of England and Wales will coordinate this mechanism, and liaise with the UN subcommittee charged with oversight of Opcat.

This sharp reminder of the principal origin of custodial inspection was one of the factors that called into question, and helped prevent, the merger of prisons inspection within a single criminal justice inspectorate. It is also helping to push the boundaries of other criminal justice inspectorates. It now mandates some important, and hitherto neglected, joint work. The Inspectorate of Constabulary did not previously inspect police custody suites as such, and certainly not regularly; it was outside its core work. Yet police custody is the place which international human rights bodies would normally be most concerned about; and where, even with the Police and Criminal Evidence Act 1984 (PACE) safeguards, there are issues around treatment and conditions (such as the state of some police cells, the healthcare service provided, the prevention of suicide, and the use of police custody as a 'place of safety' under s. 136 of the Mental Health Act 1983) which have been little ventilated, except when they go wrong and result in an investigation from the IPCC.

This gap has now been filled. Led by the Prisons Inspectorate, there is now a joint programme of regular and independent inspection of police custody suites in England and Wales. This has already revealed some issues of concern and potential tension – an aversion to risk which has meant some detainees being denied items of basic dignity, such as toilet paper or blankets, poor physical conditions in some places, and inconsistent healthcare provision. This will potentially provide the same effective feedback loop with the work of the IPCC and its investigations into police custody deaths as is currently the case with the PPO and prison deaths. Similar work is going on with the Inspectorate of Courts Administration in relation to court cells (and, incidentally, with the Ministry of Defence in relation to military detention). And proposals are being worked up with Ofsted for joint inspection of the secure training centres in which some young people are detained.

Thus, instead of the melding of the five criminal justice inspectorates into one amorphous body, there has been a much subtler process of widening, and often joint, functional inspection, focused on specific areas of activity – a horizontal rather than a vertical merger. The Prisons Inspectorate should now more properly be known as the Inspectorate of Detention – incorporating nearly all of the places in England and Wales where people may be detained, through criminal, administrative or military procedures. Interestingly, the Crown Prosecution Inspectorate is undertaking a similar expansion: inspecting other prosecuting authorities as well as the CPS.

I want to go on to focus on those things that are specific to prisons inspection, and indeed to custodial inspection in general, which reflect its particular origins and objectives. As already stated, most inspectorates, to a greater or lesser extent, have criteria which mirror the standards and objectives of the inspected agency and the government's PSA targets. Their role is to provide a consistent, independent and external validation of the agency's performance. They aim to shadow developments within the inspected agency – for example, the Probation Inspectorate moved from effective supervision inspection (ESI) to offender management inspection (OMI) when the new NOMS offender management model began to roll out. The Inspectorate of Constabulary's police performance assessments are developed jointly with the Home Office's Police and Criminal Standards Directorate. Importantly, of course, that does not prevent either chief inspector from commenting on the framework and standards which he is inspecting: as witness the Chief Inspector of Probation's critique of the increased expectations on probation, or the Chief Inspector of Constabulary's recent report on effective (and ineffective) policing. But it does tie the routine programming and methodology of inspection to agreed standards.

The Prisons Inspectorate, by contrast, inspects by independent criteria, derived from best practice and international human rights norms. We have developed 527 separate criteria (called 'expectations') which define best practice in all aspects of prison life, and which are referenced against international human rights standards. This reflects the underpinning human rights rationale of the inspectorate, and its independence from government as well as the inspected service. That is not to say that the criteria do not develop to reflect changing and rising expectations, or new legislation: for example, expectations on diversity, healthcare and resettlement have considerably expanded in the most recent edition. And in practice there is a great deal of common ground between Prison Service standards and norms and inspection criteria: as witness the fact that 95 per cent of inspection recommendations are accepted, and follow-up inspections found that between 71 per cent and 75 per cent are achieved within two to three years. There is, and needs to be, an iterative process between inspection criteria and the standards and aims of those running prisons: were this not the case, inspection would be voyeuristic, rather than effective.

Prisons inspection, I would argue, is effective on three levels: the practical outcome of individual inspections; the systemic issues covered in thematic reviews and inspections; and the overall culture and underlying purpose of prison.

The inspection timetable is a mixture of chronology and intelligence. It is vital that closed institutions are regularly inspected: even good prisons can deteriorate rapidly under poor management or new challenges. So, each adult prison is inspected at least twice in a five-year period, and each juvenile establishment at least twice in three years. This is probably not enough, though it is all that resources allow. However, if there is concern about a prison (either resulting from inspection, or from other information reaching the inspectorate) it will have more frequent, and more intense, inspection. The inspectorate's ability to go into prisons unannounced is also essential. All follow-up inspections and some full inspections take place without warning. This is important in itself, but it also to some extent mitigates the resource constraints that make inspections relatively infrequent. I have described it previously as 'virtual inspection', as it means every prison governor needs to remember that tomorrow could be the day that the inspectorate arrives. Full inspections take a week; they involve multidisciplinary teams (including healthcare and education inspectors); they include a confidential survey of all prisoners; and inspectors, with their own keys, have free access to all parts of the prison, all staff and prisoners, and all documentation. Each prison is assessed as to whether it is performing well, reasonably well, not sufficiently well or poorly against each of our four tests, and those assessments feed into the Prison Service's own performance assessment system.

So, what are the effects of all this effort? The statistics are powerful. In full inspections last year, we made 3,533 recommendations for change in 29 prisons. Of those, 3,349 were accepted, wholly or partially, by the inspected prison, which then had to produce an action plan to implement them. Unannounced follow-up inspections, between 18 and 30 months later, last year found that 71 per cent (1,950) of recommendations made in previous inspections of twenty-six establishments had been achieved, wholly or partially. Those are real and tangible effects.

Recommendations range from the relatively trivial – though nothing is trivial when everything you wear, eat or do is controlled by someone else – to the fundamentally important. It is sometimes easier for prisons to achieve the smaller, rather than the larger things. For that reason, we always have a small number of main recommendations: those things that should be priorities, as they go to the heart of the prison's work. For example, the 196 recommendations in the inspection of Norwich prison included main recommendations calling for: the demolition of a wing that was not fit for purpose, with leaking soil-stacks and filthy, cold cells; changes in a landing that held recently arrived and vulnerable young prisoners alongside identified bullies and those who were being punished for breaches of prison discipline; and a resettlement strategy specific to the many young adults held. They were followed by a raft of detailed recommendations, including for example those on cleanliness, laundry, food, race investigations and visits booking arrangements.

Sometimes we, or the Prison Service, may need help in achieving main recommendations. In the case of Norwich, our recommendation to close a wing was eagerly seized on by prison managers, who began emptying it the week after the inspection. Sadly, no sooner had it been emptied than the rising population required it to be reopened. However, the inspection report, and prisoners' continuing complaints, led to a successful action under health and safety legislation, which finally and terminally closed it. For inspection reports also serve the purpose of putting in the public domain, for legal as well as political purposes, the detail of what is going on in closed institutions and which could otherwise go unrecorded. Information about the treatment of children in prison (and immigration detention), about suicide prevention and safety, and about the lack of planning for indeterminate-sentenced prisoners, has been used in judicial reviews, coroners' courts and in pressure for changes to the law.

Systemic changes can also be nudged forward through inspectorate thematic reports. These are research-led exercises that cover a representative sample of prisons and prisoners, using a mixture of statistical survey information, questionnaires, semi-structured interviews with staff and prisoners, literature reviews and documentary evidence to provide an overview of a particular kind of provision or population. They are assisted by an advisory group, usually involving practitioners and academics. They are slow-burners: they take a long time (usually a year) to complete, and even longer to influence practice and policy.

Ten years ago, a report on prison healthcare (then an extremely second-rate service) recommended that healthcare should be provided by, and to the same standards as, National Health Service provision outside prisons. Two years ago, that was achieved, and in general the services provided in prisons are of an equivalent standard to those outside: though of course prisoners have much greater levels of physical and mental morbidity than the population in general. Similarly, thematic reports on women and juveniles were important in establishing and monitoring the need for different treatment and provision for these often marginalized groups. Recent thematics on older prisoners, race and foreign nationals have driven improvements in aspects of diversity; and the most recent, on mental health, has led to a government review of diversion from prisons as well as provision within them.

These are the tangible measures of effectiveness. But the intangible measures are also important. The inspectorate's focus on safety, decency, activity and resettlement has, by a process of osmosis, become accepted as the touchstone for prisons policy as well as individual prisons – both here and in some other countries. That is very important at a time of increased prisoner numbers and decreasing resources, with the prospect of diminishing prison regimes. The recent proposals for the building of 2,500-

place 'Titan' prisons were abandoned after a period of consultation that found no support for a prison model that offered little but containment. The inspectorate's approach introduces and sustains a human rights, as well as utilitarian, focus on the nature and objective of imprisonment. Drawing on international human rights norms, it provides a perspective that is external to the immediate priorities, or possibilities, of government and the Prison Service. It provides vital and accurate information for public and parliamentary debate, and is therefore a key part of the public accountability of these closed institutions.

I would also argue that this approach can be, and indeed needs to be, applied to other closed settings. One of the benefits of the developing National Preventive Mechanism is that it joins together those inspecting prisons, places of military detention, secure mental hospitals and secure children's homes. In some countries, NPMs have extended their remit to cover compulsory military service, and residential homes for older people, which can (as Seddon argues) in practice be as or more restrictive than some prisons. These too are places which cannot be inspected on paper, but which need to be visited and described in detail: in the words of the previous Chief Inspector of CSCI, Dame Denise Platt, 'you need to be there and smell the urine'. The NPM framework therefore offers some very interesting opportunities to extend and promote the concepts and methodologies that I describe.

Within closed institutions, the introduction of an outside eye, capable of asking 'why' as well as 'how', is both an important and necessary form of regulation. I have rarely been on a prison inspection that did not reveal something that the governor did not know about. In a good prison, those will be small things, gratefully received by managers. More generally, though, each expansion of inspection activity into new territory has acted to challenge assumptions and accepted practice, that can become trapped within the walls of the place of detention. There often follows a process of denial, attempts at justification and, usually, acceptance – at least in principle.

This has also been the case in other countries. The spread of ratifications of Opcat is leading to the setting up of NPMs in other countries, to complement internal inspection and performance management systems, and focus on conditions and treatment within places of detention. In France, this has taken the form of a Contrôleur général des lieux de privation de liberté, with the remit of inspecting all places of detention in France, specifically to ensure that human dignity and fundamental rights are respected.[7]

[7] Article 1, Loi de 30 Octobre 2007.

The Contrôleur is to be entirely independent of the correctional service, and therefore operates in a complementary fashion to the service's own Inspecteur général. The first Contrôleur général, Jean-Marie Delarue, was appointed in June 2008 and has published his first annual report, covering the six-month period to December 2008.[8]

Like the Prisons Inspectorate, he has no regulatory power, but the right to enter all places of detention, in order to produce reports and make recommendations to ministers. His only remit is to report on prisoners' and detainees' conditions and treatment, looking at staffing issues only insofar as they affect that goal. His annual report reveals some striking similarities with the experience of custodial inspection in the UK. His inspections have brought to light things that are taken for granted as accepted practice by detaining bodies: for example, the routine removal of brassieres and spectacles from those detained in police custody (*garde à vue*), who are then brought to court without those essentials. He criticizes the extent of overcrowding and the absence of proper hygiene facilities in prisons, the inconsistency and sometimes unsafeness of arrangements for medical care in police custody, the absence of sufficient purposeful activity, and the links between larger prisons and concerns about safety. Those are familiar themes in all independent custodial inspection, but in some cases were less familiar to those running, or responsible for, the places inspected.

With a small budget (recently expanded to €3m) and an extremely large remit (there are for example 576,000 *gardes à vue* alone), the task of the Contrôleur général will not be easy. Nor does he have any regulatory power. It is too early to detect what the effect will be on practice and strategy in relation to prisons and places of detention – but already he is demonstrating the importance of an independent, objective eye, and requiring detaining bodies to defend accepted practices which affect human dignity and rights.

By a separate route, there has also been recent interest in independent inspection and monitoring systems for prisons in the US. During 2005–6, after the violations at Abu Ghraib were publicized, in some cases perpetrated by people who had been correctional officers in the US itself, there was renewed interest about the conditions of incarceration in domestic jails and prisons, and the safeguards that existed to prevent and detect abuse. The most effective method of regulation in the

[8] *Rapport annuel du Contrôleur général des lieux de privation de liberté* (Paris: Dalloz, 2008).

US had been judicial: the ability of the courts, especially the federal district courts, to find conditions in prisons and jails unconstitutional and in extreme cases to order that judicial officers take over effective control for a period. This form of regulation was extremely controversial, and was significantly restricted by the Prison Law Reform Act. The respected independent organization, the Vera Institute, set up a Commission on Safety and Abuse in America's Prisons in 2005. It held a series of hearings, taking evidence from correctional staff, ex-prisoners and relatives, and agencies in the US and elsewhere that inspect or monitor prisons. The published report recommended that there should be structures for independent oversight both at state and national level, with the capacity to make improvements.

> The most important mechanism for overseeing corrections is independent inspection and monitoring. Every U.S. prison and jail should be monitored by an independent government body, sufficiently empowered and funded to regularly inspect conditions of confinement and report findings to lawmakers and the public. Today, this is the case in only a few states and localities. While independence is a crucial feature, the relationship with corrections should be collaborative: insiders and outsiders working together to ensure safe and effective facilities. (Vera Commission 2006)

There is a variety of different models in operation in the US, reflecting and responding to the legislative provisions and political priorities in different states. However, there are very few, and most prisons and jails in the US are not subject to oversight. This was shown in a fifty-state study carried out by the University of Texas (Deitch 2010). New York is an interesting example, as there are two such organizations, one in New York City and the other in New York State. They operate in different ways, illustrating the strengths and weaknesses of different forms of regulation and inspection.

The oldest is the Correctional Association of New York, established in 1844 as a citizens' watchdog with the right of entry into all prisons in New York State, with the aim of making prisons fairer, more efficient and more humane, based upon 'a belief in the inherent dignity of all human beings and a deep faith in the human capacity for change' (see 'Our Mission' on its website). It is entirely independent of the state and prison authorities, and receives little government or corporate funds. Its Prison Visiting Project monitors individual prisons and issues reports. It also carries out thematic studies on systemic issues, such as healthcare and substance-abuse treatment. There is also a project on women in prison. The Correctional Association has been a fierce critic of the Rockefeller drug laws, which imposed stringent mandatory sentences for drug crimes, and has called for their repeal. They have also criticized restrictions to post-secondary prison education programmes, deficiencies in healthcare provision and in particular the treatment of those with HIV/AIDs and of specific practices such as the shackling of women in labour. More broadly, the Correctional Association has been a vocal critic of the overuse of incarceration, arguing for investment in prevention and rehabilitation.

The New York City Board of Corrections, established in 1957 under the New York City Charter, has a different role and approach. It was created to 'provide management and planning assistance' to the New York City Department of Correction, with nine members who were appointed by the Mayor. Since 1977, it has had the responsibility of establishing and ensuring compliance with minimum standards for conditions, including healthcare, in all New York City prisons. Its standards are therefore mandatory and directly enforceable. It can also hold hearings, with subpoena powers, and make recommendations. The appointment of members was made more independent, with the mayor directly appointing only three – three others are appointees of the City Council, and the remaining three are appointed by the mayor on the nomination of judges. The Board issued its first sixteen standards in 1978, and has amended them twice since. In the 1980s, it developed mental health minimum standards, in collaboration with the departments of correction, health, mental health and the mayor's office, and in 1991 similarly developed general health standards to make prison healthcare consistent with accepted professional standards.

Its direct links to the political and administrative systems clearly give the Board direct and effective regulatory authority – standards must be complied with unless the department applies for a 'variance'. However, this process also ties standards to current realities. This was evident in 1985, when the Board amended its standards on overcrowding to deal with the reality of a prison system that had been so overstretched that remand prisoners had had to be released following a ruling by the Federal District Court. The previous standard, of 75 square feet of living place per prisoner, was amended downwards to 60 square feet. In return, the Department undertook to abide by maximum capacity numbers in dormitories, and agreed ratios for showers, toilets and sinks.

These two bodies represent different models of independent regulation: one tied to political and administrative reality, but with direct and enforceable authority, the other entirely independent of those running and responsible for prisons, with the ability to act as an advocate for change, in light of human rights and best practice – but whose recommendations are in practice often ignored by the agency.

These are important debates and dilemmas surrounding the inspection and regulation of places of detention. There is a dual purpose: to make conditions better, or as good as they can be, but also to point out the inevitable consequences of large-scale incarceration. This is a live debate in England and Wales within the Prisons Inspectorate, which spans both of the New York bodies' functions – being independent of the operational and departmental line, but setting out standards that should be, and often are, achieved.

Prisons inspection has helped to create what is certainly one of the better prison systems in the world; but also one of the most overused, certainly in western Europe. The two may not be unconnected: for the paradox of expecting, and to a considerable extent getting, better prisons, with more positive activity and more professionalized health and education services, is that it becomes more comfortable to send people there. When prisons literally smelled like drains, judges were deeply uncomfortable about using them too liberally. Prisons that offer drug detoxification, numeracy and literacy teaching, mental health in-reach and cognitive behavioural therapy become places that are perceived as being able to do good to people, and that conversely can allow other public services to evade their responsibilities for doing so. Yet prisons are essentially coercive environments, which can make people worse, or less able to cope with the realities of the real world: thus creating and expanding their customer base. Moreover, as they become more overcrowded, they become less effective, in any terms. And the more public money spent on and in prisons, the less is available upstream or downstream to tackle the causes of offending, or support those released from prison.

Despite that, I am unapologetic about the objectives and achievements of the Prisons Inspectorate, and the work of the other prison monitors and investigators, for there is an even more alarming alternative: more, but worse prisons. Given a retributive and reactive public climate, and severe restrictions on public spending, that is a real possibility, in a system planning to incarcerate 100,000 people by 2014. But the current prisons overcrowding crisis does point to the limitations, as well as the effectiveness, of a focused single agency approach on the current model.

I remain convinced that a single criminal justice inspectorate is dangerous and less effective, particularly in relation to places of detention. I believe that it would lead to reduced expertise in each area, and an oversimplification of the complexities within criminal justice: searching for a single approach and methodology and unprotected from a focus on efficiency and executive-set targets. The tensions and balances within inspectorates are as necessary as those within the system. So too are the regulatory functions of other agencies: ombudsmen, investigators and ultimately courts and inquiries.

Nevertheless, as is evident from the examples above, there are considerable risks in a blinkered, silo approach. Inspectorates run the risk of being captured by the culture and priorities of the service they inspect, or of the departments where they are lodged, which control their budgets, and to which they report. Criminal justice inspectorates in particular need to avoid becoming simply an arm of the executive, especially when it is, as often, in a reactive 'something must be done' mode. That leads me to two final points.

The first is that I believe that there should be a much stronger link between independent inspectorates (and indeed the Prisons and Probation Ombudsman) and Parliament. There is currently a proposal for chief inspectors' and ombudsmen's appointments to be subject to some limited form of parliamentary scrutiny. I would go further than that, and have inspectorates and ombudsmen reporting to parliamentary select committees – ideally a criminal justice joint committee of both Houses, mirroring the effective joint parliamentary Human Rights Committee – with their budgets set by parliamentary vote. That would create proper lines of accountability, especially when inspectorates may need to be critical of government departments, or indeed, like the Prisons Inspectorate, set their own inspection standards. It would prevent a situation in which ministers and departments could exercise indirect control through budgetary allocations, appointments and reappointments, and inappropriate or cumbersome operational requirements. I and my fellow chief inspectors, and the PPO, constantly need to police the boundaries of our independence, especially in response to newly arrived officials, agencies or policies.

Equally importantly, a parliamentary base could provide a vehicle for informed, objective and transparent commentary on the likely impact of proposed criminal justice legislation: usually passed in haste and repented at leisure. This is something which is specifically mentioned in the job description of the national preventive mechanism required under Opcat, but which would be invaluable in relation to the effectiveness of criminal justice in general.

Second, there clearly needs to be appropriate and effective cooperation and joint working – first of all between criminal justice inspectorates and ombudsmen, to flush out those areas where inefficiencies or competing priorities and targets are undermining the effectiveness of the system. This should flow from a proper understanding of public protection, which is double-edged: including both the need for a criminal justice system that protects the citizen, and the need for citizens to be protected when they are caught up in, or sanctioned by, the agencies of criminal justice. The criminal justice system needs to be effective at both.

Cooperation and challenge needs, though, to go further than that. As has already been stated (Sanders, Seddon, this book, Chapters 3 and 11 respectively), criminal justice and its agencies are increasingly seen as mechanisms for tackling social and economic ills, and for regulating behaviour which is not in itself criminal – so expanding the reach of criminal justice and enabling other agencies to evade responsibilities and costs. Indeed prisons, the most extreme end of the system, can act as mirrors: reflecting those things that are failing, or absent, in the society outside them. They are too often society's 'too difficult tray': providing relatively cheap short-term solutions to societal problems. For that reason, criminal justice inspection needs to work in alliance with, and sometimes to challenge, other public sector inspectorates, whose own agencies' targets may be best served by greater use of criminal justice.

Those are messages that politicians and the public need to hear, and that an effective regulatory system should be expected to expose – though their resolution is in the end a matter for government, Parliament and the judiciary.

References

Deitch, M. (2010) *Independent Correctional Models: A 50-State Study*. University of Texas [to be published in *PACE Law Review*, 2010].

Home Office (2002) *Justice for All* (Cm. 5563). Norwich: Stationery Office.

(2008) From the Neighbourhood to the National: Policing Our Communities Together (Cm. 7448). London: Home Office.

McConville, S. (1995) *Next Only Unto Death: English Local Prisons 1860–1900*. London and New York, NY: Routledge.

Office for Public Sector Reform (2003) *The Government's Policy on the Inspection of Public Services*. July.

Vera Commission (2006) *Confronting Confinement: Report of the Commission on Safety and Abuse in America's Prisons*.

11

Rethinking prison inspection: regulating institutions of confinement*

TOBY SEDDON

> Closed institutions of all kinds – prisons, juvenile detention centres, police lock-ups, secure psychiatric wards, immigration detention centres and similar custodial services – pose accountability challenges for democratic societies.
>
> (Harding 2007: 543)

Introduction

The need to shine a light into the closed world of prisons has been recognized for a very long time. In Britain, the 'official' inspection of prisons dates back to 1835, when its first emergence was part of the broader 'revolution in government' in the middle of the nineteenth century during which much of the administrative machinery of the modern state was assembled (MacDonagh 1958; Braithwaite 2003: 10). But the question of external scrutiny of prisons had also been widely discussed in the previous century, notably by the prison reformer John Howard in his classic *The State of the Prisons* first published in 1777 (see Stockdale 1983). Indeed, we can trace this back even further: medieval prisons were sometimes subject to inspection (Peters 1995: 29, 36), as were some in the ancient world, notably in the Roman Empire (Peters 1995: 19).

Today, the inspection of prisons is carried out across the world by a range of national bodies, as well as by supranational organizations such as the European Committee for the Prevention of Torture and the Special Rapporteur on Prisons and Conditions of Detention in Africa. The United Nations Optional Protocol to the Convention against Torture and Other

* I am grateful to participants in the seminar series for a stimulating discussion around my original contribution on prison inspection. Special thanks to John Braithwaite, Anne Owers and John Raine for constructive comments on an earlier version of this chapter. The usual disclaimer applies.

Cruel, Inhuman or Degrading Treatment or Punishment (Opcat) came into force in 2006, requiring signatories to put in place adequate inspection arrangements. In the British context, prison inspection took on its current form at the start of the 1980s following the May report into prison disturbances (May 1979). Since then, a succession of chief inspectors has come to define the role as one involving critical rigour and fearless independence. The previous incumbent, Anne Owers, continued this tradition and the achievements of her inspectorate were impressive (Owers, this book, Chapter 10). Elsewhere around the world, the picture is more mixed. The purpose of this chapter is to develop some new ideas that can inform the improvement and enhancement of prison inspection regimes and practices right across the board, regardless of their present state of development. It offers, in other words, a new generic framework for thinking about prison inspection, rather than one tied to any specific country or region. My central claim is that to do this, we need to rethink the matter in the much broader context of the regulation of public services.

The rest of this chapter proceeds as follows. I begin by considering some key conceptual issues, specifically the concept of inspection itself and its relationship to notions of regulation and accountability, and how they might be applied in the prison context. I then examine the question of how 'special' or distinctive prison inspection is and set out a basis for how we might make useful connections with studies of inspection in other fields beyond criminal justice. I then develop this point by drawing on an empirical study by John Braithwaite and colleagues of the inspection of nursing homes (Braithwaite *et al.* 2007b) and attempt to show how this might inform a rethinking of prison inspection. In conclusion, I draw together the key elements of my argument and suggest some priorities for future research and development.

Conceptual issues: regulation, accountability, inspection

Terms such as inspection, audit, regulation, scrutiny and accountability are often used almost interchangeably. It is worth clarifying a little the conceptual terrain in which prison inspection is located. I will attempt to do that in this section by looking, first of all, at the notions of regulation and accountability and then considering how they relate to inspection.

Regulation and accountability

Two related concepts are absolutely central to the idea of inspection: regulation and accountability. Regulation is the broader term and has been subject to considerable definitional debate (see Black 2002). Some adopt a narrow or restrictive definition, seeing regulation primarily as rules and standards set and enforced by the state (Ogus, this book, Chapter 2; see also Ogus 1994). Others take a more expansive view (Grabosky, this book, Chapter 4), seeing regulation simply as all attempts at 'steering the flow of events and behavior' (Braithwaite *et al.* 2007a: 3). Black (2002: 26) provides a helpful framing definition:

> Regulation is the sustained and focused attempt to alter the behaviour of others according to defined standards or purposes with the intention of producing a broadly identified outcome or outcomes, which may involve mechanisms of standard-setting, information-gathering and behaviour modification.

Clearly, in the context of prison inspection we are largely talking about what Ogus (this book, Chapter 2) calls public regulation, where one part of the state is regulating another (or, in the case of privately-managed prisons, where one part of the state is regulating a private contractor of another part of the state). But it is also necessary to look beyond the state. Around the world, NGOs can and do play a part in the regulation of prison and other custodial regimes. In Britain, for example, organizations like the Prison Reform Trust and the Howard League for Penal Reform all perform what could be termed regulatory functions in the wider sense of the term, using a range of tools, from strategic litigation to media campaigns, to try and change what happens inside prisons. As Owers (this book, Chapter 10) notes, there are also other regulatory bodies such as the Independent Monitoring Boards (formerly Boards of Visitors) and the Prisons and Probation Ombudsman . In relation to prisons, then, there is a complex regulatory space, with many different actors – 'official' inspection forms just one part of this space. Indeed, Hood and colleagues (1999: 134) observe for the British case, perhaps controversially, that in certain respects prisons are over-regulated, in the sense that there are more actors involved in their regulation than for many other public services. Scott (2000: 53) sees this instead as a 'belt and braces' approach – what he terms a 'redundancy' model of accountability – where effective regulation does not stand or fall on the performance of a single actor. The point I want to emphasize here though is simply that prison inspection does not represent the sole regulatory mechanism for prisons. I will return to this later as it touches on an important theoretical issue which has significant practical implications.

What then of accountability? On the face of it, this might seem easier to define. Scott (2000: 40), for example, refers to its core as the 'duty to give account for one's actions to some other person or body'. This implies a backward-looking focus, suggesting that accountability is primarily past-oriented and punitive or corrective. A contrast is sometimes drawn here with regulation which may be characterized as largely future-oriented and preventive. But this distinction is hard to sustain. Accountability is indeed partly about accounting for past actions but it will often also lead to prescriptions or recommendations for preventing future recurrences of the undesired behaviour in question. Similarly, while the attempt to prevent certain behaviours happening in the first place lies at the heart of regulation, in many instances this will draw from, or be combined with, responding to events that have already occurred.

This blurring of conceptual boundaries has generated considerable discussion about the relationship between regulation and accountability (Scott, 2000; Mulgan 2000; Lodge 2004; Mashaw 2006; May 2007; Smith 2009). Some have sought to distinguish the two more precisely by establishing clear points of difference. More helpful, in my view, is Scott's (2000: 39) argument that they are 'linked concepts, operating on a continuum'. In a similar vein, May (2007) describes accountability as a subset of regulation, suggesting it is a 'necessary but insufficient condition for increasing regulatory effectiveness' (2007: 11). It is important to stress though that to say that the two are 'linked' and exist on a continuum is not the same as saying they are synonymous. The concept of accountability centres on the notion of being answerable or responsible (see Bovens 2007) and this is not properly or wholly captured in the idea of regulation as 'steering the flow of events'. We need to retain an appreciation of this difference whilst at the same time understanding how the two ideas are closely linked.

This link or connection is certainly evident in the context of prisons. In an interesting essay, John Raine (2008) describes one of the major strengths of prison inspection in Britain over the last twenty-five years as the way it has enhanced what he terms 'public accountability'. But it becomes clear that what he means by this is a form of answerability that encompasses both ideas – he sees prison inspection as partly about 'placing the issues of prison conditions strongly in the public eye and consciousness' (2008: 95) but also as being 'influential in leading to significant raising of standards' (2008: 94). That Raine chooses to describe this as 'public accountability' is perhaps not surprising, as the discourse of accountability has dominated debates about prisons for some time (e.g. Maguire *et al.* 1985; Vagg 1994; Stenning 1995). One of the contributions I hope to make with this chapter is to switch the focus back onto regulation, as this in turn opens up greater possibilities for seeing inspection as a tool for improvement rather than just as an instrument for scrutiny.

Inspection

Where then does inspection fit in relation to this regulation–accountability continuum? And how can we define it more precisely? Dictionary definitions give the primary meaning of 'to inspect' as 'to look into' and the secondary as 'to examine officially'. We might say then that inspection involves authorities of one type or another examining or looking into activities or operations carried out by others. But for what purpose? In the simplest terms, inspection seeks to observe and to check whether the inspected are doing what they should be and in the way that they are supposed to.

An important article by Boyne and colleagues on public service inspection is helpful here in developing this a little (Boyne *et al.* 2002). They identify inspection as a regulatory tool or instrument and offer a 'working definition':

> Inspection is one element of a system of regulation, is likely to utilise information provided by other elements, entails site visits to service providers and has a strong focus on service standards and outcomes.
>
> (Boyne *et al.* 2002: 1198–9)

Drawing on Hood *et al.*'s (1999) work, they go on to emphasize three core components of the inspection process (Boyne *et al.* 2002: 1201):

- a *director* (a method of setting standards);
- a *detector* (a way of monitoring compliance with standards); and
- an *effector* (a means of changing future behaviour).

These three components map onto Black's definition of regulation ('standard-setting', 'information-gathering' and 'behaviour modification'). This underlines the point that public services inspection is not just about 'public accountability' but rather operates across the regulation–accountability continuum. Putting it another way, we can say that inspection is both a regulatory tool and an accountability mechanism.

We can use this tripartite framework – *directing*, *detecting* and *effecting* – to look more closely at prison inspection. Taking the first element, directing, it is fundamental to the process of inspecting prisons that the inspectorate should be able to articulate the standards by which it will appraise or evaluate prison regimes and conditions. In the British context, Owers (2004: 108) describes how these standards have been derived from the World Health Organization's 'Healthy Prison' concept and broader international human rights principles. These have produced four tests which she suggests 'define the core business of a Prisons Inspectorate': that prisoners are held in *safety*; that they are treated with *respect* and dignity; that they can engage in *purposeful activity*; and that they are prepared for *resettlement*. Building on this framework, the British inspectorate has developed a detailed set of standards, called *Expectations* (HMIP 2008). The latest published edition of the *Expectations* runs to 232 pages and provides the framework for all inspections and their reporting. It is clear then that the *directing* component of inspection, that is, the method of setting standards, is quite highly developed in Britain. I will return below to this question of standards and the *Expectations*.

What of the second component, *detecting*? In a sense, this is at the heart of the whole process of an inspection regime based on site visits. The reason that the inspection teams physically go to prisons is precisely to monitor compliance with standards. As Owers (this book, Chapter 10) describes, it does this through a mix of inspection modes:

- full inspections, both announced and unannounced;
- full follow-up inspections which are unannounced and focus on major concerns raised by a previous inspection visit; and
- short follow-up inspections which are unannounced, where there are fewer concerns.

As Owers (this book, Chapter 10) describes, inspections deploy a range of detection methods, including input from prisoners through confidential surveys and the ability to access freely any part of the prison. As she notes, resources perhaps do not allow for 'enough' inspection visits to take place each year but, nevertheless, it is undoubtedly true that there is a rigorous, thorough and substantial system in place for detecting and monitoring compliance with expected standards.

The third component, *effecting*, is less well developed than the first two (see Hood *et al.* 1999: 116). Inspection reports include recommendations, and there is some scope for monitoring their implementation, but ultimately the inspectorate cannot directly *require* 'behaviour modification' (see Owers 2009). Instead, it relies on a set of 'softer' and more indirect methods for achieving change. As will be argued later, this is a significant gap from the perspective of regulatory theory. It is partly for this reason that in the prison context it is so important to bring the concept of regulation to the forefront, instead of allowing it to be overshadowed by the all too evident need for strong accountability mechanisms.

Perhaps to some readers, this conceptual analysis may seem as little more than restating the obvious. I think though that it helps to bring out more clearly the potential commonalities in inspection across different fields and in different sites – from restaurant kitchens, to schools, to prisons. My argument, then, is that by understanding inspection in this way, as an instrument or tool for regulation and accountability, we can potentially learn lessons from inspection in very different sites extending far beyond the criminal justice system. Before exploring this claim in more detail, in the next section I will consider one of the main objections to this idea, namely that prison inspection is a 'special' case and that therefore the potential for cross-sectoral learning is in fact quite limited.

Is prison inspection 'different'?

It is no doubt possible to overstate the similarities between inspection in different fields. There are certainly some distinctive features of criminal justice, and especially the prison system, which cannot and should not be ignored. I think it is helpful though to try to specify more precisely what exactly is distinctive about criminal justice. Looking at the prison system, its fundamental nature as a closed institution with coercive powers over its inmates certainly changes the regulatory challenge that it presents. As Owers (this book, Chapter 10) observes, the United Nations Opcat protocol, which aims to ensure that prison inspections are in place in order to prevent torture and other mistreatment of prisoners, offers a sharp reminder of the special need for effective monitoring and inspection in penal institutions.

I would suggest though that even here there are some connections that can be made across different fields. Prisons are not the only coercive institutions of confinement – there are immigration centres, secure psychiatric hospitals, military facilities and so on. Indeed, I think this list could be further extended if we see institutions of confinement as operating along a continuum, from the most coercive and secure (e.g. prisons holding category A prisoners,[1] high-security psychiatric hospitals), to the least (e.g. boarding schools, hostels for the homeless). Despite obvious differences, there are also some important commonalities across these diverse institutions, in terms of the nature of the regulatory challenges they face, the use of particular inspection techniques and so on. For example, inspectors of children's homes concerned with preventing child abuse by residential

[1] Category A is the highest security classification in the English and Welsh prison system. It refers to prisoners who would be highly dangerous to public or national security if they were to escape.

care staff (see Cawson 1997) are engaged to a certain extent in a very similar exercise to prison inspectors visiting institutions holding young offenders. Indeed, there are strong resonances across both these sectors in some of the controversies in recent years about the use of particular restraint techniques by staff on children (see Smallridge and Williamson 2008). In terms of a research and policy development agenda, the idea of institutions of confinement might provide a useful cross-cutting category for looking at inspection. Other cross-cutting categories no doubt could also be developed. My point is that I think we can usefully look at things in a broader regulatory frame rather than sticking unquestioningly to the belief that the criminal justice field is 'special' and 'different'. Further work on developing a typology of inspection sites and inspection regimes might be helpful in this regard (see: Hughes *et al.* 1997; Boyne *et al.* 2002).

Looked at in this way, there are a series of research questions concerning prison inspection for which learning from inspection practices in different sectors could be helpful. Is there any evidence from other fields, for instance, about the relative effectiveness of announced and unannounced inspections? What is the most effective balance between the two? How frequent should inspections be? How significant are the styles of interaction deployed by inspectors on the ground as 'street level bureaucrats' (May and Winter 2000)? Do inspectors need to be specialist experts in the field they are inspecting? What are the characteristics of the best inspectors, not just in terms of skills but also age, background, experience and so on? What is the most effective use of follow-up inspections? What are the best ways of ensuring that those inspected promptly rectify problems identified during inspections? How useful is it to require the provision of documentary evidence either before, during or after site visits? Building up an evidence base that draws from empirical research in different fields does not mean ignoring the distinctiveness of prison inspection but, equally, we should not dismiss the similarities that exist with the inspection of other institutions of confinement.

In the next section, I want to test out this general claim about the potential for cross-sectoral learning about inspection by examining in more detail one specific area outside the criminal justice arena: the inspection of nursing homes for the elderly. I am not suggesting at all that this is the only sector with which useful comparisons can be made but it happens to have been the subject of an exceptionally detailed and extensive empirical research study characterized by rare theoretical insight and conceptual sophistication. In my view, there are unusually rich pickings here for those looking for cross-sectoral lessons.

Learning from nursing home inspection

Drawing a comparison between prisons and nursing homes for the elderly might be seen by some as at best misguided and at worst as wilfully provocative. My intention is not to say that nursing homes are 'like prisons' in a crass or sensationalist way. Rather, the comparison is an analytical one, designed to draw lessons from a major empirical research study on nursing home regulation that might be applied to the future development of prison inspection. Having said that, the comparison is not an entirely fanciful or far-fetched one, of course. In the book *Regulating Aged Care* which reports on the empirical work by Braithwaite and colleagues, a conversation is recalled between one of the authors, Toni Makkai, and her late father (then a nursing home resident):

FATHER: Why am I here?
TM: Because Mom can't look after you anymore and you need to be in a secure and safe place.
FATHER: But I can't get out.
TM: It is for your own good.
FATHER: It's a prison.
TM: No, it's a nursing home.
FATHER: Then why can't I get out?

(Braithwaite *et al.* 2007b: 4)

This rather poignant exchange highlights what we might term sociologically the ontological reality of the cross-cutting category of 'institutions of confinement'. Or, to put it more straightforwardly, from the perspective of the confined, they may not always seem as different as outsiders might think (or hope). In a sobering passage at the beginning of their book, Braithwaite *et al.* (2007b: 4–6) recall some of the worst instances of misconduct due to regulatory failure that they came across in their nursing-home research, ranging from rape, to genital mutilation, to residents being forced to eat faeces.

I will not attempt to summarize the entire study here but a brief description of its scale and scope will provide some context for what follows. The empirical work was carried out across three decades, starting in the 1980s, and covered three countries: England, the United States and Australia. It consisted of a series of linked projects on nursing home inspection through which a vast amount of data was gathered, including interviews with hundreds of inspectors, observations of routine interactions in numerous nursing homes, observation of over 150 inspection 'events', focus groups with nursing home staff, interviews with key stakeholders (from cabinet ministers to advocacy groups), as well as quantitative studies of compliance and of the validity and reliability of standards. It is an exemplar of a large-scale macro–micro, mixed-methods study of regulatory practice, all of which is brilliantly brought together in the book *Regulating Aged Care* (Braithwaite *et al.* 2007b). So what precisely can we learn from it? There are three particular aspects I will focus on here: the nature of inspection standards; responsive regulation; and building on strengths.

Inspection standards: the paradox of reliability

One of the earlier publications from the nursing home study was an important and influential article by Braithwaite and Braithwaite (1995) entitled 'The Politics of Legalism'. It explored a question which on the face of it might have seemed relatively unimportant but which turned out to be critical to the inspection enterprise: is it more effective to inspect against the yardstick of a small number of general standards/principles or against a larger number of more specific rules? While socio-legal scholars and philosophers of law have long argued the question of rules versus standards, the nursing-home research provided some rare empirical data in which to ground the debate.

Their findings were surprising. One of the central insights they drew from their empirical data concerned what they termed the 'paradox of reliability'. They made a comparison between nursing-home inspection in Australia (based on thirty-one broad and vague standards) and in the United States (based on over 1,000 detailed and precise rules). Turning their initial expectations on their head (Braithwaite and Braithwaite 1995: 310), they found that the Australian regime led not only to more reliable and consistent inspections but was also more conducive to allowing inspectors to help develop better quality of care. Furthermore, they found from their extensive qualitative fieldwork in both countries that the reason 'Australian ratings are more reliable is precisely because they are more (a) broad, (b) subjective, (c) undefined with regard to protocols, (d) resident-centred and (e) devoid of random sampling' (Braithwaite and Braithwaite 1995: 311). This was not what the researchers had expected. Indeed, it is highly counter-intuitive – one would expect that striving for greater rule precision and attempting to eliminate inspector discretion would lead to more consistency and fairness rather than less (1995: 336).

So what should we make of the 'paradox of reliability' in relation to prison inspection? Viewed in the light of these findings, the *Expectations* document developed by the British prison inspectorate is particularly interesting. At first sight, it might appear to resemble more the United States case in the Braithwaite study. It contains well over 500 separate criteria with the clear aim of comprehensively covering just about everything an inspector should be looking at during a prison visit. For example, in the section entitled 'First Days in Custody', there are twenty-eight separate standards. Each is very precisely defined and even stipulates the sources of information that inspectors should rely on in assessing compliance. Standards 17 and 18 in that section illustrate this well:

> 17. Prisoners with substance-related needs are identified at reception and given information about services available.
>
> *Evidence*
> *Observation*: those with acute substance-related needs should be given symptomatic treatment.
> *Prisoners*: check that all prisoners understood the information e.g. foreign nationals.
> *Documentation*: information leaflets.
> *Cross-reference with substance use inspector*
>
> 18. All prisoners are given information about sources of help available, including the chaplaincy team, Listeners or Insiders and Samaritans, in appropriate languages. All prisoners are explicitly offered the chance to speak to a Listener or Insider and a member of the chaplaincy on their first night and the following morning.
>
> *Evidence*
> *Questionnaire*
> *Observation*: individual interviews – speak to Listeners/Insiders. Languages covered should include sign language.
> *Documentation*: check reception packs and whether an up-to-date database on sources of appropriate help is available.
> *Cross-reference with self-harm and suicide inspector.*
>
> (HMIP 2008)

I am sure that such a comprehensive, thorough and detailed guide has been developed in order to make the inspection process as rigorous and penetrating as possible. I am equally sure that it has proved extremely useful for the inspectorate. Indeed, the idea that this level of detail might potentially be counterproductive would probably strike many readers (and prison inspectors) as rather odd. Nevertheless, we should be wary of dismissing out of hand the relevance of the 'paradox of reliability' that Braithwaite and colleagues found in their study. Their explanation for the paradox centres on the notion of regulatory ritualism, that is, the 'acceptance of institutionalised means for securing regulatory goals while losing focus on achieving the goals or outcomes themselves' (Braithwaite 2008: 141). In other words, ritualism is an adaptation to regulatory demands that looks to satisfy the letter of the 'rules' rather than being concerned about the wider outcome(s) for which each standard or rule stands as a proxy indicator. To give an example, a ritualistic approach to Standard 18 quoted above would focus on ensuring the reception packs and database meet the standard expected by inspectors, whilst being indifferent to whether prisoners in fact get a real opportunity to access help or support if they need it when they first arrive in prison. Their argument is that the proliferation of rules, attempts to make them as precise as possible and efforts to 'tighten up' protocols for measuring them, are all conducive to regulatory ritualism. Conversely, outcome-oriented standards that are more generally expressed, allow inspectors the flexibility to do their job better:

> The smaller the number of standards, the better the prospects of ensuring that (a) the most vital information for assessing the total quality of life and quality of care of residents is pursued; (b) lying behind each rating is a collective deliberative process on what that particular rating should be; (c) there is effective public accountability to audit that (a) and (b) actually occur; and (d) inspectors have the capacity to stand back to document the wider patterns in the problems they have identified, to see the wood for the trees.
>
> (Braithwaite and Braithwaite 1995: 322)

My hypothesis then is that a slimming down and simplification of the *Expectations* might facilitate a more effective inspection process by reducing this risk of regulatory ritualism. From this perspective, enabling inspectors to identify patterns, make connections and 'see the wood for the trees' would tend to enhance their ability to identify and diagnose problems and to focus on what actually matters most. On the other hand, a continuing accumulation of standards and expansion of the *Expectations* document would tend to increase the likelihood of ritualistic responses to inspection which, in the long run, would significantly dissipate its impact.

Yet, interestingly, there is another side to the *Expectations* which points in a different direction. The four 'healthy prison' tests referred to above – safety, respect, purposeful activity, resettlement – are also used by the inspectorate. These much more closely resemble the 'broad' and 'subjective' standards that Braithwaite and colleagues found in the more reliable and effective Australian nursing-home regulation regime. In fact, one of the best ways to approach reading the lengthy and detailed prison inspection reports in their published form is to begin with the 'healthy prison summary' that forms part of the introduction of each report and which summarizes inspectors' assessments of outcomes under each test. So perhaps the inspectorate is able partly to transcend regulatory ritualism by the use of these four overarching tests which allow it to 'take the temperature' of a prison without having to be too directly or closely tied by the more detailed standards. However, in the absence of empirical evidence about how these inspectors operate in practice, this remains as speculation. This is an important area for future research.

Responsive regulation

A central dilemma for regulators in all fields is to know when to punish and when to persuade. When is a quiet word or the dangling of a 'carrot' the best way to secure compliance? And when is the threat of punishment or the wielding of a 'stick' most effective? There is no easy answer to this conundrum. Over the last twenty-five years, John Braithwaite and colleagues have set about developing a solution, building a theory based on detailed empirical studies conducted in diverse sectors, from coal mine safety (Braithwaite 1985), to tax avoidance (Braithwaite 2005), to criminal justice (Braithwaite 2002) and, most recently, the nursing-home study which I am focusing on here (Braithwaite *et al.* 2007b). For inspection, it involves recognizing a fundamental point:

> Whether it is nursing home inspectors, or inspectors checking for weapons of mass destruction in Iraq, it is myopic to see inspection as something that mainly works through deterrence.
>
> (Braithwaite *et al.* 2007b: 305)

Their solution to the conundrum is encapsulated in the concept of responsive regulation, as set out in the landmark book by Ayres and Braithwaite (1992). The essence of the idea is simple: 'regulators should be responsive to the conduct of those they seek to regulate in deciding whether a more or less interventionist response is needed' (Braithwaite 2008: 88). The regulatory pyramid elegantly summarizes this (Ayres and Braithwaite 1992) – see Figure 11.1. The idea is that we begin at the base of the pyramid with the 'most restorative dialogue-based approach we can craft for securing compliance' (Braithwaite 2008: 88). Only when these efforts fail should we move, reluctantly, up to the next level of the pyramid. As we progress up the pyramid, interventions become more punitive and demanding. At each level, the knowledge that we can escalate

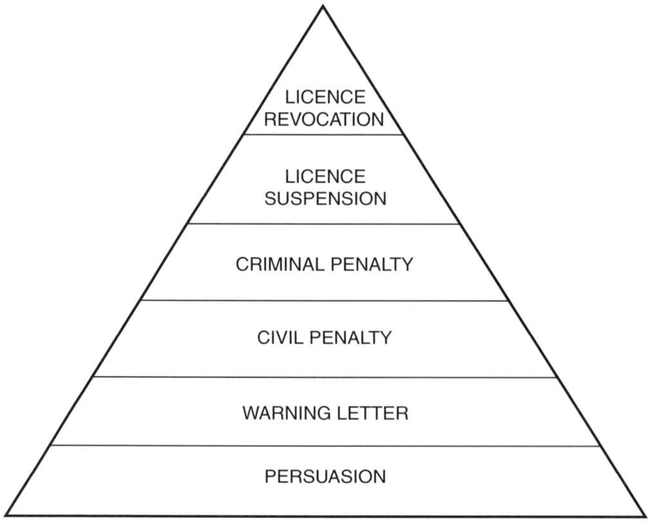

Figure 11.1 Generic regulatory pyramid (adapted from Ayres and Braithwaite (1992))

up the pyramid is part of what helps to secure compliance. When we reach a level where reform or repair starts to be achieved, we should de-escalate, moving back down towards the base again to reward that positive response.

There are several significant implications for prison inspection of the idea of responsive regulation, three of which I wish to highlight here. First, I noted earlier the weakness of the effector component within prison inspection. As Owers (2009: 16) starkly puts it, the inspectorate 'cannot require change, or close down failing institutions'. This is deeply problematic from the perspective of regulatory theory as it cuts away a vital element of a responsive regulation strategy. In effect, the upper layers of the pyramid are missing. Why does this matter? According to the theory, the effectiveness of the lower levels is dependent to a significant extent on the possibility of escalation to a more punitive response. As Braithwaite (1997) nicely puts it, it is about 'speaking softly whilst carrying big sticks'. But, of course, in the absence of big sticks, softly-spoken persuasion tends to lose its potency. The clear implication is that the development of a more responsive approach will require the prison inspectorate to be given proper enforcement powers. This would represent a major shift, requiring new legislation, but, I would argue, is something that should be seriously considered. The aim is not that such enforcement powers would be extensively used, quite the opposite in fact, as by 'signalling (without making threats) a resolve to escalate up an enforcement pyramid until a just outcome is secured, we can actually drive most of the regulatory action down to the base of the enforcement pyramid' (Braithwaite 2008: 163).

Second, as the nursing-home study clearly shows, along with many others conducted by Braithwaite and his collaborators, at the heart of a responsive regulation strategy lie dialogue and conversation. Skilled nursing-home inspectors talking to residents, staff members and managers was the foundation for effective inspection. As one would expect, for dialogue-based regulation to work at its best, inspectors need above all else to be good listeners able to make even the weakest and quietest voices be heard, a point that I will return to in the next section. One tool for conversational regulation described in the nursing-home study is the exit conference. This takes place at the end of the inspection visit and involves managers, staff and resident representatives coming together to hear the inspectors' preliminary findings and to start discussions about how any identified problems might be remedied. The approach and purpose of the conferences is reparative and restorative rather than confrontational. They should in this respect resemble the family group conferences that restorative justice practitioners convene. No doubt they are sometimes difficult for participants but they can also be immensely powerful:

> We observed a team of three Australian inspectors in 2005 give the assembled staff of the nursing home a round of applause at the end of an exit conference.
>
> (Braithwaite *et al.* 2007b: 198)

Currently, the prison inspectorate in England and Wales does hold formal debriefs with senior managers at the end of inspection visits. One way of developing this could be to trial full-blown restorative exit conferences involving all the key actors in the prison (including prisoner representatives), as a concrete means of shifting to a more responsive regulation strategy. I do not underestimate the shift in attitudes and thinking this would require, especially for prison managers, but in my view it is worth exploring as a tool that may potentially improve the effectiveness of the inspectorate as a regulator.

Third, one of the more recent developments of the regulatory pyramid has been the idea of 'networked escalation', first developed by Peter Drahos (2004) – see also Braithwaite (2008: 87–108) and Wood and Shearing (2007). This draws on the notion that we live increasingly in a world in which governance is polycentric or nodal (see Shearing and

Froestad, this book, Chapter 5; Burris *et al.* 2005), that is, that it occurs through and within networks. Drahos's insight is that weaker regulators do not always have to operate on their own. They can also enrol network partners to escalate pressure on the regulated as they move up the pyramid. In the nursing-home study, networked escalation was found to be a vital strategy:

> Empirically, Braithwaite et al (2007) found British nursing-home inspectors to be weak regulatory agencies, in both legal powers and resources. Yet they accomplished a great deal of improvement in quality of care by creative networking even of organisations as powerful as banks. Banks become reluctant to lend money to homes when inspectors put up on the Internet excoriating inspection reports.
>
> (Braithwaite 2008: 96)

It is clear that prison inspectors already practise networked escalation to some extent. An infamous example of this occurred in 1995 when the then Chief Inspector, Sir David Ramsbotham, pulled his team out of Holloway prison halfway through an inspection visit in protest at the conditions they found there and immediately wrote to the Head of the Prison Service and the Home Secretary demanding improvements be made before they would return. The resulting negative publicity placed more regulatory pressure on the prison management to improve conditions than even the most viscerally damning inspection report could have done. More mundanely, inspectors regularly draw on formal and informal links with others (e.g. non-governmental organizations – NGOs) to bring about change. My proposal here is that they should experiment further with networked escalation, viewing it as a constructive and positive regulatory weapon rather than just as a necessity borne out of weakness. By looking strategically at the range of partners with whom they might profitably network, prison inspectors could potentially expand their regulatory capacity and potency quite significantly.

Strength-building

One of the most original contributions to regulatory theory made by the nursing-home study is its development of a new pyramid designed to operate alongside the enforcement pyramid discussed above. The authors explain the new twin-track approach:

> To craft a new regulatory environment that has two complementary models – a regulatory model backed by enforcement and a strengths-based

> model backed by rewards. The former is designed to ensure that the standard of care in nursing homes reaches the minimum standard set by the regulator; the latter is designed to build out from micro and macro strengths within nursing homes and the industry to lift the standard of care beyond the minimum to continuously higher levels.
>
> (Braithwaite *et al.* 2007b: 330)

With the new strengths-based pyramid, inspection shifts away from being an accountability mechanism towards being primarily a regulatory tool. Here 'the most important thing regulators do is catalyse continuous improvement' (Braithwaite *et al.* 2007b: 322). The aim becomes to push the regulated to ever higher standards, rather than just to make sure that basic standards are met. The philosophy is to 'pick strengths and expand them' on the basis that the 'best way to improve is to build out from your strengths' (Braithwaite 2008: 152).

This philosophy transforms the inspection process. While the enforcement pyramid draws on shame, disapproval and sanctions for failures to manage risks and solve problems, the strengths-based pyramid uses praise, pride and rewards where opportunities for improvement are successfully taken (Braithwaite *et al.* 2007b: 320). Inspectors are no longer just concerned with identifying problems and recommending solutions to them; now, they are charged also with identifying strengths and opportunities to build on them. And institutions become accountable to inspectors not just for dealing with problem areas but also for proactively seeking to improve what they do, building out from existing successes.

As I argued above, listening is an important part of the inspectors' toolkit within a responsive regulation approach. When a strengths-based pyramid is added alongside it, it becomes absolutely central, as Braithwaite (2008: 154) argues:

> A key skill of the strengths-based inspector is being a good listener. You cannot build strengths without empowering those with the strength. A mistake I observed many neophyte inspectors in Australia to make when they had a strengths-based philosophy, but executed it badly, was to jump in quickly with communicating expectations on what kind of improvement is desired. More sophisticated practitioners of this philosophy were more patient, encouraging nursing-home staff to tell their own story of how they were building on their strengths, what their plans were for future improvement ...We can empower people by the simple act of listening to their stories, making their stories the point of reference for the stories we contribute to our conversation with them. Therefore, good strengths-based inspectors are accomplished listeners. Through their listening they

> help convince staff that yes they do have the power in their own hands to transcend regulatory ritualism and secure real further improvement.

I recognize that to apply the strengths-based pyramid to prison inspection involves quite an imaginative leap. For prisons, inspection has to some extent, and for entirely understandable reasons, been framed primarily as a means of preventing abuses and assuring minimum standards are attained. The idea of using inspection for continuous improvement and to aspire to excellence may seem to border on the fanciful in the face of some of the grim conditions to be found in prisons around the world. But I think it would be a failure of aspiration and imagination to reject this out of hand. Why should our prisons not be striving for excellence in what they do?

So what might a strengths-based approach to prison inspection look like? There are two features that I want to pull out here. First, it would alter what inspectors are focused on looking for during prison visits. Rather than just hunting out deficiencies, they would be trying at the same time to find opportunities for improvements based on what the inspected prison was doing well at. The *Expectations* document might include not only minimum standards but also examples of excellence from institutions across the prison estate. Exit conferences would cover both what was needed to rectify failures to meet basic standards and also ideas about creating a route towards continuous improvement. This twin focus would then be reflected in the written inspection report and in the conduct of any follow-up inspection visits. In other words, a strengths-based approach would add an entirely new dimension to the whole inspection process. Second, as we saw before with the enforcement pyramid, improvement that builds on strengths is also something that can be effected through networked governance. In an individual prison, inspectors could facilitate the networking of relevant stakeholders into a project of institutional transformation. As a national player, the prison inspectorate can also more readily grasp what Braithwaite (2008: 148) calls the 'micro–macro linkages' involved in networked governance. An innovative improvement in a privately managed prison might subsequently be taken up by other institutions managed by that particular private company. By flagging this up, the inspectorate could then help to engage NGOs and other stakeholders in a national campaign to extend that learning more widely across the entire prison estate. This is what Parker (2002) has called triple-loop learning, whereby micro-change in a single institution (or a single part of an institution) can eventually lead to macro-change at a national level. Braithwaite *et al.* (2007b) certainly found examples of this in their study.

Conclusion

An obvious, and entirely justified, response to my argument in this chapter would be to return to the claim that prisons are simply too 'different' for this type of cross-sectoral learning to be of any real use. I happily admit that this may be so but it seems to me that this is an empirical question rather than one that can be decided in advance. My own judgement is that there are sufficient commonalities within the category of 'institutions of confinement' for such comparisons to be worth pursuing. I have no doubt at all that a study of prison inspection would throw up some surprises, some issues that are truly 'different' from other institutional contexts. But this is something that can only become apparent through empirical work. It is, in any case, absolutely central to the idea of responsive regulation that I have been proposing that specific regulatory strategies need to be crafted on the basis of an understanding of their specific regulatory context. While there are generic design principles – e.g. the regulatory pyramid – regulation scholars like Braithwaite have repeatedly emphasized the need for an empirically grounded appreciation of each particular field as the basis for developing effective approaches that are suitably attuned and responsive to context.

In this sense, what I have been engaged in in this chapter has been the setting out of some hypotheses for exploration in concrete research studies. In other words, it is a research agenda, rather than a detailed blueprint for change. The latter can only come as an evidence base begins to accumulate. It is striking, in fact, how little research has been done to date on prison inspection, despite the growing global recognition of its profound importance, as indicated, for example, by the expanding list of signatories to the UN Opcat Protocol. Today, there are nearly 10 million people held in penal institutions across the world (Walmsley 2009) and problems of suicide, self-harm, overcrowding and poor conditions are endemic in many countries, with rich countries far from immune from these difficulties – in England and Wales, for example, there were over 22,000 recorded incidents of self-harm and 92 suicides in the prison system during 2007 (Prison Reform Trust 2009). The need to monitor what goes on inside prisons and to improve performance is more important and urgent than ever. An imaginative and rigorous programme of research on prison inspection, exploring the issues of compliance, responsiveness, and so on, that I have discussed here could make a genuinely significant and positive contribution.

So I want to end by making a modest proposal, or rather two proposals. First, to regulation scholars, I propose that the inspection of prisons should be the subject of comparative empirical research, as an important site for advancing regulatory theory. Second, to prison researchers, I propose that they turn at least some of their attention to the work of prison inspection which has been often praised but rarely researched to date. And, of course, to achieve either of these will require prison inspectorates to be as open to scrutiny and to the potential for improvement as they themselves hope that the prisons they inspect are.

References

Ayres, I. and Braithwaite, J. (1992) *Responsive Regulation: Transcending the Deregulation Debate*. Oxford University Press.

Black, J. (2002) 'Critical Reflections on Regulation', *Australian Journal of Legal Philosophy*, **27**, 1–35.

Bovens, M. (2007) 'Analysing and Assessing Accountability: A Conceptual Framework', *European Law Journal*, **13**(4), 447–68.

Boyne, G., Day, P. and Walker, R. (2002) 'The Evaluation of Public Service Inspection: A Theoretical Framework', *Urban Studies*, **39**(7), 1197–1212.

Braithwaite, J. (1985) *To Punish or Persuade: Enforcement of Coal Mine Safety*. Albany, NY: State University of New York Press.

(1997) 'On Speaking Softly and Carrying Sticks: Neglected Dimensions of Republican Separation of Powers', *University of Toronto Law Journal*, **47**, 1–57.

(2002) *Restorative Justice and Responsive Regulation*. New York, NY: Oxford University Press.

(2003) 'What's Wrong with the Sociology of Punishment?', *Theoretical Criminology*, **7**(1), 5–28.

(2005) *Markets in Vice, Markets in Virtue*. New York and Sydney: Oxford and Federation Press.

(2008) *Regulatory Capitalism: How It Works, Ideas for Making It Work Better*. Cheltenham, Glos.: Edward Elgar.

Braithwaite, J. and Braithwaite, V. (1995) 'The Politics of Legalism: Rules Versus Standards in Nursing-Home Regulation', *Social and Legal Studies*, **4**, 307–341.

Braithwaite, J., Coglianese, C. and Levi-Faur, D. (2007a) 'Can Regulation and Governance Make a Difference?', *Regulation and Governance*, **1**, 1–7.

Braithwaite, J., Makkai, T. and Braithwaite, V. (2007b) *Regulating Aged Care: Ritualism and the New Pyramid*. Cheltenham, Glos.: Edward Elgar.

Burris, S., Drahos, P. and Shearing, C. (2005) 'Nodal Governance', *Australian Journal of Legal Philosophy*, **30**, 30–58.

Cawson, P. (1997) 'Who Will Guard the Guards? Some Questions about the Models of Inspection for Residential Settings with Relevance to the Protection of

Children from Abuse by Staff', *Early Child Development and Care*, **133**(1), 57–71.

Drahos, P. (2004) 'Intellectual Property and Pharmaceutical Markets: A Nodal Governance Approach', *Temple Law Review*, **77**, 401–24.

Harding, R. (2007) 'Inspecting Prisons', in Y. Jewkes (ed.), *Handbook on Prisons*. Cullumpton, Devon: Willan, pp. 543–65.

Her Majesty's Inspectorate of Prisons (HMIP) (2008) *Expectations: Criteria for Assessing the Conditions in Prisons and the Treatment of Prisoners*, 3rd edn (at: www.justice.gov.uk/inspectorates/hmi-prisons/docs/expectations_2009.pdf; accessed 10/09/09).

Hood, C., Scott, C., James, O., Jones, G. and Travers, T. (1999) *Regulation Inside Government*. Oxford University Press.

Hughes, G., Mears, R. and Winch, C. (1997) 'An Inspector Calls? Regulation and Accountability in Three Public Services', *Policy and Politics*, **25**(3), 299–313.

Lodge, M. (2004) 'Accountability and Transparency in Regulation: Critiques, Doctrines and Instruments', in J. Jordana and D. Levi-Faur (eds.), *Politics of Regulation: Institutions and Regulatory Reforms for the Age of Governance*. Cheltenham, Glos.: Edward Elgar, pp. 124–44.

MacDonagh, O. (1958) 'The Nineteenth-century Revolution in Government: A Reappraisal', *Historical Journal*, **1**, 52–67.

Maguire, M., Vagg, J. and Morgan, R. (eds.) (1985) *Accountability and Prisons: Opening up a Closed World*. London: Tavistock.

Mashaw, J. (2006) 'Accountability and Institutional Design: Some Thoughts on the Grammar of Governance', in M. Dowdle (ed.), *Public Accountability: Designs, Dilemmas and Experiences*. Cambridge University Press, pp. 115–56.

May, Mr Justice (1979) *Report of the Committee of Inquiry into the United Kingdom Prison Services*. London: HMSO.

May, P. (2007) 'Regulatory Regimes and Accountability', *Regulation and Governance*, **1**, 8–26.

May, P. and Winter, S. (2000) 'Reconsidering Styles of Regulatory Enforcement: Patterns in Danish Agro-Environmental Inspection', *Law and Policy*, **22**(2), 143–73.

Mulgan, R. (2000) 'Accountability: An Ever-Expanding Concept?', *Public Administration*, **78**, 555–73.

Ogus, A. (1994) *Regulation: Legal Form and Economic Theory*. Oxford: Hart.

Owers, A. (2004) 'Prison Inspection and the Protection of Human Rights', *European Human Rights Law Review*, **2**, 107–16.

(2009) 'Reforming Prisons: The Role of Inspection', *Criminal Justice Matters*, **77**, 16–17.

Parker, C. (2002) *The Open Corporation: Effective Self-regulation and Democracy*. Cambridge University Press.

Peters, E. (1995) ‘Prison Before the Prison: The Ancient and Medieval Worlds’, in N. Morris and D. Rothman (eds.), *The Oxford History of the Prison: The Practice of Punishment in Western Society*. Oxford University Press, pp. 3–43.

Prison Reform Trust (2009) *Bromley Briefings: Prison Factfile, June 2009*. London: Prison Reform Trust.

Raine, J. (2008) ‘Inspection and the Criminal Justice Agencies’, in H. Davis and S. Martin (eds.), *Public Services Inspection in the UK*. Research Highlights in Social Work 50. London: Jessica Kingsley, pp. 87–101.

Scott, C. (2000) ‘Accountability in the Regulatory State’, *Journal of Law and Society*, **27**(1), 38–60.

Smallridge, P. and Williamson, A. (2008) *Independent Review of Restraint in Juvenile Secure Settings*. London: Ministry of Justice and Department for Children, Schools and Families (at: www.justice.gov.uk/publications/docs/restraint_review.pdf; accessed 11/01/10).

Smith, G. (2009) ‘Citizen Oversight of Independent Police Services: Bifurcated Accountability, Regulation Creep and Lesson-Learning’, *Regulation and Governance*, **3**(4), 422–42.

Stenning, P. (ed.) (1995) *Accountability for Criminal Justice: Selected essays*. University of Toronto Press.

Stockdale, E. (1983) ‘A Short History of Prison Inspection in England’, *British Journal of Criminology*, **23**(3), 209–28.

Vagg, J. (1994) *Prison Systems: A Comparative Study of Accountability in England, France, Germany and the Netherlands*. Oxford: Clarendon Press.

Walmsley, R. (2009) *World Prison Population List*. 8th edn. London: International Centre for Prison Studies, Kings College London.

Wood, J. and Shearing, C. (2007) *Imagining Security*. Cullompton, Devon: Willan.

12

Regulating democracy: justice, citizenship and inequality in Brazil*

BARBARA HUDSON

Introduction

My paper for the Manchester ESRC Seminar Series, Regulation and Criminal Justice, was part of the session on 'responsivity'. 'Responsivity' has many connotations, but in this chapter I am concerned with the issue of responsiveness to diversity and division. Systems of criminal justice and regulation are increasingly called upon to recognize the claims to inclusion of the formerly excluded or marginalized, and to respond to conflicts and harms involving persons whose perspectives may be so different as to appear irreconcilable. Theories put forward to deal with these demands include *deliberative democracy* and *cosmopolitan justice*. The idea common to both is that of *discourse*: response to diversity, division and difference in perspectives demands greater openness of discourse than is found in established formal justice proceedings. Participants should be able to present their claims, their harms and the circumstances of their transgressions in their own words.

The idea of 'responsive regulation' is particularly associated with John Braithwaite, and responsivity is at the heart of the restorative justice paradigm he advocates (Braithwaite 2002). In this model, justice processes should respond to harms, disruptions, wrongs discursively: they should define the problem they are dealing with in terms of its effects on victims, offenders and the community, and process participants must seek solutions appropriate to all parties rather than fitting the problem into pre-existing legal categories and applying the relevant rules and precedents. Restorative justice is, therefore, discursive justice – the acts that occasioned the proceedings, their effects and the circumstances in which

* I am grateful to the Ministério Público of Paraná for assistance with research, for sharing so openly their ideals and their anxieties, and for generous and convivial hospitality.

they occurred, measures to remedy harms and reduce the likelihood of recurrence need to be discussed freely.

While restorative justice projects have become much more widespread in recent years, they have tended to remain on the periphery of criminal justice, or they have become incorporated into mainstream criminal justice. Along with other forms of community justice, they are ceded a place in the criminal justice system dealing with young offenders, minor offences within minority communities, for example, rather than replacing it. The idea of restorativeness as a 'replacement discourse', displacing retributive justice rather than being accommodated within it or on its fringes, is seldom raised outside a small circle of restorative justice theorists. Recent debates on the 'institutionalisation of restorative justice' (Aertsen *et al.* 2006) have raised issues about its place in relation to established criminal justice. In my own contribution to this debate I have discussed the potential for generalization of the ethics and the modality of discourse within criminal justice, as more appropriate than established formal criminal justice to the diversity of contemporary societies, rather than discursive justice remaining as justice for young offenders and minor offences, or as a rung on the penal ladder (Hudson 2007). I am, therefore, interested in innovations at state level as well as in projects on the periphery of justice.

Critiques of existing justice processes in settled, stable democracies tend to tackle issues of exclusion or of ineffectiveness one by one. Thus, for instance, there are demands for justice to become more 'womanwise', or to pay attention to race discrimination, or to ensure that the administration of justice complies with human rights legislation. More wide-ranging changes, that adopt more regulatory style approaches and encompass multiple aspects of diversity and inequality, usually come about in post-conflict situations. The constitutions of post-conflict societies such as South Africa after the end of apartheid; the new constitution and the Charter of Rights and Freedoms introduced in Canada in 1983, prompted in large part by the growing strength of the separatist movement in French-speaking Quebec combined provisions to ensure democratic government, with specifications of rights and aspirations for equality of citizenship (Tully 1995).

In this chapter I discuss one such new constitution, the 1988 post-military regime Constitution of Brazil. The focus is on aspects of the Constitution which are relevant to the inclusion of the marginalized and excluded, and on the role of one particular institution, the Ministério Público (Public Prosecutor) in promoting and defending these aspects of the Constitution. I suggest that the Ministério Público uses discursive approaches to its promotion of justice, that it represents the sort of institution consistent with *deliberative democracy*, and that it is developing an ethos of *democratic professionalism*.

The idea of discursive justice

The idea of discourse as a principle and mode of justice does not only arise in relation to restorative justice. Writers such as Habermas (1984, 1987, 1996) Benhabib (1992) and Young (1990) have proposed discourse as a fundamental, universalizable principle of justice. They advocate discursive justice as the means of responding to the claims for inclusion of social groups who have been marginalized and excluded from established justice. Indigenous peoples, women, religious, cultural and ethnic minorities, non-citizens and other 'outsiders' have justice claims that need recognition and response, and these writers argue that this recognition and response can only be realized by justice becoming more discursively open. Discursive justice means that all participants should be able to raise any topic, and that they should be able to discuss their concerns in their own terms, not remain within the restricted parameters of legal discourse.

As societies become more diverse, and as radical diversity is increasingly acknowledged, existing models and processes of justice and regulation have come under strain as they respond to difference. Protection of women and children from violence; dealing with racial violence and discrimination, for example, are areas where established law has proved deficient. Cultural questions such as the wearing of hijabs, burkhas and religious symbols in public as well as private spheres; recognition of polygamous marriages, marriage and divorce according to the rules and ceremonies of different religions; the rights that should be extended to non-citizens, are proving difficult to resolve in societies where radical difference has tended to be glossed over or repressed (Hudson 2008).

Iris Young (2002) has argued that diversity should be recognized as a resource for justice, rather than as a difficulty. Established liberal justice tends to consider people only as individuals, with the relevance of social groups ruled 'out of court'. In many instances where justice is called upon, however, group membership is relevant. People suffer inequalities and discrimination because the groups of which they are members are marginalized, impoverished, repressed or discriminated against. Justice and regulation need to be able to respond to group as well as to individual circumstances and experiences.

The idea of discourse as a fundamental principle of justice involves the move from Kant's stipulation that rules should be those that *could* be agreed by all members of a community of shared rationality to the principle that rules should be those that actually *are* agreed. In political theory, this idea of justification by actual discourse is the core of the model of *deliberative democracy*, in which rules are debated and defended. Deliberative democracy is:

> A conception of democratic politics in which decisions and policies are justified in a process of discussion among free and equal citizens or their accountable representatives...Its fundamental principle is that citizens owe one another justification for the laws they collectively impose on one another.
>
> (Gutman and Thompson 2000: 161)

Gutman and Thompson (1996) endorse deliberative democracy because its discursive mode makes it more able than other models to accommodate moral conflicts. Habermas (1999) has argued for deliberative democracy in similar terms, describing democracies as 'communicative contexts' where conflicts can be accommodated and minorities included. In contemporary societies characterized by radical diversity, consensus may not always be possible. Justice has to obtain between groups and individuals whose difference may be irreducible: a common perspective may be unattainable, but accommodation nonetheless has to be found.

Discursive justice and cosmopolitan justice

Thinking about the inclusion of formerly marginalized and excluded groups within the community of justice, and protecting the interests and promoting the rights of the irreducibly other, some proponents of discursive justice have moved to advocating *cosmopolitan justice*. As they have turned their attention from expounding the theory of discourse as a generalizable principle of justice to actual dilemmas of resolution of moral conflicts arising from radically different perspectives, and to difficult issues for regulation and justice such as migration, terrorism and diffused citizenship, advocates of discursive justice have also become adherents of cosmopolitan justice (Benhabib 2004, 2006; Habermas 1999, 2003; Young 2002). The central idea of cosmopolitan justice is that of doing justice to the *stranger*, the person who is beyond our borders of geographical, political or moral community (Hudson 2008).

Contemporary cosmopolitan justice theory often takes as its starting point Kant's essay 'To Perpetual Peace' (1983, first published in 1784). As well as his ideas of justice in societies of shared mentalities, which are inscribed in the justice systems of post-Enlightenment western states, Kant developed ideas for responding with justice to people encountered through trade (including the slave trade of which he was highly critical), exploration and imperialism. He calls for a 'cosmopolitan federation' of nations to maintain peaceful relations between states, and he also argues for a right and corresponding duty of universal hospitality. By hospitality in this context, he means 'the right of a stranger not to be treated as an enemy in someone else's country' (Kant 1983: 118). This right of hospitality is the essential proposition of the contemporary theory of cosmopolitan justice.

Kant's political cosmopolitanism has been drawn on by contemporary theorists. Habermas (1999, 2003) and Benhabib (2004, 2006) take up the proposition of 'cosmopolitan federalism'; for Derrida (2001, 2003) and Bauman (2004) the idea of hospitality is the most important. For these latter theorists, Kant's duty–right of hospitality gives a political aspect to Levinas's principle of moral responsibility to the Other just because of her presence. This responsibility, for Levinas, precedes any relationship of reciprocity, and even precedes understanding. The idea of hospitality makes this moral relationship available to the political sphere of justice rather than being confined to the face-to-face sphere of ethics.

All the people of the world

'Cosmopolitan' as commonly used today denotes a 'citizen of the world' (Beck 2006). The cosmopolitan is the businessperson, or indeed the academic, who stays in identical hotels in cities throughout the world; who eats Mexican food in London, Chinese food in New York; who watches 'world cinema' and listens to 'world music'; who can converse about the best and worst experiences in airports and airline food, and who feels more sophisticated than the simple 'provincial'. In theories of cosmopolitan justice, however, the word is used in its older philosophical sense of 'all the citizens of the world' (Appiah 2006). This means that all the citizens of the world wherever they may be, persons of all groups, traditions, cultures; it means all races, men and women, the traditional and the progressive, the powerful and the powerless, the rich and the poor, have rights and are owed justice.

My interest in cosmopolitan justice as an appropriate model for single states as well as for international and cross-national justice has been stimulated by my working for part of each year since 2004 in Brazil. As well as being home to cosmopolitans in the newer sense, Brazil is home to people from all over the world. It is a land of immigrants, from Europe, from Asia and the Middle East, from elsewhere in the Americas; it has descendants of slaves and of slave traders, and, of course, it has its own 'first peoples', the Amazonian Indians and other river peoples. In terms of theories of justice, Brazil represents both kinds of societies envisaged by the Enlightenment philosophers. Colonization by the Portuguese and immigration by other western Europeans means that Brazil belongs to the community of countries sharing a common reasoning because of similar cultures and experiences, and its law is based on the code system of Portugal. On the other hand, the presence of its original population, its descendants of slaves, and the tremendous diversity among the generations of migrants, means that it also represents the society of strangers for which cosmopolitan principles of justice were developed. Justice in Brazil has to be able to respond to individuals and groups with diverse traditions, diverse experiences, and within a context of continuing gross inequalities.

The new constitution and the re-democratization process

In 1985, Brazil returned to democratic rule after twenty-one years of military government. The first military government was led by Marshall Castelo Branco, who in March 1964 withdrew mandates of members of the Brazilian legislative body, and arrested opponents of the military regime. Increasing levels of censorship and repression culminated in the Institutional Act no. 5, 1968, introduced by President Costa e Silva, which ended democratic freedoms in Brazil. In 1985, the death of Tancredo Neves, the indirectly elected presidential candidate approved by the military, led to the assumption of the presidency by the Vice-President, Sarney, on 21 April. This ended the cycle of military governments.

A new Federal Constitution came into effect in 1988. Like other constitutions enacted in post-dictatorship, post-conflict situations in the latter part of the twentieth century, the Brazilian 1988 Constitution articulates principles and mechanisms of democratic governance, and also incorporates a contemporary charter of rights. The Brazilian Constitution expresses the ideals of a newly democratized country, aspiring to accommodate all demands relevant to the 'democratic spirit'. It also attempts to implement a political, social and economic order very different from the previous authoritarian regime (Sadek and Cavalcanti 2000).

Article 3 of the Constitution lists the 'fundamental objectives' of the Federal Republic of Brazil as:

I to build a free, just and solidary society;
II to guarantee national development;
III to eradicate poverty and substandard living conditions and to reduce social and regional inequalities;
IV to promote the well-being of all, without prejudice as to origin, race, sex, colour, age and any other form of discrimination.

Article 4 decrees that the international relations of Brazil will be governed by the following principles, among others:

II prevalence of human rights;
III self-determination of the people;
VII peaceful settlement of conflicts;
VIII repudiation of terrorism and racism;
X granting of political asylum.

After the declaration of basic principles, the Constitution delineates a range of basic rights and freedoms which encompass all the rights we understand as due process rights (fair trials, no punishment without conviction, etc.); personal freedoms/civil rights (freedom of expression, freedom of worship, etc.); social rights including rights to education, health and welfare benefits; protection of workers against dismissal, minimum wage; maternity and paternity leave; health and safety protection; assisted childcare for children from birth to 6 years of age. There are fourteen sections detailing specific rights, with between them over 300 clauses, so that Brazil's Constitution is one of the most detailed in the western hemisphere, regulating practically all aspects of collective life (Sadek and Cavalcanti 2000: 2–3).

Since the return to democratic rule, and the introduction of the new Constitution, Brazil has been undergoing what is referred to as a 're-democratization project'. This has two key elements. The first is that of making the rights and freedoms promised by the Constitution into realities; the second is that of re-awakening the Brazilian people to democracy. In Brazil, the strongest theme in promoting the Constitution to the people has been that of democracy.

Emphasis on promulgation of the new Constitution as a re-democratization process makes it appropriate to think of developments in post-military Brazilian institutions in terms of *transitional justice* (Teitel 2000). Invocation of democracy rather than legality suggests that law is not perceived as an instrument of democracy: in transitional justice, law has to change in order to serve democracy. The term 'transitional justice' first referred to processes to call to account officials and politicians responsible for human rights violations by the previous regimes, with trials of violators and purges to ensure that they did not retain their positions in the new regime.

Brazil has not had criminal trials, truth and reconciliation commissions, or purges following the ending of the military regime. Transitional justice, however, is not only concerned with dealing with the past, but also with building the future, bringing about reconstruction and reconciliation (Bell and Campbell 2004). Transitional justice is involved in using law to install and entrench democratic freedoms and human rights, and in re-establishing the rule of law itself. With authoritarian rule, law and legal institutions are disregarded or disrespected. Either authoritarian regimes take and maintain power without law, or they manipulate law to these ends. At the least, law is usually seen as compliant, the instrument of power, used against the powerless. Transitional justice tries to move from this position of disempowered or compromised law, to a law that can support constitutionalism on behalf of all the people.

Packaging the Constitution and juridical actions to deliver its promised rights and freedoms as democracy rather than legality, demonstrates the low regard in which law was held by substantial sections of the Brazilian people at the end of military government. The re-democratization process, then, has addressed the transitional justice tasks of delivering rights and freedoms promised by the Constitution; relegitimizing law as the instrument of all sections of Brazilian society, and making governmental processes democratic and accountable.

The Ministério Público

The new Constitution was innovative in two important respects. First, as well as recognizing individual rights, it recognizes 'diffuse and collective rights'. As Arantes (2003) explains, transindividual rights are those which are indivisible in nature, whether the persons holding the rights are indeterminate in nature (diffuse rights) or a group of individuals with some sort of legal relationship (collective rights). Environmental rights, rights to cultural and historical heritage, and consumer rights have been defined as diffuse and collective rights since 1985, and subject to class action litigation. The law creating the *ação civil pública* (public civil action suit) in 1985 provided the judicial instrument which could be used to secure diffuse and collective rights. Class action suits have become one of the most important mechanisms for the promotion and defence of constitutional rights.

The second innovative feature of the 1988 Constitution is the enlargement and redefinition of the role of the Public Prosecutor, the Ministério Público. According to some assessments, the Ministério Público can 'be considered as the main institutional novelty in Brazil since the return to democracy' (Arantes 2003: 4). The Ministério Público has become, in effect, the defender of the Constitution:

> The Public Prosecution is a permanent institution, essential to the jurisdictional function of the State, and it is its duty to defend the juridical order, the democratic regime and the inalienable social and individual interests.
>
> (Federal Constitution, 1988, Chapter IV, s. 1, Art. 127)

The wide role of the Ministério Público defined by the Constitution is broken down into several functions, listed in Article 129:

I to initiate, exclusively, public criminal prosecution;
II to ensure effective respect by the Public Authorities and by the services of public relevance for the rights guaranteed in this Constitution, taking the action required to guarantee such rights;
III to institute civil investigation and public civil suit to protect public and social property, the environment and other diffuse and collective interests;
IV to institute action of unconstitutionality or representation for purposes of intervention by the Union or by the states, in the cases established in this Constitution;
V to defend judicially the rights and interests of the Indian populations;
VII to exercise external control over police activities.

There are also functions (VI, VIII) which give ombudsman-like powers to investigate the use of their powers by state organizations, including the police. Clause IX allows for 'other functions' provided they are compatible with the Ministério's purposes. Together, these functions give the Ministério very wide powers and responsibilities in respect to the provisions and aspirations of the Constitution.

Studies of prosecutors by Hensler (2005),[1] Arantes (2003) and by Sadek and Calvaceti (2000), show that they regard themselves as necessary defenders of the public interest and guardians of the re-democratization process because of their perception (widely shared throughout Brazil)

[1] I am grateful to Salo Coslovsky for giving me a copy of this insightful paper.

that although the Constitution expresses high ideals, the institutions of government are weak and corruption is widespread.

Political corruption is a marked feature in Brazilian society, with corrupt dealings in campaign financing, decision making and policy implementation rife in the post-military redemocratization period. Hensler concludes that 'It is hardly an overstatement to suggest that Brazil's recent political history is the story of the impact of, and resistance to, corruption in public life' (Hensler 2005: 8). Explanations of the extent of political corruption in Brazil usually highlight poor accountability mechanisms within government institutions, lack of regulation in areas such as campaign financing, and the lack of activism by the judicial system. Investigations into corruption in the post-dictatorship regimes of Sarney and Collor were sparked by media campaigns and taken forward by congressional commissions of enquiry. During the impeachment of Collor in 1992 the public prosecutors were accused of incompetence and inexperience; by the end of the decade they had transformed themselves into a much more vigorous and competent organization for fighting corruption.

Much of the Ministério's activism has concerned local mayors, who in Brazil have powerful functions. In Rio Grande do Sul, Paraná and Sao Paulo state, in particular, large numbers of mayors have been prosecuted for misuse of public funds, fraud and links with organized crime. In Rio Grande do Sul, there were so many prosecutions that a special court had to be established; in Sao Paulo prosecutors investigated corruption not just by mayors, but at all levels of the state's political machinery. One famous case concerned Sao Paulo mayor Paulo Maluf, who has been accused of fraud, money laundering, diversion of funds for broadcasting sporting events, a tunnel-construction project and the supply of chicken to schools (chicken-gate).

In the state of Paraná, the mayor of the city of Londrina ('little London'), Antonio Belinatti, was accused of corruption in 1999. He had set up a scheme which encompassed several kinds of fraud and appropriation of public funds into private bank accounts which would, among other things, fund the electoral campaigns of family members and political allies. The Ministério Público worked with a social movement 'Red Feet, Clean Hands' (which refers to the rich red earth for which the state is well known), and the mayor was impeached by the City Council in June 2000. He (and over 100 people and companies charged with him) faced more than thirty class action suits and fourteen criminal action suits for the embezzlement of large sums of public money (Arantes 2003: 22–3). The public prosecutors and the Red-feet movement were awarded the 2001

Integrity Award from Transparency International, who in their report on Brazil's 'integrity systems' gave the Ministério the only wholly positive assessment among all the major institutions of government and civil society (Hensler 2005).

Protector of the powerless

The responsibility to promote public civil actions for the protection of diffuse and collective interests has been particularly important for the development of the Ministério's role of 'political law enforcer' (Arantes 2003: 5). Laws created since 1988 that recognize diffuse and collective rights and give a leading role to the Ministério Público for their enforcement include the Handicapped Persons Act (1989); the Statute of the Child and Adolescent (1990) and the Consumer Protection Code (1990). These laws, added to their responsibilities for defence of the Constitution, and for defence of the rights and interests of Indian populations have encouraged those prosecutors who have most fully and eagerly embraced the possibilities of their institutional role to resemble 'cause lawyers' rather than state prosecutors in other countries (Coslovsky 2007).

Coslovsky (2007) has reviewed existing research on the Ministério Público, and has also conducted interviews with many prosecutors. He sees the development of their role as 'protectors of the powerless' not only as the result of the possibilities given under the 1985 Public Action Suit and the responsibilities inscribed in the 1988 Constitution, but also as the continuation of a trend partially established a century earlier. The *Lei do Ventre Livre* of 1871 (the 'Born Free Law') gave the prosecutors the duty to ensure that the sons and daughters of slaves did not become enslaved themselves. This role expanded to other groups from the 1970s, when it was proposed that a government agency should be charged with protection of the interests of *hipposufficientes*, those less than able to look after themselves, including widows, orphans, the legally insane and indigenous people. From the 1970s, prosecutors, particularly in Sao Paulo state, expanded this role, and in interviews with Coslovsky, prosecutors described the Ministério Público's mission as 'not to jail criminals but to protect society' and described themselves as 'not a prosecutor of criminals' but as 'protectors of the powerless' (Coslovsky 2007: 12–14). What is agreed is that the years since the 1988 Constitution have seen a steady and considerable increase in the powers of the Ministério Público prosecutors to bring civil actions in defence of the interests of powerless groups.

The field of children's rights and interests, regulated by the 1990 Statute of the Child and Adolescent, is one area where the activities of the Ministério Público has expanded. Among its provisions, the statute states that:

> Article 4. It is the duty of the family, the community, society in general and the public authority to ensure, with absolute priority, effective implementation of the rights to life, health, nutrition, education, sports, leisure, vocational training, culture, dignity, respect, freedom, and family and community living.
>
> Article 5. No child or adolescent will be subject to any form of negligence, discrimination, exploitation, violence, cruelty and oppression, and any violation of their fundamental rights, either by act or omission, will be punished according to the state of the Law.
>
> (Law no. 8,069, 13 July 1990)

Prosecutors have acted when they have found children's rights being violated or ignored by municipal and state governments in areas of health, education and welfare. Often they have acted by calling public meetings, lobbying and other means to raise awareness of children's issues, only commencing lawsuits when non-judicial approaches fail to produce results. They have allied themselves to organizations such as UNICEF and also to local campaigners for improved provisions and respect for the rights of children and adolescents.

The Ministério Público has also intervened in cases of use of child and adolescent labour, which is forbidden by law. In one example, prosecutors in the region of Ribeirao Preto, in Sao Paulo state, organized surprise inspections of farms and plantations thought to be using underage labour. These inspections resulted in the removal of about 4,000 child or adolescent workers (Silva 2000). Agreements were secured with employers to refrain from using underage labour, and in other instances prosecutors have secured agreements with municipal and state governments to institute policies for the protection and advancement of the rights of children and adolescents.

Article 232 of the Constitution declares that 'Indians, their communities, and organizations are legitimate parties to demand juridical protection of their rights and interests'. Before this, indigenous peoples' interests could only be represented through a state agency, the National Foundation for Indigenous Peoples (FUNAI), which worked with the state under the 1973 Indian Statute to implement coercive assimilationist policies (Rodrigues 2002). Ministério Público actions have been taken against seizures of indigenous peoples' lands in several areas, including Matto Grosso, Amazonas and Maranhao. In some instances, the actions resulted in contested areas being declared off-limit for mining and timber-felling. Most of the actions have been taken against the federal government, for failure to protect the territories of indigenous peoples. Prosecutors have used their powers to compel production of documents and other forms of information to verify abuses of land and other rights. They have also investigated the federal government's lack of diligence in pursuing policies to secure the rights of indigenous peoples. For example, in 1993 federal prosecutors examined the causes for the 'non-compliance by the federal government of the constitutional time frame … to conclude the procedures for demarcation of indigenous lands' (Instituto Socioambiental 2004).

As Rodrigues (2002) records, indigenous peoples' groups were active in lobbying during the constitutional debates of 1987 and 1988. Indigenous representatives were present at the Brazilian Congress whenever there were discussions and voting on issues of interest to them. Indigenous organizations have continued in the democratic era to press for more legal protection of their lands and their way of life, and they have sought support of national and international bodies, and of the Ministério Público. The prosecutors are valuable allies in that they have the duty to instigate actions in defence of collective rights, and unlike other groups or individuals who might wish to bring suits, they do not have to pay the costs of cases if they lose. As well as supporting indigenous groups in bringing actions, prosecutors have assisted them in exercising their rights to democratic participation, taking voting machines to Amazonian peoples, and helping people who cannot read and write to vote.

Law enforcement and criminal justice

It is in the area of law enforcement and criminal justice that the Ministério Público's defence of rights and its campaigns against corruption of public officials appear to have been least effective. Although there have been public civil action suits taken against state authorities in respect of the detention of juveniles in adult facilities, and the absence of community-based facilities which would offer young offenders educational and social measures as well as penal sanctions, conditions in prisons and detention centres continue to be deplorable. Policing also continues to be characterized by corruption and brutality. Prisoners and detainees, the urban poor; street and favela (shanty town) dwellers are groups who need, but do not receive, any significant degree of protection under the responsibilities assumed by the Ministério Público for groups unable to protect themselves.

Amnesty International has issued a series of critical reports on the policing of Brazilian city centres, especially Rio de Janeiro and Sao Paulo, claiming that Brazil has abandoned its shanty-town dwellers to the control of criminal gangs and drugs traffickers, with police contributing to rather than controlling violence. It accuses police of acting in poor communities through violent invasions, killing around 2,000 people a year in Rio de Janeiro and Sao Paulo (Amnesty International 2005). The Amnesty investigation found that incidents were usually labelled 'resistance followed by death' and were rarely investigated. High-profile invasions of favelas have shocked the world, the report notes, but what remains largely unremarked is the day-to-day violence experienced by poor communities at the hands of the police.

The Ministério Público has not been as active and as successful in engaging with police brutality as it has in relation to political corruption. For example, although torture is generally outlawed by the 1988 Constitution and specifically forbidden in criminal justice in a 1997 amendment to the Penal Code, in 2001 the United Nations Special Rapporteur on Torture found that torture is a 'widespread and systematic' police practice in Brazil (United Nations 2001). Although hundreds of cases have been documented, there have been very few prosecutions of police officers since 1997. Fiona Macaulay (2002: 4) in a review of police oversight in Brazil concludes that: 'It would appear that overall the Brazilian police have become less efficient, more corrupt, more abusive and less controllable than in the period of military rule' (1964–1984). Macaulay quotes a survey of prosecutors carried out in 1997 which showed that they themselves rated their performance in curbing gross human rights abuses by police as poor.

The most commonly given explanation for lack of effectiveness in controlling the police is that nearly 80 per cent of state police personnel are military police, who are controlled by a parallel system of military justice which has survived from the military regime. Military police are responsible for keeping order and fighting crime, and so are responsible for most of the street homicides. Civilian police are responsible for investigations, however, and torture and inhumane treatment continue to be reported during interrogation and detention. Oversight of military and civil police is carried by their internal affairs departments (*corregedoria*), which have no external input; in some states there is a police ombudsman's office (*ouvidoria*), but although civilians monitor police complaints, they have no powers to bring charges, and the police carry out the investigations and decide any sanctions. The prosecutors are therefore the only truly external control mechanism.

Constitutional responsibility for police oversight by the Ministério was only fleshed out in secondary legislation in 2000, so before that it was not difficult for police to claim that the public prosecutors had no jurisdiction, and to refuse to cooperate with investigations. Several states are, however, beginning to become more activist in relation to police abuses, with Sao Paulo state establishing the widest powers to inspect both prisons and police stations. Bahia, somewhat unusually, has been relatively more active in opposing police abuse than in investigating political corruption, and the state of Goias has taken a more activist stance than most states in eradicating torture by the police (Macaulay 2002: 20).

Although the Statute of the Child and Adolescent provides for the treatment of young offenders to be in line with the best international standards, this has not been achieved in practice. An Amnesty International (2000) investigation into Sao Paulo's juvenile detention system found that ten years after the enactment of the statute, adolescents were being abandoned to 'torture, ill-treatment and cruel, inhuman and degrading conditions of detentions'. Punishments for minor infractions, such as speaking during meals, could result in severe beating; inmates have died from beatings by warders and by fellow inmates. Public prosecutors have allied with Sao Paulo's juvenile court in bringing actions against the state government, and against the state juvenile detention system, but in most cases the State Appeals Court has upheld government appeals.

Prosecutors have also brought cases in several states against the holding of young offenders in adult prisons. One case that was reported widely inside and outside of Brazil concerned a young woman who was held in a police cell with twenty adult men for a month and repeatedly sexually abused. It was reported that the young woman may only have been 15 years old, so the case highlights the plight of both young offenders and females. Amnesty International (2007) commented that it receives extensive reports from Brazil about detained women suffering sexual abuse, torture, substandard healthcare and inhuman conditions. Its most recent report, covering the year 2008, says that the number of women prisoners continues to rise, and that women prisoners continue to face ill-treatment, overcrowding, inadequate support during childbirth and lack of childcare provision (Amnesty International 2009).

Conditions in Brazil's prisons, as well as its high imprisonment rates, are well known, and demonstrate that rights of prisoners – especially black prisoners – to freedom from degrading and inhumane treatment, are very far from being recognized, let alone realized. Loic Wacquant has said that Brazil's prisons are akin to '*concentration camps for the dispossessed*, or public enterprises for the storage of social refuse' (Wacquant 2003: 200, emphasis in the original). According to Wacquant, Brazilian policy towards the poor and towards prisoners is the very opposite of a strategy for establishing human rights and policies to promote social rights. The right to freedom from detention without conviction, for example, is flouted by the terrible conditions in which remand detainees are held. He describes the conditions at one remand institution in Sao Paulo:

> staggering overcrowding resulting in abominable living conditions and catastrophic hygiene, characterized by lack of space, air, light and food (in police lockups, detainees, who are more often than not innocent, are crammed in for months and even years on end, in complete illegality, as many as eight to a cell designed for one, like at the Casa da Detencao in Sao Paulo, where they can be recognized by their sickly appearance and jaundiced complexions, which has earned them the nickname '*os amarelhos*' 'the yellow ones').
>
> (Wacquant 2003: 200)

In spite of the Torture Law amendment to the Penal Code, and Brazil's acceptance of United Nations criticisms and recommendations, brutal police invasions of shanty towns continue; torture in police and prison detention continues; and police corruption and involvement in organized crime continues. Wacquant charges that failure to tackle prison conditions, and to eradicate police violence, means that in spite of its new Constitution, Brazil has 'yet to construct a state of laws worthy of the name'.

From transitional justice to democratic professionalism

Unlike other countries emerging from authoritarian regimes and civil conflicts, Brazil did not experience the trials, truth and reconciliation processes, or purges that have been characteristic of transitional justice elsewhere. Many of the violators of human rights in the military dictatorship period remain in post in Brazil in the police, armed forces and other public bodies (Macaulay 2002). The Ministério's efforts to curb these abuses of power by police and criminal justice officials, and to disrupt the impunity formerly enjoyed by them and by corrupt politicians, have earned the prosecutors the hostility of other branches of government. Prosecutors have been accused of acting irresponsibly, of acting on political bias, and there have been constant calls for their powers and their right to speak directly to the public to be curbed. Hensler (2005) notes that the present Workers' Party government led by President Ignácio 'Lula' da Silva, who were principal allies of the public prosecutors when in opposition, has accused them of political bias and impropriety in their investigations of highly placed officials. There have been various attempts to introduce new laws to prevent the prosecutors informing the public about their investigations, and removing the Ministério's powers to instigate their own investigations.

Some of the debates about the Ministério Público's powers and its actions reflect the sense that the period of transition, the redemocratization period, is at its end. Twenty years on from the introduction of the new Constitution, democratic processes seem to be well embedded, and the Ministério Público is trusted and respected among the public. Political corruption prosecutions demonstrate that the Ministério Público has embraced its constitutional task of holding public officials to account, showing that the law is used against the rich as well as the poor. Through its class action suits on behalf of children and adolescents, the prosecution has also gained acceptance as an institution concerned with social as well as legal justice, recognized for its independence from government and from the judiciary.

Some of the criticisms currently made of the Ministério Público by other organs of government certainly suggest that its role as an agency of transition is regarded as ended. Demands being made now are that, rather than energetically defending the powerless and guarding the public patrimony, the prosecution should 'grow up' and take its proper place among the institutions of justice. Phrases such as 'behaving responsibly', 'avoiding recklessness' are used, words which have connotations of adolescence. The prosecution is called upon to strengthen its internal hierarchy, to become more responsive to government interests and more accountable to government. The Ministério Público, however, is concerned to protect its independence and its role of defender of democracy and of the powerless.

Perhaps the most appropriate model for the Ministério Público at the end of the transition phase is that of *democratic professionalism* (Olson and Dzur 2004; Dzur 2008). In their article Olson and Dzur noted the lack of attention to the professionals involved in restorative justice projects, with most research focus being on victims and offenders. The nature of restorative justice proceedings is that professionals involved as facilitators, chairs, mediators have to adapt themselves to the concerns, the viewpoints and the discourse of participants in the search for constructive and acceptable outcomes, while bringing to the debates legal values such as due process, proportionality, respect for rights. In his further development of the idea of democratic professionalism, Dzur has advocated building bridges between professionals in fields such as law, medicine and journalism to enhance public involvement in deliberations on major social issues. He examines fields in which collaboration between professionals and citizens have produced advances in democracy and social justice.

The Ministério Público is an organization of professional lawyers; like other branches of the legal profession and in fields such as medicine, state employment does not erode professional status and adherence to the values of the profession. The Ministério Público has constitutional guarantees of independence from other branches of the state, of permanence for its employees (subject of course to the possibility of dismissal for illegal activity or similar cause), and of irreducibility of earnings. Prosecutors are not elected, nor are they political appointees: entry is by competitive examination following acquisition of academic and professional law qualifications, and promotion is on merit. Although it has a structure – prosecutors, senior prosecutors, Attorney General – the Ministério Público is a fairly loose hierarchical structure which gives a large measure of autonomy to individual prosecutors (Sadek and Cavalcanti 2000). Prosecutors are very aware of themselves as legal professionals, whose responsibility is to give their best legal opinion, rather than an opinion which accords with the interests of other government branches. They are, moreover, democratic professionals who bring actions against government on behalf of citizens, look after the powerless, and work in alliance with human rights groups, campaigners for child welfare, and groups such as the Red Feet movement in the Londrina case.

In most states, the Ministério Público has now developed strategic plans to guide their work, and to generate clearly stated objectives against which their performance can be measured. The plan of the Ministério Público of Paraná state, confirms commitment to the democratic values and responsibilities given under the Constitution, and lays out the means by which these are to be taken forward.[2] Under the heading 'Legal Order and Citizenship', the objectives refer to defence of the interests of people and groups in situations of familial, social and economic vulnerability; protection of children and adolescents; defence of diffuse and collective

[2] I am grateful to Eliezer Gomes da Silva, Special Assistant to the Attorney General, Ministério Público of Paraná, for giving me a copy of the strategic plan.

interests, the democratic regime, and the implementation of constitutional policies; to guarantee sustainable environmental policies and practices; they aim to intensify actions to combat organized crime and control police activities, and to defend the proper use of public assets. Procedures to achieve these objectives include increasing non-judicial resolution of conflicts; improving interaction with society; improving relations with republican institutions and social organizations.

Paraná's Ministério Público, like that of other states, has renewed its commitment to the democratic objectives of protecting the rights and interest of vulnerable groups, making public officials accountable for any misconduct and protecting diffuse and collective interests, including environmental concerns. Mention of non-judicial resolution of conflicts, improving interactions with society and relations with republican institutions and social organizations demonstrate its discursive approach to justice, and show it to be a democratic professional institution consistent with the idea of deliberative democracy. It is striving to increase its effectiveness by strengthening its professionalism, without losing its democratic purpose through becoming an agent of the state akin to public prosecutors in most other countries.

Concluding comments: discourse, democracy and cosmopolitan justice

A danger for democracy is that it can descend into majoritarianism or populism, and the risk for democratic professionalism is that it will pay most attention to causes for which there is popular demand, or at least for which popular understanding can be generated through discourse. The Ministério Público has achieved public approval through pursuing causes such as prosecutions of politicians for misappropriation of public funds. They are far less effective in relation to unpopular causes: reforms on behalf of the poor and the criminal. Restraining police brutality, of the kinds practised by both the military and civil police, and improving prison condition, have not received backing by the public, or by populist governments.

The approving response of Brazilian audiences to the drama-documentary film *Elite Squad*, which won the Golden Bear at the Berlin Film Festival in 2008, which portrays a Rio de Janeiro police unit using methods of extreme brutality, illustrates the lack of concern about police violence (Gomes da Silva 2008). Similarly, public reaction to reports of deplorable prison conditions, violence in prisons and lack of rehabilitative opportunities, does not demonstrate sympathy or concern. Prison disturbances, reports by international bodies and Brazilian human rights activists, do not seem to generate any widespread public or political demand for reform.

Not only do the poor suffer brutal policing and prison conditions, but the favelas where they live lack sanitation and other services, and suffer from high levels of gang violence. Landless workers, migrant workers (mainly internal migrants from the poorest regions of Brazil but also from poorer Latin American countries) suffer from appalling living and working arrangements, and are often in slave-like conditions of indentured labour. In rural areas landless workers have been subject to intimidation and forced evictions, and in the cities the poor have been left with inadequate social protection, discrimination in urban development policies, and lack of security. In the rural areas, landless workers and indigenous people have been victims of discriminatory development projects and unchecked agro-industrial expansion. The poor in both urban and rural areas have, instead of receiving protection of public police, suffered violence from private security companies as well as from state police (Amnesty International 2009).

Wacquant (2003) says that Brazil is moving towards a dictatorship over the poor. He points out that for the majority of the affluent middle classes, defence of constitutional rights of the poor signifies tolerance of criminals. They have shown little support for any moves to provide protection for poor communities, full access to education, health and other 'social rights'. Although there have been improvements in access to housing and amenities such as treated water since the new Constitution, given added force by the Statute of the City in 2001 (Avritzer 2007), there has been no reduction in residential segregation and the middle-class preference to live in heavily gated communities and apartment blocks. Sao Paulo has been labelled a 'city of walls' (Caldeira 2000), and in 2008 the governor of the city of Rio de Janeiro proposed building a wall around the favela districts.[3]

The Ministério Público of Paraná's plan includes protection of the interests of those vulnerable socially and economically. Although the Ministério sees itself as the protector of the powerless it remains to be seen whether or not the prosecutors can increase their effectiveness on

[3] This proposal was criticized by the UN. I understand from Tom Cahill, Amnesty International, that it is actually being built (private conversation, 1 August 2009).

behalf of the urban and rural poor. The movement for urban reform and the landless workers' movement have used the tactics of deliberative democracy, forming strong civil society associations, lobbying, taking part in constitutional debates, developing alliances with other organizations, but the poor in Brazil continue to live in deplorable conditions and with little protection of law (Avritzer 2007; Meszaros 2000).

Where societies are characterized by radical diversity and gross inequality, democratic processes need to be underpinned by a strong commitment to human rights. An important part of the discourse of democratic professionalism needs to be that of championing the rights of the most vulnerable, even (especially, perhaps) of vulnerable groups who are feared and despised. The rural poor are seen as threatening the economic development of the country, and as they migrate into the more prosperous cities they are seen as threatening the safety and security of respectable citizens. In the cities, the poor are seen as predatory criminals, responsible for murder, drug dealing and robbery.

In Brazil's case, democratic discourse needs to include vigorous advocacy of the view that all persons, and all social groups, have rights which must be defended, and that all groups and all persons should be able to participate in the society as full citizens. The ethics of cosmopolitan justice, that all humans have rights, and must be responded to without violence, however different, however incomprehensible, however threatening and fearsome they seem, and the understanding that justice is owed to strangers as well as to those with whom we feel a sense of community, are appropriate moral underpinnings for the task of regulating democracy in such diverse, divided and unequal societies.

References

Aertsen, I., Daems, T. and Robert, L. (eds.) (2006) *Institutionalizing Restorative Justice*. Cullompton, Devon: Willan.

Amnesty International (2000) *Sao Paulo's Juvenile Detention System – A Human Rights Crisis, Not a Public Security Issue*. London: Amnesty International.

(2005) *They Come in Shooting: Policing Socially Excluded Communities*. London: Amnesty International.

(2007) *Brazil: Prison Rape Exposes Increasing Abuse of Women*. London: Amnesty International.

(2009) *Brazil Report* (at: http://amnesty.org/regions/Americas/brazil; accessed 13/07/09).

Appiah, K. A. (2006) *Cosmopolitanism: Ethics in a World of Strangers*. London: Penguin/Allen Lane.

Arantes, R. B. (2003) 'The Brazilian "Ministerio Publico" and Political Corruption in Brazil', working paper CBS-50–04, Centre for Brazilian Studies, University of Oxford.

Avritzer, L. (2007) *Urban Reform, Participation and the Right to the City in Brazil*, Institute of Development Studies (at: www.ids.ac.uk/ids/Part/proj/pnp.html; accessed 15/07/09).

Bauman, Z. (2004) *Europe: An Unfinished Adventure*. University of Chicago Press.

Beck, U. (2006) *The Cosmopolitan Vision*, trans. C. Cronin. Cambridge: Polity.

Bell, V. and Campbell, K. (2004) 'Out of Conflict: Peace, Change and Justice', *Social and Legal Studies*, **13**(3), 299–304.

Benhabib, S. (1992) *Situating the Self: Gender, Community and Postmodernism in Contemporary Ethics*. Cambridge: Polity.

(2004) *The Rights of Others: Aliens, Residents and Citizens*. Cambridge University Press.

(2006) *Another Cosmopolitanism* ed. R. Post. Oxford University Press.

Braithwaite, J. (2002) *Restorative Justice and Responsive Regulation*. Oxford University Press.

Caldeira, T. (2000) *Sao Paulo, City of Walls*. Berkeley, CA: University of California Press.

Coslovsky, S.V. (2007) *From Prosecutors to Cause Lawyers*. Boston, MA: MIT, Department of Urban Studies and Planning.

Derrida, J. (2001) 'On Cosmopolitanism', in *Cosmopolitanism and Forgiveness*, trans. M. Dooley and M. Hughes. London: Routledge.

(2003) 'Autoimmunity: Real and Symbolic Suicide', in G. Borradori (ed.), *Philosophy in a Time of Terror: Dialogues with Jurgen Habermas and Jacques Derrida*. University of Chicago Press.

Dzur, A. W. (2008) *Democratic Professionalism: Citizen Participation and the Reconstruction of Professional Ethics, Identity and Practice*. Pennsylvania, PA: Penn State University Press.

Gomes da Silva, E. (2008) 'The penal system, democracy and human rights: A Brazilian issue or a global one?', paper presented to the annual meetings of the Law and Society Association, Montreal, May 28–31.

Gutman, A. and Thompson, D. (1996) *Democracy and Disagreement*, Cambridge, MA: Belknap Press of Harvard University Press.

(2000) 'Why Deliberative Democracy is Different', *Social Philosophy and Policy*, **17**(1), 161–80.

Habermas, J. (1984, 1987) *The Theory of Communicative Action*, vols. 1 and 2, trans T. McCarthy. Cambridge: Polity.

(1996) *Between Facts and Norms*, trans. W. Rehg. Cambridge: Polity.

(1999) *The Inclusion of the Other*, (eds.) C. Cronin and P. de Grieff. Cambridge: Polity.

(2003) 'Fundamentalism and Terror', in G. Borradori (ed.), *Philosophy in a Time of Terror: Dialogues with Jurgen Habermas and Jacques Derrida*. University of Chicago Press.

Hensler, B. (2005) 'The Ministerio Publico and the politics of prosecuting corruption in Brazil', unpublished paper, on file with the author.

Hudson, B. (2007) 'The Institutionalisation of Restorative Justice: Justice and the Ethics of Discourse', in E. van der Spuy, S. Parmentier and A. Dissel (eds.), *Restorative Justice: Politics, Policies and Prospects*. Cape Town: Juta.

(2008) 'Re-imagining Justice: Principles of Justice for Divided Societies in a Globalised World', in P. Carlen (ed.), *Imaginary Penalties*. Cullompton, Devon: Willan.

Instituto Socioambiental (2004) *Indigenous Peoples in Brazil*. Sao Paulo: Instituto Socioambiental.

Kant, I. (1983) 'To Perpetual Peace', in *Perpetual Peace and Other Essays*, trans. T. Humphrey. Cambridge: Hackett Publishing.

Macaulay, F. (2002) 'Problems of police oversight in Brazil', working paper CBS-33–02, Centre for Brazilian Studies, University of Oxford.

Meszaros, G. (2000) 'Taking the Land into their Hands: The Landless Workers' Movement and the Brazilian State', *Journal of Law and Society*, **27**(4), 517–41.

Olson, S. M. and Dzur, A.W. (2004) 'Revisiting Informal Justice: Restorative Justice and Democratic Professionalism', *Law and Society Review*, **38**(1), 139–76.

Rodrigues, M. G. M. (2002) 'Indigenous Rights in Democratic Brazil', *Human Rights Quarterly*, **24**, 457–512.

Sadek, M. T. and Cavalcanti, R. B. (2000) 'The new public prosecution and the efficacy of accountability mechanisms', paper presented to the conference Political Institutions, Accountability and Democratic Governance in Latin America, Notre Dame, 8–9 May.

Silva, C. A. (2000) 'Brazilian prosecutors and the collective demands: bringing social issues to the courts of justice', paper presented to the meeting of the Latin American Studies Association, Miami, 16–18 March.

Teitel, R. G. (2000) *Transitional Justice*. Oxford University Press.

Tully, J. (1995) *Strange Multiplicity: Constitutionalism in an Age of Diversity*. Cambridge University Press.

United Nations (2001) *Report of the Special Rapporteur [on Torture] Sir Nigel Rodley submitted pursuant to Commission on Human Rights Resolution 2000/3 Addendum. Visit to Brazil. 30 March 2001*. Geneva: UNHRC.

Wacquant, L. (2003) 'Toward a Dictatorship of the Poor? Notes on the Penalization of Poverty in Brazil', *Punishment and Society*, **5**(2), 197–206.

Young, I. M. (1990) *Justice and the Politics of Difference*. Princeton University Press.

(2002) *Democracy and Inclusion*. Oxford University Press.

INDEX

Note: names of national institutions and items of legislation are UK unless otherwise stated